Competitive Advantage and Competition Policy in Developing Countries

THE CRC SERIES ON COMPETITION, REGULATION AND
DEVELOPMENT

Series Editors: Paul Cook, *Professor of Economics and Development
Policy* and Martin Minogue, *Senior Research Fellow, Institute for
Development Policy and Management, University of Manchester, UK*

Titles in the series include:

Leading Issues in Competition, Regulation and Development
Edited by Paul Cook, Colin Kirkpatrick, Martin Minogue and David Parker

The Politics of Regulation
Institutions and Regulatory Reforms for the Age of Governance
Edited by Jacint Jordana and David Levi-Faur

Regulating Development
Evidence from Africa and Latin America
Edited by Edmund Amann

Regulatory Governance in Developing Countries
Edited by Martin Minogue and Ledivina Cariño

Regulatory Economics and Quantitative Methods
Evidence from Latin America
Edited by Omar Osvaldo Chisari

Regulation, Markets and Poverty
Edited by Paul Cook and Sarah Mosedale

Competitive Advantage and Competition Policy in Developing Countries
Edited by Paul Cook, Raul Fabella and Cassey Lee

Competitive Advantage and Competition Policy in Developing Countries

Edited by

Paul Cook

Director of the Centre on Regulation and Competition (CRC), University of Manchester, UK

Raul Fabella

Professor of Economics and Dean, School of Economics, University of the Philippines

Cassey Lee

Associate Professor of Industrial Economics, Nottingham University Business School, University of Nottingham (Malaysia Campus), Malaysia

THE CRC SERIES ON COMPETITION, REGULATION AND DEVELOPMENT

Edward Elgar

Cheltenham, UK • Northampton, MA, USA

Published by
Edward Elgar Publishing Limited
Glensanda House
Montpellier Parade
Cheltenham
Glos GL50 1UA
UK

Edward Elgar Publishing, Inc.
William Pratt House
9 Dewey Court
Northampton
Massachusetts 01060
USA

A catalogue record for this book is available from the British Library

Library of Congress Cataloging in Publication Data

Competitive advantage and competition policy in developing countries /
edited by Paul Cook, Raul Fabella and Cassey Lee.
    p.   cm. – (CRC series on competition, regulation and development)
    Includes bibliographical references and index.
1. Competition–Developing countries. 2. Developing countries–Economic
policy. I. Cook, Paul. II. Fabella, Raul V. III. Lee, Cassey.
    HC59.7.C624 2007
    338.6′048091724–dc22   2006028691

ISBN 978 1 84542 627 9 (cased)

Printed and bound in Great Britain by MPG Books Ltd, Bodmin, Cornwall

Contents

Contributors

Paul Cook is Professor of Economics and Development Policy and Head of the Institute for Development Policy and Management at the University of Manchester. He is also Director of CRC and the Competition Research Programme at the CRC, University of Manchester, UK.

Kamala Dawar is Trade Policy and Representation Officer at Consumers International, London, UK.

Germano Mendes de Paula is Associate Professor of Economics at the Federal University of Uberlandia, Brazil.

Joachim Ewert is Associate Professor in the Department of Sociology at the University of Stellenbosch, South Africa.

Raul Fabella is Professor of Economics and Dean of the School of Economics, University of the Philippines and a regional research partner with CRC, University of Manchester, UK.

Trudi Hartzenberg is Executive Director of the Trade Law Centre for Southern Africa (TRALAC).

Jeffrey Henderson is Professor of International Economic Sociology at the Manchester Business School and Institute for Development Policy and Management, University of Manchester, and Research Fellow at the CRC, University of Manchester, UK.

Kim Kampel is Case Manager at the Competition Tribunal of South Africa, Pretoria, South Africa.

Cassey Lee is Associate Professor of Industrial Economics at the Nottingham University Business School, University of Nottingham Malaysia Campus, Malaysia and a regional research partner with the CRC, University of Manchester, UK.

John Stanley Metcalfe is Stanley Jevons Professor of Economics and Director of the Centre for Research in Innovation and Competition (CRIC), University of Manchester and a Research Fellow at the CRC, University of Manchester, UK.

Selim Raihan is University Lecturer at Dhaka University, Bangladesh and an associate of the CRC, University of Manchester, UK.

Ronnie Ramlogan is a Research Fellow at the Centre for Research in Innovation and Competition (CRIC), University of Manchester, UK.

Yuichiro Uchida is a Research Associate at the CRC, University of Manchester, UK.

Efa Yonnedi is a doctoral student and an associate of the CRC, University of Manchester, UK.

Preface

Issues of competition and regulation have long been matters of both public policy debate and academic research in developed economies, but until recently were relatively unexamined in relation to developing economies. The Centre on Regulation and Competition (CRC) of the University of Manchester, UK, has been conducting research into regulatory developments and competition issues since 2001, with a primary focus on changes and reforms in developing countries, working together with partners both in the United Kingdom and overseas in China, Ghana, India, Malaysia, the Philippines, South Africa and Sri Lanka. This work has been funded primarily by the United Kingdom's Department for International Development, with other support from the UK Foreign and Commonwealth Office's Global Opportunities Fund, and from the British Council. Other collaborating agencies include the Foreign Investment Advisory Service of the World Bank and the Competition Division of the United Nations Committee on Trade and Development (UNCTAD).

This book series is one of the many ways in which the work of the CRC and its partners is disseminated, complementing conferences, workshops, journal publication and policy briefs. This volume incorporates the research of CRC on competition and competition policy. The contributors focus on the meaning and understanding of the relation between competition and development and the implications for competition policy. The volume also gives attention to the difficulties associated with measuring competition and uses a range of quantitative techniques to assess the competitiveness of markets. These new research insights will provide a stimulus to reflexive policy-making in international development institutions, and a focus for further contextual research in the academic development community.

Paul Cook
Martin Minogue
Series Editors

Acknowledgements

We are grateful for the financial support provided by the UK Department for International Development (DFID) to the CRC. This has enabled the CRC to fund research and host conferences from which the contributions for this book have been drawn. We would also like to express our thanks to Pam Johnson who has provided support in the preparation of this book.

1. Introduction

Paul Cook, Raul Fabella and Cassey Lee

In recent years there has been an acceleration of interest in competition policy for developing countries. This interest is most evidently seen in the number of countries that have revised old competition laws or have developed new ones. This trend towards the introduction of new competition laws has been accompanied by the development of dedicated competition agencies designed to tackle anti-competitive practices and review cases of mergers and acquisitions. Competition has also been part of the remit of the spate of newly established dedicated regulatory bodies responsible for ensuring economic efficiency and protecting the welfare of consumers arising from the activities of enterprises in the utilities sector, particularly those that have been privatized.

This rise of interest in competition in developing countries has a number of explanations (Cook, 2004). Undoubtedly, the interest in the competitiveness of domestic markets and the attention to antitrust-type competition policy has to some extent resulted from the failures of economic reforms in the 1980s, that overly relied on trade liberalization to promote domestic market competition. During that time, World Bank structural adjustment loans did not stipulate conditions for competition policy (Gray and Davis, 1993). The conclusion reached was that trade liberalization by itself did not achieve all it was expected to in terms of increasing productive efficiency and competitiveness in external markets (Tybout, 1992). The idea that trade liberalization would improve domestic competition has led to a reassessment, addressed in this book, that indicates that success in international trade is itself linked to establishing a competitive domestic market environment. This, in turn, is associated with a view that competition policy not only incorporates notions about the potential abuses of economic power, but needs to act to promote competitive conditions and adopt a broader perspective that encompasses the competitive infrastructure such as communications, financial and fiscal systems and regulatory constraints.

Further, the interest in competition has been heightened as a consequence of the recent spate of mega-mergers and the increased potential for cross-border anti-competitive practices (Evenett, 2002). In relation to these events, concern has been expressed over the ability of developing country governments to deal with these, and to the role that global institutions can play in setting rules to ensure competitive conditions are maintained (Holmes, 2004). While there are numerous bilateral and regional agreements on competition policy between countries, most multilateral principles for competition continue to rely on voluntary action.

The issue of competition has also gained ascendancy as a result of the wave of privatization since the early 1980s across the world. In particular, the shift towards the privatization of utilities in developing countries in the 1990s raised new concerns about the economic regulation of private utilities into markets that were not fully competitive. Would regulators provide surrogate competition for monopoly utilities and how would competition be developed in these industries? These questions also extended the debate over competition into an examination of the respective roles between dedicated economic regulators and competition agencies.

The new interest in issues of competition and the implications for policy exposed how little was known about the ways in which the competitive process works in developing countries and of what types of policy would be most effective in creating a competitive environment. These are the issues addressed in the various chapters of this volume.

The book is divided into three parts. The first consists of chapters reviewing the notion of competition and the implications for competition policy in developing countries. The first chapter in Part I, Chapter 2 by Stan Metcalfe and Ronnie Ramlogan, examines competition as the regulator and promoter of economic development, arguing that competition and development are processes for the transformation of economies from within. This view of the role of competition is in sharp contrast to that portrayed in the static theory of resource allocation, which is grounded in the notion of equilibrium as the organizing concept. The authors argue that viewing competition as a process of transformation and therefore placing it firmly in a development context, challenges many of the ideas that shape existing antitrust-based approaches to competition policy. Metcalfe and Ramlogan indicate that adopting the wrong model of competition, particularly when it is drawn from the experiences of advanced industrialized economies, may not only stifle development but is also likely to clash with local institutions and embedded business culture.

In Chapter 3, Cassey Lee compares and contrasts two models of competition law put forward by the major international development agencies, the OECD-World Bank model and the UNCTAD model laws. The chapter compares the objectives and definitions contained in each model and how each proposes to tackle issues relating to market dominance and mergers. Lee discusses the implications for developing countries of drawing on these frameworks and how in practice this may affect implementation and enforcement.

Following on from this, Cassey Lee in Chapter 4 analyses the relationship between legal origins and the development of competition policy. The differences between civil and common law approaches are reviewed and their relation to economic development and growth is discussed. After reviewing some of the cross-country and econometric-based studies on the determinants of competition policy and its likely effects, Lee develops a framework to examine the links between legal tradition and competition policy. The review of the literature indicates that the relationship between legal tradition and competition policy is complex and multidimensional. The attempt by Lee to model the relationship is beset, as with other quantitative studies, with problems concerning the adequacy of the data, the smallness of sample sizes and poorly developed proxy variables. Despite the limitations and preliminary nature of this research, Lee concludes that variations in legal traditions appear to have a limited effect on competition law.

Chapter 5, by Kamala Dawar, develops a consumer perspective on competition. Rather than simply viewing the competition as a process where enterprises compete to influence consumers to purchase their goods and services, Dawar argues that more attention ought to be given to the demand side in the competitive process. Dawar contends that consumer welfare and the ability of individuals to use their resources efficiently, is not a priority in national development strategies. Correspondingly, there is a need to draw consumers into the competition policy process so that their welfare is considered and markets are made to function more competitively. Dawar proposes a strategy to draw consumers as participants into policy-making through various ways of institutionalizing consumer representation.

The final chapter in Part I is by Raul Fabella. In Chapter 6, Fabella develops a model drawing on the East Asian experience that characterizes the relationship between entrepreneurs and government. Fabella analyses property rights and contractual conditions within a weak governance environment. The model depicts the *guanxi* system, referred to as relational contracting, to examine the possibilities for solving contract enforcement problems where there is weak state enforcement. Fabella then shows how entrepreneurial behaviour modelled in this way can result in anti-competitive outcomes, which have important implications for the type of competition policy that will be effective.

In Part II, attention is shifted to consider the experience with competition policy in a range of developing countries. Three chapters in this part examine countries where a competition law has been introduced, namely Brazil, South Africa and Indonesia. In contrast, two further chapters review the experience with competition policy in general but where no specific law has been enacted. In Chapter 7, Germano Mendes de Paula reviews the historical evolution of competition policy in Brazil. The 1990s represented a turning point in economic policy for Brazil, which was to have significant implications for the role of competition policy. de Paula analyses competition policy in Brazil with reference to the changes that were taking place in the steel industry. A key finding of de Paula's review relates to the speed with which competition policy decisions are reached and enacted upon. It is argued that the procedures for competition policy are drawn out and slow. This appears to be in part due to the reluctance of the bureaucracy to accept change; to overlapping responsibilities of various agencies dealing with competition and to fundamental problems with the judicial system, which is slow and open to lengthy appeal processes.

Competition policy and specifically the role of public interest objectives are examined in Chapter 8 by Trudi Hartzenberg. This chapter focuses on South Africa's new Competition Act, which was introduced in 1998. Hartzenberg provides a detailed account of the development of the competition law and of the public interest test, which is explicitly included within it. Hartzenberg argues that public interest considerations embodied in competition law are necessary to meet the challenges in terms of transition and sustainable development facing South Africa. In this chapter Hartzenberg uses examples to illustrate the use of public interest objectives over employment, black empowerment and smaller enterprise development and to draw lessons for other countries. Hartzenberg concludes that public interest considerations are necessary but must be applied cautiously if the long-term credibility of competition agencies is to be maintained.

Chapter 9 by Efa Yonnedi considers the competitive environment and competition policy in Indonesia, which was introduced in 1999. Yonnedi reviews the available evidence on market concentration and concludes that, although this is high by international comparisons, it has generally been declining. Yonnedi also reviews the factors that account for relatively high levels of concentration in Indonesia. In the second part of the chapter, Yonnedi traces the historical evolution of economic policy in Indonesia from the nationalization programme of President Sukarno to the current spate of market opening policies pursued after the economic crisis of 1997. An important component of the most recent reforms have concerned reducing the extent of policy-induced barriers to domestic competition and the introduction of a formal competition law. Finally, Yonnedi discusses some of the challenges confronting the government in terms of effectively implementing the new competition law.

Attention in the next two chapters turns to countries where issues of competition have become important but where no formal competition law has yet been developed. In Chapter 10, Cassey Lee reviews the experience of Malaysia. Lee documents the rise of sector regulation in Malaysia, with a particular emphasis on the competition elements. Lee examines the impact of a range of economic policies on competition and points to the difficulties raised by not having a clear and coherent view on competition policy. This has often resulted in a heavy-handed approach to regulating market behaviour on an ad hoc basis, rather than one developed within a consistent framework.

Like Malaysia, Bangladesh does not have a formal competition law. In Chapter 11 Selim Raihan critically examines the range of economic policies that constitute competition policy in its broader context. These principally consist of trade and industrial policies, but competition is also affected by privatization and foreign direct investment. Raihan assesses the competitive environment by developing a number of measures that indicate the extent of competition in Bangladesh. Raihan's econometric analysis indicates that the tendency towards capital intensity has reduced the degree of competition in the domestic market, although external competition has had the opposite effect.

Part III of the book places greater emphasis on examining the effects of competition policy and determining the extent of competition in various markets. This is achieved through reviews and case studies drawing on the experience in South Africa and econometric analysis across a range of countries. In Chapter 12, Kim Kampel examines the effect of South Africa's competition law on the development of small and medium-sized enterprises. Initially, Kampel outlines the intentions of the competition law, and despite showing how small and medium-sized enterprise interests are accommodated in the law, Kampel explores instances that can occur where this goal conflicts with the need to consider other wider interests. A number of examples are used to illustrate the complexity of this issue.

Joachim Ewert and Jeffrey Henderson present a further case study of competition and its effects in South Africa in Chapter 13. Ewert and Henderson examine the implications of government competition and regulatory policies on growth and equity in the wine industry. It is shown that while some progress has been made in South Africa towards poverty alleviation in urban areas, the same cannot be claimed for rural areas where farm workers remain one of the poorest and most marginalized groups. Ewert and Henderson show that while regulatory reforms and the global integration of the industry has brought about fundamental change that has benefited some, there are many workers in the industry that have lost permanent work and whose welfare is less secure. Ewert and Henderson argue that the existing policy environment, which seeks to address issues of poverty and equity, is too narrowly focused on employment and workplace transformation. Instead, Ewert and Henderson suggest that the viability of the industry and its welfare implications will also be determined by the motives and actions of oligopolistic enterprises operating on the demand side and by a wider set of other government policies aimed at improving international competitiveness.

The next two chapters in the final part of the book use quantitative methods to examine the extent of competition in developing countries. In Chapter 14 Selim Raihan examines the impact of foreign competition on the growth of manufacturing in Bangladesh. Raihan selects a range of variables that provide indicators of the extent of competition being faced in the domestic industry and finds that the relationship between foreign competition and growth in the manufacturing sector using the five indicators is somewhat ambiguous. Raihan provides a number of explanations for this result.

In Chapter 15 Yuichiro Uchida and Paul Cook examine trade and technological competitiveness and the role played by domestic competition. Using country- and industry-based analysis Uchida and Cook investigate changes in patterns of technological and trade comparative advantage and link these to changes in the level of domestic competition. Not surprisingly the levels of domestic competition within industries vary but are increasing in medium and high-tech industries, particularly in East Asia. Uchida and Cook show increases in the level of domestic competition are correlated with improvements in international competitiveness, particularly on the trade side.

REFERENCES

Cook, P. (2004), 'Competition Policy, Market Power and Collusion in Developing Countries', in P. Cook, C. Kirkpatrick, M. Minogue and D. Parker (eds), *Leading Issues in Competition, Regulation and Development*, Cheltenham, UK and Northampton, MA, USA: Edward Elgar.

Evenett, S. (2002), 'How Much Have Merger Review Laws Reduced Cross-border Mergers and Acquisitions', mimeo, February, Bern: World Trade Institute.

Gray, C. and A. Davis (1993), 'Competition Policy in Developing Countries Pursuing Structural Adjustment', *The Antitrust Bulletin*, Summer, 425–67.

Holmes, P. (2004), 'Trade and Competition Policy at the WTO: Issues for Developing Countries', in P. Cook, C. Kirkpatrick, M. Minogue and D. Parker (eds), *Leading Issues in Competition, Regulation and Development*, Cheltenham, UK and Northampton, MA, USA: Edward Elgar.

Tybout, J. (1992), 'Linking Trade and Productivity: New Research Directions', *World Bank Economic Review*, **6** (2), 189–212.

PART I

Competition policy and development

2. Competition and the regulation of economic development

John Stanley Metcalfe and Ronnie Ramlogan

INTRODUCTION

The theme of this chapter is competition as the regulator and promoter of economic development and that competition and development are processes for the transformation of economies from within. This process view of competition links development to new uses for resources, to the creation of new activities, to the formation of new patterns of consumption and demand and to innovation and rivalry. We contrast this view with the more familiar idea of regulating states of competition, arguing that the static theory of resource allocation, in which the conventional 'antitrust' case is grounded, is a distorting mirror in which to reflect the competition policy needs of developing economies. Indeed the central thrust of our argument is that the promotion of competition as a process of rivalry is not the same as the regulation of the market behaviour of errant firms. Traditional views of the abuse of market power and the definition of markets are displaced by a concern with open markets, the prevention of exclusionary practices by incumbent firms and the stimulation of enterprise (Krattenmaker, Lande and Salop, 1986; Charles River Associates, 2002). The consequences of this shift to a developmental perspective are considerable, for it rules out of consideration many of the existing frames of thought that relate to the idea of economies as equilibrium states of affairs. First, it should be obvious that any system that is in equilibrium has exhausted all the internal tendencies to change and that any alteration in its state can only be imposed from outside of it by some external agency that cannot, by definition, be part of the conditions determining that equilibrium state. Yet it is scarcely controversial to suggest that development takes place from within an economy and therefore, that an economy cannot be in equilibrium if it is to experience development. If we have learnt that economic systems exhibit self-organization and that this is what market institutions achieve, it is a short step to argue that development and competition are similar and interlinked processes of self-transformation.

Second, self-transformation is an evolutionary process and evolutionary processes are ordered, they exhibit structure, and in creating those orders, generate the internal reasons to change. As we shall see, markets play a very important role in this perspective but markets are not enough if we are to link development to competition. Enterprise and innovation, the stimuli to self-transformation, depend on more than market institutions and the organization and regulation of these wider institutional frames is an essential element in competition policy.

Third, economic development is a process of structural and qualitative transformation out of which arises measurable economic growth. No economy has ever grown in the fashion of proportional, semi-stationary growth in which all activities increase pari passu as if that economy conducted one single, integrated activity. Such a macro approach is entirely at odds with the developmental view expressed here and although we can measure macro aggregates we cannot comprehend development from a macro perspective. For then we have not only averaged away the diversity that describes the potential for development, we have also hidden from view the very processes that matter causally. This does not deny that there are macro constraints on the development process only that economies do not develop as macro economic wholes (Metcalfe, Foster and Ramlogan, 2004).

Fourth, closely connected to the transformational view is the notion that development reflects a growth of knowledge and that competition is a process that depends on and responds to the growth of knowledge. This is why if, as generally agreed, all economies are knowledge-based, then they cannot be in equilibrium unless knowledge is in equilibrium. No meaning can be attached to the idea of knowledge in equilibrium if we take human agency seriously. To say the converse is to take economics out of time, to imagine it to be possible for time to pass, and for nothing to happen; not a useful way of approaching the problem of development. This is the real challenge posed by the problem of development to understand how knowledge increases and how new knowledge is applied to improve the use of resources to meet human need. Can there be any decline in poverty, for example, without the growth and application of useful knowledge?

In incorporating the growth of knowledge as one of the crucial determinants of development we are led directly to the role of innovation, the relationship with inventive creativity and the competitive processes that ensure the spread of innovations in technique, organization and product throughout the economy. Innovation is a process of generating economic variety, a process that cannot be handled by the notion of representative behaviour unless that notion is statistical and what is representative becomes a measure taken on some distribution of behaviour. The dynamic consequences of economic variety are handled naturally in an evolutionary framework, a framework that provides causal explanations of structural change and links these changes to the improvement in the use of resources that defines development. In this process, innovation and the growth of knowledge are largely endogenous, new knowledge arises through the market process and through the deliberate allocation of resources directed to the conduct of experiments in business, science and technology (Kuznets, 1977). The development of knowledge and the development of an economy co-evolve and the competitive process is central to any understanding of this claim.

Finally, innovations depend greatly on new technological knowledge but they also require new knowledge of markets and organization. A policy for science and technology may be necessary but it is not sufficient for development. Knowledge has to be put to practical economic use and markets are the principal but not the only context in which application occurs. Markets matter in the evolutionary account but markets mean much more than getting the prices right. No one will argue that prices should be wrong but what the right prices are is contingent on the objectives in mind and subject to continual change in a developing economy. Prices that measure marginal costs, for example, will not be found in any activity where investment in knowledge is essential to economic conduct (Stiglitz, 1997; Fisher, 2000).[1] Even when the prices are right, that is only part of the story and possibly the lesser part. Market arrangements are the prerequisite for prices and markets do not come for free, they presuppose organization and an organizing agency. How market arrangements are instituted and regulated is thus a central issue in appraising the prospects for a competitive process. An efficient price mechanism gives confidence not particularly in relation to the current allocation of resources but rather that the allocation of resources will be changing in a pro-development direction. Enterprise can only conjecture pro-development innovations if the worth of existing practices is accurately reflected in the existing pattern of prices. From this viewpoint market structure is not the issue; rather what matters is a process of rivalry driven by alternative conjectures about how economic problems can be solved in better ways. It is the supply of new conjectures, the capability to apply them in practice and the open nature of markets in adapting to these new opportunities that matter for competition and development. Moreover, it is because innovation-led development entails adaptation to changing circumstances that markets have the central role they have; the economic problem is never solved because the solutions to problems only serve to define new problems.

However, in respect of development and competition, markets alone are not enough. Other instituted arrangements matter as well in relation to innovation and competition, not least of which are the arrangements through which innovation systems are established to connect firms with other knowledge-holding and -generating organizations. Thus there is a possibility that a competition policy for development may have relatively little to do with the agendas of competition authorities in the traditional sense of concerns over the abuse of monopoly power. Given the concerns currently expressed in the OECD, WTO and other agencies in relation to creating competition authorities in developing countries this is an issue we return to in the final section below.

The rest of the chapter is organized as follows. First, we sketch the elements of an evolutionary process of innovation-based competition and then introduce a framework to account for all the elements of evolutionary change. This provides the basis for the discussion in the final section on competition policy for developing economies.

COMPETITION AS EVOLUTION

The contrast between competition as a state of market equilibrium characterized by a structure, and competition as a process characterized by a rate and direction of change, is scarcely new, but a reading of much of the competition policy literature in relation to development suggests that old ideas have not been jettisoned. Even leaving aside Schumpeter, other economists of note have indicated forcefully that all is not well with the idea of competition as a state of equilibrium. Thus J.M. Clark (1961) claimed that the shift in perspective from equilibrium to process was the most challenging question in the theory of competition. Competition as a process depended for him on competent customers able to accurately appraise the products on offer, freedom to trade in any market, access to the means of production and independence of attitude among competitors. In this context what makes for competition is change in the nature of what is supplied, that is to say, innovation. Brenner (1987) is also a notable contributor to this literature with his claim that competition is a process of putting bets on new ideas as if we were analysing a horse race. That competition has the attributes of a contest was the theme explored by Knight (1935) and the implication that the outcome of the competitive process is open and unpredictable. What all of these writers are pointing to is competition as a process of rivalry and for rivalry to be meaningful the competitors need to be different. It is this that connects us immediately to the evolutionary foundations of competition and development.

All economies are developing economies and the issue we have to address is that of the framework that can draw together these ideas into an account of a competitive process consistent with the processes of self-transformation and development. It will need to incorporate entry, exit and innovation and the structural change that flows from the competitive dynamic. It should show how these processes are connected to shifting patterns of resource utilization and the growth of productivity and it should explain the presence of significant profits in the presence of intense competition, leading to the view that profits are not uniquely to be interpreted as the result of abuses of economic power. In short, the framework should be broadly evolutionary and provide the frame for the notion explored below that innovation policy is the strongest form of competition policy.

As with all modern evolutionary approaches the appropriate framework is based on the population method, for it is in populations that adaptation takes place in response to selection working on material provided by variety in relevant characteristics. To be precise, a population is defined by a set of economic activities taking place in productive plants where inputs are transformed into outputs. These plants are operated by profit-seeking firms and any firm may operate more than one plant producing more than one commodity. However, it is the plants that are selected for or against; selection for the associated firms is indirect. Each plant has a set of selective characteristics, those dimensions of its activity that are causally related to differential profitability and the growth of the capacity of the operating firm. These are the characteristics that are evaluated by the market environment and lead to the levels of input and output and prices associated with the operation of each plant. Thus what makes the different plants part of the same population is their experience of the same processes of market evaluation. A plant for example, producing multiple products for different markets will be operating in different populations and its overall performance will be an average of performance across the different market contexts. Population analysis provides a rich approach to the dynamics of competition in these many cases but here we focus on the base case, the single plant operated by a single plant firm, producing a commodity that is identical to that produced by rivals while drawing on the same factor markets. The market environment that defines the population is clearly identified, and in this case so are the relevant characteristics that underpin selection. For each firm there are three broad kinds of process at work, in relation to which competition is linked to differences in selective characteristics across the population of firms. The three sets of characteristics, a developmental triad, are as follows:

- Characteristics that causally influence the productive activity of the firm and determine its productive efficiency and the quality of the product it produces. Some of these are grounded in matters of technology but others are matters of organization, capability and workplace culture; the internal rules of the game that determine how each individual member of the firm interacts with the others, together with the objectives motivating behaviour at all levels.

- Characteristics that causally influence the ability of the firm to expand its productive capacity in the population through processes of investment in physical and human capital. These relate to questions of motivation and the ability to manage change processes as well as the ability to access the free capital to finance investment programmes.
- Characteristics that causally influence the ability of the firm to innovate in terms of technology or organization and thus to alter the first set of characteristics above. All innovation presupposes a growth of knowledge and this will depend on the firm's ability to access external knowledge as well as the effort it devotes internally to innovation.

Each firm is defined in these three dimensions, and characteristics in each dimension may not be independent, creating multiple trade-offs between efficiency, investment and innovation. As in all evolutionary argument, what matters is that the firms differ in the three dimensions, that there is variety in behaviour on which selection can do its work. Competition is multidimensional even in this much simplified account and cannot be reduced to behaviour in relation to the first set of characteristics. For example, it is not unknown for a firm to possess excellent technological or organizational capabilities that give it large cost advantages in its population and yet for the owners of that firm to refuse to grow and invest to capitalize on these advantages. Similarly, there are firms that have excellent technology but fall behind their rivals through an unwillingness or inability to innovate as effectively as their rivals, eventually consigning themselves to history.

As soon as we recognize that competition takes place in three dimensions, much of the record of business rivalry falls into view, as does the accuracy of Schumpeter's bon mot that it is a process of creative destruction. Moreover, the concept of the market environment involves much more than is covered by product and factor markets that evaluate the current distribution of activity. It extends to the capital markets and the supply of finance for investment and innovation as well as the markets for skills important in relation to innovation. Immediately, non-market institutions come into view for the ability to innovate for example, or to access skilled individuals they will be dependent on the surrounding knowledge environment in universities or the education and training system more generally. It will depend upon public policies in relation to the innovation and investment process. These considerations take us beyond our immediate brief but we clearly cannot understand the competitive process in markets solely in terms of markets (Bruton, 1998; Nelson and Pack, 1999).

If markets define the populations of rival firms, how are we to represent the competitive process in a way that allows for entry of new firms, exit of incumbent firms and the growth, decline and differential innovative performance of incumbent surviving firms?. How can we translate these processes into measures of average rates of development say in terms of the rate of structural change or the average change of resource productivity in a population? The answers are provided by the population method and we begin first with a pure accounting schema that accounts for all possible sources of change in the population.

ACCOUNTING FOR COMPETITION AND DEVELOPMENT

The population method is a remarkably general tool of analysis in that it provides an exhaustive way to account for all the changes that occur in a population of economic activities over a time interval of length, Δt. Let the population consist of a group of firms, being members of this population by virtue of being subject to the same selective process, each one with its set of selective characteristics. Four processes exhaust the possibilities of population change:

- pure replication of the continuing (surviving) entities that remain in the population over the interval, Δt, measured in terms of changes in the scale of output (activity) of each firm;
- the entry (birth) of new firms in that population within the time interval, Δt;
- the exit (death) of firms, alive in the population at the beginning of the interval Δt but departing the population within the interval;
- innovations (mutations) in the characteristics possessed by the continuing entities so that they vary individually between the initial and terminal dates defining the interval.

By partitioning the population of firms into survivors, entrants and exits we can perform a complete analysis of the change in the population between the two dates. An analysis of selection only in terms of the surviving firms, a standard approach in evolutionary analysis, is not satisfactory, for it loses sight of extremely important processes in relation to the birth and death of firms and indeed the birth and death of entire economic activities. Innovation in the surviving firms is an essential element in economic evolution, for it corresponds to a change in the characteristics of the entities and thus a change in the distribution of selective advantage in the population (Foster and Metcalfe, 2000). As with all evolutionary arguments, the focus of concern is upon the differential growth rates of the different activities in the population.

Let the first census date be at date t, and the second at date $t + \Delta t$. Let X $(t + \Delta t)$ and $X(t)$ be the aggregate output rates across the whole population at the two census dates. Define compound growth rates such that $g\Delta t$ is the growth rate of total activity, $g_c\Delta t$ is the growth rate of the activity of the surviving firms and $g_e\Delta t$ is the growth rate of the activity of the firms that exit during the interval. Thus for example, $X_c(t + \Delta t) = X_c(t)(1 + g_c\Delta t)$ defines the output profile of the surviving firms. Let $N(t + \Delta t)$ be the output contributed by those firms that enter the population in the interval Δt. Define the entry rate, $n \cdot \Delta t$, such that $N(t + \Delta t) = n \cdot \Delta t \cdot X(t + \Delta t)$. Similarly, define $e \cdot \Delta t$ as the fraction of output $X(t)$ accounted for by the firms that subsequently exit in the interval. Let $E(t + \Delta t)$ be the output contributed by the exiting firms while they remain alive, whence, $E(t + \Delta t) = e\Delta t \cdot X(t)$ $(1 + g_e\Delta t)$. It follows that

$$X(t + \Delta t) = X_c(t) + E(t + \Delta t) + N(t + \Delta t)$$

or

$$X(t + \Delta t) = X(t)\left\{\frac{(1 - e\Delta t)(1 + g_c\Delta t) + e\Delta t(1 + g_e\Delta t)}{1 - n\Delta t}\right\}$$

It is convenient to assume that all the exit events occur at the beginning of the interval, in which case, $g_e\Delta t = -1$, and we find that the growth rates, entry and exit rates are related by

$$\frac{(1 + g\Delta t)}{(1 + g_c\Delta t)} = \frac{(1 - e\Delta t)}{(1 - n\Delta t)} \tag{2.1}$$

Whenever the entry rate is the same as the exit rate then the growth rate of the surviving firms is the same as the growth rate in the population as a whole. More generally as e is greater or smaller than n, then g is greater or smaller than g_c, which accords with common sense provided we remember that the exit and entry rates are defined as proportions of aggregate activity not as numbers of firms.

We can now identify the dynamic of population change in respect of the surviving firms and the population as a whole. If we define $c_i(t)$ as

$X_i(t)/X_c(t)$ the share of each surviving firm in the aggregate output of the survivors, it follows that

$$c_i(t + \Delta t) = c_i(t)\left\{\frac{1 + g_i\Delta t}{1 + g_c\Delta t}\right\}$$

and

$$\frac{\Delta c_i}{\Delta t} = \frac{c_i(t + \Delta t) - c_i(t)}{\Delta t} = c_i(t)\left\{\frac{g_i - g_c}{1 + g_c\Delta t}\right\} \qquad (2.2)$$

with

$$g_c(t) = \sum c_i(t)g_i$$

Equations (2.2) are primitive replicator dynamic relations that hold exactly for surviving entities and they tie the rate of change of the structure of the sub-population to the diversity of growth rates contained within it. If the population is to evolve it must be a population defined by growth rate diversity, which is to say nothing more than the obvious statement that evolution is a dynamic process. If entity i is to increase its share of the activity of the surviving group it is necessary and sufficient that it grows more quickly than the average for its population, $g_i > g_c$, and conversely, if i is to decline in relative importance over the interval. Notice for completeness that since $\Sigma c_i(t) = 1$ it follows that $\Sigma \Delta c_i(t) = 0$, always a useful check on the internal consistency of the replicator process.

Now consider the total population and define $s_i(t)$ as $X_i(t)/X(t)$, the share of a continuing firm in the total output produced in the time interval, after taking account of entry and exit, and it follows that

$$s_i(t + \Delta t) = s_i(t)\left\{\frac{1 + g_i\Delta t}{1 + g\Delta t}\right\}$$

$$= s_i(t)\left\{\left(\frac{1 + g_i\Delta t}{1 + g_c\Delta t}\right)\left(\frac{1 - n\Delta t}{1 - e\Delta t}\right)\right\} \qquad (2.3)$$

and therefore, the two measures of population change are related by

$$\frac{s_i(t + \Delta t)}{s_i(t)} = \frac{c_i(t + \Delta t)}{c_i(t)}\left(\frac{1 - e\Delta t}{1 - n\Delta t}\right) \qquad (2.4)$$

If the exit and entry rates coincide then the two measures of structural change coincide and $g = g_c$. In general they will not, and although a surviving firm may be increasing its share in that sub-population ($g_i > g_c$) it may still be experiencing a declining share in the total output if n is sufficiently greater than e. Relations (2.2), (2.3) and (2.4) provide the elements of a replicator dynamic corrected for processes of entry and exit.

In many cases it is more transparent to work with the replicator dynamic in continuous time, in which case, letting the time interval Δt tend to zero, we can replace (2.1) to (2.3) by

$$g = g_c + n - e \tag{2.1'}$$

$$\frac{dc_i}{dt} = c_i(t)(g_i - g_c) \tag{2.2'}$$

$$\frac{ds_i}{dt} = s_i(t)(g_i - g) = s_i(t)(g_i - g_c - n + e) \tag{2.3'}$$

These relations provide a complete description of the different sources of evolution that restructure any population as a result of the growth rate diversity contained within it. They are compatible with any theory of the underlying processes, whether deterministic or stochastic. Like any accounting scheme they are a filing system in which to locate the various forces that jointly exhaust the competitive process, a filing system that serves to provide a complete partitioning of the processes that describe the development of a population at the most inclusive level. They tie together four kinds of competitive change, which in practice we expect to give rise to causally effective explanations in relation to development of the population. They also provide a frame in which to place competition policy in its developmental context. What we see through this population method is the fundamental evolutionary theme that change is contingent on variety. The structures of the populations change because the growth rates of the survivors are distributed around a population average growth rate and because the entry and exit rates differ. In short, development is an evolutionary process of displacement and replacement, a process of self-transformation in which the population in question becomes something different. It is in this sense that competition is a regulator of development, a method of reallocating resources to different uses, a method for generating structural change. From this perspective an economy is a set of interdependent interacting populations of activities that utilize resources and the accounting method will apply at any level of disaggregation we choose. Developmental change is nested and we can focus the lens of population change according to the problem in hand.

To illustrate this point consider a familiar, if limited, index of development, the growth in resource productivity in an industry over some time interval. Using the accounting framework, we can group the factors at work into 'selection processes' defined in terms of the differential growth or decline of survivors and the elimination of exiting firms and 'innovation processes' defined in terms of the entrants and the changes in the characteristics of the surviving firms. Suppose that the characteristic in question is average labour productivity in this population of firms, labelled z, and we want to know how the population average value, labelled $\bar{z}$, changes over our time interval. It follows from the definitions above that in relation to the 'selection processes'

$$\bar{z}(t) = (1 - e)\bar{z}_c(t) + e\bar{z}_e(t)$$

where $\bar{z}_c(t) = \Sigma c_i(t)z_i(t)$ and $\bar{z}_e(t)$ is the average value of $z(t)$ for those entities that will exit over the interval Δt. Similarly, in relation to the 'innovation processes'

$$\bar{z}(t + \Delta t) = (1 - n)\bar{z}_c(t + \Delta t) + n\bar{z}_n(t + \Delta t)$$

where $\bar{z}_n$ is the average value of $z(t + \Delta t)$ for the entrants over the interval. The change in $\bar{z}$ follows as

$$\Delta\bar{z} = \bar{z}(t + \Delta t) - \bar{z}(t) = (1 - n)\Delta\bar{z}_c + n[\bar{z}_n(t + \Delta t) - \bar{z}_c(t + \Delta t)]$$
$$- e[\bar{z}_e(t) - \bar{z}_c(t)] \qquad (2.5)$$

Expression (2.5) is a complete accounting for the change in average population value of labour productivity. On the right-hand side the first term is the selection effect operating on the surviving firms, adjusted for the impact of entry. The second and third terms reflect the productivity levels in entrants and exits, expressed as deviations from the average productivity value for the continuing entities at the appropriate dates.[2]

Now the change in average productivity among the survivors can be expressed more fully by taking account of the so-called Price equation, a well-known result in evolutionary population analysis (Price, 1970; Frank, 1998; Metcalfe, 1998; Gintis, 2002; Andersen, 2004). This method decomposes the change in average value into two additive effects, one due to selection and the other due to innovation. Thus, following a proper accounting at the two dates, we find

$$\Delta\bar{z}_c = \sum c_i(t + \Delta t)z_i(t + \Delta t) - \sum c_i(t)z_i(t)$$

$$= \sum \Delta c_i z_i(t) + \sum c_i(t + \Delta t)\Delta z_i$$

$$= \frac{1}{1 + g_c}\left\{ \sum c_i(t)(g_i - g_c)z_i(t) + \sum c_i(t)(1 + g_i)\Delta g_i \right\}$$

or

$$(1 + g_c)\Delta \bar{z}_c = C_c(g_i z_i) + E_c[(1 + g_i) \cdot \Delta z_i] \qquad (2.6)$$

Expression (2.6) is the Price equation; in which, $C_c(g_i z_i)$, the measure of the selection effect, is the (c_i weighted) covariance between fitness values (the growth rates g_i) and the values of z_i at the initial census date. This captures the idea that the change in the average value of the characteristic depends on how that characteristic co-varies with growth rates across the population. The second term, $E_c[(1 + g_i) \cdot \Delta z_i]$, the measure of the innovation effect, is the expected value (again c_i weighted) between the growth rates and the changes in the characteristic values at the level of each firm. Notice the recursive nature of this formulation; for if the entities are also defined as sub-populations of further entities we can apply the Price equation successively to each sub-population. For example, if entity i itself consists of a population of j sub-entities we can apply the Price method and write

$$(1 + g_i)\Delta \bar{z}_i = C_{cj}(g_{ij}, z_{ij}) + E_{cj}[(1 + g_{ij})\Delta z_{ij}]$$

and apply this to each of the i entities in the original population. As Andersen (2004) suggests, the Price equation 'eats its own tail', an attribute of considerable significance in the analysis of multilevel evolutionary processes. It means that we can decompose population change into change between any number of sub-populations and change within sub-populations in an identical fashion, so that at each level of aggregation we can reflect the forces of adaptation whether through selection or innovation.

The force of this approach can be simply summarized. Though selection is only one level of explanation for population change, it cannot be separated from innovation. Innovation creates the variety on which selection depends and the ensuing process reshapes the conditions for further innovation. It is an ensemble-level rather than an individual-level explanation, but one that is based on the specifics of individual variation (Matthen and Ariew, 2002).

We have applied the accounting across two generations of a population of firms, and of course we can iterate the procedure indefinitely. As we do so the composition of the population of the firms will change and a date may be reached when not one of the original members of the population remains alive. In changing the members of the population we naturally change the distribution of capabilities and propensities to grow and to innovate so that the causal nature of the evolutionary process varies in the background. However, the activity continues and provided that the forces of selection remain the same we can continue to speak of a given population.

COMPETITION POLICY FOR DEVELOPING ECONOMIES

Within the last decade there has been a steadily growing interest in the matter of applying competition law in developing economies, stimulated by the general decline in tariff barriers to trade and stoked by the concerns of UNCTAD, the WTO and the OECD (Tarullo, 1999; Holmes, 2002; Janow, 2003). We do not consider the specific issues of multilateral or bilateral approaches to require developing countries to adopt competition law, or the administrative competences that are required to create and operate a competition authority. Rather we ask, in the light of the above, what kind of competition law should frame competition policy? Alternatively, what rules of the competition process are pro-development? Put simply, the real danger is enforcing the adoption of a 'wrong model of competition', one that is inimical to economic development. In practice the exercise of competition law is a deeply practical matter. In the telecoms market for example, it involves questions of interconnection access to an infrastructure and charging in a system of great complexity. Again our concern is with the general framework, not the specifics of individual cases that vary greatly. As De Leon (2000) makes clear there is little prospect of translating competition law and practice from advanced Western economies to the developing world. Local institutions matter and competition policy may clash irreconcilably with the established business culture and be undermined as a consequence. Moreover, a dynamic view of competition and its relation to innovation results in a very different take on the competition problem.

Innovation is a correlate of increasing returns and the latter undermines any resort to the precepts of perfect competition as a guide for policy. In a similar vein, Singleton (1997) argues, persuasively in our view, that competition policy should recognize the discovery-based nature of competition; it should not assume that the economic problem is already solved in its final form. To argue thus would be to deny the presence of a development problem.[3]

We too shall argue that the best competition policy is a pro-innovation policy and that this takes the debate over competition policy into a far broader domain, one consistent with a process view of competition and the instituted context of competition. The general objective is to support development and so raise average standards of living and reduce the inequality of its distribution. Innovation and the growth of practical knowledge is the necessary condition for this transformation to occur.[4]

A policy to encourage competition and facilitate economic development in terms of the framework sketched above clearly looks very different from a conventional 'antitrust' policy. It is wider in scope and dynamic in focus, it is a set of policies to stimulate change in one or more of the four categories outlined above. It is not a set of policies to pass negative judgement on the structure of markets or the alleged excess profitability of some firms but rather to stimulate the market process positively and to connect that to superior profitability and its converse (Audretsch, Baumol and Burke, 2001). A competition policy for development places at its core, ongoing structural change, the exit of unprofitable activities and the entry of new innovation-based activities. Development results from this evolutionary process if and only if activities with superior characteristics displace less productive activities, and this only occurs to the extent that the distribution of the growth rates of activities is positively correlated with the distribution of the pro-development characteristics of productive activities. If there is no correlation there is no development, at best only random drift, and so a top-level requirement of a competition policy is that it should facilitate the emergence of the appropriate patterns of correlation. The consequence would be for example, that firms with better products in the perception of users, or firms with better methods of production, can grow their share of the relevant markets by growing faster than their rivals. In turn this leads to a set of questions about the instituted rules of the game that cut to the core of the efficacy of the competitive process. Do product and factor markets operate such that the firms with superior process technology are also the lowest-cost, most profitable firms? Do markets work such that the activities with superior profitability are also the faster-expanding activities? Do markets and the institutions supporting innovation work such that the faster-expanding firms are also the more innovative firms? Do markets work to eliminate activities that are no longer profitable, do they work to facilitate the entry of firms with superior new technologies or ways of organizing a business?

These are questions about the ability of the market process to support development. In its broadest sense what is required is that better activities are more profitable, and whether or not this is the case depends on the price-setting process in a fundamental way. As a general rule, firms set prices and the issue is what determines their freedom so to do. In part this depends on the degree of perfection of the market, which in turn depends on the organization of the market and the capacity to disseminate information among market participants. It also depends on the speed with which market participants are able to react to different offers, either as consumers or suppliers of resources. As a general rule, price structures for outputs and inputs of the same quality that are uniform are more efficacious from a dynamic viewpoint than price structures that are non-uniform or arbitrary. A perfect market achieves this result in that information is disseminated so widely and the recipients of it can respond so quickly that firms are forced to set the same prices, with the consequence that the differential rates of growth of their activities are tied to differential access to resources and markets to the maximal degree. Better product quality and lower price attract customers more quickly and higher wages and better employment conditions more quickly attract employees. The outcomes in terms of profitability influence the ability to invest in productive capacity to match the growth of the market, either through profit retention or access to external capital. But a balance needs to be drawn. Lower prices and higher wages provide greater opportunity for expansion but reduce the wherewithal to invest in capacity to meet that expansion of market. This dilemma is resolved differently in each individual firm in a way that reflects their underpinning technological and organizational capabilities. Better methods of production and or higher-quality products or net employment advantages provide the space to offer lower prices, higher wages and invest more rapidly than rivals.

Several general consequences follow for the competitive process. Firms with above-average technical and organizational characteristics will enjoy above-average growth when markets are more perfect.[5] Of course, the growth rates are not intrinsic characteristics of the firms but are the consequence of the market process and they are mutually determined; how one firm's activities expand or contract cannot be separated from the performance of the other firms in the population. Thus to speak of the competitiveness of the individual firm as if that is an attribute of that firm is meaningless, whatever competitive performance it enjoys depends on where it stands in the entire population of competitors and the particular nature of the market environment. This is the nature of a selection process, growth rates are the degrees of fitness of the different activities and the degrees of economic fitness of rival activities are mutually determining.

Efficient markets and adaptive behaviours in the sense discussed above are only part of the problem. What is at least as important is that markets are open, that they facilitate and create incentives to challenge established positions and that they eliminate activities that are no longer viable in the prevailing environment. Barriers to entry, whether created by incumbents or by the regulation of the market process, have adverse effects on development as does the operation of activities that are below the survival margin and that are kept 'alive' through subsidy or other intervention. However, this involves much more than a traditional concern with artificial barriers to entry and exclusionary practices in general. Much more significant is the 'supply' of potential entrant activities, the stimulus to enterprise more generally and to innovation-based enterprise in particular. Without a flow of entrants challenging existing positions, the continued basis of an evolutionary competitive process is undermined. Left to itself competition consumes its own fuel and leads to market concentration and ultimately to the survival of firms with broadly similar characteristics. Keeping competition active is thus contingent on rules of the game that facilitate the formation of new businesses and ensures that they have access to capital for expansion and other resources in their early stages of growth. In turn, the rate of activity creation will depend on the rate at which innovative business opportunities can be identified and this will depend to a considerable degree on the wider context of innovation and enterprise in the economy.

We turn now to the claim that the most effective competition policy is a general innovation policy. The innovation processes identified above provide the fuel that drives competition and the regulation of development as to rate and direction. They depend to a degree on the support for the formation of scientific and technological capabilities but this is not sufficient. Innovation involves much more than invention and the recognition of technological possibility; it also requires an ability to identify possible markets, an ability to lead and organize the business process and ready access to productive inputs (Witt, 1998; Metcalfe, 2004). Moreover, as Schumpeter ([1911] 1934) recognized so clearly, the barriers to enterprise, whether economic, social or cultural, can be formidable and the effect of tradition a major limitation on innovation. Thus the ability of policy to facilitate enterprise, to connect the science and technology base to opportunities for commercial exploitation, lies at the core of the competitive process. Recently, evolutionary scholars and others have developed this idea through an analysis of innovation systems (Teubal, 1996; Edquist et al., 2004), expressed in terms of the activities external to the firm that condition their innovative capabilities. Like markets, innovation systems cannot be presumed, they have to be organized and sustained and it is appropriate to think of them not simply in terms of national level organizations but as locally organized sets of interactions (Edquist et al., 2004). Systems of innovation imply different component knowledge-based organizations and they also presume connections, interactions between these organizations usually focused upon the pursuit of particular innovation problems in particular market and sector contexts. This is not the place to expand on this rich literature except to make two points. First, those innovation systems provide instituted support for the competitive process; not all the dimensions of competition can be reflected through markets. Second, innovation systems are embedded in the market process and to this degree will be expected to self-organize and self-transform as the innovation problems change. If the market processes outlined above do not work well it is not likely that innovation processes will work well either and innovation systems are more likely then to degenerate into science and technology support systems with little connection with business and development.

It is traditional in these literatures to focus on the connection between development and innovation-based market entry. It is too easy to forget the converse process, that of ensuring the exit of non-viable activities or firms. The rules regarding insolvency and bankruptcy are to this degree essential to competition policy in the process sense. Similarly, public policies of subsidizing non-viable activities, for whatever reason, may have the consequence that development is slowed and distorted as resources more valuable in other activities are locked into inappropriate uses. A broader issue is relevant here. It is not unusual to find business activities that would be governed better by a different firm and so one stimulus to the competitive process is the trading of distinctive activities among firms so that they meet their strategic objectives better. The market for corporate control is so often seen as a negative control mechanism for wayward management that the more positive role of the market for corporate control as part of the business innovation mechanism is too readily overlooked. Especially in industries subjected to rapid technological change the trading of integrated business activities is one essential component in the building of competitive capabilities.

Having drawn a broad definition of the scope of competition policy as regulator of development it is appropriate to reflect on its connections with the regulation of competition in the narrower sense. Consider first the focus on excess profits attributable to the exploitation of a monopolistic or monopsonistic market structure. That this is possible is not denied but in situations in which competition is active in the sense used here these positions are unlikely to last long unless supported by artificial restrictions on market entry. Moreover, profits are, from this view, not the result of market power but of superior competitive advantage grounded in superior business knowledge. To regulate them away is to put at risk the incentives to innovate in any substantial degree and, to the extent that these profits are premised on superior innovative ability, to prejudice the further progress of innovation. As Richardson (1960) pointed out long ago, all manner of static market imperfections can be justified if they lead to superior paths of investment and innovation, objectives that perfect competition by its nature cannot serve well.[6] The consequence of the competitive process is almost inevitably concentration and market dominance unless this is offset by innovation-based entry. Monopoly is the prize in the competition draw, which is why innovation and entry are so important, not because of the effect on price-cost margins but because of the potential effects of monopoly in limiting the sources of innovation. If there is a genuine problem with monopoly it is in relation to the diminution of innovation that the policy concerns should be addressed. We are not aware that this practice is the case among competition authorities in general.

What then is the test for the presence of competition if the market structure test is ruled out? It is that the market structure is changing as measured say by the rate of change of a concentration index such as the Herfindahl. What then is the test for competition being pro-development? It is that the market structure is evolving in such a way as to increase the efficiency and effectiveness with which resources are used. If these tests are met, we suggest that 'antitrust', per se, is not a reliable basis for intervention in the competitive process.

CONCLUSION

We have suggested that the competition process and the development process are so intertwined as to be indistinguishable to all intents and purposes. An economy that is dormant is unlikely to be competitive, it will not be characterized by the creation and application of new knowledge, it will be asleep and it will offer no escape from poverty. By contrast an innovation-based economy, in which new knowledge is continually generated and applied, will be competitive. It will be characterized by ongoing structural and qualitative change, by selection, by entry and exit so that the economy continually becomes a new economy. In this process, competition policy is far broader and more significant than is encompassed by the notion of antitrust. It covers the regulation of the market process, the determination of the scope of markets and the rules of the game within them, together with the openness of markets. However, it extends beyond markets too, in particular, the wider conditions that influence innovation and enterprise. In this context it seems unlikely that the recent debates in the WTO and elsewhere on establishing competition law in developing economies will be fruitful unless a narrow 'within market' perspective on competition is abandoned. By contrast, if energies were devoted to the promulgation of the need for innovation and enterprise then the task of ensuring competition would be better done.

NOTES

1. This theme is the foundation of the Schumpeterian trade-off, in which monopoly power provides the resources to fund innovation; the losses from restrictions of output must then be balanced against the gains from better products or more efficient methods of production (Littlechild, 1981; Nelson and Winter, 1982).
2. In his survey of industry dynamics processes in LDCs, Tybout (2000) discusses some limited empirical evidence in favour of relatively high rates of turnover in plants and employment, finding that efficiency, compared with survivors, is lower in exiting plants and in entrant plants, and that these categories rarely account for more than 5 percent of total output in any year. This suggests that some entrants fail to survive, and that those that do soon overcome the liability of newness and achieve at least average levels of productivity in the relevant populations.
3. As Singleton (1997) also points out, in many developing countries the focus of the attention of competition authorities would be on the activities of the State in allocating resources, controlling prices and managing production and distribution.
4. Space precludes discussion of the ethical aspects of this stance. The blunt fact is that innovation-based competition creates losers as well as winners. If average standards of life improve they do so in the context of much distress and hopes falsified. Restless systems are uncomfortable systems so there is a policy dimension of welfare protection that we do not address here.
5. A context in which every firm is a local monopolist would be a system in which market shares would be frozen and development suspended. The degree of perfection of markets is a quite different concept from the degree of perfection of competition, a point that Makowski and Ostroy (2001) seem to fail to recognize.
6. See Stiglitz (1997) for the more general argument that innovation and investment activities incur knowledge overheads that make imperfect competition (in the Chamberlin sense) the norm. In this view the so-called Harberger triangles and wastes of rent-seeking fall into insignificance relative to the consumer surpluses created by innovation (Littlechild, 1981).

REFERENCES

Andersen, E.S. (2004), 'Evolutionary Econometrics: From Joseph Schumpeter's Failed Econometrics to George Price's General Evometrics and Beyond', mimeo, Aalborg University.

Audretsch, D.B., W.J. Baumol and A.E. Burke (2001), 'Competition Policy in Dynamic Markets', *International Journal of Industrial Organization*, **19**, 613–34.

Brenner, R. (1987), *Rivalry: In Business, Science, Among Nations*, Cambridge University Press.

Bruton, H.J. (1998), 'A Reconsideration of Import Substitution', *Journal of Economic Literature*, **36**, 903–36.

Charles River Associates (2002), *Innovation and Competition Policy*, Office of Fair Trading, London.

Clark, J.M. (1961), *Competition as a Dynamic Process*, Brookings Institute, Washington.

De Leon, I. (2000), 'The Role of Competition Policy in the Promotion of Competitiveness and Development', *World Competition*, **23** (4), 115–36.

Edquist, C., F. Malerba, J.S. Metcalfe, F. Montobbio and W.E. Steinmueller (2004), 'Sectoral Systems: Implications for European Technology Policy', in F. Malerba (ed.), *Sectoral Systems of Innovation*, Cambridge University Press.

Fisher, F.M. (2000), 'The IBM and Microsoft Cases: What's the Difference?', *American Economic Review*, **90** (2), 180–83.

Foster, J. and J.S. Metcalfe (2000), *Frontiers of Evolutionary Economics*, Cheltenham, UK and Northampton, MA, USA: Edward Elgar.

Frank, S.A. (1998), *Foundations of Social Evolution*, Princeton University Press.

Gintis, H. (2002), *Game Theory Evolving*, Princeton University Press.

Holmes, P. (2002), 'Trade, Competition and the WTO', in B. Hoekman, A. Mattoo and P. English (eds), *Development, Trade and the WTO*, Washington: World Bank.

Janow, M.E. (2003), 'Developing Competition Policy: A Role for the WTO', *Consumer Policy Review*, **13** (1), 17–24.

Knight, F. (1935), *The Ethics of Competition and other Essays*, London: George Allen and Unwin.

Krattenmaker, T.G., R.H. Lande and S.C. Salop (1987), 'Monopoly Power and Market Power in Antitrust Law', *The Georgetown Law Journal*, **76**, 241–69.

Kuznets, S. (1977), 'Two Centuries of Economic Growth: Reflections on US Experience', *American Economic Review*, **67**, 1–14.

Littlechild, S.C. (1981), 'Misleading Calculations of the Social Cost of Monopoly Power', *Economic Journal*, **91**, 348–63.

Makowski, L. and J.M. Ostroy (2001), 'Perfect Competition and the Creativity of the Market', *Journal of Economic Literature*, **39**, 479–535.

Matthen, M. and A. Ariew (2002), 'Two Ways of Thinking about Fitness and Natural Selection', *Journal of Philosophy*, **99** (2), 55–83.

Metcalfe, J.S. (1998), *Evolutionary Economics and Creative Destruction*, London: Routledge.

Metcalfe, J.S. (2004), 'The Entrepreneur and the Style of Modern Economics', *Journal of Evolutionary Economics*, **14** (2), 157–75.

Metcalfe, J.S., J. Foster and R. Ramlogan (2006), 'Adaptive Economic Growth', *Cambridge Journal of Economics*, **30** (1), 7.

Nelson, R.R. and H. Pack (1999), 'The Asian Miracle and Modern Growth Theory', *Economic Journal*, **109**, 416–36.

Nelson, R.R. and S. Winter (1982), *An Evolutionary Theory of Economic Change*, Belknap: Harvard University Press.

Price, G.R. (1970), 'Selection and Covariance', *Nature*, **227**, 520–21.

Richardson, G. (1960), *Information and Investment*, Oxford University Press.

Schumpeter, J. [1911] (1934), *The Theory of Economic Development*, Oxford University Press.

Singleton, R.C. (1997), 'Competition Policy for Developing Countries: A Long-run Entry-based Approach', *Contemporary Economic Policy*, **15** (2), 1–11.

Stiglitz, J. (1997), *Whither Socialism*, Cambridge, MA: MIT Press.

Tarullo, D.K. (1999), 'Competition Policy for Developing Markets', *Journal of International Economic Law*, **2** (3), 445–55.

Teubal, M. (1996), 'R&D and Technology Policy in NICs as Learning Processes', *World Development*, **24**, 449–60.

Tybout, J.R. (2000), 'Manufacturing Firms in Developing Countries: How Well Do They Do, and Why?', *Journal of Economic Literature*, **38** (1), 11–44.

Witt, U. (1998), 'Imagination and Leadership – the Neglected Dimension of an Evolutionary Theory of the Firm', *Journal of Economic Behavior and Organization*, **35**, 161–77.

3. Model competition laws

Cassey Lee

INTRODUCTION

The number of countries that have implemented competition law has risen significantly in the past two decades. More than half of such countries enacted competition laws within the 1990–99 period – the decade of extensive economic reforms. The drafting of competition laws in these countries benefited from the experiences of some of the more developed countries or communities such as the United States, Japan, Germany and the European Community. There is in fact a discernable legal lineage in the competition laws of some countries (Table 3.1). For example, Thailand, in drafting its own competition law, borrowed from South Korea, which in turn was influenced by the competition laws of Japan and Germany. It is well known that both Japan and Germany implemented their competition laws during the occupation period by the United States.

International aid and development agencies such as the OECD, the World Bank and UNCTAD have also been influential in prompting developing countries to implement competition laws. Both Indonesia and Thailand implemented their competition laws as part of their commitments in the structural adjustment programmes in the aftermath of the Asian financial crisis in 1997/98. Similarly, South Korea made significant reforms in its competition law under similar circumstances.

Table 3.1   Country influence in competition law design

Country	Influence From
Japan (1947)	USA (1890)
Australia (1974)	USA (1890)
South Korea (1980)	Japan (1947), Germany (1957)
Taiwan (1992)	Japan (1947), Germany (1957)
Thailand (1999)	South Korea (1980)
Indonesia (1999)	USA (1890), Japan (1947), Germany (1957), EC

Such international agencies have also played another important role, namely in providing technical assistance in the drafting of competition laws. An aspect of this is the formulation of a 'model competition law', which serves as a template for developing countries that are drafting their own laws. The World Bank published its model in 1999, while UNCTAD's latest version was published in 2003. The Commonwealth Secretariat has also issued its own model competition law in 2002.

There are very few discussions on the similarities and differences between these model competition laws. This gap in the comparative competition law literature is surprising given their importance as potential templates for countries drafting their own competition laws. This chapter attempts to address this gap by comparing the two major model competition laws published by the World Bank-OECD and UNCTAD. Apart from discussing the similarities and differences between these two model laws, the chapter attempts to draw implications for policy-makers involved in the drafting of competition laws.

The outline for the rest of the chapter is as follows. A comparison between the model competition laws of World Bank-OECD and UNCTAD is undertaken in the next section. In the sub-sections the focus is on the objectives of competition law, its scope and definitions, restrictive agreements, abuse of dominance and merger controls. The final section concludes. The relevant excerpts of the model laws are provided in the appendices.

THE WORLD BANK-OECD AND UNCTAD MODEL COMPETITION LAWS

There are some standard features of competition laws that are usually present in almost all competition laws that have been enacted (Table 3.2). These include the following:

- a statement on the objective of the competition law;
- a delineation of the scope of the law and definitions therein;
- a list of prohibited agreements and arrangements;
- abuse of dominance; and
- merger controls and notification.

The discussions on the above points in each document are quite distinctive. The World Bank-OECD provides a more broad-based and foundational discussion on each item, with occasional references to the experiences of a few developed countries such as the United States, Canada and France. The UNCTAD document on the other hand, devotes a considerable amount of

Table 3.2 Basic structure of model competition laws

Main Areas	World Bank-OECD (1999)	UNCTAD (2003)
Objective	Chapter 1	Chapter 1
Definition	Chapter 2	Chapter 2
Restrictive agreements	Chapter 3	Chapter 3
Abuse of dominance	Chapter 5	Chapter 4
Merger controls	Chapter 4	Chapter 5

space to country experience, including many developing countries. One gets the impression that the World Bank-OECD approach is generally more substantive (in the basic foundation) while UNCTAD is more inclusive (recording a wide range of experiences). This is consistent with perceptions on the modus operandi of the two organizations – the former seeks to influence policy implementation directly (e.g., financial aid with structural reform requirements), the latter more persuasively (via advisory technical assistance). In the following sub-sections, the recommendations from both the World Bank-OECD and UNCTAD model competition laws are compared.

Objectives of Competition Law

The objective of competition law is stated in the World Bank-OECD (1999, p. 142) in the following manner: 'This Law is intended to maintain and enhance competition in order ultimately to enhance consumer welfare.' Similarly, in UNCTAD (2003, p. 13) as: 'To control or eliminate restrictive agreements or arrangements among enterprises, or acquisition and/or abuse of dominant positions of market power, which limit access to markets or otherwise unduly restrain competition, adversely affecting domestic and international trade or economic development.'

The World Bank-OECD's approach is to define the objective of competition law in broader terms, namely to protect and enhance the competition process. UNCTAD focuses on the actions that are needed to achieve this. These two statements are different sides of the same coin. This is recognized in the World Bank-OECD (1999, p. 2): 'The most common of the objectives cited is the maintenance of the competitive process or of free competition, or the protection or promotion of effective competition. These are seen as synonymous with striking down or preventing unreasonable restraints on competition.'

Despite such similarities there are differences in the rest of the statements of definition in the two documents. These refer to the 'ultimate' targets or beneficiaries of competition law enforcement. For the World Bank-OECD, the ultimate objective is the enhancement of consumer welfare. Some may contend that this may be too restrictive, preferring social welfare instead. UNCTAD's approach to defining the ultimate beneficiaries of competition policy is somewhat broader, emphasizing the domestic and international trade and economic development. A consequence of this broader approach is that the ultimate beneficiary in UNCTAD's definition is vague or can even be interpreted as left undefined.[1] This has the advantage of implicitly incorporating a wide range of objectives such as consumer welfare, social welfare, economic efficiency and the protection of small business. The disadvantage is that some of these implicit objectives may conflict with each other.

There is a general consensus amongst economists that one of the potential benefits of competition is economic efficiency. However, economic efficiency may also be consistent with non-competitive situations, for example, in cases involving natural monopoly, network effects and innovation (dynamic efficiency).

As shall be seen later, the choice between narrow and broad statements of competition law objectives may have implications for the instruments, criteria and legal and economic standards in administering and enforcing competition law (World Bank-OECD, 1999).

How should countries frame their statement on competition law objectives? Should they adopt the more focused but narrow approach of the WB-OECD or the broader but conceivably vaguer approach of UNCTAD? A brief survey of 23 countries (Table 3.3) indicates that the enhancement of competition (19 countries), the elimination/prevention of Restrictive Business Practices (RBPs) (11), economic efficiency (10), consumer welfare (8) and economic freedom (6) are the five most cited objectives of competition laws in the countries surveyed.

Scope of Competition Law

The scope of competition law specifies the entities (enterprises, natural persons etc.) to which the law applies. It can also specify any exclusion from the law. Excerpts from the WB-OECD and UNCTAD model competition laws are presented in Appendix 3.1 at the end of the chapter.

Typically, competition law covers all commercial economic activity in its myriad forms. These include actions, transactions, agreements and arrangements involving goods, services and intellectual property. Both the WB-OECD and the UNCTAD model laws have this basic statement.

There are some interesting differences between the two model laws. The WB-OECD model law includes acts undertaken outside the country but

Table 3.3   Statement on competition law objectives in selected countries

Country	Promote Competition	Eliminate RBPs	Economic Efficiency	Economic Freedom	Consumer Welfare
Algeria	X		X		X
Armenia	X				X
Canada	X		X		
Denmark	X		X		
Estonia	X	X			
Gabon		X		X	
India	X	X		X	X
Hungary	X		X		
Mongolia	X	X			
Norway	X		X		
Panama		X	X		X
Peru		X			X
Russia		X	X		
Spain	X			X	
Sweden	X				
Switzerland	X	X			
USA	X		X	X	
Taiwan	X				X
Tunisia	X	X		X	
Ukraine		X			
Venezuela	X		X	X	X
Zambia	X	X	X		X
EC	X				
Total	19	11	10	6	8

which have substantial effect in the country. It also excludes workers' and employees' union-related activities.

In its model competition law, UNCTAD includes 'natural persons' (as distinct from and in addition to enterprises) as a separate entity to which the law applies. Such natural persons include the owners, managers or employees of enterprises. UNCTAD also excludes all acts of the State and State-related agencies from the application of the competition law. The discussions in UNCTAD (2003) appears to suggest that State-owned enterprises may be included but this varies from country to country.

The extraterritorial element in the WB-OECD model law is an interesting one. While relevant, it remains to be seen how such provisions can be enforced, particularly in small developing countries. Unlike UNCTAD the WB-OECD defines 'firms' as including natural persons. The exclusions related to the State that are provided for in the UNCTAD model law also require careful consideration. Developing countries may pursue development strategies that require significant state intervention in the economy that may compromise competition (at least in the short and medium term). Even if such strategies are to be pursued and State-related acts are excluded in the competition law, some mechanisms of consultation (with the competition authority) should be implemented, at the very minimum.

Definitions in Competition Law

The importance of definitions in competition law becomes apparent in the process of enforcing a competition law. Characterizations and measures of market structure depend on the definitions employed in the law. Definitions can be set out generally in the initial part of the statute or more specifically in the relevant sections of the statute such as mergers and abuse of dominance.

Appendix 3.2, at the end of the chapter, sets out some of the basic definitions in the model competition laws of both the WB-OECD and UNCTAD. Both the WB-OECD and UNCTAD are in agreement on the choice of two major definitions in competition law, namely firms or enterprises and the (relevant) market. The WB-OECD uses the term 'firms' in a broader sense to include 'any natural or legal person, government body, partnership or association in any form engaged directly or indirectly in economic activity'. UNCTAD defines 'enterprises' in a similar way to the WB-OECD's meaning of the term 'firm'. Both the WB-OECD and UNCTAD also agree on the two elements in the definition of the market/relevant market. These are substitutability of goods (product market) and geographic delineation (geographic market).

In addition to the above, the WB-OECD's model competition law also defines very basic terms such as 'competition' and 'good'. UNCTAD on the other hand, provides a specific definition on the 'dominant position of market power'. The WB-OECD also defines dominant position but in the subsection pertaining to the abuse of dominant position. Overall, both model competition laws agree on the basic definitions used in competition laws.

Restrictive Agreements

Transactions between firms are often governed by implicit or explicit agreements amongst themselves. These agreements can be classified as either horizontal or vertical agreements (UNCTAD, 2003, p. 20):

- Horizontal agreements are concluded between firms engaged in the same activities.

- Vertical agreements are concluded between firms at different stages of the manufacturing or distribution process (i.e., between an upstream and a downstream firm).

Such agreements tend to be 'restrictive' in the sense of reducing the independence of firms involved to undertake alternative business decisions. When such agreements significantly lessen competition, they are said to be 'anti-competitive'. The five major types of restrictive agreements identified in both the WB-OECD and UNCTAD model competition laws are as follows:

- price fixing (includes tariffs, discounts, surcharges and any other charges);
- quantity fixing;
- market allocation (includes geographic and customer allocation);
- refusal to deal (comprising both refusal to purchase and refusal to supply); and
- collusive bidding/tendering.

With the exception of collusive bidding, all the above agreements can take place either horizontally or vertically. The term 'vertical restraints' is also used to denote the various types of restrictive vertical agreements such as retail price maintenance (a form of price fixing), quantity forcing (quantity fixing), exclusive dealing (where a manufacturing firm prohibits a distributor firm from dealing with competing products or distributors, subject to the threat of refusal to supply), and tying (also subject to the threat of refusal to supply).

While both the WB-OECD and UNCTAD model competition laws are in agreement on the types of restrictive agreements (see Appendix 3.3), there are some differences in terms of the provisions for:

- horizontal vs. vertical restrictive agreements; and
- per se vs. rule of reason prohibitions.

The WB-OECD model law makes an explicit distinction in their model law between prohibitions subjected to per se illegality and rule of reason. In the model law, horizontal restrictive agreements (i.e., agreements between competitors) that are subjected to per se illegality include:

- price fixing;
- quantity fixing;
- market allocation;
- refusal to deal;

- collusive bidding/tendering; and
- elimination of actual or potential sellers or purchasers from the market.

Restrictive agreements other than those listed above are subjected to rule of reason. The application of rule of reason consists of two elements (WB-OECD, 1999, p. 144):

1. A threshold criteria:
   (i) for competing firms (i.e., horizontal agreement). The restrictive agreement cannot be found to significantly limit competition unless shares of the firms participating in the agreement collectively exceed 20 percent of a market affected by the agreement.
   (ii) for non-competing firms (i.e., vertical agreement). The restrictive agreement cannot be found to significantly limit competition unless:
        (a) at least one of the parties holds a dominant position in a market affected by the agreement;[2] or
        (b) the limitation of competition results from the fact that similar agreements are widespread in a market affected by the agreement.
2. A cost–benefit comparison between 'the effects of any limitation on competition that result or are likely to result from the agreement' and 'gains in real as opposed to merely pecuniary efficiencies', applying either a total welfare standard (giving equal weight to consumers and producers) or a consumer welfare standard.

The rule of reason also relates to the exemption of such restrictive agreements with the provision that 'the burden of proof lies with the parties seeking the exemption'.

The treatment of restrictive agreements is somewhat simpler in UNCTAD's model competition law. There is a list of the restrictive agreements that are prohibited but any of these may be exempted or authorized if it can be shown that it will produce 'net public benefit' (UNCTAD, 2003, p. 19). As a result of UNCTAD's emphasis on exemptions, there is an extensive discussion on exemptions and authorizations in its model competition law document.

Even though the UNCTAD's model law does not make the distinction between horizontal and vertical agreements and between per se and rule of reason, such differences are discussed in the context of selected country experiences. Some of these experiences are summarized in Table 3.4.

In general, restrictive horizontal agreements tend to be considered more serious than restrictive vertical agreements. Thus, restrictive horizontal

Table 3.4   Prohibitions on restrictive agreements

Type of Agreement	Per Se Illegal	Rule of Reason
Market allocation	USA, UK	
Refusal to deal	Australia	India
Collusive bidding	USA, Kenya	

agreements, particularly cartel agreements, tend to be considered per se illegal in some countries (e.g., in the United States), while restrictive vertical agreements are mostly subjected to rule of reason. This is reflected in the WB-OECD model law but not in the UNCTAD (even though the later document contains discussions on these issues).

In addition, the WB-OECD considers the distinction between cartel and non-cartel horizontal agreements to be an important one (WB-OECD, 1999, p. 143):

> Certain types of horizontal agreements, collectively described as cartel agreements, are subjected to stricter control than other types. In many countries this distinction is not found in the law itself but in enforcement practice and regulations. Countries that are first adopting competition laws, however, are better off making the distinction explicitly in the law.

Presumably this concern over cartel agreements is dealt with in the WB-OECD model law via the per se approach to horizontal restrictive agreements. In such cases, fines and even imprisonment may be the appropriate forms of sanctions. This aspect is, however, not dealt with in both of the model competition laws.

Abuse of Dominance

Abuse of dominance occurs when a 'dominant firm' in a market undertakes an action that significantly lessens competition in that market. The two basic provisions on abuse of dominance are:

● definition of dominance or dominant position; and
● a listing of actions by a dominant firm that are considered to be abuses of dominance.

Defining dominance
There is a difference in the treatment of the first between the WB-OECD and the UNCTAD model laws. The WB-OECD has a quantitative dimension in its approach to dominance while UNCTAD adopts an entirely qualitative

approach. In defining dominance the WB-OECD model law adopts 'a necessary but insufficient condition' in a numerical form relating to a market share threshold of 35 percent. In contrast, UNCTAD merely defines 'dominant position of market power' as 'a situation where an enterprise, either by itself or acting together with a few other enterprises, is in a position to control the relevant market for a particular good or service or group of goods or services' (UNCTAD, 2003, p. 14.).

Which is more commonly adopted in competition laws around the world? In a survey of 50 countries, the World Bank noted that 28 out of 50 countries surveyed have a qualitative definition of dominance while the remaining 22 countries have adopted quantitative benchmarks (World Bank, 2002, p. 140). In the latter group of countries, there are significant differences in the level of quantitative benchmarks adopted for dominance (see Table 3.5 below).

The World Bank suggests that for developing countries, quantitative benchmarks may be easier to apply than a qualitative approach for dominance – the latter requiring sophisticated information and human resource capacity (World Bank, 2002). This may be true to some extent but there is still the question of the benchmark level, which appears to be quite arbitrary.

Types of abuse of dominance
The WB-OECD model law does not specify a list of behaviour that constitutes abuse of dominance. This is probably because the types of behaviour associated with abuse of dominance are not necessarily always anticompetitive. Furthermore, firms that behave in such manner may not have any criminal or anti-competitive intent. Nevertheless, there are discussions on the specific types of behaviour associated with abuse of dominance in the World Bank-OECD (1999, Chapter 5). In this regard the WB-OECD makes a distinction between:

Table 3.5   Quantitative benchmarks of product market dominance

Country Group	Market Share of Firm
Developing and transition countries	
East Asia	50–75%
Eastern Europe & Central Asia	30–40%
Africa	20–45%
Industrialized countries	
United States	≥ 33%
European Union	40–50%

- exploitative abuses – in which a firm takes advantage of its market power by charging excessively high prices to its customers, discriminating among customers, paying low prices to suppliers or through related practices;
- exclusionary abuses – in which a firm attempts to suppress competition – for example, by refusing to deal with a competitor, raising competitors' costs of entering a market, or charging predatory prices.

Due to the ambiguity of most exploitative abuses, the World Bank-OECD (1999, pp. 72–3) suggests that the focus should be on preventing dominant firms from engaging in exclusionary abuses. The UNCTAD model law provides a list of abuse of dominance behaviour but does not make a distinction between the two classes of abuse of dominance behaviour. Table 3.6 summarizes the list of behaviours associated with abuse of dominance in the UNCTAD model and those inferred from the World Bank-OECD (1999).

While there are similarities in both model laws in terms of the list of behaviour identified as normally associated with abuse of dominance, the two model laws differ slightly in terms of their treatment of behaviours that are not anti-competitive. The WB-OECD excludes such actions if they are brought about by an increase in the level of efficiency by firms or if the benefits of such efficiencies are passed on to consumers. In contrast UNCTAD provides for authorization or exemptions via notification. An approach that could be said is more open-ended than a focus on efficiency and consumer welfare.

Finally unlike the UNCTAD model law, the WB-OECD provides for remedial measures to be taken in abuse of dominance cases. These measures are listed as the reorganization and division of the firm(s).

What can be concluded about the differences between the two model laws in their treatment of abuse of dominance? The trade-off between a

Table 3.6   Behaviours associated with abuse of dominance

Main Areas	World Bank-OECD (1999)	UNCTAD (2003)
Price discrimination	X	X
Tie-ins	X	X
Refusal to deal	X	X
Predatory pricing	X	X
Raising rivals' costs	X	
Vertical restraints	X	X
Price fixing		X

qualitative and quantitative approach to the dominance benchmark is a difficult issue to address. It is obviously easier for competition agencies to apply a quantitative dominance benchmark in assessing dominance. However, the complexity of behaviours associated with abuse of dominance requires a careful case by case analysis. The two aspects need not be inconsistent with each other since the dominance benchmark is merely a necessary but insufficient condition. However, since it is a necessary condition the benchmark should not be set too high as to automatically exclude too many cases. (See Appendix 3.4 for an outline of the WB-OECD and UNCTAD approaches to abuse of dominance.)

Merger Controls

Mergers occur when two independent companies combine into one. Mergers can be either horizontal or vertical mergers. Horizontal mergers involve firms that are actual or potential competitors, while vertical mergers involve firms at different levels in the chain of production (World Bank-OECD, 1999, p. 42).

Mergers change market structure by reducing the number of independent firms in the market. They also result in the merged entity having a larger market share than each of the two merging firms before the merger. Thus some mergers can result in a dominant firm (where none existed before the merger) or/and it can increase the merged entity's market power. Both can be detrimental to consumers if the merged entity abuses its dominant position or exercises its market power. Merger controls are put in place to prevent such situations from arising. While most merger controls are preventive, in the sense of being pre-merger controls, competition agencies are sometimes given post-merger powers to rectify mergers that are not beneficial to society by dissolving such mergers. Thus pre-merger controls are primarily structural in nature while post-merger controls can be structural or behavioural.

A basic component of pre-merger controls is the pre-merger notification process. Both the WB-OECD and the UNCTAD model laws contain pre-merger notification (see Appendix 3.5). However, they differ in terms of the application of the pre-merger notification. The WB-OECD model law sets a transaction size threshold, below which mergers are exempted from notifying the competition agency. In the UNCTAD approach there are no suggestions on threshold provisions in its model law.

Pre-merger notification thresholds are used in a number of developed countries (see Table 3.7). However, there appears to be neither agreement on the appropriate type of threshold to be adopted (assets or turnover) nor on the level of threshold to be applied.

Table 3.7   Pre-merger notification threshold in selected countries

Country	Type of Threshold	Size of Threshold
United States	Assets	US$200 million
Canada	Assets or turnover	C$50 million ≈ US$38 million
Germany	Turnover	€25 million ≈ US$31 million
Rep. Korea	Turnover	KRW100 billion ≈ US$86 million
Japan	Asset	¥10 billion ≈ US$90 million
	Turnover	¥1 ≈ US$9 million
Brazil	Turnover	R$400 million ≈ US$133 million

Source: Global Competition Review (2003).

While both model laws include post-merger remedies, such provisions in WB-OECD's model law are more detailed compared with those observed in the UNCTAD model law. The WB-OECD also spells out in a detailed manner the circumstances that can justify an exemption from the law. These may include industry consolidation that increases real efficiency gains or prevents actual or potential financial failure.

CONCLUSIONS

There are a number of differences between the WB-OECD and the UNCTAD model competition laws, but are these differences important? UNCTAD's model competition law incorporates broader developmental objectives while the WB-OECD is more likely to focus on economic efficiency and consumer welfare objectives. In addition, the WB-OECD extensively uses quantitative benchmarks and thresholds while UNCTAD eschews discussions of quantitative benchmarks and thresholds.

Developing countries that are drafting competition laws face difficult choices. There may be trade-offs between the ease of enforcement with the accuracy of enforcement. Per se illegality is relatively easy to enforce but runs into the risk of penalizing an optimal business practice. Quantitative benchmarks and thresholds have similar effects – they may be easy to use but can be wrongly applied. There is also little consensus on how the levels of these quantitative measures ought to be computed.

It may be that the appropriate choice can be determined by the capacities of the competition agency. The irony is of course, the broader and the more qualitative the objectives of a competition law are, the more difficult it may be to enforce such a law.

NOTES

1. Interestingly, there are also contrasting differences between the 'positive statement' approach of the World Bank-OECD (i.e., 'enhance') and the 'negative statement' approach of UNCTAD (i.e., 'adversely affecting').
2. Elsewhere in the model law, dominance is defined as a firm having at least 35 percent of the relevant market share. See WB-OECD (1999, p. 142).

REFERENCES

UNCTAD (2003), *Model Law on Competition*, Geneva: United Nations.
World Bank (2002), *World Development Report 2002*, Washington, DC: World Bank.
World Bank-OECD (1999), *A Framework for the Design and Implementation of Competition Law and Policy*, Washington, DC: World Bank and OECD.

APPENDIX 3.1 SCOPE OF COMPETITION LAW IN MODEL COMPETITION LAWS

A3.1.1 WB-OECD

1. This Law shall be enforceable on the whole territory of the Republic of X and applies to all areas of commercial economic activity. The Law shall be applicable to all matters specified in [section(s) of the law containing the prohibitions of restrictive agreement, abuse of dominance, and merger review], having substantial effects in the Republic of X, including those that result from acts done outside the Republic of X.
2. This Law does not derogate from the direct enjoyment of the privileges and protections conferred by other laws protecting intellectual property, including inventions, industrial models, trademarks, and copyrights. It does apply to the use of such property in such a manner as to cause the anti-competitive effects prohibited therein.
3. This Law shall apply neither to the combinations or activities of workers or employees nor to agreements or arrangements between two or more employers when such combinations, activities, agreements, or arrangements are designed solely to facilitate collective bargaining in respect of conditions of employment.

A3.1.2 UNCTAD

1. Applies to all enterprises as defined above, in regard to all their commercial agreements, actions or transactions regarding goods, services or intellectual property.
2. Applies to all natural persons who, acting in private capacity as owner, manager or employee of an enterprise, authorize, engage in or aid the commission of restrictive practices prohibited by law.
3. Does not apply to the sovereign acts of the State itself, or to those of local governments, or to acts of enterprises or natural persons which are compelled or supervised by the State or by local governments or branches of government acting within their delegated power.

APPENDIX 3.2   DEFINITIONS IN COMPETITION LAW

A3.2.1   WB-OECD

Competition – the process by which economic agents, acting independently in a market, limit each other's ability to control the conditions prevailing in the market.

Firm – any natural or legal person, governmental body, partnership, or association in any form engaged directly or indirectly in economic activity. Two firms, one of which is controlled by the other, shall be treated as one firm. Two or more firms that are controlled by a single firm shall be treated as one firm. The competition office shall adopt a regulation setting out what constitutes control.

Good – all property, tangible and intangible, and services.

Market – a collection of goods among which buyers are or would be willing to substitute, and a specific territory, which could extend beyond the borders of the Republic of X, in which are located sellers among which buyers are or would be willing to substitute.

A3.2.2   UNCTAD

Enterprises – means firms, partnerships, corporations, companies, associations and other juridical persons, irrespective of whether created or controlled by private persons or by the State, which engage in commercial activities, and includes their branches, subsidiaries, affiliates or other entities directly or indirectly controlled by them.

Dominant position of market power – refers to a situation where an enterprise, either by itself or acting together with a few other enterprises, is in a position to control the relevant market for a particular good or service or group of goods and services.

Relevant market – refers to the general conditions under which sellers and buyers exchange goods, and implies the definition of the boundaries that identify groups of sellers and of buyers of goods within which competition is likely to be restrained. It requires the delineation of the product and geographical lines within which specific groups of goods, buyers and sellers interact to establish price and output. It should include all reasonably substitutable products or services, and all nearby competitors, to which consumers could turn in the short term if the restraint or abuse increased prices by a not insignificant amount.

APPENDIX 3.3   RESTRICTIVE AGREEMENTS

A3.3.1   WB-OECD

Prohibited agreements between firms

1. An agreement, concluded in any form including by concerted practice, between competing firms (including firms that could easily become competitors) is prohibited if such an agreement has or would likely have as its principle effect:
    (a) fixing or setting prices, tariffs, discounts, surcharges, or any other charges;
    (b) fixing or setting the quantity of output;
    (c) fixing or setting prices at auctions or in any other form of bidding, except for joint bids so identified on their face to the party soliciting bids;
    (d) dividing the market, whether by territory, by volume of sales or purchases, by type of goods sold, by customers or sellers, or by other means;
    (e) eliminating from the market actual or potential sellers or purchasers; or
    (f) refusing to conclude contracts with actual or potential sellers or purchasers.
2. An agreement, other than those enumerated in Section 1 of this article, concluded in any form including by concerted practice, is prohibited if it has or would likely have as its result a significant limitation of competition:
    (a) an agreement among competing firms, including firms that could easily become competitors, other than those agreements enumerated in Section 1 of this article, cannot be found to significantly limit competition unless the shares of the firms participating in the agreement collectively exceed 20 percent of a market affected by the agreement;
    (b) an agreement solely among non-competing firms cannot be found to significantly limit competition unless:
        (i) at least one of the parties holds a dominant position in a market affected by the agreement; or
        (ii) the limitation of competition results from the fact that similar agreements are widespread in a market affected by the agreement.
3. (a) An agreement prohibited under Section 2 of this article is nonetheless legal if it has brought about or is likely to bring about gains in real as opposed to merely pecuniary efficiencies that are

greater than or more than offset the effects of any limitation on competition that result or are likely to result from the agreement.

Or

An agreement prohibited under Section 2 of this article is nonetheless legal if it has brought about or likely to bring about such large gains in real as opposed to merely pecuniary efficiencies that consumer well-being is expected to be enhanced as a result of the agreement.

(b) The burden of proof under this section lies with the parties seeking the exemption, and includes demonstrating that if the agreement were not implemented it is not likely that the relevant efficiency gains would be realized by means that would limit competition to a lesser degree than the agreement.

A3.3.2　UNCTAD

1. Prohibition of the following agreements between rival or potential rival firms, regardless of whether such agreements are written or oral, formal or informal:
   (a) agreements fixing prices or other terms of sale, including in international trade;
   (b) collusive tendering;
   (c) market or customer allocation;
   (d) restraints on production or sale, including by quota;
   (e) concerted refusals to purchase;
   (f) concerted refusals to supply;
   (g) collective denial of access to an agreement, or association, which is crucial to competition.
2. Authorization or exemption
   Practices falling within paragraph 1, when properly notified in advance, and when engaged in by firms subject to effective competition, may be authorized or exempted when competition officials conclude that the agreement as a whole will produce net public benefit.

APPENDIX 3.4   ABUSE OF DOMINANCE

A3.4.1   WB-OECD

Abuse of dominance
1. Dominant position – a firm has a dominant position if, acting on its own, it can profitably and materially restrain or reduce competition in a market for a significant period of time. The position of a firm is not dominant unless its share of the relevant market exceeds 35 percent. A firm having a market share exceeding 35 percent may or may not be found to be dominant depending on the economic situation in that market, including the firm's market share, competing firms' market shares and their abilities to expand those shares, and the potential for new entry into the market.
2. Actions of a dominant firm – including creating obstacles to the entry of competing firms or to the expansion of existing competitors or eliminating competing firms from the market – that have or may probably have as their result a significant limitation of competition are prohibited.
3. Section 2 of this article does not prohibit actions by a firm that creates obstacles to the entry of new firms or reduce the competitiveness of existing firms solely by increasing the efficiency of the firm taking those actions, or that pass the benefits of greater efficiency on to the consumers.

Power to break up a firm abusing its dominant position
1. When a firm has abused its dominant position and no other remedy under this law or under an applicable regulatory statute would be likely to rectify the situation or prevent recurrence of the abuse, the competition office may reorganize or divide the firm provided there is a reasonable likelihood that the resulting entity or entities would be economically viable.
2. The power to reorganize or divide contained in this article shall be exercised in a manner designed to minimize any increases in costs of providing the good.

A3.4.2   UNCTAD

1. Prohibition of acts or behaviour involving an abuse, or acquisition and abuse, of a dominant position of market power.

    A prohibition on acts or behaviour involving an abuse or acquisition and abuse of a dominant position of market power:

(a)   where an enterprise, either by itself or acting together with a few other enterprises, is in a position to control a relevant market for a particular good or service, or groups of goods or services;

(b)   where the acts or behaviour of a dominant enterprise limit access to a relevant market or otherwise unduly restrain competition, having or being likely to have adverse effects on trade or economic development.

2.   Acts or behaviour considered as abusive:

(a)   predatory behaviour towards competitors, such as using below cost pricing to eliminate competitors;

(b)   discriminatory (i.e., unjustifiably differentiated) pricing or terms or conditions in the supply or purchase of goods or services, including by means of the use of pricing policies in transactions between affiliated enterprises which overcharge or undercharge for goods or services purchased or supplied as compared with prices for similar or comparable transactions outside the affiliated enterprises;

(c)   fixing the prices at which goods sold can be resold, including those imported and exported;

(d)   restrictions on the importation of goods which have been legitimately marked abroad with a trademark identical with or similar to the trademark protected as to identical or similar goods in the importing country where the trademarks in question are of the same origin, i.e., belong to the same owner or are used by enterprises between which there is economic, organizational, managerial or legal interdependence, and where the purpose of such restrictions is to maintain artificially high prices;

(e)   when not for ensuring the achievement of legitimate business purposes, such as quality, safety, adequate distribution or services:

   (i)   partial or complete refusal to deal on an enterprise's customary commercial terms;

   (ii)   making the supply of particular goods or services dependent upon the acceptance of restrictions on the distribution or manufacture of competing or other goods;

   (iii) imposing restrictions concerning where, or to whom, or in what form or quantities, goods supplied or other goods may be resold or exported;

   (iv)   making the supply of particular goods or services dependent upon the purchase of other goods or services from the supplier or his designee.

3. Authorization or exemption

Acts, practices or transactions not absolutely prohibited by the law may be authorized or exempted if they are notified, as described in article 7, before being put into effect, if all relevant facts are truthfully disclosed to competent authorities, if affected parties have an opportunity to be heard, and if it is then determined that the proposed conduct, as altered or regulated if necessary, will be consistent with the objectives of the law.

APPENDIX 3.5   MERGER CONTROLS

A3.5.1   WB-OECD

Review of concentrations

Definition
  1. 'Concentration' shall be deemed to arise when:
     (a) two or more previously independent firms merge, amalgamate, or combine the whole or a part of their businesses; or
     (b) one or more natural or legal persons already controlling at least one firm acquire, whether by purchase of securities or assets, by contract or by other means, direct or indirect control of the whole or parts of one or more other firms.
  2. 'Control' for the purpose of this article, is defined as the ability to materially influence a firm, in particular through:
     (a) ownership or the right to use all or part of assets of an undertaking; or
     (b) rights or contracts that confer decisive influence on the composition, voting, or decisions of the organs of a firm.

Notification
  3. When an agreement or public bid will produce a concentration larger than the minimum size as provided in regulations issued pursuant to section 7 of this article, the parties to the agreement or bid are prohibited from consummating such concentration until _____ days after providing notification to the competition office, in the form and containing the information specified in regulations issued pursuant to section 7.
  4. Before the expiration of the _____ day period referred to in section 3 of this article, the competition office may issue a written request for further information. The issuance of such a request has the effect of extending the period within which the concentration may not be consummated for an additional _____ days, beginning on the day after substantially all of the requested information is supplied to the competition office.
  5. Parties to an agreement or public bid not subject to the notification requirement in section 3 of this article may voluntarily notify and, if they do so, be subject to the same procedures, restrictions, and rights as are applied to cases of compulsory notification.
  6. If, before consummation of a concentration, the competition office determines that such concentration is prohibited by section 8 of this

article and does not qualify for exemption under section 9 of this article, the competition office may:

(a) prohibit consummation of the concentration;

(b) prohibit consummation of the concentration unless and until it is modified by changes specified by the competition office;

(c) prohibit consummation of the concentration unless and until the pertinent party or parties enter into legally enforceable agreements specified by the competition office.

Regulations regarding concentrations

7. The competition office shall from time to time adopt and publish regulations stipulating:

(a) the minimum size or sizes of concentrations subject to the notification requirement in section 3 of this article;

(b) the information that must be supplied for notified concentration;

(c) exceptions or exemptions from the notification requirement of section 3 for specified types of concentrations;

(d) other rules relating to the notification procedures in sections 3, 4, and 5 of this article.

Permitted and prohibited concentrations

8. Concentrations that will probably lead to a significant limitation of competition are prohibited.

9. Concentrations prohibited under section 8 of the article shall nonetheless be free from prohibition by the competition office if the parties establish that either:

(a) the concentration has brought about or is likely to bring about gains in real as opposed to merely pecuniary efficiencies that are greater than or more than offset the effects of any limitation on competition that result or are likely to result from the concentration; or

(b) one of the parties to the concentration is faced with actual or imminent financial failure, and the concentration represents the least anti-competitive uses for the failing firm's assets.

The burden of proof under this section lies with the parties seeking the exemption.

A party seeking to rely on the exemption specified in (a) must demonstrate that if the concentration were not consummated it is not likely that the relevant efficiency gains would be realized by means that would limit competition to a lesser degree than the concentration.

A party seeking to rely on the exception specified in (b) must:
  (i)   demonstrate that reasonable steps have been taken within the recent past to identify alternative purchasers for the failing firm's assets;
  (ii) fully describe the results of that search.

10. The competition office may determine, within three years after consummation, that either a non-notified concentration or a notified concentration in which the provisions of sections 3–5 of this article are not fully complied with, has led or will probably lead to a significant limitation of competition and does not qualify for either of the two exemptions set out in section 9 of this article. If it so determines, the competition office may:
  (a)   undo the concentration by dissolving it into its constituent elements;
  (b)   require other modifications of the concentration, including sale of a portion of its operations or assets;
  (c)   require the surviving firm or firms to enter into legally enforceable agreements specified by the competition office and designed to reduce or eliminate the competition-limiting effects of the concentration.

11. Notifiable concentrations that the competition office determines are prohibited by section 8 of this article and do not qualify for exemption under section 9 may subsequently be authorized by a published decision of the Government of _____ for overriding reasons of public policy involving a unique and significant contribution to the general welfare of the citizens of _____.

A3.5.2   UNCTAD

Notification, examination and prohibition of mergers affecting concentrated markets:

1. Notification
   Mergers, takeovers. Joint ventures or other acquisitions of control, including interlocking directorships, whether of a horizontal, vertical, or conglomerate nature, should be notified when:
   (a)   at least one of the enterprises is established within the country; and
   (b)   the resultant market share in the country, or any substantial part of it, relating to any product of service, is likely to create market power, especially in industries where there is a high degree of market concentration, where there are barriers to entry and where

there is a lack of substitutes for a product supplied by firms whose conduct is under scrutiny.

2. Prohibition

Mergers, takeovers, joint ventures or other acquisitions of control, including interlocking directorships, whether of a horizontal, vertical or conglomerate nature, should be prohibited when:

(a) the proposed transaction substantially increases the ability to exercise market power (e.g., to give the ability to a firm acting jointly to profitably maintain prices above competitive levels for a significant period of time); and

(b) the resultant market share in the country, or any substantial part of it, relating to any product or service, will result in a dominant firm or in a significant reduction of competition in a market dominated by very few firms.

3. Investigation procedures

Provisions to allow investigation of mergers, takeovers, joint ventures or other acquisitions of control, including interlocking directorships, whether of a horizontal, vertical or conglomerate nature, which may have competition could be set out in a regulation regarding concentrations.

In particular, no firm should, in the cases coming under the preceding subsection, effect a merger until the expiration of a _____ day waiting period from the date of the issuance of the receipt of the notification, unless the competition authority shortens the said period or extends it by an additional period of time not exceeding _____ days with the consent of the firms concerned, in accordance with the provisions of Possible Elements for Article 7 below. The authority could be parties from enterprises in the affected relevant market or lines of commerce, with the parties losing additional time if their response is late.

If a full hearing before the competition authority or before a tribunal results in a finding against the transaction, acquisitions or mergers could be subject to being prevented or even undone whenever they are likely to lessen competition substantially in a line of commerce in the jurisdiction or in a significant part of the relevant market within the jurisdiction.

4. Legal traditions and competition policy

Cassey Lee

INTRODUCTION

The two decades beginning from the early 1980s witnessed significant institutional changes in many economies in the world. Socialist countries in Eastern Europe and Central Asia underwent political transformation into democracies and embraced the market system. Other socialist countries that did not undergo political transformation, such as China and Vietnam, began using market mechanisms selectively to enhance their economic performance. At the same time, countries that have already adopted the market system undertook to give market forces a greater role in their economies by divesting state-owned enterprises through large-scale privatization.

Economists have also become more interested in the role of institutions in economic growth and development. In the context of the institutional changes that have taken place, economists are pondering over the type of institutions such as property rights protection that should be considered to be essential for the proper functioning of market economies. However, the questions are not just about market institutions but of state interventions that are required to address problems of market failures. One such intervention is competition policy.

Currently more than 100 countries around the world have implemented national competition laws. There is sufficient theoretical and empirical support to motivate the implementation of competition policy (UNCTAD, 1997). What is debatable, especially from the viewpoint of developing countries, is the form and timing of implementation, that is, whether multilateral competition rules are useful and whether more exemptions ought to be allowed for conflicting industrial policies.

For countries that have decided to implement competition law there remains the immense task of formulating a competition law that can be effectively enforced. At first glance, the content of a competition law may not be too difficult, as the UNCTAD's model law on competition would have us believe (UNCTAD, 2003). In reality, country-specific factors such as legal and administrative traditions, stage of economic development and political realities are likely to have significant impact on the efficacy of the enforcement of competition law in any country. This observation has led the OECD to conclude that there is no single (or one size fits all) optimal design of competition institution (OECD, 2003).

This chapter attempts to further analyse the importance of one such country-specific characteristic, namely, legal tradition, in the implementation of competition law. The outline of the rest of the chapter is as follows. The following section provides a brief discussion of the major legal traditions in the world. The next section summarizes the empirical literature on legal traditions and its impact on economic growth and development. The next section examines the relationship between legal tradition and competition policy and the final section concludes.

LEGAL TRADITIONS OF THE WORLD

A legal system refers to an operating set of legal institutions, procedures and rules (Merryman, 1985). Legal systems can be grouped into different families based on cultural dimensions:

> A legal tradition . . . is a set of deeply rooted, historically conditioned attitudes about the nature of law, about the role of law in society and the polity, about the proper organization and operation of a legal system, and about the way law is or should be made, applied, studied, perfected, and taught. (Merryman, 1985, p. 1)

Types of Legal Traditions

David and Brierley (1985) list at least three types of major legal tradition (or legal family), namely, the Romano-Germanic (civil) law, common law and socialist law. Others include Talmudic, Islamic, Hindu and Asian legal traditions. There are some differences within some legal traditions that require further reclassification. For example, within the Romano-Germanic legal tradition, scholars distinguish between the French, German and Nordic (Scandinavian) civil law traditions. The French civil law is regarded to be more distrustful of judges (the Napoleonic code) and hence places more emphasis on judicial formalism compared with the German civil law. Table 4.1 presents the World Bank's (2004) classification of countries in terms of the five major legal traditions in the world, namely: English (common law), French (civil law), German (civil law), Nordic and socialist. The list is based on the origin of the company law or commercial code in each country.

Table 4.1 Countries and legal traditions

English Common Law (36)	French Civil Law (64)		German Civil Law (18)	Socialist Law (11)	Nordic Law (4)
Australia	Albania	Madagascar	Austria	Armenia	Denmark
Bangladesh	Algeria	Mali	Bosnia and	Azerbaijan	Finland
Botswana	Angola	Mauritania	Herzegovina		
Canada	Argentina	Mexico	Bulgaria	Belarus	Norway
Ethiopia	Belgium	Morocco	China	Georgia	Sweden
Ghana	Benin	Mozambique	Croatia	Kazakhstan	
Hong Kong, China	Bolivia	Netherlands	Czech Republic	Kyrgyz Republic	
India	Brazil	Nicaragua	Germany	Moldova	
Iran, Islamic Rep.	Burkina Faso	Niger	Hungary	Mongolia	
Ireland	Burundi	Oman	Japan	Russian Federation	
Israel	Cambodia	Panama	Korea, Rep.	Ukraine	
Jamaica	Cameroon	Paraguay	Latvia	Uzbekistan	
Kenya	Central African	Peru	Macedonia, FYR		
Lesotho	Republic	Philippines	Poland		
Malawi	Chad	Portugal	Serbia and		
Malaysia	Chile	Puerto Rico	Montenegro		
Namibia	Colombia	Romania	Slovak Republic		
Nepal	Congo, Dem. Rep.	Rwanda	Slovenia		
New Zealand	Congo, Rep.	Senegal	Switzerland		
Nigeria	Costa Rica	Spain	Taiwan, China		
Pakistan	Cote d'Ivoire	Syrian Arab			
Papua New Guinea	Dominican Republic	Republic			
Saudi Arabia	Ecuador	Togo			

56

Egypt, Arab Rep.	Sierra Leone	Tunisia
El Salvador	Singapore	Turkey
France	South Africa	Uruguay
Greece	Sri Lanka	Venezuela
Guatemala	Tanzania	Vietnam
Guinea	Thailand	
Haiti	Uganda	
Honduras	United Arab Emirates	
Indonesia	United Kingdom	
Italy	United States	
Jordan	Yemen, Rep.	
Kuwait	Zambia	
Lao PDR	Zimbabwe	
Lebanon		
Lithuania		

Source: World Bank (2004).

Differences Between Legal Traditions

A civil law vs. common law example

The differences between legal traditions can be illustrated by comparing two major legal traditions, namely, the civil law tradition and the common law tradition. The most salient differences are in the independence of the judiciary (from the state), the professional status of judges, their role in the trial process, the use of juries, legal instruction and records, and the importance of precedence and appeal. Table 4.2 summarizes some of these differences between the two legal traditions.

The judiciary in a civil law system is generally considered to be less independent from the state compared with the common law system. Judges in the civil law system follow a specific career track that culminates in their appointment by the state. In contrast, common law judges are appointed from the community of practising lawyers. Juries are also more often used in common law than in civil law. The function of prosecution and judgement are combined in civil law whereas the two functions are separated in common law. The combination of prosecution and judgement in civil law also means that judges in a civil law system assume an inquisitorial role, undertaking the investigative part of the prosecution process. In contrast, lawyers and judges assume adversarial roles, lawyers undertake investigations, collect evidence and present their case before the judge (and jury). Legal codes also play a more important role in civil law, the judge's role is to apply faithfully the existing statutory law and render a judgement that is narrowly consistent with it. In contrast, the law is fashioned in terms of broad legal principles in common law. Here judges interpret, in the best manner possible, the 'spirit' of the law. This allows

Table 4.2   Differences between civil law and common law

Characteristic	Civil Law	Common Law
Independence of judiciary from state	State controlled	Independent
Professional status of judge	Professional judges	Lay judges
Use of juries	Less frequent	Frequent
Role of judge in trial process	Inquisitorial	Adversarial
Legal instruction	Legal codes	Broad legal principles
Precedent	Less important	Important
Appeal/re-litigation	Less important	Important
Certainty of law?	Legal standards	Rules

common law judges to 'make' laws by setting precedents (*stare decisis*) that are considered to be an important interpretation of the law for subsequent and related cases. It is hence not surprising that appeal or re-litigation is an important process in a relatively open legal system such as the common law.

THE IMPACT OF LEGAL TRADITION ON ECONOMIC DEVELOPMENT

The impact of legal tradition on economic development has recently received some attention in the empirical studies of comparative institutional economics (Shirley, 2003). In this section we review the evidence from such studies. This is undertaken to assess the significance of the legal tradition as a factor in economic development before we propose and test a similar role in the case of competition policy.

Legal Tradition and Finance

The recent work on the impact of legal tradition on economic development comes from investigations into the relationship between law, financial development and economic growth. This approach, dubbed the 'law and finance theory' builds on the basic empirical evidence that financial development has a first-order impact on economic growth (Levine and Zervos, 1998; Demirgüç-Kunt and Maksimovic, 1998; Rajan and Zingales, 1998 and Kunt and Levine, 2001). The theory attempts to uncover the determinants of financial development (La Porta et al., 1997, 1998). It argues that international differences in financial development can be explained by differences in legal institutions (system, tradition).

Beck and Levine (2003) summarize the main findings of the theory as countries where legal systems enforce private property rights, support private contractual agreements, protect legal rights of investors and where savers are more willing to finance firms and financial markets flourish. They further argue that the different legal traditions that emerged in Europe and were spread internationally through conquest, colonization and imitation help explain cross-country differences in investor protection, the contracting environment and financial development.

There are two components in the law and finance theory. First, legal traditions have a significant impact on the effective protection of private property rights such as enforcement of private contract agreement and investor protection. Second, the protection of private property rights contributes towards financial development. Essentially the protection of private property rights provides confidence to savers, lenders and investors to participate in the financial markets.

In terms of the different legal traditions, common law is considered to be more conducive to financial development compared with civil law. Proponents of this theory have advanced at least two reasons to explain this observation. The first is political: civil law protects the rights of the state more than the rights of private investors, while the reverse holds in common law. The second is adaptability of legal systems: civil law, which relies on case law and empowers judicial discretion (interpretation), is more adaptive to changes in economic conditions (compared with civil law, which relies on judgements based on statutes).

Not surprisingly, the subsequent debates on the validity of the findings of the law and finance theory have focused on the two set of linkages: (1) between legal tradition and basic market institutions, and (2) between basic market institutions and financial development. Even though the proponents of the law and finance theory have described research in this area as ongoing, the accumulated evidence in favour of the theory is fairly impressive (Beck and Levine, 2003).

Legal Tradition, Regulation and Court

Proponents of the law and finance theory have also extended their work to encompass regulation and courts. There is a difference between regulation and courts. Regulation restricts private conduct while the court resolves disputes. Two recent examples include Djankov et al. (2002 and 2003) where data is used on the regulation of entry of start-up firms in 85 countries to examine the determinants of the cost of entry. They find that civil law countries (with the exception of Scandinavian countries) tend to regulate entry more heavily compared with common law countries.

Interestingly, the authors did not find any correlation between legal tradition and political factors such as executive de facto independence, constraints on executive power, effectiveness of legislature, competition nominating, autocracy and political rights. The exception is the socialist legal tradition, which showed correlation with autocracy (positive) and political rights (negative).

Djankov et al. (2003) measure the procedures used by litigants and courts to evict a tenant for non-payment of rent and collection of bounced cheques and used these data to construct an index of procedural formalism for 109 countries. The authors define procedural formalism as the ways in which the law regulates the operation of courts. These include the use of lawyers and professional judges, litigation procedures etc. Their intention is to study the effectiveness of courts as mechanisms of dispute resolution.

The authors find that civil law countries tend to exhibit higher formalism in adjudication compared with common law countries. Higher formalism is also associated with lower enforceability of contracts, higher corruption, lower honesty, lower consistency and a less fair legal system.

Legal Origin and Legal Transplant

The next natural step after uncovering the indirect influence of legal traditions on financial and economic development would of course be the explanation of the choice of legal systems. Economists have applied the rational choice framework to understand the problem of legal origins. The explanation thus far has been a rational and political one – the adoption of a given legal system is understood to be an 'optimal' or 'efficient' outcome given the adopting country's political circumstances.

Glaeser and Shleifer (2002) for example, argue that the original choice of a given legal system by a country is an outcome of the political situation in that country in which these laws originated. More specifically, a country would 'choose' a legal system that is most efficient given the balance of power between the king and the nobility. The influence of local nobles vis-à-vis the king was greater in France than in England (a dictator-controlled country). Hence local magnates in France preferred civil law – in which the judges are state controlled – because they feared independent juries (as in common law) would be compromised by other local interests. The situation in England was the reverse – a dictatorial king required independent judges that may reduce the bias of the courts towards the royals. Hence, the community engaged in a 'Coasian bargain' (i.e., the Magna Carta) whereby the community and the king agreed on the cash transfers needed to support the efficient outcome, that is, choice of legal system.

The choice of legal systems by other transplant or 'non-origin' countries is also an interesting problem (origin countries include England, France and Germany). There are significantly more countries to consider and the story is complex. Legal codes have been transplanted to the rest of the world via a variety of mechanisms including conquest, colonialization and imitation. Economic inquiry into the question of legal transplant has thus far focused on the impact of the type (i.e., legal tradition) and process of legal transplant on economic development.

With regard to legal tradition, Berkowitz, Pistor and Richard (2003) found empirical evidence that the impact of transplanting a particular legal tradition on economic development is not robust to different legality measures. Legality measures include efficiency of judiciary, rule of law, absence of corruption, risk of appropriation and risk of contract repudiation. Furthermore, the overall impact of the transplanting process (via its impact on legality) is stronger than the impact of transplanting a particular legal tradition. The policy implications that the authors draw from their work are also worth quoting in full:

> The policy implications of these results are fundamental: a legal reform strategy should aim at improving legality by carefully choosing legal rules whose meaning can be understood and whose purpose is appreciated by domestic law makers, law enforcers and economic agents, who are the final consumers of these rules. In short, legal reform must ensure that there is a domestic demand for the new law, and that supply can match demand. . .a cautious suggestion would be that legal borrowing should take place either from a country with a similar legal heritage, or substantial investment should be made in legal information and training prior to adoption of a law, so that domestic agents can enhance their familiarity with the imported law and make an informed decision about how to adapt the law to local conditions. (Berkowitz et al., 2003, p. 192)

The above recommendations suggest that the transplant of law requires careful considerations that extend beyond mere adoption of legal rules and principles from other countries (Pistor et al., 2003). In particular the importance of 'legality' provides some clues on how to improve the transplant process. We take these insights to motivate our investigations into the importance of legal tradition for the implementation and enforcement of competition policy.

Legal Tradition and the New Comparative Economics

The literature on comparative institutional economics, in which legal tradition is included as an important element, has evolved towards discovering the political determinants of institutional choice (including legal origin). In Djankov et al. (2003a), the label of 'new comparative economics' is used to describe a framework of analysis for institutional choice. According to this framework, institutional choice involves a political trade-off between the cost of disorder (in the form of appropriation by private parties) and those of a dictatorship (appropriation by the state). Depending on the enforcement environment, one or more of four (non-mutually exclusive) forms of business controls (i.e., private ordering, private litigation, regulation and state ownership) might be chosen.

The enforcement environment depends on a variety of factors under the general term of 'civic capital', which encompasses broad aspects such as culture, ethnic heterogeneity, factor endowments, physical environment as well as more specific ones such as the distribution of wealth and power, political freedom and the effectiveness of government.

With regard to the importance of legal tradition, Djankov et al. (2003a) reaffirm Glaeser and Shleifer's (2002) arguments for legal origin and argue that some of the problems observed in developing countries stem from the transplantation of legal traditions that are inconsistent with the conditions of the society.

The characterization of the trade-off between disorder and dictatorship also receives some attention in Acemoglu and Johnson (2003). In their paper they differentiate between two types of institutions: 'contracting institutions' that support private contracts (which would include private ordering) and 'property rights institutions' that constrain government and elite expropriation. Legal tradition is considered to be a proxy for contracting institutions. In the study, property rights institutions have a first-order effect on long-run economic growth, investment and financial development. On the other hand, contracting institutions matter only for the form of financial intermediaries. The reason for this is that it is difficult to write contracts that prevent the state from expropriation, while private contracting is flexible enough to overcome the problems of legal formalism.

The importance of politics in the choice of institutions also figures prominently in the comparative law literature as well. For example, Djankov et al.'s (2003a) reference to Hobbes (1651), who favoured a strong state to reduce disorder, and Montesquieu (1748), who was mindful of taking by the state, finds some resonance in the interpretation of law in the comparative law literature as well. As Tetley (2000, p. 24) observes:

> In civil law jurisdictions, the first step in interpreting an ambiguous law . . . is to discover the intention of the legislator by examining the legislation as a whole. . . . In common law jurisdictions, by comparison, statues are to be objectively constructed according to certain rules standing by themselves, such as that an enactment must be read as a whole, and that special provisions will control general provision, so as to meet the subjects' reasonable understandings and expectations. . . . Two reasons can be advanced to explain this difference in interpretation. Firstly, common law statutes have to be read against a case law background, while civil law codes and statutes are the primary source of law under Montesquieu's theory. Secondly, civil law judges are influenced by Rousseau's theory that the State is the source of all rights under the social contract, while English judges favour Hobbes' theory that the individual agreed to forfeit to the State only certain rights.

The reference to Montesquieu also leads us to another important aspect of institutional choice, namely, the separation of powers between legislature (parliament), executive and judiciary (courts). This is necessary to ensure that the power of the state does not fall into one person or a small group in society. What is the relationship between separation of powers and legal tradition? The work of Glaeser and Shleifer (2002) certainly suggests that the two are related. For example, the judiciary in a civil law system (by virtue of being an extension of the executive) has less separation of powers than in the common law system.

LEGAL TRADITION AND COMPETITION POLICY

Many countries have recently implemented competition law and at least 70 per cent have implemented their law between 1990 and 2003 (see Table 4.3). The implementation of competition laws are fairly evenly distributed across the different legal traditions.

Based on the distinctions that legal scholars draw between the different traditions, as well as from the evidence gathered by the law and finance theorists, it is plausible that legal traditions do have some impact on the implementation of competition policy. Precisely in what forms these impacts take will require further thought. In this matter we draw some clues from existing empirical work related to competition policy and from law and finance theory.

Cross-country Empirical Work on Competition Policy

Cross-country and econometric-based studies on competition policy have thus far been relatively diverse, focusing on issues relating to the reasons for and impact of implementing competition policy. There has also been an attempt to construct an index for competition law regimes that can be used as an indicator of governance. We briefly review some of the main findings from this kind of research.

Palim (1998) examines the reasons for implementing competition policy in 70 countries. The author finds that the implementation of competition policy is associated with economic reform and increased level of development. In this work, the economic reform variable is derived from the economic freedom index developed by Gwartney, Lawson and Block (1996). The level of development is measured by GDP per capita. In terms of the influence of events and institutions, Palim finds that the implementation of competition law is significantly associated with Europe's market unification (for relevant countries), dramatic economic crisis (debt default) and the transition from planned to market economy. Interestingly, Palim finds no evidence of foreign aid having a positive influence on the implementation of competition policy. Furthermore there is no evidence that the implementation of competition policy is related to international trade.

Dutz and Vagliasindi (2000) look at the experience of implementing competition law amongst 18 transitional economies. They relate three dimensions of the effectiveness of competition law (enforcement, competition advocacy and institutional effectiveness) to indicators measuring the intensity of competition (measured by economy-wide enterprise mobility). The authors find a robust positive relationship between effective implementation of competition law and the intensity of competition. The most

Table 4.3 Competition legislation around the world, 1889–2003

Legal Tradition	1880–89	1890–1944	1945–69	1970–79	1980–89	1990–99	2000–03	No.
English common law	Canada (1889)	UK (1890) US (1890)	South Africa (1955) India (1969)	Pakistan (1970) Australia (1974) Thailand (1979)	S. Lanka (1987) Israel (1988) Kenya (1988)	Ireland (1991) Fiji (1993) Iceland (1993) Jamaica (1993) Malta (1994) Tanzania (1994) Zambia (1994) Zimbabwe (1996) Malawi (1998)	Namibia (2003)	21
French civil law				Guatemala (1970) Chile (1973) France (1977) Greece (1977) Cote d'Ivoire (1978)	Argentina (1980) Spain (1989)	Cyprus (1990) Dominican R. (1990) Italy (1990) Peru (1990) Dominican R. (1990) Belgium (1991) Peru (1991) Tunisia (1991) Venezuela (1991) Colombia (1992) C.Rica (1992) Lithuania (1992) Mexico (1992) Portugal (1993) Brazil (1994)		33

Table 4.3 (continued)

Legal Tradition	1880–89	1890–1944	1945–69	1970–79	1980–89	1990–99	2000–03	No.
German civil law			Japan (1947) Germany (1957)	Luxembourg (1970)	Korea (1980) Switzerland (1985) Austria (1988)	Senegal (1994) Turkey (1994) Albania (1995) Algeria (1995) Panama (1996) Romania (1996) Netherlands (1997) Gabon (1998) Mali (1998) Indonesia (1999) Morocco (1999) Poland (1990) Bulgaria (1991) Czech (1991) Latvia (1991) Slovakia (1991) Slovenia (1991) Taiwan (1992) China (1993) Estonia (1993) Croatia (1995) Hungary (1996)		17

	1	2	4		9	8	60	3
Socialist law							Kazakhstan (1991) Russia (1991) Belarus (1992) Moldova (1992) Tajikistan (1992) Uzbekistan (1992) Azerbaijan (1993) Mongolia (1993) Kyrgyzstan (1994) Georgia (1996)	Armenia (2000) 12 Ukraine (2001)
Nordic law			4				Finland (1992) Norway (1993) Sweden (1993) Denmark (1997)	
Total	1	2	4		9	8	60	3

87

Source: UNCTAD (2003) and Palim (1998).

important element of effective competition is institutional effectiveness, which highlights the importance of independence (from pressure groups), transparency and effectiveness of appeals.

Kee and Hoekman (2003) investigate the effect of competition law on the contestability of markets in 42 countries over a period of 18 years. They find that competition law has no direct impact on industry mark-ups. However, they find some evidence of competition law having an indirect impact on industry mark-ups in the long run by promoting a larger number of domestic firms. The authors also make the startling suggestion that the reduction of trade barriers and government regulation over entry–exit conditions yields a higher level of benefit compared with the implementation of competition policy.

Nicholson (2004) attempts to 'quantify' competition laws by developing an 'antitrust law index' that can serve as a further measure of governance. The index for each country is constructed by summing up the points given for various aspects of competition law such as extraterritoriality, fines, divestitures and merger notifications. The author finds a non-linear (U-shaped) relationship between the antitrust law index and GNP.

None of the empirical studies cited above have examined the effect of legal tradition on the implementation and enforcement of competition policy. In the rest of this chapter we attempt to examine this issue.

RELATING LEGAL TRADITIONS TO COMPETITION POLICY

How is competition policy related to legal traditions? We can examine this issue through the lens of the existing literature on the economic impact of legal traditions that was reviewed earlier. It is easier to focus on competition law rather than the broader concept of competition policy. A useful framework for analysing the various issues involved is presented in Figure 4.1

The first component of the framework concerns the choice of legal tradition – either by the country of the legal origin or transplant by other countries. Broader political issues covering aspects such as separation of powers, the role of regulation vs. courts and contract vs. property rights institutions are important. Obviously we ought to expect differences between the origin and transplant cases, particularly when transplant cases involve colonialized countries.

The second component relates to the implementation of competition law. Here it is useful to distinguish between origin and transplant countries. The United States, a civil law country, can be regarded as an 'origin country' for competition policy. Whether there are other 'origin' countries

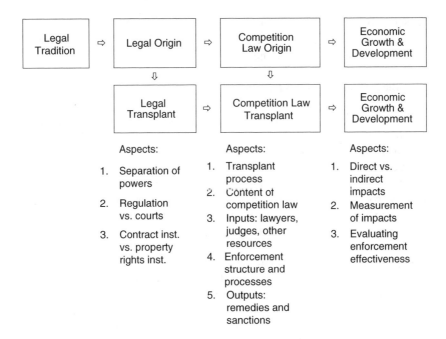

Figure 4.1   Framework for analysing the relationship between legal tradition and competition law

is an important question. An 'origin' country with regard to legal tradition may not be an 'origin' country with respect to competition law. Interestingly, civil law countries (such as France) only began implementing competition law in the late 1970s. Civil law countries such Japan and Germany may have adopted US-type competition law. Hence legal tradition may not have a one-to-one relationship with a competition law type. More specific questions can also be asked, for instance, how does legal tradition affect the various aspects of the implementation of competition law such as the transplant process, the content of the law, input resources applied (such as lawyers and judges), the enforcement structure and process and the outcome (or output) of enforcement in the form of remedies and sanctions?

The third component in the framework should examine the direct or indirect impacts of competition policy within the context of legal tradition. The measurement of such impacts is obviously an important topic. Does legal tradition affect the effectiveness of a country's competition law?

The above framework is used as a guideline to evaluate empirically the links between legal tradition and competition policy. Obviously it is not possible to do this exhaustively. The following sub-sections examine both the qualitative and quantitative evidence on the relationship between legal tradition and competition policy.

Qualitative and Anecdotal Evidence

There is qualitative and anecdotal evidence on the impact of legal tradition on competition law. Scholars have recognized the importance of legal tradition when discussing competition law but very few have articulated this as a central issue. As a result, the qualitative and anecdotal evidence is scattered and varied. We review some of the evidence in this sub-section. It ranges from specific discussions on competition law in a common law setting to the issue of convergence in competition law and enforcement problems across OECD countries.

Competition law in common law jurisdictions

Hylton (2003) analyses competition law from a common law perspective and raises several key issues relating to the certainty of law, the relative merits of rules vs. legal standards, the process of legal evolution and the capacity of courts to apply reasonableness standards to business practices. Even though Hylton's discussions are one-sided, in the sense of addressing only common law, they provide an insight into the type of issues that might be relevant in comparing competition law in different legal traditions.

Hylton highlights the tension between the economic conception of a reasonableness inquiry and the administrative concerns of courts and enforcement agencies. The asymmetry of information between firms and courts (and enforcement agencies) makes it difficult for the latter to undertake a full assessment of the costs and benefits of a challenged practice (e.g., resale price maintenance).

One solution is to remove from the plaintiff the burden of demonstrating that the challenged practice is economically unreasonable, for example, via a per-se-type clause.[1] This option however, is difficult to implement in common law countries because the common law process relies on precedents that are generated over time, based on equating legal validity with the notion of reasonableness (Hylton, 2003). In the United States this constraint is reflected in the changes from a reasonableness-based inquiry to a per se standard and back to the reasonableness-based inquiry. These changes are also documented in Kovacic and Shapiro (2000), as well as Gifford and Kudrle (2003).

The difficulty in reconciling economic reasonableness and legal administrative concerns also relates to the role of economic theory. Hylton (2003, p. xv) for example, quotes Judge Breyer's opinion that reflects how law in the common law tradition is incomplete, cumulative and adaptive, 'For, unlike economics, law is an administrative system, the effects of which depend on the content of the rules and precedents only as they are applied by judges and juries in courts and by lawyers advising their clients' (Justice Breyer in *Barry Wright* vs. *ITT Grinnell Corporation*).

When law is administrated in such a manner, there is always the possibility of the courts making either mistakes of false conviction or false acquittals. The choice of rule of reason vs. per se illegality then depends on the expected costs of making the different type of mistakes. If the expected costs of false convictions for a challenged practice exceed those of false acquittals, we ought to prefer to adopt legality in cases for the challenged practice.

Hylton's (2003) analysis seems to suggest that legal tradition (e.g., common law) has an impact on the structure or content of competition policy (e.g., rule of reason vs. per se illegality) and their effectiveness (e.g., errors, costs). Hylton's work can also be related to Londregan (2002) who addresses the issue of ex ante predictability in the enforcement of laws in civil law and common law. Londregann discusses court predictability in the two legal traditions in the context of redistributive politics. Yet another interesting area that may be relevant is the relationship between the evolution of competition law in the United States and the ascendancy of the 'Chicago School of Antitrust'.

Convergence of competition laws

There are some indications of the differences between competition laws under different legal traditions in the literature on convergence of competition laws. Gifford and Kudrle (2003) argue that convergence of European competition law with American competition law is constrained by history, ideology, politics and legal tradition. The authors focus on differences between the two competition regimes in terms of substantive decision standards (e.g., efficiency and consumers' welfare). With regard to legal tradition, the authors noted that European competition law is largely administered in the civil law tradition in which laws are set forth in legislation. This approach is more legislation-bound compared with the common law tradition, which relies on adjudication and the precedents created. Although judicial precedent does play some role in the interpretation of competition law statutes in civil law, presumably this is less important than in common law jurisdictions. Hence they argue that European competition law is less flexible in the sense that any changes require legislative changes. It is further argued that the continued divergence between the two competition laws (in terms of the substantive decision standards) is partly due to the differences in legal tradition.

Judicial enforcement
The judiciary is an important institution in the enforcement of competition law. The OECD (1997) highlights the two functions of the judiciary in the enforcement of competition law, namely: ensuring that procedural due process is observed; and applying the underlying substantive principles of the competition law in a correct and consistent manner.

There are some differences in the mechanisms for judicial enforcement in countries with different legal traditions. In common law countries, the strong emphasis on the separation of powers in the constitution implies that the administration of justice is exclusively undertaken by the courts. However, constitutions under common law (e.g., Australia, Ireland) usually allow for the establishment of independent bodies (e.g., tribunals) that examine factual issues in competition cases (OECD, 1997). In contrast, bodies in civil law countries (e.g., the Competition Council in Belgium) are established within ministries and can decide on whether an anti-competitive conduct has occurred or not. The courts are involved when and if there are appeals against such decisions. There are also countries such as Canada where the Competition Tribunal is a hybrid institution comprising judges and lay members (OECD, 1997). The Tribunal is an adjudicative body for non-criminal competition matters. Here the judicial members of the Tribunal decide on 'questions of law' while questions of fact and of mixed law and fact are decided by all members of the Tribunal. The relationship between legal tradition and the judicial enforcement process of competition law is obviously a complex one. Because competition law is only one law (and a newer one) amongst many in a country, we should expect some variations in how competition law is enforced in countries with different legal traditions.

Preliminary Quantitative Evidence

There is very little secondary data available for cross-country analyses of competition regimes. The available data is also subject to debates in terms of their appropriateness and quality. These weaknesses should be borne in mind in interpreting the quantitative analysis of the impact of legal tradition on competition law presented below.

Competition law implementation and legal tradition
Three simple logit regressions are used to find out if the implementation of law is influenced by gross national income (GNI) per capita and legal tradition. The data for GNI per capita and the classification of countries by legal tradition is derived from the World Bank (2004). Table 4.4 summarizes the regression results. GNI per capita is a significant determinant

Table 4.4   Determinants of competition law implementation

	Logit Specification Competition law (Yes = 1, No = 0)	Logit Specification Competition law (Yes = 1, No = 0)	Logit Specification Competition law (Yes = 1, No = 0)
GNI per capita	0.00093*	0.000094*	0.00010*
	(0.00003)	(0.000033)	(0.00003)
French		− 0.01742	
		(0.44853)	
German		1.38981	
		(0.74354)	
French +			0.23764
German			(0.43499)
Intercept	− 0.0805	− 0.46038	− 0.51008
	(0.2153)	(0.39445)	(0.39483)
LR	13.98	19.07	14.1
Log likelihood	− 82.31	− 71.22	− 73.55
Number of obs	132	117	117

Note: * Indicates statistical significance at the 10 percent level.

of the implementation of competition law. This is consistent with existing results, such as Palim (1998). However, legal tradition does not appear to be a significant determinant of the implementation of competition law.

Legal tradition and content of competition law
To examine the influence of legal tradition on the content of competition law, we focus on three variations of a simple variable, namely, merger notifications. Data for pre-merger, post-merger and voluntary merger notifications comes from UNCTAD (2003). Table 4.5 summarizes the results. Interestingly, legal tradition may be influential only in the case of pre-notification mergers. The odds ratio (not reported here) indicates that switching from English common law to German civil law doubles the probability of implementing pre-merger notification.

Legal tradition and structure of competition agencies
We examine two variables that highlight the structure of competition agencies, namely the length of the head of agency's appointment and political appointments in the agencies. The data is derived from the *Global Competition Review* (2003a). The regression results are summarized in Tables 4.6 and 4.7. Legal tradition does not seem to have any influence on either of these variables.

Table 4.5   Determinants of merger notification in competition law

	Logit Specification Pre-merger notification (Yes = 1, No = 0)	Logit Specification Post-merger notification (Yes = 1, No = 0)	Logit Specification Voluntary merger notification (Yes = 1, No = 0)
French	0.7621	1.3581	−0.5465
	(0.6256)	(1.1519)	(0.8022)
German	3.1600*	1.3398	Dropped
	(1.1403)	(1.2230)	(perfect prediction)
Intercept	−0.4520	−2.6391	−1.0116
	(0.4834)	(1.03510)	(0.5839)
LR	12.92	1.93	0.46
Log likelihood	−33.48	−22.99	−19.33
Number of obs	60	52	38

Note: * Indicates statistical significance at the 10 percent level.

Table 4.6   Determinants of length of head of agency term of office

	OLS Specification Length of head of agency term of office (years)
English	−0.9423
	(4.14445)
French	1.0250
	(3.9701)
German	−0.2500
	(4.1095)
Nordic	-1.02×10^{-14}
	(5.1254)
Socialist	Dropped
Intercept	9.25
	(3.6242)
R-square	0.0124
Number of obs	55

Legal tradition and enforcement of competition law

Does legal tradition affect the performance of the enforcement of competition law? We use the *Global Competition Review's* (2003b) rating index as a measure of the performance of competition law enforcement. Aside from legal tradition, we include variables such as GNI per capita (from the World Bank, 2004), competition agencies' budget per staff (computed from the

Table 4.7 Determinants of appointment of top posts in competition agencies

	Logit Specification Political appointment of posts in agency (Yes = 1, No = 0)	Logit Specification Political appointment of posts in agency (Yes = 1, No = 0)
French	0.6286	
	(0.7692)	
German	− 0.6242	
	(0.7966)	
French + German		0.0896
		(0.6752)
Intercept	0.4700	0.4700
	(0.5701)	(0.5701)
LR	2.84	0.02
Log likelihood	− 28.88	− 30.29
Number of obs	46	46

Global Competition Review, 2003a) and age of competition agency (from UNCTAD, 2003 and Palim, 1998). The results are reported in Table 4.8. Interestingly, legal tradition is not significantly related to the performance of competition law enforcement. Only budget per staff and GNI per capita are significant determinants of the performance of competition law enforcement.

Limitations and future work
The quantitative analysis carried out in this section is obviously limited. There are many aspects of competition law that have not been examined. Important omissions include transplant effects and the impacts of competition law (direct and indirect). More work needs to be done on the judiciary vs. competition agency role in competition law enforcement. In the future we may also want to examine the links between per se vs. rule-of-reason provisions for various practices and legal traditions. It may also be important to include the impact of other laws on competition. For example, Tirole (1999) argues that proper legal enforcement of contracts can enhance competition either: (1) directly (market entry is encouraged when the ability to enforce contracts makes it easier for firms to vertically disintegrate or outsource); (2) indirectly (new or young firms can borrow more and on more favourable terms when creditors' and shareholders' interests are legally protected, similar to the law and finance literature). In this light there is also a need to go beyond the narrow investigation of competition policy in terms of competition law. One

Competition policy and development

Table 4.8   Determinants of enforcement of competition law

	OLS Specification *Global Competition Review*'s rating (index)	OLS Specification *Global Competition Review*'s rating (index)	OLS Specification *Global Competition Review*'s rating (index)	OLS Specification *Global Competition Review*'s rating (index)
English	0.3875 (0.5227)	0.6776 (0.3977)	0.2622 (0.4910)	Dropped
French	−0.7722 (0.5114)	Dropped	−0.8834 (0.4797)	−0.7860 (0.4885)
German	Dropped)	−0.0404 (0.4908)	Dropped	−0.0474 (0.5081)
Nordic	0.1375 (0.6151)	−0.1163 (0.5530)	0.1360 (0.5734)	0.2781 (0.5991)
Socialist	Dropped)	Dropped	Dropped	Dropped
GNI per capita		0.00006* (0.00002)		
Budget per staff			5.36×10^{-6}* (2.58×10^{-6})	5.12×10^{-6}* (2.54×10^{-6})
Age of comp. law				0.0085 (0.0063)
Intercept	3.3000* (0.4101)	1.8394* (0.3284)	2.8264* (0.4450)	2.6191* (0.5398)
R-square	0.25	0.51	0.38	0.43
Number of obs	26	26	26	26

Note: * Indicates statistical significance at the 10 percent level.

significant limitation of this and other quantitative studies has been data constraints, resulting in poor proxies and measures and small sample sizes.

CONCLUSIONS

The relationship between legal tradition and competition policy is a multi-dimensional and complex one. Qualitative arguments on the relationship have revolved around the evolution of competition laws in the United States and Europe and the difficulty of convergence between the two. The issue is further complicated by institutional variations in the structures and processes of competition law enforcement. Preliminary quantitative analysis, based on a small number of variables and limited data, have indicated that legal tradition has a very limited effect on competition law.

NOTE

1. Different terminologies are sometimes used. Per se clauses are also known as prohibitions provisions. Economic reasonableness is applied in interpreting 'rule of reason' clauses. 'Abuse principles' relate to conduct-based prohibitions that are subject to reasonableness-based inquiry.

REFERENCES

Acemoglu, D. and S. Johnson (2003), 'Unbundling Institutions', mimeo, MIT.

Beck, T. and R. Levine (2003), 'Legal Institutions and Financial Development', World Bank Policy Research Paper No. 3136, September.

Berkowitz, D., K. Pistor and J.-F. Richard (2003), 'Economic Development, Legality and the Transplant Effect', *European Economic Review*, 47, 165–95.

David, Rene and John Brierley (1985), *Major Legal Systems in the World Today*, Third Edition, London: Stevens & Sons.

Demirgüç-Kunt, A. and V. Maksimovic (1998), 'Law Finance and Firm Growth', *Journal of Finance*, 53(6), December.

Demirgüç-Kunt, A. and R. Levine (eds) (2001), *Financial Structure and Economic Growth: A Cross-country Comparison of Banks, Markets, and Development*, Cambridge, MA: MIT Press.

Djankov, S., R. La Porta, F. Lopez-de-Silanes and A. Shleifer (2002), 'The Regulation of Entry', *Quarterly Journal of Economics*, **CXVII** (1), 1–38.

Djankov, S., R. La Porta, F. Lopez-de-Silanes and A. Shleifer (2003), 'Courts', *Quarterly Journal of Economics*, **CXVIII** (1), 453–518.

Djankov, S., E. Glaeser, R. La Porta, F. Lopez-de-Silanes and A. Shleifer (2003a), 'The New Comparative Economics', mimeo, Harvard University.

Dutz, M. and M. Vagliasindi (2000), 'Competition Policy Implementation in Transition Economies: An Empirical Assessment', EBRD working paper 47, London, European Bank for Reconstruction and Development.

Gifford, D.J. and R.T. Kudrle (2003), 'European Union Competition Law and Policy: How Much Latitude for Convergence with the United States?', *Antitrust Bulletin*, Fall, 727–80.

Glaeser, E.L. and A. Shleifer (2002), 'Legal Origins', *Quarterly Journal of Economics*, **CXVII** (4), November.

Global Competition Review (2003a), *The 2003 Handbook of Competition Enforcement Agencies*, London.

Global Competition Review (2003b), *Rating Enforcement Survey*, London.

Gwartney, J.D., W. Block and R. Lawson (1996), 'Economic freedom of the world, 1975–1995', Varcouver, BC: Fraser Institute.

Hylton, Keith N. (2003), *Antitrust Law: Economic Theory and Common Law Evolution*, Cambridge: Cambridge University Press.

Kee, H.-L. and B. Hoekman (2003), 'Imports, Entry and Competition Law as Market Disciplines', mimeo, World Bank.

Kovacic, W.E. and C. Shapiro (2000), 'Antitrust Policy: A Century of Economic and Legal Thinking', *Journal of Economic Perspectives*, **14** (1), 43–60.

La Porta, R., F. Lopez-de-Silanes, A. Shleifer and R. Vishny (1997), 'Legal Determinants of External Finance', *Journal of Finance*, 52, 1131–50.

La Porta, R., F. Lopez-de-Silanes, A. Shleifer and R. Vishny (1998), 'Law and Finance', *Journal of Political Economy*, 106, 1113–55.
Levine, R. and S. Zervos (1998), 'Stock Market Development and Long-run Growth', The World Bank, Policy Research Working Paper Series: 1582 1999.
Londregan, J. (2002), 'Common Law vs. The Civil Code: Precedent and Predictability', mimeo, Princeton University.
Merryman, J.H. (1985), *The Civil Law Tradition: An Introduction to the Legal Systems of Western Europe and Latin America*, Second Edition, Stanford, CA: Stanford University Press.
Nicholson, M. (2004), 'Quantifying Antitrust Regimes', FTC Working Paper, 5 February.
OECD (1997), 'Judicial Enforcement of Competition Law', Proceedings of Seminar on Enforcement of Competition Law, OCDE/GD(97)200.
OECD (2003), 'Optimal Design of a Competition Agency', Secretariat Note, CCNM/GF/COMP(2003)2.
Palim, M.R.A. (1998), 'The Worldwide Growth of Competition Law: An Empirical Analysis', *Antitrust Bulletin*, Spring, 105–45.
Pistor, K., Y. Keinan, J. Kleinheisterkamp and M.D. West (2003), 'Evolution of Corporate Law and the Transplant Effect: Lessons from Six Countries', *World Bank Research Observer*, **18** (1), 89–112.
Rajan, R. and L. Zingales (1998), 'Financial Dependence and Growth', National Bureau of Economic Research, NBER Working Papers 5758 1996.
Shirley, M. (2003), 'Institutions and Development', mimeo.
Tetley, W. (2000), 'Mixed Jurisdictions: Common Law vs. Civil Law', *Louisiana Law Review*, 677–738.
Tirole, J. (1999), 'The Institutional Infrastructure of Competition Policy', mimeo.
UNCTAD (1997), 'Empirical Evidence of the Benefits from Applying Competition Law and Policy Principles to Economic Development in Order to Attain Greater Efficiency in International Trade and Development', UNCTAD Paper No. TD/B/COM.2/EM/10, 18 September.
UNCTAD (2003), *Model Law on Competition*, Geneva: United Nations.
World Bank (2004), *Doing Business in 2004: Understanding Regulation*, Washington DC: Oxford University Press for World Bank.

5. Establishing consumers as equivalent players in competition policy

Kamala Dawar

INTRODUCTION

Competition is good for consumers. In markets where firms have to compete to persuade consumers to buy their products, consumer welfare is increased through greater choice and lower prices. In a competitive market, supply and demand determines the price and output of a good or service rather than the dominant behaviour of any one firm or the collusive behaviour of a group of firms.

Many examples can be given to illustrate this general point. However, the purpose of this chapter is not to restate the virtues of competition for consumers or for economies but, primarily using research drawn from Consumers International members, to consider why competitive markets are difficult to achieve, particularly in developing economies, and to examine the tension between the stated objectives and the actual impact of competition laws, especially in relation to consumer welfare.

The evidence suggests that competition policies that give priority to the supply of competition, ensuring rivalry or contestability in the structure of markets (such as preventing barriers to entry or ensuring the fair conduct of firms) will not by themselves be sufficient to ensure a competitive outcome. These issues are primarily producer-oriented and do not directly affect the demand for competition. Competition policy needs to incorporate complementary consumer policies aimed at ensuring that consumers can make informed and active choices in the marketplace. These choices send signals to producers, and in doing so trigger the development of more competitive markets. Thus, competition policy will be more effective where it includes action to develop the demand side of the market. This applies whether the country is developing or developed. The chapter further argues that consumers are not automatically able to respond to competitive markets, and considers policies in relation to individual consumers, consumer organizations and consumer protection agencies to rectify this.

Consumer welfare and the ability of individuals to use their (limited) resources efficiently is not a priority in many national strategies for growth and development. Countries certainly need the flexibility to choose their own balance between producers and consumers. But positive outcomes require attention to the demand side of the equation, for example, through consumer protection laws and consumer-driven investigations of anti-competitive practices. Using a 'bottom-up' approach to activate competition also makes the consumer a full participant in the competition policy-making processes. Such a strategy not only increases consumer welfare and enables markets to function more competitively but also enhances democracy within the polity and the marketplace.

Following this introduction, the second part of the chapter looks at the difficulties experienced in achieving competitive markets, particularly in newly liberalizing economies, and then examines the predominant thinking behind competition policy. The third section considers weaknesses in competitor/supplier-oriented competition policy. The fourth section discusses how the demand side to competition policy can be institutionalized. The fifth calls for demand-side policies to be included in competition policy-making processes. Examples of recent developments are given, such as in the use of US litigation practice regarding consumers as 'demand-side' complainants and the EC Consumer Strategy. This strategy includes new initiatives to inform consumers about competition policy and its impact on them, in addition to enabling consumers to identify anti-competitive activities and to bring them to the European Commission's attention. The sixth section provides concluding comments.

DIFFICULTIES IN ACHIEVING COMPETITIVE MARKETS

There is an abundance of evidence that trade liberalization does not by itself guarantee competitive markets in terms of increasing efficiency or becoming competitive internationally. Within projects such as the Consumers in the Global Market Programme, Consumers International members have been conducting research and analysis into national competition regimes in developing and transition economies.[1] The problems identified by this research illustrate the lack of success these countries have had in creating and in maintaining competitive markets, due to tensions between seeking to protect domestic producers as players in the market and seeking to promote consumer welfare.

Conflicting Policy Priorities

In conditions of scarcity and underdevelopment, competition policy seldom takes centre stage in government policy. If total income is very low, a government may decide that the most appropriate national trade strategy is to increase its domestic industries' overall competitiveness by allowing dominant players to emerge in the market that are capable of achieving economies of scale and undertaking research and development.

In the Ukraine for example, legislation allows for a concentration of economic entities, which would otherwise be prohibited by the Antimonopoly Committee, if the positive effect for the public interests of the concentration is judged to be greater than the negative consequences for competition caused by the market restriction. Ukrainian competition policy therefore focuses on contestability in the marketplace, with a consumer protection clause in recognition of the public interest. However, this clause has not been effectively institutionalized. Without a transparent system of consultation with consumer representatives, and with no clear legal guidance on how 'benefits' should be assessed or any indication of what should constitute a 'fair share' of those benefits, it is rather the potential for conflict between the benefits for producers and consumers that has been institutionalized, along with poor governance in the marketplace.

A similar problem is highlighted by Consumers International's research into the Colombian aviation sector. In this instance, the decision by the Superintendencia to reject a merger between Avianca, SAM and ACES was reversed after the three companies appealed and a different 'ad hoc' Superintendent was appointed. Before the merger the national market shares stood at: Avianca 26 per cent, SAM 11 per cent and ACES 29 per cent. After the merger the new entity held 80 per cent, with control of 24 of the 27 (89 per cent) of national routes. The justification for the merger was the need for scale in the aviation industry in order to compete in a global market where demand is fragile. However, the new decision was controversial because it was ad hoc, dubious in the evidence used to support it, and insufficient consideration was given to the public interest. The case prompted the resignation of the Superintendent of Industry and Commerce, further undermining both the credibility and impartiality of the competition authority because the public interest override was based on a non-transparent and seemingly undemocratic decision-making process. Effectively, the competition authority was told to go away and come back with a different verdict. Thus, although competition policy existed, it had its focus on producer concerns, and was ultimately unable to provide credible support for either competition or consumer welfare.

Competition and Privatization

In transition and developing economies, privatization and other market-oriented economic reforms have often been undertaken without appropriate regulation and competition laws in place. This has commonly resulted in the transfer of monopoly power from the public sector to the private sector, which can be referred to as false liberalization. Although in principle, market-oriented reforms should increase competition and serve the consumer interest, much of the research indicates that privatization has simply allowed firms to take advantage of weak governments to monopolize markets, with little resulting benefit for consumers. If sound competition policy does not exist, government intervention can appear arbitrary and irrational, and ultimately erodes confidence in the market.

In Indonesia, a long history of state control of the most important sectors of the economy has inhibited the development of competitive markets. The Prohibition of Monopoly and Unfair Business Competition Practices Law, which came into force in 2000, did not address the issue that it was government regulation that determined domestic competition and trade policy, rather than the anti-competitive conduct of private enterprises. For example, when the government sold off the monopoly clove industry, the transaction favoured a single private purchaser who then became both the sole buyer and the sole seller of cloves. In this case, government intervention actually created a private monopoly, and further prevented any benefits from the privatization from reaching the consumer. Again, the priority of producer concerns overrode due consideration of consumer interest or the demand side of competition policy.

The research also shows that many laws have been poorly formulated, with a lack of clarity between the 'ends and means' to achieve a specific objective. There is, for example, a tendency to fail to make a distinction between anti-competitive business conduct on the one hand, and the form of market structure on the other. And in some, laws are unclear as to the definition of the vertical integration of business activities. Laws that set an arbitrarily maximum market share limit as a benchmark for fair competition, ignore issues such as the fact that large-scale firms do not automatically have market power if the markets in which they operate have no barriers to entry or exit. So high market share or monopoly is prohibited even though it may encourage technological progress and economic growth, or it results from the inventor of a unique new technology automatically dominating the market they have created. Rather than prohibiting monopolistic enterprises, laws should have focused on 'harmful' monopolistic conduct and specify the various types of anti-competitive business practice most detrimental to the goal of fair and open competition that enhances consumer welfare.

Thus, while competitive markets benefit consumers, if privatization and liberalization are embarked upon without sound competition and consumer policy, these newly liberalized markets will not function to the benefit of economic efficiency or consumer welfare. As competition becomes more acute, businesses have attempted to cut their costs and secure their market position by reducing the standards of their product and services to an unsafe level, or by undertaking fraudulent practices.

Competition and Regulation

Competition policy and regulation both address the concern to limit the exercise of market power and to facilitate the efficient allocation of resources. Many industries, particularly natural monopoly industries or those said to be 'clothed in the public interest' such as water, energy, fixed line local telecommunications, and transport, need to be regulated to ensure the benefits of economies of scale while protecting consumers from high prices or abuse of dominant positions. Regulation is understood to be appropriate, either as a substitute for competition, or as a short- to medium-term strategy until competition can be introduced to the market. However, in developed economies such as the United States, difficulties over assessing what is a 'fair' rate of return within regulation have also raised concern that the process itself reflects a complex mixture of political and economic considerations, where the consumer interest may well be subsumed by politically organized groups that can more effectively negotiate a higher rate of return (Kahn, 1995).

Evidence has emerged in the United States suggesting that nascent regulated industries have used regulation and the creation of state regulatory agencies to insulate existing firms from competition (Jarrell, 1978). As incumbents allocate resources to protect their position, new entrants may have to deplete resources to enter the market, while others may have to enter the political marketplace in response to the political activity of others. The extra advocacy pressures from other interest groups results in further politicization, and rent seeking can become a significant diversion of resources away from more productive activities. If this is a documented problem in the United States, then the opportunity cost of similar expenditures and pressure to rent seek in economies characterized by scarcity is an even greater concern.

Even the best-designed economic regulatory process imposes costs on society for its establishment and administration, through its distorting effect on economic efficiency, and because of the time, effort and expense associated with its removal (Crampton and Face, 2002). In one study, deregulation was found to provide consumers with benefits of at least $50 billion annually (Crandall and Ellig, 1996). Research has consistently demonstrated that deregulation has been accompanied by large price reductions to consumers and substantial improvements in quality and service. Regulatory frameworks should only limit competition to the minimum extent necessary to achieve their goals. This can be aided by ensuring that domestic competition agencies work with regulators on regulatory proceedings, and participate in the process of developing laws or policies that have the potential to impact adversely upon competition (Crampton and Face, 2002).

LACK OF COHERENT LEGISLATION AND EFFECTIVE INSTITUTIONS AND AGENCIES

With general consensus as to the benefits of competition policy in underpinning both liberalization and regulation, the following section highlights the importance of political will for strengthening the structure, application and implementation of laws and policies that incorporate not only the supply side, but also the demand for competition.

Consumer research in Panama has highlighted the importance of a strong judiciary and the role that public interest organizations can play in monitoring competition. Competition policy in Panama was, in principle, strengthened by a brewery merger decision insisting that the benefits of greater efficiency must be passed on to the public. Yet while this ruling strongly indicated that consumer welfare was to be considered within competition policy, it appears to have had little impact on how the competition authorities monitored other industries, such as wheat flour.

Following price liberalization in 1991 the Panama market in wheat flour was dominated by four large domestic miller companies who had benefited from an import duty of 32.5 per cent. In 1996, the Panamanian consumer association lodged a formal complaint with CLICAC (the competition authority), using evidence it had secured to suggest that the four millers had been colluding to fix flour prices and apportion market shares since 1994. CLICAC favourably responded by demanding an immediate end to illegal agreements and indemnities, but the court case took five years and eventually failed to reach a conclusion. In 2001, the millers made an out of court settlement accepting that they had acted illegally and pledging to stop colluding regardless of the court. The inability of the court to come to a decision seriously undermined public perception of its ability to defend the rule of law, as well as of the role of competition authorities and the work of consumer organizations.

Had this case been successfully concluded in the courts, it would have brought together an effective demand for competition and its successful enforcement. The demand was evident when consumers complained about the price of wheat flour and sought a fair price. And the case utilized the cost-effective strategy of drawing upon the evidence produced by consumer organizations about the impact of anti-competitive practices on consumer welfare. The study highlights the need for competition authorities to look beyond unfair trading as practices against competitors and/or the specific scope of consumer protection laws. The focus should be on ensuring effective rights of access for relevant public interest groups and enabling these potential allies to present *amicus curiae* briefs to the courts, or even better, to bring collective actions as full parties before the courts in order to institutionalize securely the demand for competition.

In the Ukraine, research has identified many press articles and foreign business complaints denouncing the poorly developed concept of what constitutes a conflict of interest within the legislative and judiciary branches, particularly when so many officials retain their commercial interests while in power. This creates barriers to entry for less influential and less-resourced businesses as well as to the emergence of transparent and rational market mechanisms. In addition there is no mechanism for giving rights of access to the consumer to pursue their legitimate interest. Thus both the supply and demand for competition are seriously undermined. Removing vested interests from the marketplace is a long-term objective for ensuring contestability in any domestic system, but enhancing the demand for competition is an immediately less politically destabilizing strategy for improving competition and democratic governance. Institutionalizing demand-side policies within the competition regime will provide information, evidence and a means of mobilizing the public to send signals to business that can counteract vested interests. In addition, demand-side strategies can be shown to be cost-effective relative to agency enforcement. Dysfunctional markets and widespread corruption mean that there is little protection for consumers, despite the existence of laws. In such situations, bottom-up demand-side policies, including direct actions by consumers, are even more important to counterbalance the lack of effective supply-side competition policy.

Lack of Complementary Consumer Policy

The highest level of demand-side competition policy is consumer protection law. While some countries such as Australia, Poland and the United Kingdom have joint agencies and laws, others have not introduced complementary consumer policy or harmonized policy objectives. For example, Slovenia's competition policy was motivated by EU accession. The necessary legal framework and apparatus for the execution of the EU antitrust regulation and regulation of state aid was introduced, but without enhanced consumer protection and education components.

Without adequate and relevant regulation protecting the welfare of consumers, increased competition in, for example, the Slovenian road freight transport sector, has proved problematic. This sector has been undergoing liberalization and deregulation since 1989, during a period of large losses in transport volume and widespread bankruptcies. There was little legislation regulating new businesses and drivers who had previously lost their jobs found it easy to set up new small enterprises by buying trucks from their previous employers at very competitive rates; 72 per cent of the market was held by new small enterprises with only one employee. The increased number of business operators resulted in cutthroat price competition and in lower transport prices. There was, for example, an estimated 30 per cent decline in the price of a 25-ton transportation on the Ljubljana–Hamburg link between 1995 and 2000. However, there was deterioration in transport safety, with the number of accidents involving freight vehicles increasing more than 30 per cent between 1994 and 2000. The average age of freight vehicles owned by individuals was almost double those owned by companies, at ten years compared with just over five years. While this development decreased prices and eased the burden of the expected increase in unemployment, it took place without adequate regulation and consumer protection measures to complement the sudden increase in competition, to the detriment of the industry and public safety.

Competition agencies need constantly to monitor changes in markets that will affect efficiency and consumers. The rise of e-commerce in South Korea has brought new issues to the attention of the competition authorities and the online market system has been specifically charged with using exaggerated advertisements and with swindling. Legislation such the Fair Labelling and Advertising Act has not yet been able to redress these negative developments. This has a negative effect on consumer confidence in electronic transactions, and the level of competition in the market. Ultimately it inhibits the growth of the industry. In Indonesia, consumer protection from injurious monopolistic practices only covers the packaging and advertisements of cigarettes, pork-free labelling of canned goods and the censoring of pornography or scenes offensive on cultural or religious grounds.

Given the potential complementarity of objectives within competition and consumer protection policy, competition will be enhanced if the remit of consumer protection policies is enlarged and further resourced whether or not there is a joint competition and consumer protection agency.

Predominant Thinking Behind Competition Policy

With experts agreed on the benefits of competition, policy needs to translate theory into practice for both the economy and consumers, particularly in developing and transition economies where 'policy transfer' has not often been successful (Cook et al., 2004). Yet the economic analysis that underpins the work of competition authorities has shown a strong tendency to privilege producer concerns (the supply of competition), while the issues about consumer behaviour (the demand for competition) are secondary or in some cases non-existent.

Not all countries give a high priority to consumer efficiency and welfare because of the need to preserve domestic capacity to compete, as seen in many development strategies, or because of the inherent need to preserve flexibility to choose between policy objectives. These can include choosing between competition and regulation, and between competitors and consumers, for example. Competition authorities tend to be largely concerned about whether policy should focus on rules and procedures to prevent anti-competitive practices, dominance or abuse of dominance, the reduction of barriers to entry and/or facilitating optimal conditions. However, even if governments do choose to implement laws that focus on reducing competitor protection by promoting rivalry, or by eliminating excessive divergences from an industry structure, the outcomes can and should be enhanced by increasing the impact of consumer behaviour, in sending signals to the market that trigger competition.

There tends to be too little analysis of consumer behaviour and welfare in making policy, law enforcement and investigations. In a series of studies conducted in the United States in the early 1970s, economists compared the markets where government was enforcing antitrust laws with the markets where government should enforce the laws, if consumer well-being were the paramount concern. The studies concluded unanimously that the size of consumer losses from monopoly played little or no role in government enforcement of the law (Demsetz, 1973). While the United States, Australia, the United Kingdom and other developed countries have been moving more towards consumer efficiency models of competition policy, demand-side policies have still not been meaningfully institutionalized throughout the different levels of consumer interest. In less developed economies, industrial policies remain focused predominantly on competitor protection.

INSTITUTIONALIZING DEMAND-LED COMPETITION POLICY

In this section, the three levels of consumer interest and the role each can play in raising the demand for competition, are examined. The first level of demand-side competition policy focuses on the individual consumer. Just as the behaviour of firms impacts on consumers, consumer behaviour directly impacts on competition. How consumers search the market, how many firms they survey before making decisions, and how much they will pay (in time or money) to search the market are important factors. Allied to this is consideration of how they respond to products and prices offered in the market; whether they switch firms, whether they make formal complaints, or seek redress if necessary. This raises the question of whether or not policy could or should influence consumer search behaviour and whether there is a greater role for emphasizing the similarities between products and services, in order to aid consumers in making choices.

Policy can influence both the costs to consumers and the actions firms can or cannot take. In addition to the tangible costs of searching and switching, consumer behaviour may be the result of intangible factors, such as cultural taboos. Consumer perceptions or misperceptions of searching and switching costs can be manipulated by those who supply the good or service. Firms can choose, for example, whether or not to mark prices clearly at the point of sale, or whether to provide freely the information required to facilitate switching between firms or products. Frictions in markets, such as barriers to entry, may also be caused by consumer behaviour manipulated by advertising.

Within Waterson's (2001) work on the role of consumers in competition and competition policy, he puts forward five propositions to demonstrate the importance of searching and switching costs for the outcome in a market. For example, if each consumer searches only one firm before the purchase decision, the pricing outcome is at the monopoly level regardless of the number of firms in the market. Thus, the higher the proportion of active searchers, all other things being equal, the greater the proportion of low-cost firms, with searchers also imparting information to non-searchers. Waterson (2001) also argues that in firms where no discrimination between new and old customers is feasible, firms' prices are generally higher with switching costs than in their absence. In examining the UK energy market after liberalization, Waterson's work indicates the value of understanding what can facilitate consumers in making rational and informed market decisions, and in doing so, build the demand for competition, or a competition culture, from the bottom up.

The implications of the behaviour of consumers are wide-ranging. Consumers will only engage in additional searches if the expected benefits are greater than the costs. Yet the consequence of this is that if consumers believe it is not worthwhile searching a market, it will not be worthwhile because firms will get signals that they do not have to compete with each other in order to gain customers. In the case of Bates (US Supreme Court, 1976), a low-price law practice won a case to allow it to advertise lower fees because it became clear that its business could not survive in the absence of information provided to consumers about its low-cost centre. This is because consumers would not have otherwise learned about the law firm and be motivated to use it.

Conversely, if consumers believe searching is going to be worthwhile, it will probably be the case because informed and active consumers seeking out cheaper provisions of a standard good or service will send firms signals they will respond to by reducing prices and/or improving quality. A Bill was introduced into the UK House of Commons in 1984 proposing to end the solicitors' monopoly on conveyancing (house ownership transfer). Despite the Bill being withdrawn and legislation being delayed until 1987, reductions in conveyancing charges actually first appeared in 1984. As the public became sensitized to possible changes in prices, some solicitors responded to new expectations and initiated price cuts before competition was actually institutionalized (Domberger and Sherr, 1989). In the United Kingdom in the early 1990s, British Telecom also brought down its telephone charges before, but in anticipation of, the termination of the duopoly market.

Therefore, in addition to the need for greater political will in implementing and maintaining the supply side of competitive markets, there is an equal requirement for ensuring consumer action in the market. Both aspects need to be in place in order to ensure that the framework for contestable markets is triggered by informed and active consumers. Law and policy can create the conditions for competition to flourish but it is consumers who ultimately set it in motion. Even when a market has the potential to be competitive, it may not be so in operation largely because of the behaviour of consumers.

Establishing Consumers as Equivalent Players in Competition Policy

It is suggested here that the stimulation of the demand for competition needs to be institutionalized at three interconnected levels: in policy and investigations, in the work of consumer organizations and at the level of the individual consumer. By taking a more bottom-up approach and creating an administrative mechanism that can ensure rights of access to consumer representatives, through consultations and *amicus curiae* briefs, for example, policy-makers can complement quantitative consumer behaviour data with qualitative insight into consumer attitudes, knowledge, satisfaction and complaint levels to understand market responses better.

A notable development at a regional level is the EC Consumer Policy Strategy 2002–2006, which initiates a decision to integrate consumer interests tangibly into the implementation of Community competition rules and develop lasting capacities allowing them to be genuine and effective representatives of consumer interests within the decision-making process. This focuses directly on the demand side by seeking to support consumers at member state level in order to increase their capacity to participate before national competition authorities.[2] In particular, the strategy seeks to promote the possibility of collecting information and evidence about practices that may be particularly injurious to the consumer, but where competitors may not be injured due to their capacity to pass the costs of restrictions to the ultimate consumers. Thus for antitrust and merger control areas, network services, mass-marketed products or the liberal professions, it may be that the Commission is seeking to bring the consumer, as represented in organizations at the domestic level, directly into the national authority case decision-making structure.[3] If so, this assists not only the consumer, who is enabled by the programme to obtain the resources to complete market research, but authorities as well, who otherwise are restricted by lack of resources to deal with complaints by competitors against other competitors. Different domestic systems rely in different parts on agencies and private rights of enforcement. Thus, demand-side developments can be tracked not only by agency-oriented strategies such as the Commission policy above but also by court developments.

A recent Trinko case in the United States showed that private actions by consumers remain a ripe area for legal development. Here the indirect but ultimate purchaser of an office telephone system asserted their right to recover damages caused by the anti-competitive behaviour of the supply firm to their own local provider.[4] Besides consideration of the practice itself and its relation to federal regulatory enactments, the demand-side issue of standing by the ultimate consumer right to bring the action to court was also at issue. The 2nd US Circuit Court of Appeals found that the plaintiff did have standing. This case was supported by *amicus curiae* briefs by the two largest consumer organizations in the United States, on the grounds that 'it is vital that consumers, who are often the immediate focus and always the ultimate victims of anti-competitive conduct, have standing to vindicate their rights under the antitrust laws' (*The American Lawyer*, 10 August 2003).

Thus, even in developed countries with a highly advantageous system, the extent to which that system is available for consumers is still an aspect of judicial development. In addition to supporting individual consumers, national consumer organizations can play a cost-effective role in aiding competition authorities' investigations by providing evidence and the consumer welfare perspective to counterbalance producer concerns. In Mali, the consumer organization ASCOMA undertook a price survey of the meat industry after an unexpected price hike in 1994. This market surveillance and information dissemination drive was directed at the government and the evidence gathered was subsequently used by the government to bolster its competition drive. In Zambia, the national consumer organization, ZACA, set up Consumer Water Watch groups to monitor the water and sanitation sector following privatization. ZACA now regularly lobbies the Zambian National Water Supply and Sanitation Council, offering information and consumer representation.

The information gathering and dissemination function of consumer organizations can be further enhanced as a primary component of the demand side. Not only are consumer organizations closer to the individual consumer than government agencies, but they are usually seen as more independent than government and their advice and information is consequently more trusted. In Senegal, the consumer organization, Arête, undertakes regular media alerts during controversial tenders such as the Shell, Total and Elf joint tender to run the Senegalese oil refinery. These media campaigns raise public awareness about each particular case, acting to ensure that tenders serve consumers and not only the firms involved and to increase transparency and accountability.

CONCLUSION

Institutionalizing consumer representation in competition authorities' policy-making processes is necessary to incorporate and advocate procedures that will take account of the impact of both consumer behaviour in activating competition and of business behaviour on consumer welfare. Competition authorities can incorporate mechanisms that will help consumers to encourage, or even force businesses to act more effectively by working with national consumer organizations to disseminate information, mobilize consumers and undertake consumer research to input a consumer welfare perspective into investigations and policy-making. This presents not only a cost-effective means of enhancing competition but, perhaps more importantly, it increases consumer welfare, provides legitimacy to consumer welfare objectives and ultimately enhances the democratic process itself.

NOTES

1. The consumers in the Global Market Programme are supported by the Dutch government, the International Development Research Centre and Oxfam. Full case study reports can be obtained from www.consumersinternational.org.
2. European Commission Consumer policy strategy 2002–2006 (COM(2002) 208 final)(2002/C 137/02).
3. These are the sectoral themes for competition analysis set out in the EC DG Sanco 2004 call for tenders. SANCO-2004-01307-00-0.
4. That the telecommunications company violated Section 2 of the Sherman Act by using its monopoly power to keep rivals out of the marketplace. The increased costs of the practice were by the purchaser, thereby warranting treble damages and injunctive relief.

REFERENCES

Cook, P., C. Kirkpatrick, M. Minogue and D. Parker (eds) (2004), *Leading Issues in Competition, Regulation and Development*, Cheltenham, UK and Northampton, MA, USA: Edward Elgar.

Crampton, P.S. and B.A. Face (2002), 'Revisiting Regulation and Deregulation through the Lens of Competition Policy', *World Competition*, **25** (1).

Crandall, R. and J. Ellig (1996), *Economic Deregulation and Customer Choice: Lessons for the Electric Industry*, Fairfax, VA: Centre for Market Processes.

Demsetz, H. (1973), 'Industry Structure, Market Rivalry and Public Policy', *Journal of Law and Economics*, **16**, 1–9.

Domberger, S. and A. Sherr (1989), 'The Impact of Competition on Pricing and Quality of Legal Services', *International Review of Law and Economics*, **9**, 41–56.

Jarrell, G.A. (1978), 'The Demand for State Regulation of the Electricity Utility Industry', *Journal of Law and Economics*, **21** (2), October.

Kahn, A. (1995), *The Economics of Regulation, Vol 1*, Cambridge: The MIT Press.

Waterson, M. (2001), 'The Role of Consumers in Competition and Competition Policy', University of Warwick Working Paper No. 607, July.

Waterson, M. (2003), 'Consumers and Competition', University of Warwick Working Paper No. 679, May.

6. *Guanxi* and *taipans*: market power and the East Asian model of competition

Raul Fabella

INTRODUCTION

Solutions to idiosyncratic and non-standard obstacles to production and exchange are par for the course for a special set of players known as entrepreneurs. These hurdles may be technological, organizational and financial or risk-related. In frontier or underdeveloped areas, the common missing ingredient is the absence or the severe inadequacy of formal or state-provided contract enforcement and property rights protection (North, 1990; Barzel, 2002). Ex-post opportunism makes for a prohibitive transaction cost that results in highly fragmented or even missing markets. Not only is the state remiss in contract enforcement, it may itself serve as a vehicle for expropriatory tendencies among the political elite. For an entrepreneur to thrive, it must solve these twin weak governance problems.

The *guanxi* system, also known as relational contracting, solves the contract enforcement and ex-post opportunism problem by limiting exchanges among players who are also members of a group or community that is subject to an existing, informal but effective, system of sanctions. *Guanxi*-based contracts face lower opportunism risk and transactions cost than, and thus can drive out, those contracts dependent only on absent or weak state-provided or third-party enforcement (TPE). In North's (1990) phraseology, *guanxi* is a second-party enforcement mechanism (SPE), drawing its power from community sanction. Williamson (1983) called this genre of effort private ordering in the absence of adequate public ordering.

Because political power may be lodged outside this group or community, the *guanxi* entrepreneur, if successful, also faces considerable expropriation risk. The wielders of political power can either selectively enforce certain laws or pass new laws to effect partial or total expropriation. The entrepreneur solves this by coupling with or capturing the state's rule-making apparatus. In this case, property rights protection is effectively internalized.

The entrepreneur that successfully deals with these dual problems of weak governance is a *taipan*. The very process of their emergence in the weak governance setting ought to explain the many stylized facts about *taipans* and their operations. Before proceeding, some known facts about *taipans* in East Asia are reviewed.

MODERN *TAIPANS*

The economic landscape in most of East Asia is dominated by very large conglomerates headed by powerful tycoons or *taipans*, largely overseas Chinese (*huaquio*). Between 50–80 percent of market capitalization is in their hands in Indonesia, Thailand, Malaysia and the Philippines (*The Economist*, 2001). The stylized facts about the *taipans* and their operations are the following:

1. They operate largely on the basis of *guanxi* – contracting on the basis of relations and connections rather than written rules, the relational contracting mode.
2. They preside over sprawling business empires without the blessing of clear synergistic logic, for example, Robert Kuok of Malaysia is into food, manufactures, banking, property and media; Lucio Tan of the Philippines is into airlines, banking, tobacco, breweries and property.
3. Each company in the empire is run by a family member and outside auditors and professional managers are a rarity.
4. The use of complex pyramids of share- and cross-holdings of companies anchor their legendary penchant for secrecy. Books of accounts, when available, are opaque and uninformative. For example, Lucio Tan of the Philippines thrives on such pyramids.
5. The delegation of authority is meager and information is a closely guarded monopoly of the patriarch.
6. Wherever *taipans* operate they enjoy a monopoly or near-monopoly position.
7. The cultivation of political powers via rumored shady but mutually beneficial relations is par for the course. (Harry Stonehill was run out of the Philippines in the 1960s to keep his payola black book from being opened and implicating many figures. Lucio Tan was a close associate of then President Joseph Estrada of the Philippines; Danding Co-Juangco of the Philippines, said to be a close Marcos crony, and was also a favorite of Estrada; the Salims of Indonesia were linked to President Suharto.)
8. The *taipans* have a very pronounced ethnic minority (usually Chinese) flavor.

The feature that this chapter focuses on is the need for and the acquisition by the entrepreneur of contract enforcement and property rights protection to support market exchange where the state is weak.

The Economist (7 April 2001), on the clash of Asian business cultures, observes:

> Developed economies have rule-based governance systems that incur enormous fixed costs but negligible incremental costs . . . By contrast, the poor countries of Asia have not been able to afford the investment in high fixed costs of such a system, and have, therefore, settled for the large incremental costs of a *guanxi*-based system.

The *guanxi* system, like the Maghribi system (Greif, 1993, 2001) and even the merchant law (Grief, Milgrom and Weingast, 1994) is a second-party contract enforcement system developed in the absence of adequate third-party enforcement (TPE) (North, 1990; Barzel, 2002). But the *guanxi* system is only one side of the *taipan* coin. The other side is the acquisition of private property rights protection capability. While only a faint penumbra of their nineteenth-century counterparts, the stylized facts about the current crop of *taipans* nonetheless, echo most pronounced aspects of nineteenth-century *taipans* – vertical integration into second-party property rights enforcement in the absence of weak governance (see Criswell, 1981). It is also evident, however, that as some East Asian countries progressed rapidly in the wake of opening up, the grip of *guanxi* and second-party enforcement has slowly loosened in favor of more rules-based contracting.

VERTICAL INTEGRATION INTO SPE

The motivation for vertical integration is myriad. Coase (1937), addressing the boundaries of the firm, proposed the umbrella concept of high transactions cost of arm's length market exchange. Subsequent proposals have elaborated on Coase. Williamson (1975), following Coase but with sharper lenses, threw in ex-post opportunism, lock-ins and asset specificity as the driving forces behind the high transactions cost of market exchange. Klein, Crawford and Alchian (1978) added the threat of quasi-rent appropriation and its avoidance as a motivator. Barzel (1982) placed the difficulty of measurement and the disputes it triggers at the roots of integration. Grossman and Hart (1986) identified residual rights of control as one motivator. Holmstrom and Roberts (1998) revisiting the boundary of the firm issue found that the universe of motives cannot all be accounted for by the transactions cost (Coase and Williamson) or the property rights (Grossman and Hart, 1986) paradigms.

The absence of an adequate supplier of a particular input or service essential for the production or distribution of a final product signals the high transactions cost of arm's length exchange and motivates vertical integration. This market for the input or service may be missing or the state tasked to provide it may be weak and unable to deliver. Third-party enforcement (North, 1990) of property rights and the enforcement of contracts are supposedly all-important state-provided services. The boundary of the firm in the frontiers where public ordering is weak, thus extends into the provision of Williamson's private ordering (1983).

In the Middle Ages, third-party enforcement was inadequate in Europe and had to be supplemented by second-party mechanisms, such as the Community Responsibility System (Greif, 2001) and Maghribi trading or merchant law based on network (Greif et al., 1994). In the Wild West of America, the railroad tycoons maintained their own private enforcement force as well as financed occasional posses and bounty hunters to deal with bandits and troublemakers. They also sometimes 'privatized' public enforcement agencies to deal with unions. In the Far East through the Victorian period, the *taipans* of the Princely Hongs maintained virtual private armies and navies to protect their trade and mete occasional punishments on bandits and pirates (Criswell, 1981). Their influence on the Foreign Office meant access to the Royal Navy's capability to cow even sovereign states. Entrepreneurship in this environment required vertical integration into second-party enforcement. Second-party enforcement however, conduces toward less competition even as it resolves the 'missing market' problem.

This type of vertical integration is very special because enforcement becomes private and excludable. Other players cannot avail of it and thus, cannot operate. These effectively form barriers to competition. Since enforcement has considerable economic scale potential, this has a serious implication for the structure of the market.

This chapter proposes a nexus of contract explanation for the emergence of a *taipan*, based loosely on the characterization described above. The background is a weak third-party enforcement environment where entrepreneurs, to operate and survive, must acquire enforcement capacity. The underlying model used is based on Fabella (2005), where contracts involve a cash advance in Period 1 from a principal P to an agent A who delivers effort or repayment in Period 2. This is referred to as a cash in advance contract. The idea is that a *taipan* is primarily a market-exchange-oriented entrepreneur who, in a weak TPE environment, is forced to integrate vertically into second-party enforcement to survive. While TPE is public, SPE is private and excludable. Thus, the *taipan* is on the one hand Schumpeterian, in that it brings otherwise infeasible markets into existence through its command over an SPE, and on the other a potential predator, in that this command may be trained against potential competitors. In particular, pursuit of an SPE may lead to the capture of the state decision-making apparatus, which may retard institutional change. In this respect the robber barons of the nineteenth-century industrializing American come to mind. Whether the *taipan* stays Schumpeterian (growth-enhancing) or becomes a predator (growth-retarding) is an important question.

The next section develops a model of the contract environment that is characterized by weak TPE and results in a 'missing market'. The *guanxi* approach is then developed as a contract theoretic response. The following two sections cover the birth of a *taipan* as an entrepreneur who captures the state enforcement and rule-making apparatus in order to internalize property rights protection. The fifth section examines anti-competitive mechanisms and the sixth and seventh discuss the implications for policy. The eighth concludes.

THE CASH-IN-ADVANCE CONTRACT

Weak Third-party Enforcement

Consider a production contract where the principal P advances the agent A a portion $w_1 = bw$, $0 \leq b_1 \leq 1$ of the agreed-on fee w in Period 1. A supplies observable and contracted effort e in Period 2 and, when the output X is observed in Period 2, receives the rest of the fee $(1 - b)w = w_2$. It is assumed that the division 'b' is fixed. It is assumed that spot contracts, i.e., $b = 1$, are not feasible. The perfect function is $pF(e) - w$, where the price p is parametric.

A, after receiving w_1 and enjoying $u(w_1)$ may, however, decide to renege, that is, refuse to supply e and instead supply e to their next best alternative, which gives them their outsider reservation utility U^0 in Period 2. Let the probability of being punished be Q and the punished be $L > 0$. The expected second-period utility with reneging is $Q(u^0 - L) + (1 - Q)U^0 = U^0 - QL$. If they renege, their total two-period utility becomes $U^0 + [u(w_1) - QL]$. The parenthesized expression refers to the incentive for ex-post opportunism. When $u(w_1) > QL$, there is, in North's terminology, weak third-party enforcement (TPE) and opportunism pays. When $u(w_1) < QL$, TPE is strong and opportunism does not pay. Q is the index of efficiency of state-supplied TPE. Thus, A abides by the contract only if

$$(i) \quad u(w_1) + u(w_2) - v(e) \geq U^0 + u(w_1) - QL = U^{00}. \qquad (6.1)$$

This becomes under weak TPE and strong TPE, respectively,

$$\text{(i)} \quad u(w_2) - v(e) \geq U^0 - QL$$

$$\text{(ii)} \quad u(w_1) + u(w_2) - v(e) \geq U^0. \tag{6.2}$$

(6.2i) is the augmented participation constraint (APC) for the model. If (6.2i) is true, then the ordinary participation constraint (6.2ii) is automatically satisfied. If (6.1) is satisfied, A will never renege despite weak TPE, since it does not pay to forfeit the second-period payment w_2. An analogous condition has also been called the enforcement proofness constraint (see, e.g., Laffont and Mortimart, 2002) in an adverse selection context. To highlight the governance problem, let effort be observable and unique, that is, $3 = e^0$.

The principal offers a contract $C(w, e)$ to A where (w, e) solves the following:

$$\max_{w} pF(e) - w$$

s.t. either (6.2i) or (6.2ii). $\tag{6.3}$

Let $C(w^*, e^0)$ be the weak TPE contract and $C(w^{**}, e^0)$ be the strong TPE contract. The following is obvious:

Lemma 1: (i) The optimal contract is costlier for P under weak than under strong TPE, that is, $w^* > w^{**}$. (ii) As QL rises, w^* falls towards w^{**}.

Proof: (i)   Since $U^0 + [u(w_1) - QL] > U_0$ and the APL binds strictly under optimal contracts, $u(w_1^*) + u(w_2^*) - u(w_1^{**}) - u(w_2^{**}) > 0$. Thus $w^{**} < w^*$. (ii) As QL rises $[u(w_1) = QL]$ falls and the relevant difference approaches zero.

QED

As QL falls it is obvious that $[pF(e^0) - w^*]$ falls and the principal may decide to cease operation altogether. Governance failure can result in a missing market failure.

The difference $(w^* - w^{**}) > 0$ constitutes a 'bribe' to keep the agent from exercising their option to renege. In an imperfect capital market, weak TPE can constitute an entry barrier.

THE *GUANXI* CONTRACT

Suppose a potential entrepreneur observes that a subset of the population of agents exists for whom 'informal sanctions' against ex-post opportunism are binding. That is, for this subset of agents, contract violation entails an added personal or social penalty G unrelated to QL. G is a certainty. They can limit their choice of agent to this subset perhaps because they also belong to this subset. The trade-off is that the 'technical aptitude' of the average agent in this subset is inferior to that of the average agent from the whole population and this impacts on the prospective revenue of the enterprise. Indeed, one can continue trading off 'technical aptitude' for higher G by a progressive narrowing of the subset.

Let $f, 0 \leq f \leq 1$, be the index of the restrictiveness of the set of agents from whose ranks A is drawn. If the set is the whole population, $f = 0$. Let $g(f)$ be the technical aptitude associated with f, and $g'(f) \geq 0, g(1) =$ max g, $g(0) = 0$. Thus 'technical aptitude' is at its highest when $f = 0$. For $f > 0$, the effective production technology becomes $F(e)[1 - g(f)]$. But as the set of agents progressively shrinks (f rises), the personal cost G also rises, that is, $G(f)$ and $G' > 0$, $G(0) = $ max G, that is, the reneging likelihood also falls. Again let $e = e^0$.

The optimal *guanxi* contract $C(w^g, e^0)$ for this entrepreneur solves the following:

$$\max_{w, e} pF(e)[1 - g(f)] - w \tag{6.4}$$

$$\text{s.t.} \quad u(w_2) - v(e) > U^0 - QL - G(f).$$

Optimal w^g is solved from the APC:

$$u(w_2) - v(e^0) = U^0 - QL - G(f) = U^g < U^{00}. \tag{6.5}$$

w^* monotonically decreases as f (or QL) rises. The maximized profit written as a function of f alone is:

$$\Pi^*(f) = pF(e^0)[1 - g(f)] - w^*(f). \tag{6.6}$$

As f rises the response of Π^* is ambiguous, since f is costly to the firm via $g(f)$. Note that for some high $f = f^0$, $u(w^1) - QL - Q(f^0) < 0$ and the APC becomes $u(w_2) - v(e) \geq U^0$.

The role of entrepreneurship here is to find the proper (g, G) profile that results in (6.6) being positive. The entrepreneur who does this is a

guanxi entrepreneur. *Guanxi* thus allows entrepreneurs who may otherwise stay out due to inadequate contract enforcement and ex-post opportunism to become viable. The *guanxi* approach consists of judicious
limiting of the choice of agents to a subset of the population whose
personal reneging cost G is prohibitive enough and independent of the
TPE penalty QL. The set may be limited to close blood relations, a cohes-
ive religious minority or to the same close-knit ethnic group among
whom 'face' or other informal sanctions are important. But this approach
does not come free as it trades off average technical aptitude for
less opportunism. Since *guanxi* limits the number of players to those with
access to f, it therefore serves as an entry barrier and may underpin
market power.

The cost of *guanxi* becomes revealed however, as the economy mod-
ernizes and QL rises. Clearly where QL has become large enough to by
itself deter reneging, only 'technical aptitude' will matter. When competing with products of other producers operating under adequate TPE,
that is, where QL is sufficiently high, the opportunity cost of *guanxi*
becomes telling and burdensome. If they buy inputs only from their small
guanxi circle while a competitor buys inputs from a larger circle that
includes the *guanxi* circle, the competitor gets their inputs at a lower, but
at worst no higher, price (if the larger circle is the world, e.g., in an open
economy).

The *guanxi* entrepreneur, having solved the contract enforcement
problem and with market power become wealthy, must then address
another property rights protection problem. The *taipan* is the one who goes
beyond the *guanxi*.

TAIPAN: BEYOND *GUANXI*

A *guanxi* entrepreneur must also solve the risk of expropriation, a problem
very eminent in the environment of weak governance. This risk may orig-
inate from the holders of state powers themselves. Suppose the entrepreneur faces an expropriation tax t, legal or illegal, the level of which is a
decreasing function of the intensity of pressure, r, applied in *taipan* T's
behalf by the Leviathan or political power authority K. That is,
$t = t(r)$, $t' < 0$ and $t(0)$ is large. That is, if $r = 0$, the *taipan* is not viable.
To be viable T must buy r from K. Let K's utility function be
$U_k = u_K(m) - v_K(r) \geq U_k^0$, where $u_k(m)$ is K's utility defined over payoff
$m > 0$ from T, $v_k(r)$ is the disutility to K of pressure r in favor of T and
U_k^0 is K's reservation utility. Thus, the full contract design problem facing
T involves:

$$\max_{w,e,m,r} \quad pF(e)(1 - g(f)) - w - t(r) - m$$

$$\text{s.t.} \quad u(w) - v(e) \geq U^0 - QL - G(f)$$

$$u_k(m) - v_k(r) \geq U_k^0. \tag{6.8}$$

Again letting $e = e^0$ for simplicity, (6.8) generates two optimal contracts: $C(w^*, e^0)$ and $C(m^*, r^*)$. The first contract is opportunism proof vis-à-vis the agent A and the second is expropriation proof beyond $t(r^*)$ vis-à-vis the Leviathan K. The *taipan* is the entrepreneur who finds the profile (g, G) and the contract $C(m^*, r^*)$, which makes the market exchange viable. The second contract in effect privatizes the public enforcement under K.

The *taipan* vertically integrates into property rights protection by either (1) privatizing the state rule-making and enforcement apparatus under K or (2) by hiring private property rights enforcers. It is this aspect that the *taipan* shares with the nineteenth-century robber barons of America. Since the payoffs are normally illegal, they should never appear in the books of accounts. This results in secrecy and double book-keeping.

It is however possible for t to be simply a legitimate tax. K may be the tax collection and/or judicial apparatus, and m may be the payola to K. This is simple tax evasion. Indeed, for even higher r, $t(r) < 0$, which means that the *taipan* gets subsidized by favorable treatment. It is possible for all to coexist at any given time.

ANTI-COMPETITION OUTCOME

These defensive mechanisms, once established, can be turned into anti-competitive instruments. The capture of rule-makers can result in laws favoring the *taipan* and legitimizing entry barriers. Their largely private character means that other players cannot use them and therefore operate at a disadvantage. The structure of the Philippine specific tax on cigarettes, claimed to highly favor the products of Fortune Tobacco Corporation, is maintained by a phalanx of legislators beholden to owner-*taipan* Lucio Tan. This is clearly in accordance with Stigler's (1971) idea of state regulation. Currently there is a suit brought to the Supreme Court by Anglo-American, a smaller rival, claiming that the specific tax structure illegally favors Fortune Tobacco. New players are especially disadvantaged by the structure.

In a *guanxi*-dominated environment, contracts other than spot contracts are effectively limited to a subset of the population where informal sanctions have a significant effect. The business profile tends to have an ethnic and/or religious hue. The SM Group owned by *taipan* Henry Sy, which runs the largest chain of supermarkets in the Philippines is said to favor Iglesia ni Kristo sect members for whom unionism is a 'sin'. Labour unions complain loudly about this practice and businesses in turn accuse labour unions of pursuing an extraneous agenda. Inter-marriages within the group only strengthen the informal sanction mechanisms and reinforce *guanxi*. The tendency towards market power concentration and collusion is pronounced, especially when the two or three competitors are of the same ethnic and/or social group. Market power and wealth in turn become highly concentrated and attract expropriatory overtures from political powers. These must then be softened or captured.

REGULATORY DILEMMA

The common approach, known as the 'inhospitability' or 'antitrust' tradition, is to pass laws directly to counter the usual manifestations of collusion such as price manipulation. In a strong governance environment, this can be effective. In a weak governance milieu, this law can itself lack teeth and become yet another rent tollgate for political powers. Antitrust laws designed to break up concentrations of market power may only attack the symptoms. They do not attack the source of the problem. The 'inhospitability rule' may not, as Williamson (1983) observed, be welfare improving. The Sherman Act of 1890 in the United States was observed more in breach than in compliance in its first two decades of existence. Affected firms find it cheaper to subvert public enforcement than to comply. The result is regulatory capture rather than a level playing field.

The real entry barrier is the weak TPE of contracts and property rights. If QL is strengthened then entrants from outside the *taipan* and *guanxi* circle can raise competition and reduce concentration. The courts of law could be upgraded to protect property. Thus investing in the rule-of-law could be the best competition policy initiative. This is, of course, easier said than done. How did this happen in East Asia in the second half of the twentieth century?

MARKET ENHANCEMENT AS COMPETITION POLICY

The East Asian model's emphasis (see Fabella, 1999) on export and foreign investment promotion spearheaded by export processing zones (EPZs) in East Asia may have served the cause of competition and regulation policy reform very well as an unintended consequence. There are several reasons for this to have occurred. First, export promotion meant a shift in the incentive structure in favor of the export sector. Those who dared to test the waters (mostly *guanxi* types in the beginning) found themselves competing for export shares with rivals whose goods were, in contrast, not weighed down by *guanxi*-related costs. The *guanxi* circle was no longer a help in the distribution segment of these firms in the world market, while they may have carried *guanxi*-related costs at home. These players, in time, became effective advocates for stronger TPE. Other non-*guanxi* players may also have found foreign export niches that were not open to them in the *guanxi*-dominated local market. The local distribution and marketing segments are where ex-post opportunism has been rife. Export markets have been relatively immune. In this way, export promotion may have given a political constituency to better rule-of-law in export-oriented East Asia.

Second, the export promotion via foreign investment strategy took another very effective form – the export processing zones – which helped foreign and local non-*guanxi* players along. The EPZ was not only a set of export-friendly hard infrastructures. It was even more a commitment to better, faster and largely faceless procedures; a new set of rules and even a new set of enforcers with which foreign investors were familiar. This was a crucial part of the attraction of EPZs. Indeed the Subic Bay EPZ (Philippines) sells itself to investors less as an infrastructure-enabled hub than as a new set of institutions that are familiar to foreign locators.

Thus, the so-called East Asian model was not only a trade posture; it was a competition and regulation policy posture brought about not by direct confrontation with the *taipans* but by market-enabling policies. It created strong rule-of-law enclaves where non-*guanxi* and non-*taipan* players did not have to deal with unfair advantages that *taipans* could steer their way. The EPZ culture, because it spawned winners such as the IT sector in Taiwan, gradually infected the whole polity.

Third, gradual import liberalization forced *guanxi* players to compete with foreign rivals unburdened by *guanxi* costs. This made the tradable sector less congenial for *guanxi*-based business. Most retreated to the non-traded goods sector, namely, banking property and retail trade, where the external pressure was only tangentially felt.

Fourth, the relaxation of entry of foreign investment in these service areas again forced the *guanxi* business people to further modernize, either by joint ventures or by 'Harvardizing' the next generation, as did Li Kashing of Hong Kong. The rules of engagement in the service sectors had to be rewritten to entice foreign players. The case of the privatization of Manila Waterworks and Sewerage System (MWSS) is a pronounced case in point (see Fabella, 2005). The dispute resolution mechanism involved an Appeals Panel, which is international in composition. This took local politics and judicial pliancy out of the picture.

Thus, competition and regulation policy was eminently served by enabling the market through openness, which was central in the East Asian model. The 'inhospitability rule' could not have done better.

SUMMARY

In weak third-party enforcement environments, entrepreneurs have to confront additional idiosyncratic hurdles of ex-post opportunism by business partners and the absence of adequate property rights protection from predatory political elites. *Guanxi* serves to address the first by shrinking the set of potential partners to those for whom non-formal sanctions and even second- or first-party enforcement is binding. Thus, the business activity takes on an ethnic, religious or familial color, which is true of East Asia. To address predatory property expropriation, the entrepreneur enlists state officials and politicians in a web of payoffs and favors. Who succeeds in both, is characterized as the *taipan*. Bringing to vigorous life otherwise missing or highly fragmented markets is their Schumpterian role.

The *taipan* has been modeled as a nexus of contracts involving a vertical integration into second-party enforcement and property rights protection. Many of the accepted stylized facts about East Asian *taipans*: tax pyramids, legendary secrecy, an aversion for outside auditing, monopoly or shared monopoly positions, business sprawl, shadowy cultivation of politicians and the capture of rule-making apparatus, can all be traced to this vertical integration into second-party enforcement. The boundary of the firm is different in the periphery than in the center.

Since second-party enforcement is private and excludable, it tends to foster market power and entry barriers. Second-party capability is therefore a second-best substitute to good third-party enforcement: it can underpin the existence of markets but it can also truncate those markets once extant.

The usually prescribed regulatory remedies include confronting market power and cartels with new laws directly penalizing so-called unfair 'restraint of trade' practices. This is the 'inhospitability tradition' in regulation. Heavier taxes are also par for the course. In weak governance environments, this is either ineffective or counterproductive since enforcement is what is precisely lacking. They serve to deter only those without connections, thus raising entry barriers and enriching unscrupulous bureaucrats. Extant *taipans* respond by committing more resources to developing political leverage, resulting in even more uncertain political economy. This largely explains the resistance from the business sector to a proposed antitrust agency in the Philippines.

New laws surrounding contract enforcement such as bankruptcy laws are helpful only insofar as the enforcement apparatus (officials and judges) are rule-of-law-minded enough. If they are not, the cost of doing business rises with hardly an improvement in quality.

In East Asia, throughout the second half of the twentieth century, competition and regulation policy appeared to have taken a backseat to the so-called imperatives of the East Asian model. This is true only insofar as the competition policy was understood in the inhospitability tradition, which requires strong enforcement to be effective. But weak enforcement was still widespread in the early second half of the twentieth century. The market-enabling features of the East Asian model, through export promotion, export-processing zones, direct foreign investment liberalization and gradual import liberalization, served as the better regulation and competition policy package in weak governance environments. Where the model was a great success, these features did serve to weaken *guanxi* and transform *taipan*-ism into its more modern reincarnation. Market-enabling policies and openness served to indirectly advance the first best policy – the provision of adequate third-party enforcement. Direct confrontation would have been only harmful. This could explain why institutional quality seemed to have played such a crucial role in the development of East Asia at the time when the East Asian model held sway (see, e.g., Rodrik, 1996). This also suggests an institutional interpretation of the East Asian model.

REFERENCES

Barzel, Y. (1982), 'Measurement Cost and the Organization of Markets', *Journal of Law and Economics*, 25, 27–48.

Barzel, Y. (2002), *A Theory of the State: Economic Rights, Legal Rights and the Scope of the State*, Cambridge: Cambridge University Press.

Coase, R.H. (1937), 'The Nature of the Firm', *Economica*, 4, 386.

Criswell, C. (1981), *The Taipans: Hong Kong's Merchant Princes*, Hong Kong: Oxford University Press.

Fabella, R. (1999), 'The East Asian Model and the Currency Crisis: Credit Policy and Mundell–Fleming Flows', *The Manchester School*, 67 (5), 475–95.

Fabella, R. (2005), 'Shifting the Boundaries of the State: The Privatization and Regulation of the Metropolitan Waterworks and Sewerage System (MWSS)', a UPecon-CRC Regulation and Competition Policy Series.

Greif, A. (1993), 'Contract Enforceability and Economic Institutions in Early Trade: The Maghribi Traders', *American Economic Review*, 83, 525–48.

Greif, A. (2001), 'Institutions and Impersonal Exchange: From Communal to Individual Responsibility', unpublished monograph, Stanford University.

Greif, A., P. Milgrom and B. Weingast (1994), 'Coordination, Commitment and Enforcement: The Case of the Merchant Guild', *Journal of Political Economy*, 102, 745–76.

Grossman, S.J. and O.D. Hart (1986), 'The Costs and Benefits of Ownership: A Theory of Vertical and Lateral Integration', *Journal of Political Economy*, 94, 691–719.

Holmstrom, B. and J. Roberts (1998), 'The Boundaries of the Firm Revisited', *Journal of Economic Perspectives*, **12**, 73–94.

Klein, B., R.G. Crawford and A.A. Alchain (1978), 'Vertical integration, appropriable rents, and the competitive contracting process', *Journal of Law and Economics*, October.

Laffont, J.-J. and M. Meleu (2000), 'Enforcement of Contracts with Adverse Selection in LDCs', mimeo, IDEI, Toulouse.

Laffont, J.-T. and D. Mortimart (2002), *The Theory of Incentives: The Principal–Agent Model*, Princeton: Princeton University Press.

North, D. (1990), *Institutions, Institutional Change and Economic Performance*, Cambridge: Cambridge University Press.

Rodrik, D. (1996), 'Institutions and Economic Performance in East and Southeast Asia', Round Table Conference: The Institutional Foundation of Economic Development in East Asia, International Economic Association, Tokyo, December 1996.

Stigler, G. (1971), 'The theory of economic regulation', *Bell Journal of Economics and Management Science*, **2**, 3–21.

The Economist (2001), 7 April, 'Asian Business Survey'.

Williamson, O. (1975), *Markets and Hierarchies: Analysis and Antitrust Implications*, New York: The Free Press.

Williamson, O. (1983), 'Credible Commitments: Using Hostages to Support Exchange', *American Economic Review*, **74** (4), 519–54.

PART II

Experience with competition policy

7. Competition policy and the legal system in Brazil

Germano Mendes de Paula

INTRODUCTION

Brazil used to be a very closed economy regarding international trade. Like many other developing countries, Brazil adopted an import substitution industrialization (ISI) strategy. In this context, competition policy was misplaced, for several reasons. A substantial proportion of large companies were state-owned and therefore the government did not need to control pricing practices through the use of antitrust policy. Moreover, the most important state-owned enterprises (SOEs) were set up in order to mitigate the weaknesses of the domestic private sector rather than put limits on cartelization or mergers and acquisitions (M&As). The government fostered market domination by a few large SOEs.

However, Brazil, as many other Latin American nations, experienced a very important shift in terms of economic policy in the 1990s. Indeed, the country engaged in intense trade liberalization and also deregulated and privatized companies. In this new environment, a massive wave of mergers and acquisitions occurred in which multinationals were in the acquiring corner for around two-thirds of all transactions (Amann, de Paula and Ferraz, 2002). As a consequence, the share of the foreign companies in the top 100 non-financial firms in Brazil increased from 26 per cent to 40 per cent in the period 1990–98.

The 1990s was a turning point for the Brazilian economy, after which the government and the corporate sector have faced a very different economic environment. Instead of restricting competition, the government began to encourage it, mainly via trade liberalization and to a lesser extent, through antitrust policy. The latter has implied a new set of challenges for the Brazilian State. While deregulation required the elimination of rules and privatization demanded asset sales or leasing, the revitalization of competition policy necessitated a large effort in reorganizing, creating and consolidating institutions. In fact it is very hard to invigorate any role of the State, during a time when any form of governmental intervention is under tremendous attack. This task is particularly difficult when the bureaucratic team in charge of developing the new guidelines for competition policy is inherited from agencies that used to operate under the 'old regime'. Furthermore, in a country where the education and health systems are very problematic, it is hard to believe that the budget approved for agencies responsible for the competition policy would be increased substantially, since the results of competition policy are usually only delivered in the medium to long term.

The main goal of this chapter is to analyse Brazilian competition policy since the early 1990s, when the country fundamentally changed its economic policy. It can be argued that a change from a closed to a more open economy could bring to the fore the role of competition policy. However, using the steel industry as a case study, it will become clear that such a transition is far from simple. Brazil, like other Latin American nations, has a very complex and slow-moving legal system. According to Rabelo and Coutinho (2001), the Brazilian judicial system is excessively bureaucratic, slow and expensive. In a similar vein, as the legal system permits the decisions to be postponed, law enforcement is very weak. Pinheiro (1998) underlines the point that the Judiciary in Brazil is a luxury good, restricted to the most affluent sectors of the population.

In order to discuss the improvements and limitations of Brazilian competition policy since the early 1990s, the legal tradition is a key issue to be tackled. The steel industry appears to be an appropriate choice of sector to address this discussion, as it has experienced a strong wave of mergers and acquisitions (M&As) and three steel companies have received the largest fines for cartelization ever applied in Brazil.

This chapter is divided into five sections, including this brief introduction. The next provides a review of the main characteristics of Brazilian competition policy. The third section analyses the M&A issue in the Brazilian steel industry, while the fourth section discusses cartelization in the steel sector. The final section summarizes the main conclusions.

EVOLUTION OF COMPETITION POLICY IN BRAZIL

Regarding industrialization, Brazil can be considered a late late-comer country. In such a country the State, instead of limiting large companies' market power, has tended to encourage firms to achieve the optimum minimum scale. Therefore, at least in the Brazilian case, from the 1930s to the 1980s, industrial policy was oriented to help companies become bigger rather than stimulating competition among them. Moreover, the ISI strategy usually required robust protectionist measures as a means to defend infant industries.

In almost all Latin American countries, the corporate governance patterns differed markedly from the Anglo Saxon paradigm. While in the latter, companies tend to be specialized and based on a pulverized ownership structure, in Latin America the leading firms are in fact family-owned ones, most of them with a large degree of productive diversification (de Paula, 2003). In other words, Latin American enterprises have preferred to grow by entering new industries, due to the opportunities opened by the ISI, rather than enlarging their market presence in one business area. Indeed, various Latin American companies have adopted a conglomerated diversification strategy. In this sense it can be argued that different corporate governance patterns have influenced the attention paid by the government to competition policy. In the case of Brazil, it was only in the 1960s that the government began to take competition policy into account. Indeed, the antitrust watchdog Conselho Administrativo de Defesa Econômica (CADE) was constituted through Law 4.137, issued in September 1962. This law regulated the abuses of economic power, such as disloyal competition, abusive speculation, collusion, agreement among competitors, abusive price increases and so on (Considera and Corrêa, 2002). CADE began to operate in 1963. The following year President Goulart's leftist government was terminated by a military coup d'état.

Salgado (1995) stresses that the Brazilian antitrust legislation was based on US norms. Nevertheless, in the latter, antitrust policy was conceived as a way of preserving a conception of democracy based on the trilogy of individual freedom, privately owned property and equality of opportunities. In Brazil, on the contrary, antitrust legislation was issued just before the inauguration of a military regime that exercised authoritarian control during the 1964–84 period.

Since the installation of CADE in 1963, competition policy in Brazil can be divided into three phases. The first was observed in the 1963–90 period. During this stage competition policy played a minor role in Brazil, if any at all. Indeed, Considera and Corrêa (2002) observe that for a long time there was not much concern for competition and antitrust issues in Brazil. In reality the State became a monopolist in infrastructure services and in strategic industries, either by creating new SOEs or by nationalizing the existing ones in activities such as mining, oil refining, steel, energy and telecommunications.

The State exercised a tremendous control over the Brazilian economy during the 1960s and the following two decades. As mentioned, in many industries SOEs played a very prominent role. In the steel industry for instance, the government-owned firms were responsible for 70 per cent of the country's production. Additionally, as a consequence of increasing inflation, the Brazilian government adopted a price control system in the most important industries. Regarding the experience of the steel industry, this system was utilized in the period 1967–1990. In reality price control served as a cartel, because (1) for products already in the market, the policy was aimed at readjusting prices according to cost increases, guaranteeing the stability of the profit margin and thus, the crystallization of a certain relative price structure; (2) prices tended to be relatively rigid, with each firm maintaining its market share; and (3) the government tried to avoid predatory competition (Considera and Corrêa, 2002). It should also be remembered that medium and large projects, even without any public participation, required governmental approval. Due to the fact that Brazil was a closed economy regarding international trade and the State coordinated prices and investments, there simply was not room for competition policy.

Cook (2002) observes that competition policy is distinct from competition law, because the first is influenced by a wide range of policy measures including policies directed towards trade and industry, employment and investment. Privatization, deregulation, foreign investment policy, regional and international agreements are some of the factors that affect competition policy. Competition law is a subset of competition policy and aims to establish the rules and guidelines governing market power and dominance. In the first phase, although Brazil had a competition law, the reality was that competition policy was quite irrelevant.

The incoherence of Brazilian competition policy during this period, with the most important goals pursued by the government, naturally impacted – negatively – on CADE's performance. In the first phase CADE did not examine M&As, being limited just to the analysis of anti-competitive conduct. In particular the main purpose of competition policy was to defend small and medium-sized enterprises (SMEs) from large firms' disloyal competition such as predatory pricing. Nonetheless, CADE could not play this role appropriately. Figure 7.1 shows that, on average, CADE analysed just 1.4 cases per month. Furthermore, from 337 accusations, only 117 turned into administrative actions. This means that CADE denied around two-thirds of initial accusations. Considering 117 administrative actions, only 16 companies were fined. Not only were the fines quite small but they were all suspended by the Judiciary (Farina, 1990; Salgado, 1995).

As indicated, the main motivation for competition policy in the period 1963–90 was to preserve SMEs. Unfortunately CADE totally failed in this respect because not only were few fines applied (and not paid) but also the administrative actions took more than four-and-a-half years, on average, to be completed (Figure 7.2). Obviously, if a large company was really practising predatory pricing, it would be totally impossible for an SME to survive for so long. The slowness was partly related to CADE's own deficiencies at that time, including small budgets, reduced numbers of technical personnel

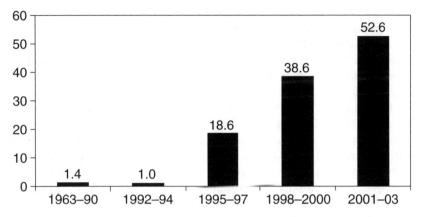

Source: CADE Annual Reports.

Figure 7.1 CADE's number of judgements per month, 1963–2003

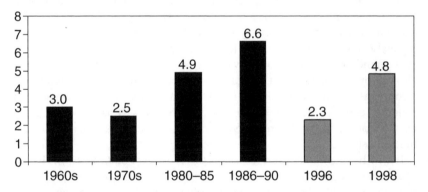

Note: In 1996 and 1998, the average time also includes the period utilized by other organs involved in the competition policy and excludes the analysis of M&As.

Sources: Farina (1990), CADE Annual Report.

Figure 7.2 CADE's average time to conclude an administrative action, 1963–98 (years)

and lack of prestige. However, the Brazilian legal system also made it possible for companies to postpone decisions, a fact that contributed strongly towards the slowness of the process. In sum during the three first decades of competition policy in Brazil, CADE judged few cases per month and the time required to conclude an administrative action was extensive.

The second period of competition policy in Brazil started in the 1990s, when the government pursued trade liberalization in order to put pressure on companies to become more competitive. In this new environment, competition policy began to have coherence with other economic policies. Law 8.078, which was issued in 1990, established the Customer Rights Code. Law 8.158, promulgated in 1991, was at the time usually termed as a New Competition Law. The main institutional change was the establishment of the Secretaria de Direito Econômico (SDE) as an organ of the Ministry of Justice.

This second period can be considered a transition stage for competition policy in Brazil. On one hand this policy began to gain momentum as, according to Nascimento (1996), in only three years, 128 administrative actions were analysed. On the other hand, a large proportion of accusations were made by government agencies instead of companies. Moreover, competition policy continued to be restricted to the analysis of anti-competitive practices. Only in 1994, when Law 8.884 was issued, did M&As come to be considered by the antitrust watchdog in Brazil.

The third and most important period of competition policy in Brazil began in 1994. Besides the amplification in its scope (including M&A and joint venture cases), CADE gained administrative and financial autonomy, although it continued to be linked to the Ministry of Justice. CADE's decisions are taken by a plenary session of seven members, all nominated by the President of Republic and approved by the Federal Senate for a two-year mandate. An additional two-year mandate for the counsellors is allowed by statute (in fact this is a frequent occurrence). The Secretaria de Acompanhamento Econômico (SEAE), an organ of the Ministry of Finance, came to be part of the so-called Sistema Brasileiro da Defesa da Concorrência (or Brazilian System of Competition Defence) in this third phase.

It will be useful to describe briefly the attributes of CADE, SDE and SEAE. Regarding M&As and joint ventures, Law 8.884 establishes that the transaction should be notified obligatorily to CADE for its deliberation in the 15-day period after its accomplishment, if: (1) as a consequence of the transaction, one company obtained more than 20 per cent of the relevant market (defined in terms of a combination of product and geographical dimensions); (2) one of the companies involved is part of a business group with revenues higher than US$130 million (at the current exchange rate). In the event that the 15-day notification period rule is not followed by the acquirer, an 'untimeliness' fine is charged.

The M&A and joint venture analyses begin at SEAE, which is entrusted with providing an official finding on the economic impact of the transaction. Usually SEAE organizes preliminary meetings to obtain additional information on the relevant market and the product. SEAE has a 30-day period to conclude its opinion. However, the 30-day period is suspended whenever SEAE asks the firms for more information. Then SDE has an additional 30-day period to produce its official finding, stressing the juridical aspects of the transaction. SEAE and SDE have analytical and investigative functions. Finally, the transaction is subject to a vote by CADE, which has a 60-day period in which to pass judgement. CADE's decisions can only be reviewed by the courts. The period can be interrupted if supplementary information is required. Usually the average time taken for approval (or disapproval) surpasses 120 days. In 1998 (the last year for which official information is available) it took an average of 360 days for an M&A or joint venture transaction to be judged. In the same year however, the anti-competitive conduct cases judged by CADE required an average of 4.8 years (Figure 7.2).

In terms of anti-competitive conduct, such as cartelization and disloyal competition, an investigation is traditionally opened as a consequence of a complaint made by a customer or a competitor. A complaint can also be elaborated by CADE itself or by any other public administration institution. The complaint is presented to SDE, which has a 60-day period to complete the necessary investigations and to determine if the information is sufficient to justify the beginning of an administrative action. In this manner SDE will proceed with the investigations and it will grant rights of defence to the defendant. This phase includes the hearing of witnesses and should be concluded within 45 days. Several levels of negotiations with the antitrust authority are allowed, including the instigation of an agreement requiring the ceasing of anti-competitive conduct (AMCHAM, 2003). The cartel fine, when applied, should be within the 1 per cent to 30 per cent range in relation to the companies' total revenues in the previous year.

Since the promulgation of Law 8.884 in 1994, there have been attempts to improve the efficiency of competition policy in Brazil. Two initiatives deserve special attention. First, in December 2000, Law 10.149 established the implementation of a leniency programme, designed to encourage parties involved in antitrust conspiracies to cooperate with the authorities, providing them with evidence of illegal activities. The legislation grants the Brazilian antitrust authorities the power to concede administrative amnesty associated with full, automatic criminal immunity for conspirators cooperating with antitrust investigations (Considera and Corrêa, 2002).

Second, new procedures were conceived in order to reduce slowness. One of them was called 'early termination' in M&A and joint venture transactions. If such criteria are observed, SDE and SEAE should each be able to reach a simplified finding in 15 days. This procedure was created in February 2003, and amplified in February 2004.

Transactions that involve the purchase of franchises, the setting up of joint ventures for entering new markets, internal ownership restructurings, entry to the Brazilian market or M&As involving the generation of a reduced market share ought to be beneficiaries of these procedures. Also under study is the possibility that in the most important M&A cases, SEAE and SDE should produce a unified report, in order to diminish the time consumed and to improve the quality of the analyses.

Concerning performance, CADE's monthly judgements have increased substantially, as can be observed in Figure 7.1. On average during the first phase of its existence, CADE judged only 1.4 cases per month. In the period 2001–03, this figure reached 52.6. A large proportion of this outstanding growth was derived from the fact that M&As and joint ventures needed to be approved by the antitrust authorities from 1994 onwards. Figure 7.3 shows that the number of M&As and joint ventures analysed by CADE rose from 21 in 1994 to 526 in 2003. It should be remembered that the companies have a 15-day period to notify their M&As and joint ventures, otherwise they would be fined for 'untimeliness'. Thus the burden of the proof lies in the companies' hands. In the case of cartelization however, it is more difficult to collect sufficient information to begin an administrative action and ultimately to punish enterprises.

The average time consumed by the judgement of M&As and joint ventures in Brazil was 1.4 years in 1996 and 360 days in 1998. Unfortunately these data represent the latest available information. Even considering that the time was smaller than that required for administrative actions (2.3 and 4.8 years, respectively), again slowness is a marked characteristic of competition policy in Brazil.

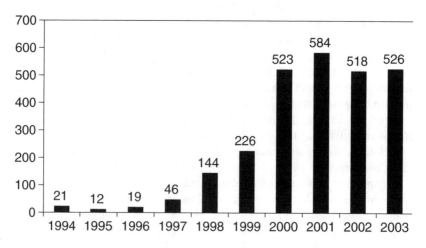

Source: CADE Annual Reports.

Figure 7.3   Number of mergers, acquisitions and joint ventures judged by CADE, 1994–2003

It is important to note that the growth of M&As and joint ventures judged by CADE reveals an increasing share of multinational corporation involvement in Brazil. In the context of 1834 transactions judged by CADE in the period 1996–2002, around 85 per cent of the acquiring companies were foreign (Table 7.1). In each year, the smallest share of non-domestic acquiring firms was 79 per cent. It is worth noting that M&As involving two or more enterprises in Third Countries, but with impacts in the Brazilian market, need to be approved by CADE. For whatever reason, experience demonstrates that if the acquiring company has not been operating on Brazilian soil, the transaction tends to be approved more easily, as the degree of domestic concentration will not be increased.

According to Silva (2004), among the 1844 transactions judged by CADE in the period 1996–2002, 94 per cent were wholly approved, 2 per cent were partially approved, 1 per cent were conditionally approved (with a performance commitment clause) and 3 per cent were classified as 'other cases'. Only two transactions were totally denied. In 2002, CADE judged 518 M&A cases, of which 474 (or 92 per cent) were approved without any restrictions. However, CADE imposed fines in 44 cases of this group, because the firms submitted their notifications after the legal time had expired (hence the levying of an 'untimeliness fine'). Nine transactions (or 2 per cent) were approved with some conditions. Oliveira (1999) declares that the non-approval rate regarding M&As and joint ventures in Brazil, which is lower than 5 per cent, is in line with practice in other countries. This diagnosis is shared by Clark (2000), who states that in a majority of OECD countries the intervention rate by the competition agency in M&As is 5 per cent or less.

CADE analysed 30 cases of possible anti-competitive actions during 2002. Of these the main accusations were related to collusion (ten cases), abuses of dominant positions (six cases), exclusivity covenants regarding professional associations (three cases), price fixing among competitors

Table 7.1   *Home country of acquiring companies in mergers, acquisitions and joint ventures judged by CADE, 1996–2002*

	1996	1997	1998	1999	2000	2001	2002	Total
Domestic	4	7	14	n.a	79	90	68	262
Foreign	15	39	130	n.a	443	492	447	1576
Domestic + Foreign	0	0	0	n.a	1	2	3	6
Total	19	46	144	n.a	523	584	518	1834

Sources: Silva (2004), CADE Annual Reports.

(three cases), refusal to deal (two cases), price discrimination (two cases) and others (four cases). From the total of 30 cases, 12 were found guilty, resulting in the imposition of fines and other sanctions. Sixteen were considered not guilty, and the cases were consequently closed. One case was terminated before its judgement and another was sent back to SEAE for further analysis (OECD, 2003).

The revision of CADE's decisions is only possible by appealing to the Judiciary. Nevertheless, in many cases, the companies do not utilize this possibility because of: (1) the slowness of the process; (2) the high costs incurred by the companies; and (3) the uncertainty about the future results derived from the absence of the judges' familiarity with the matter. Furthermore, firms enjoy a 30 per cent discount if the fines are paid without any appeal (Salgado, 2003). However, in recent years, the number and the value of the fines have increased considerably, as well as the amount of companies that appeal to the Judiciary to revise CADE's decisions. Rocha, Santos and Alves (2003) point out that there has been a proliferation of judicial appeals against CADE, in which about 90 per cent of them have started since 1998. More importantly the authors note that the Judiciary has been accomplishing widespread revision of CADE's decisions, regardless of merit. On average, companies have won 65.2 per cent of the preliminary cases (through seeking injunctions) and 59.1 per cent of sentences. Nonetheless, in the case of M&As no judicial decision has found against CADE's original judgement. It can be argued that enterprises have strong incentives to appeal against CADE. Not only is the legal system in Brazil very unhurried, but also the Judiciary frequently accepts injunctions and even changes sentences dished out by the antitrust watchdog.

The Brazilian Judiciary is an institution with serious problems. In spite of the great increase in public spending on it, the Judiciary has remained slow and distant to the great majority of the population. This is partly explained by the high growth in the demand for judicial services, which means that Brazilian magistrates continue to be forced to judge thousands of actions annually. Other structural problems can also be noted, such as: (1) the instability of the country's juridical framework; (2) the excessive formalism of Codes; (3) poor training of a substantial part of the magistracy; and (4) the excessive appeal to procedural arguments, to the detriment of substantive decisions on the subject's merit. Due to the fact that these problems have strong historical roots, the slowness and the heavily bureaucratic and formalist mode of operation have become a cultural characteristic, with an associated low probability of change (Pinheiro, 2003).

The legal system impacts on the performance of the economy in ways other than its effects on competition policy. According to Pinheiro (1998), there are four main channels through which judicial inefficiency affects the nation's economic performance. These include technological progress, companies' efficiency, investment and economic policy. In August 2004 the Brazilian government released, in all probability, the most important official report to date concerning the Judiciary (Ministério da Justiça, 2004). Making an international comparison, the report sheds unfavourable light on the Brazilian Judiciary, showing it to be associated with large expenses and low productivity. According to Figure 7.4 judicial expenditures as a proportion of total public spending in Brazil is the largest (3.66 per cent) among 35 countries, surpassing, for instance, Argentina (1.55 per cent), Italy (1.50 per cent), Mexico (1.01 per cent), Spain (0.66 per cent), South Africa (0.63 per cent) and Japan (0.38 per cent). In terms of judges per 10 000 inhabitants, Brazil's figure is 7.73, quite similar to the international average (7.34). Even so, its number is higher than countries such as Denmark (6.42), South Korea (2.57) and Japan (1.05). Regarding senior judge's salaries, in purchasing power parity terms, in a sample consisting of 30 countries, Brazil has the second highest, just behind Canada and in front of the United States, Spain, Japan and India. In fact, Brazilian salaries are 200 per cent higher than this sample average and 640 per cent higher than the Indian. Finally, the average cost of a lawsuit has reached US$600, while the minimal wage in Brazil is currently US$87. Consequently, poor people in Brazil are effectively barred access to the Judiciary.

Definitely, slowness is the key characteristic of the Brazilian legal system. According to Paduan (2004) it takes an average of 12 years to resolve a judicial case. It is estimated that 70 per cent of this time is consumed by bureaucracy, 20 per cent by lawyers and only 10 per cent by the judges' consideration itself. This result is naturally related to the legal system tradition

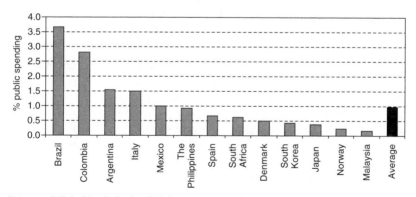

Source: Ministério da Justiça (2004).

Figure 7.4   Expenditures on the Judiciary as a proportion of total public expenditure, selected countries, 2000

in Brazil. According to La Porta et al. (1998), in general, commercial laws come from two broad traditions: common law and civil law. Most English-speaking countries belong to the common law tradition, based on the British Company Act. The rest of the world belongs to the civil law tradition, a derivative of Roman law, which has three main families: French, based on the Napoleonic Code of 1804; German, based on Bismarck's Code of 1896; and Scandinavian, which legal scholars describe as less derivative of Roman law but 'distinct' from the other two civil families. The French legal family includes France, Spain, Portugal and their former colonies, including Brazil and other Latin American countries. Even though La Porta et al. (1998) are concerned about commercial law and its impact on corporate governance, it can be argued that this distinction is useful in highlighting peculiarities among countries regarding the legal system. In other words, the legal system tradition has a large impact on how conflicts between companies and governments and among companies themselves are resolved.

It can be stated that the low efficiency of the Brazilian legal system places strong limitations on the further development of competition policy in the country. It seems very difficult to change this reality, because it has been reinforced by a long tradition. Bearing this aspect in mind the analysis of competition policy in a less developed country ought to highlight institutional path dependence issues, such as the legal system tradition, corruption levels and dictatorship and democracy periods. In the following sections, the analysis will shift to a sectoral level, by analysing the experience of competition policy in the Brazilian steel industry.

COMPETITION POLICY AND ACQUISITIONS IN THE BRAZILIAN STEEL INDUSTRY

The steel production chain constitutes a very important industry in Brazil, in particular as it relates to exports. In 2003 the exports of the Brazilian steel industry totalled US$3.9 billion. In the same year, iron ore exports reached an additional US$3.3 billion and pig iron exports amounted to US$572 million. Jointly the Brazilian iron and steel production chain generates more than US$8 billion in exports, equivalent to 11.4 per cent of the country's total export revenues.

The Brazilian steel industry originated in the early twentieth century, registering continuous growth since the 1930s. In that decade, Belgo-Mineira, a subsidiary of the Luxembourg-based company Arbed, constructed a new mill in João Monlevade, in the State of Minas Gerais. Simultaneously Barra Mansa, a subsidiary of the Brazilian diversified group Votorantim, erected another mill in the city of Barra Mansa, in the State of Rio de Janeiro. These and other steel companies, until the early 1940s, were restricted to the production of long steel products, such as rebars, demanded in the construction industry and railways.

In the 1940s Brazil engaged in flat steel production – whose main customer came to be the automobile industry through an SOE, Companhia Siderúrgica Nacional (CSN). In the following decades the State constructed large steel mills, owing to the lack of financial capability among domestic private sector companies. The State also took over private sector firms on the edge of bankruptcy. Nationalization was the key characteristic of the Brazilian steel industry until the 1980s. As mentioned, SOEs used to represent 70 per cent of the country's crude steel production. However, in the late 1980s the government decided to resell the SOE steel companies that used to be privately owned. Most of these steel firms were medium-sized, although as is noted later, their privatization implied a larger degree of concentration. Furthermore, in the early 1990s, the so-called 'big six' (Usiminas, Companhia Siderúrgica de Tubarão/CST, Acesita, CSN, Cosipa and Açominas) were privatized too.

According to data provided by the OECD (2002), in the period 1994–2000, the steel and metalworking sector accounted for 14 per cent of all M&As and joint ventures judged by CADE. It ranked in fourth place, just behind autoparts (16.7 per cent), food (14.6 per cent) and information technology (14.4 per cent). Indeed, the Brazilian steel industry has been marked by numerous corporate control changes, since the late 1980s. Besides privatization, between 1993 and 2004, there were 28 ownership changes and three asset leasings in this industry. Table 7.2 summarizes the diversity of ownership by separating transactions into eight categories.

Around two-thirds of the corporate control changes in the Brazilian steel industry during the post-privatization period have not led to an increase in the degree of concentration. For instance, on five occasions financial institutions sold their stakes without any impact on market structure. In the other seven transactions, the composition of the main shareholders changed without any effect on market structure. The same happened when five newcomers (four international and one domestic enterprises) purchased shares in Brazilian steel enterprises.

It should also be stressed that the real impact on the market structure for steel has tended to be differentiated among segments. For example, in the special flat steel business, Acesita is the only producer in Brazil. Although its corporate control changed substantially in 1998, when a French steel company became the largest shareholder, there was no impact on market structure. The opposite was observed in the common long steel business, because the two largest companies, Gerdau and Belgo-Mineira, have

Table 7.2　Ownership changes in the Brazilian post-privatized steel industry, by category, 1993–2004

Type of Ownership Change	Number of Transactions	Number of Transactions that Increased the Degree of Concentration
Changes in the internal composition of main shareholders	10	3
Financial institution sale of equity stakes	5	–
New international entrants	4	–
Acquisition of always private-owned sector companies	4	3
Leasing of assets	3	2
Acquisition of majority stake of a former SOE	2	2
New domestic company entrants	1	–
Other cases	2	–
Total	31	10

Source:　Own compilation.

increased substantially their market control. Table 7.3 shows the acquisitions carried out by these two enterprises in the Brazilian steel industry. Considering both companies together, in nine instances the acquisitions implied an enlargement in the degree of concentration. The other cases corresponded to a plant closure (which also augmented the market power of the leading companies), an entry into a new market, an internal change in the composition of the main shareholders and a vertical integration. No other segment in the Brazilian steel industry has experienced such market structure transformation. Significantly, it was exactly in this business that a relatively small transaction (US$62 million) caused the most serious case to date regarding competition policy.

Another way to express the massive concentration process that the Brazilian common steel market has undergone is shown in Figure 7.5. According to data supplied by Instituto Brasileiro de Siderurgia (IBS), the joint share of the four largest companies increased from 51 per cent in 1972 to 100 per cent in 2001, while the same index for the eight largest steelmakers jumped from 77 per cent in 1972 to 100 per cent in 1996 (left axis). The degree of concentration as measured by Herfindahl–Hirschmann Index (HHI) also rose from around 1200 points in 1972 to some 2000 points in 1989, 3000 points in 1994, 4000 points in 1995 and 4500 points in 2003

Table 7.3 *Gerdau and Belgo-Mineira's acquisitions in the Brazilian steel industry, 1988–2003*

Acquiring Company	Acquired Company	Date	Type of Transaction	Impact on Market
Gerdau	Cimetal	1988	Privatization	Higher concentration
Gerdau	Usiba	1989	Privatization	Higher concentration
Gerdau	Cosinor	1991	Privatization	Plant closure
Gerdau	Piratini	1992	Privatization	Entrance in a new market: long special steel
Belgo-Mineira	Cofavi	1993	Acquisition of the rolling mill	Higher concentration
Gerdau	Pains	1994	Acquisition of majority stake	Higher concentration
Belgo-Mineira	Dedini	1994	Acquisition of minority stake	Higher concentration
Gerdau	Fi-El	1994	Acquisition of all shares	Higher concentration
Belgo-Mineira	Mendes Jr.	1995–2003	Leasing followed by acquisition	Higher concentration
Belgo-Mineira	Cofavi	1997	Acquisition of the steelshop	Higher concentration
Belgo-Mineira	Dedini	1997	Acquisition of additional 51% stakeholding	Changes in the internal composition of main shareholders
Gerdau	Açominas	1997–2003	Acquisition (six transactions)	Backward vertical integration
Belgo-Mineira	Itaunense	2000	Leasing	Higher concentration

Source: Own compilation.

(right axis). Indeed, the number of steel companies that operate in this particular market has dropped significantly from around 30 in the mid-1970s to just three at the time of writing this chapter.

It is precisely in the common long steel business that the most important event relating to antitrust policy and the legal system has been observed. The rest of this section is dedicated to analysing this experience: the acquisition of Pains by Gerdau. In the other cases of M&A, similar events could have occurred, but their intensity and repercussions were definitely not so strong.

In February 1994 Gerdau bought, through its Uruguayan subsidiary Laisa, all the shares of the German company Korf, whose main asset was a 64.7 per cent stakeholding in Siderúrgica Pains (Table 7.4). The transaction

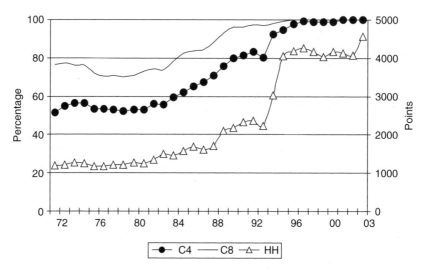

Source: Own compilation, using data supplied by IBS.

Figure 7.5　Degree of concentration in the Brazilian common long steel sector, 1972–2003 (percentage and points)

Table 7.4　Timetable of Pains' acquisition by Gerdau

Date	Event
Feb 1994	Gerdau bought an indirect 64.7% stakeholding in Pains
Mar 1994	Gerdau asked CADE's authorization to buy Pains
Nov 1994	Gerdau increased its participation to a 99.1% stakeholding in Pains
Mar 1995	CADE ruled against the acquisition for the first time
May 1995	Gerdau asked CADE to reconsider its first decision
Oct 1995	CADE judged against the transaction again
Nov 1995	The Minister of Justice accepted officially the company's appeal
Dec 1995	Judicial contest confronting CADE with the Minister of Justice
Nov 1996	CADE offered three options to Gerdau in order to finish the case
May 1997	CADE approved the transaction
Oct 2001	The action was formally concluded

Source: Own compilation.

value reached US$62 million, of which around US$50 million was related to the participation in Pains. This acquisition also included a 100 per cent stakeholding in the engineering company KTS and a 60 per cent participation in the pig iron producer Companhia Brasileira de Ferro (CBF). Later in November of 1994, Gerdau raised its participation to 99.1 per cent of voting shares of Pains, by investing an additional US$5.8 million. Although the first transaction corresponded to a purchase of a foreign company by another firm based abroad, it was analysed by CADE, due to its impact on the Brazilian steel industry. Indeed, this transaction was extremely controversial and took more than three years to be approved.

According to Brazilian competition legislation, a transaction that amplifies market concentration may be approved if it generates an improvement in economic efficiency (defined in the Law in terms of technological development, capacity expansion, export increase, additional job creation, production cost reduction or price reduction) that more than compensates for its negative effects. In the first instance Gerdau proposed to invest an additional US$50 million in Pains, of which US$36 million was in the metallurgical operation itself, US$4 million in environmental projects and US$10 million in forest plantations. However, CADE's counsellors understood that this was insufficient to compensate for the fact that Gerdau would increase its share from 39.6 per cent to 46.2 per cent in the Brazilian common long steel market. Moreover, this market was characterized by high barriers to entry – derived from the then high degree of concentration and the large nominal installed capacity – and insignificant import levels (CADE *Annual Report*, 1996). Therefore, in March 1995, CADE ruled against the acquisition, obliging Gerdau to resell the company in a 60-day period.

In May 1995 Gerdau asked CADE to reconsider this first decision, something not foreseen in CADE's procedural norms. Based on the principle that every administrative decision can be reconsidered by the same organ, CADE agreed to reanalyse the acquisition. This time Gerdau proposed that 50 per cent of Pains' production would be converted into special long steel products. CADE judged once more against the transaction in October 1995, when four of the seven counsellors voted to block the purchase.

As a result, Gerdau presented an administrative appeal to the Minister of Justice. In November 1995 the Minister accepted the company's appeal, suspended CADE's second decision and requested a second official finding from SDE. In December 1995 CADE's counsellors decided to ask the Judiciary to guarantee that its decision would be implemented. In other words what resulted was a judicial contest involving CADE (an autonomous organ linked to the Ministry of Justice) and the Ministry of Justice proper. In April 1996 new members of CADE, including the President, took their places. The new composition of CADE allowed for a new kind of solution.

In November 1996, CADE made a proposal to Gerdau, consisting of three options, in order to finish the case. The first option consisted of ten measures to reduce the transaction's negative impacts upon market competition. The more important were: (1) a programme of retraining and re-employment of workers that were sacked after the acquisition of Pains; (2) the sale of Transpains, a transport company; (3) the prohibition that Commercial Gerdau, the company's trading arm, sell any more than 20 per cent of Pains production; and (4) open access to the technologies developed by KTS, which had already been sold to the Germany company Mannesmann Huttentechnik. More importantly, the idle rolling mill located in Contagem (Minas Gerais State) to be modernized in order to be resold. The second option comprised the leasing of the Divinopólis (Minas Gerais State) and Contagem mills for a 20-year period. The third option involved the reselling of Pains' assets as a whole (CADE *Annual Report*, 1996). Gerdau opted for the first proposal and CADE approved the transaction in May 1997, effectively mandating a 39-month period between acquisition and approval. Finally, the action was formally ceased in October 2001.

CEBRAB (1997) concludes that the main measure in the option chosen by Gerdau consisted of the modernization and reselling of Contagem rolling mill. Nevertheless, this was equivalent to only 20 per cent of the Divinópolis mill's installed capacity and around 1 per cent of the Brazilian common long steel market. Therefore, the remedy proposed in this third decision was much weaker in relation to the first two. According to the CADE *Annual Report* (1996), during the period between the first and the third decisions, some new facts emerged, in particular, the impressive growth of Belgo-Mineira, which bought a 49 per cent stakeholding in Dedini and leased Mendes Jr. Regarding the stake purchase of Dedini, CADE approved the transaction in February 1996. Considering that this acquisition had occurred in August 1994, it took 18 months for CADE to reach a decision. The transaction was approved unanimously by CADE's counsellors, allowing the company to expand its participation from 18.8 per cent to 37.2 per cent in the common long steel market. This enabled Belgo-Mineira to confront the 41.1 per cent market share held by Gerdau. However, the approval was conditional on the fulfilment of a performance commitment clause, containing production goals, sales and prices (CEBRAB, 1997). This term was signed in October of 1996, with a four-year duration, stipulating half-yearly situation reports.

CARTELIZATION CASES IN THE BRAZILIAN STEEL INDUSTRY

The most important case regarding cartelization in Brazil has occurred in the steel industry. It is related to a supposed price agreement reached in 1996. The involved companies were sentenced in 1999, but until now the firms have yet to pay the fines (Table 7.5). This provides an illustration of

Table 7.5   Timetable of the Brazilian common flat steel cartel case

Date	Event
Jul 1996	Meeting between SEAE, IBS, CSN, Usiminas and Cosipa regarding price increases
Aug 1996	Price increases carried out by CSN, Cosipa and Usiminas
Jun 1997	SEAE official finding: cartelization in the common flat steel business
Jun 1997	Meeting between CADE, SEAE, SDE and IBS regarding price increases
Oct 1999	CADE fined steel companies for cartelization and distorted information
Feb 2000– July 2004	CADE refused administrative appeal and subsequently a judicial fight breaks out

Source: Own compilation.

the slowness of the antitrust system and how enterprises have possibilities to forestall penalties handed down by the legal system.

This first cartel case in the Brazilian steel industry involved three flat common steel producers: CSN, Usiminas and Cosipa. All of them were established as SOEs and were privatized in the 1991–93 period. Moreover, as a consequence of the privatization, Usiminas became the largest shareholder of Cosipa. Until 2002 these three companies were responsible for all flat common steel products fabricated in Brazil. In addition to the small import penetration (around 4 per cent), this market was highly concentrated, being under the control of three companies – or even just two, if the dominance of Cosipa by Usiminas is taken into consideration.

The high degree of concentration cannot be understood as a negative development per se, in an industry characterized by high economies of scale. Furthermore, even if Usiminas had not bought a stake in Cosipa, the market would have been highly concentrated. This situation should not be disassociated from the fact that these three companies were set up as SOEs previously because domestic privately owned firms were unable to achieve the optimum minimum scale. In other words, if the economies of scale were irrelevant, there would not have been any justification for the State to have established these enterprises in the first place. In addition, companies dedicated to the flat common steel business became involved in megamergers in Western Europe and Japan from the late 1990s. A high degree of concentration in this business is a rule, not an exception (de Paula, 2002).

Not only was a highly concentrated business inherited from the closed economy period, but also some practices related to price control. Until 1990 the Brazilian steel companies were obliged to ask for government authorization to increase prices. The price control system was only abolished when the government decided to privatize the enterprises. However, in July 1996, the IBS, the trade association that represents the steel companies, requested a meeting with SEAE. Officials from SEAE, IBS, Usiminas, Cosipa and CSN took part in the meeting. During that occasion the companies notified the government that they would increase their prices in early August. Indeed, they applied quite similar readjustments in a very few days (Table 7.6).

It is worth remembering that Brazil used to live with very high inflation rates. In the early 1990s, for example, the official inflation index reached 84 per cent in just one month. Not surprisingly, governments tried many stabilization plans, some orthodox, others heterodox. In July 1994 the government launched the 'Plano Real', which was very successful in terms of restricting inflation, at least considering the historical experience. Viewed from a developed economy perspective, a price increase of some 4 per cent of steel products in one month might seem excessive. Nevertheless, this was not the perception in Brazil. For instance, in 1996, the wholesale price index rose 9.1 per cent, whereas the steel wholesale price index increased 4.3 per cent. Therefore, the Brazilian common flat steel companies were not accused of abusive pricing but rather of price collusion.

Almost one year later in June 1997, SEAE finished its official findings and concluded that the three companies had cartelized the common flat steel business. In the same month IBS requested another meeting with

Table 7.6   Price increases announced by Brazilian common flat steel companies, August 1996

	CSN – 1 Aug %	Cosipa – 5 Aug %	Usiminas – 8 Aug %
Hot rolled sheets	3.63	3.59	4.09
Cold rolled sheets	4.34	4.31	4.48
Heavy plates		8.32	
Electro-galvanized sheets			3.38
Hot dip galvanized sheets	4.23		

Source: Santacruz (1999).

CADE, SEAE and SDE, in order to communicate that the steel companies had decided to raise prices again. This time the steel companies learned from their previous mistake and did not take part in the meeting.

In October 1999 CADE decided to punish CSN, Usiminas and Cosipa for cartel formation and the release of distorted information. The counsellors' decision was unanimous. According to Santacruz (1999), who was the designated counsellor, the evidence against the enterprises comprised: (1) the high cost of importing the flat common steel products that gave them additional market power, in a high barrier to entry industry; (2) over the period 1993–98, the companies' maintenance of a stable market share; (3) the denial of the price leadership hypothesis because in 1997, the company that was the first to elevate prices was different from that of the previous year; and (4) the meeting requested by IBS in July 1996 constituted an indirect proof of cartelization because obviously the executives had met before this meeting.

This was the first time that CADE applied a large cartelization fine in Brazil. According to the legislation the fines were supposed to vary from 1 per cent to 30 per cent of the total sales in the previous year. The joint cartelization fines totalled US$25.9 million. Moreover, Usiminas and Cosipa were also condemned to pay an additional fine (US$3.5 million) because they had initially denied that their directors took part in a meeting, which in fact was the starting point of this case.

In its defence Usiminas declared that the above-mentioned meeting was intended to notify the government about the price increase. More importantly it noted 'that such a practice was a habit in the country' (Santacruz, 1999, p. 19). If the participation in the meeting could be attributed to a mistake linked to a path dependence convention, then the firms learned quite fast. In June 1997 when a new meeting was requested by IBS to communicate that a new price readjustment would be made, the companies did not take part. The three steel companies were also accused of collectively increasing prices in September 1999. They justified at that point that they were merely following the inflation rate. In February 1999 another readjustment was implemented, between 9 per cent and 11 per cent, under the justification that it was a correction derived from the strong currency devaluation realized in the previous month. There was no condemnation resulting from these cases, because there was no proof that the steel enterprises had agreed previously to the price rises.

The reality is that almost five years after the application of fines, the steel companies have still to pay them. This situation is obviously associated with a legal system that allowed – or to be honest, stimulated – postponements. After the condemnation the steel companies interposed administrative appeals to CADE, which were refused in February 2000. Following this, the firms appealed to the Judiciary. In Brazil, generally, enterprises are granted preliminary decisions (injunctions) from the judges. In February 2002 for instance, a Federal Judge determined the suspension of the fine applied to Usiminas for issuing distorted information. In July 2003 another Federal Judge decided to maintain the cartelization fines, although he understood that it had not been proved that the companies had arranged a price agreement. This opened another possibility for new appeals.

A second cartel case in the Brazilian steel industry affected the common long steel market (in particular, rebars), which is highly concentrated in the hands of Gerdau, Belgo-Mineira and Barra Mansa. In September 2000 two trade associations, SindusCon/SP and SECOVI/SP, accused these companies of market division via price discrimination in São Paulo, the most important state in Brazil. SindusCon/SP represents the civil construction companies, while SECOVI/SP represents the real estate sellers. Two weeks later SDE opened an administrative action against the three mentioned companies (Table 7.7).

Only in August 2002 did SEAE present its official findings, which concluded that three companies had organized a cartel. During the investigation process, besides the price discrimination (whose objective was to guarantee market division), it was observed that the companies had established retail prices through the imposition of 'table prices' to the distributors. Moreover, effective sanctions were applied to the non-followers' agents. Without doubt it is never an easy task to prove the existence of a

Table 7.7   Timetable of the Brazilian common long steel cartel case

Date	Event
Sept 2000	SindusCon/SP and SECOVI/SP accused steel companies of market division
Sept 2000	SDE opened an administrative action against Gerdau, Belgo-Mineira and Barra Mansa.
Aug 2002	SEAE suggested the condemnation of the three companies for cartelization
Feb 2003	SDE preliminary finding also suggested the condemnation of the three companies for cartelization; a final finding was issued in September 2003
Feb 2003– July 2004	A judicial battle began, which has impeded CADE from judging the case

Source: Own compilation.

cartel. In this particular case a former manager of Belgo-Mineira alleged that the steel companies' managers frequently met, aiming to carve up the market and to reach agreements about retail prices.

In February 2003 SDE released a preliminary finding also suggesting that CADE condemn Gerdau, Belgo-Mineira and Barra Mansa for cartelizing the common long steel market. Since then the companies have been asking for provisional decisions by the Judiciary, to avoid – or postpone – CADE's decision. In the same month Belgo-Mineira won a preliminary judicial decision in order to suspend this administrative action. This decision was reversed in March 2003.

Afterwards, Gerdau, Belgo-Mineira and Barra Mansa were accused of a price increase implemented on the same date (5 March, 2003) and to the same value (12.9 per cent). As a consequence SDE required that these companies inform it of every price readjustment, in terms of dates and values. It also prohibited the release into the public domain of any kind of information about price increases that could facilitate the functioning of a cartel. Belgo-Mineira tried again to stop the suit in July 2003 but a Federal Judge considered its appeal unfounded. SDE eventually released its final finding with the same conclusions in September 2003. The latest available information is that Gerdau won a preliminary decision in May 2004, blocking CADE's judgement.

FINAL REMARKS

Cook (2002) observes that at the end of the 1980s only a handful of developing countries had effective competition legislation. From the 1990s on, this situation has changed, in particular among the higher-income developing nations that have recently strengthened their approach to competition policy. Nevertheless, the author stresses that due to various reasons – for example, misunderstanding among policy-makers regarding the nature of competition itself, the lack of capacity to implement competition policy, the failure of 'imported models' to work in the local environment, or the need to maintain the status quo – many countries continue with a weak system and process for monitoring competition.

For a number of reasons the Brazilian experience regarding competition policy has shown quite important improvements since the beginning of the 1990s. Although the country has counted on competition legislation since the early 1960s, competition policy per se was quite irrelevant, because the contemporary orientation of political economy was marked by trade autarchy and weighty State intervention. In fact, the government used to control prices and investments, even for non-SOEs. In the 1990s, economic reform was based on deregulation, privatization and trade liberalization. Therefore, competition policy came to fit in with other governmental policies, rather than to be incompatible with them.

In the 1990s, new competition legislation was issued on two occasions. In 1994 the antitrust watchdog CADE began to analyse M&As, amplifying its scope, which used to be restricted to the anti-competitive practices. Other procedural improvements were made, such as the introduction of the leniency programme and the arrival of the 'early termination' option. Over time, competition policy has gained more public attention and companies have become more preoccupied with it. The number of cases judged monthly by CADE has also expanded. Moreover, a very positive feature of the Brazilian experience has been that competition policy has gained in importance since the early 1990s and no significant retreat has been observed. In a decade Brazil has relaunched and consolidated a quite sophisticated apparatus concerning competition policy for a developing nation. According to Clark (2000), the level of expertise and analytical skills of professionals employed in three agencies exceed those in many other countries, including some that have been actively enforcing competition laws for a much longer time than Brazil.

However, even though some attempts have been made to circumvent the bureaucracy since 1996 (something that has accelerated from 2003 on) as the experience examined has demonstrated, the competition policy system in Brazil has remained very slow. Not only has the time involved in the formulation and release of CADE's judgement continued to be high but also there have been considerable delays in implementing the decisions themselves. In this regard the steel industry case should be considered emblematic and certainly not an exception. The goal of this chapter has been not to scrutinize the steel case per se, but rather to provide an illustration of how the legal system can place strong limitations on the quite substantial effort that government has pursued in order to develop an effective competition policy. Moreover, the companies tend to have a fast learning capability, especially in a country that traditionally has proved very unstable. Adaptation is the key to survival in such a challenging environment. One might say that firms have learnt two main golden rules, the first being, never ask to meet government officials! Examining the case of cartels in the common flat steel business, the proof first used following the accusation could not be used again because only the trade association took part in the meeting. The second golden rule for large companies seems to be that an appeal to the Judiciary pays off! This is because even if cases are eventually lost, valuable time is gained. Although Brazilian companies have traditionally criticized the bureaucracy, they are very well aware of how to be beneficiaries of it.

At least three important features contribute to the slowness of competition policy procedures in Brazil. First, it is a hard task to change bureaucrats' minds, especially when the same group that used to control prices has now taken charge of promoting competition policy. Time and patience is demanded to create new institutions, especially in a context of lack of financial resources. Moreover, Clark (2000) also observes that there is a shortage of personnel at CADE, but possibly even more seriously, there is a lack of a permanent, stable group of career officials whose presence preserves 'institutional memory' and enhances enforcement expertise over time.

Second, there is an overlapping of competences among SEAE, SDE and CADE. Salgado (2003) affirms that this overlapping has been frequently criticized, both by the companies and by bureaucrats themselves, due to the inefficiency related to the duplication of work and the costs imposed to the private sector. The author terms this situation 'bizarre' and advocates that all the functions distributed among the three organs should be unified in CADE. Clark (2000) agrees that there is duplication of effort in the Brazilian competition policy system. However, he suggests that the relationships between SEAE and SDE on the one hand, and CADE on the other, are on the whole formal, which is undoubtedly a necessary aspect of CADE's status as an independent agency. The result nevertheless, is a loss in efficiency; in general, CADE is unable to take full advantage of the experience and expertise of its sister agencies. Although each specialist tends to reinforce its proposition, it might be said that there is a consensus that further steps towards simplification should be taken. It must be stressed that some of the problems mentioned previously should be eliminated – or, most probably, attenuated – through the reform of the competition policy legal framework currently under examination in the National Congress.

Third, competition policy cannot be disassociated from the country's legal system. On the one hand competition legislation is a part of competition policy. On the other the Judiciary can restrict the scope and efficiency of the organs in charge of competition policy. In the case examined in this chapter, companies have appealed to the Judiciary to avoid the implementation of CADE's decisions and even to impede CADE's judgement. It can be argued that one of the most important obstacles for the further development of competition policy in Brazil is the legal system. In Brazil, far more often than not, it is rational to appeal to the Judiciary, which in its turn is extremely slow. It is a national consensus that judicial reform is urgently needed but the National Congress has been discussing this issue for 12 years. In such an environment how could anybody expect competition policy to be a paragon of swiftness and agility?

REFERENCES

AMCHAM (2003), *Relatório sobre o Sistema Brasileiro de Defesa da Concorrência*, São Paulo, Câmara Americana de Comércio – AMCHAM.

Amman, E., G.M. de Paula and J.C. Ferraz (2002), 'UK Corporate Acquisitions in Latin America in the 1990s: Lost Opportunities in a New Economic Environment?', *Annals of Public and Cooperative Economics*, **73** (4), 577–602.

CADE (Conselho Administrativo de Defesa Economica) (1996), *Annual Report*.

CEPRAB (1997), *Centralização de Capitais na Siderurgia Brasileira e Política Antitruste*, São Paulo: CEPRAB.

Clark, J. (2000), *Competition Policy and Regulatory Reform in Brazil: A Progress Report*, Paris: OECD.

Considera, C.M. and P. Corrêa (2002), 'The Political Economy of Antitrust in Brazil: From Price Control to Competition Policy', Rio de Janeiro, SEAE (Documento de Trabalho, 11).

Cook, P. (2002), 'Competition and its Regulation: Key Issues', *Annals of Public and Cooperative Economics*, **73** (4), 541–88.

de Paula, G.M. (2002), 'Cadeia Produtiva da Siderurgia', *Estudo de Competitividade por Cadeias Integradas: Um Esforço de Criação de Estratégias Compartilhadas*, Brasília, Ministério de Desenvolvimento, Indústria e Comércio.

de Paula, G.M. (2003), *Governança Corporativa no Brasil e México: Estrutura Patrimonial, Práticas e Políticas Públicas,* Santiago do Chile: CEPAL.

Farina, E.M.M.Q. (1990), 'Política Antitruste: a experiência brasileira', *Anais do 18° Encontro Nacional de Economia*, 1, 455–4374.

La Porta, R. et al. (1998), 'Law and Finance', *Journal of Political Economy*, **106** (6), 1113–55.

Ministério da Justiça (2004), *Diagnóstico do Poder Judiciário*, Brasília: Ministério da Justiça.

Nascimento, C.A. (1996), 'A Política de Concorrência no Brasil e o Novo Paradigma Regulatório', *Revista BNDES*, 5, 155–69.

OECD (2002), *Brazil 2001–2002 Competition Analysis Annual Report*, Paris: Organisation for Economic Co-operation and Development.

OECD (2003), *Brazil 2002–2003 Competition Analysis Annual Report*, Paris: Organisation for Economic Co-operation and Development.

Oliveira, G. (1999), 'Defesa da Livre Concorrência no Brasil: Tendências Recentes e Desafios à Frente', *Revista de Administração de Empresas*, **39** (3), 17–25.

Paduan, R. (2004), 'Solução Rápida', *Exame*, **38** (12), 98–100.

Pinheiro, A.C. (1998), 'A Reforma do Judiciário: Uma Análise Econômica', *Seminário Internacional Sociedade e a Reforma do Estado*, São Paulo: Ministério do Planejamento, Orçamento e Gestão.

Pinheiro, A.C. (2003), *Judiciário, Reforma e Economia: A Visão dos Magistrados*, Rio de Janeiro: IPEA (Text under discussion).

Rabelo, F.M. and L. Coutinho (2001), 'Corporate Governance in Brazil', *Policy Dialogue Meeting on Corporate Governance in Developing Countries and Emerging Economies*, Paris: OECD Development Centre.

Rocha, B.M., A.M. Santos and I.M.M. Alves (2003), *Memorando sobre Jurisprudência Judicial Relativa a Decisões do CADE*, Brasília: Levy & Salomão Advogados.

Salgado, L.H. (1995), *Política de Concorrência: Tendências Recentes e o Estado da Arte no Brasil*, Brasília: IPEA (Text under discussion).

Salgado, L.H. (2003), *Agências Regulatórias na Experiência Brasileira: Um Panorama do Atual Desenho Institucional*, Brasília: IPEA (Text under discussion).

Santacruz, R. (1999), *Voto no Processo Administrativo n° 080000.015337/97-48*, Brasília: CADE.

Silva, K.M. (2004), *Análise da Política Antitruste no Brasil*, Uberlândia: Instituto de Economia.

8. Competition policy and enterprise development: the role of public interest objectives in South Africa's competition policy

Trudi Hartzenberg

INTRODUCTION

Competition policy reform was high on the agenda of South Africa's new government after the first democratic elections in 1994. The African National Congress (ANC) had espoused strong socialist principles during the years preceding South Africa's democratic transition. However, by the time the ANC came to power, the winds of political and policy change had shifted substantively, internationally and in South Africa too. Instead of a policy of nationalization of private enterprises, the ANC looked to competition policy as an instrument to regulate private enterprise and to address the legacy effect of apartheid and economic isolation on domestic markets. South Africa's Competition Act No. 89 of 1998, which was drafted and promulgated after an extensive and inclusive policy-making process of consultation and debate, reflects the political concerns of the ANC.

In addition to economic efficiency, the Competition Act explicitly includes equity and distributive goals. The preamble to the Act notes the high levels of concentration of ownership and control, ineffective checks on anti-competitive practices and restrictions on economic participation, especially by black South Africans due to apartheid laws and policies, and articulates a conviction that credible competition law and institutions to implement the law effectively are necessary for an efficiently functioning economy. Furthermore, the Act says that an economic environment balancing the interests of workers, owners and consumers will benefit all South Africans. A hallmark of the Act is thus its concern with public interest issues, equity and justice, balanced with the traditional economic efficiency concerns.

This chapter focuses broadly on the role of competition policy in enterprise development in South Africa, and more specifically on South Africa's new Competition Act and particular public interest objectives such as the promotion of small and medium-sized enterprise (SME) development and empowerment of previously disadvantaged individuals. The purpose of this exercise is to draw lessons for developing countries regarding the role of competition policy in enterprise development.

Although South Africa's history is in many respects unique, there are important lessons that can be drawn from the legacy effect on markets, enterprises and consumers, and the implications for the competitive process for other developing countries. High levels of concentration are common, for example, not only in South Africa, but also in other Southern and Eastern African countries. Markets are small, consumers are not well informed of their rights and capacity to implement competition policy effectively and law is scarce. Challenges of unemployment, low levels of domestic and foreign investment, as well as the history of excessive government regulation and the adverse effects on competition are also common to many developing countries.

DEVELOPING A COMPETITION POLICY FOR A NEW SOUTH AFRICA

South Africa's apartheid legacy and its consequent marginalization from the global economy produced very specific market structural characteristics and concomitant competition policy challenges. In addition to the insular nature of the South African economy resulting from global marginalization, domestic policy stance further compounded the competition challenges. Import substitution industrial policy and capital controls, for example, promoted local enterprise development through local content programmes and limited outward investment opportunities.

High levels of concentration, both in ownership and control, and conglomerate organization structures coupled with strong vertical integration were typical of many industries and markets. Many enterprises had diversified their activities, investing in a variety of unrelated economic activities and focused almost exclusively on the domestic markets as a result of economic sanctions.

The South African economy was characterized by a dual structure with a modern, almost exclusively white formal economy and a less developed, almost exclusively black, predominantly informal economy. This dichotomous economic structure and the apartheid laws that prevented black South Africans from participating in certain economic activities and geographic areas meant that participation in the formal economy and opportunities to develop formal and growing businesses were limited for black

South Africans. By contrast, the formal economy developed markets and industries that became in many cases highly concentrated with effective economic barriers to entry, in addition to the racial regulatory barriers of the apartheid regime.

It was recognized by the ANC that these challenges would have to be addressed by a range of economic and social policies and, in addition to a substantive focus on trade and industrial policies for transformation of the economy, competition policy became the policy option for the regulation and development of enterprise to enhance the economic opportunities and participation in the formal economy of black South Africans.

The ANC mapped out an extensive policy reform programme in the early 1990s, before the first democratic elections in 1994. The 1992 Policy Guidelines for a Democratic South Africa provided an overview of the policy revamp envisaged. As part of this process an assessment of South Africa's competition challenges and the efficacy of the existing competition law was undertaken. A complementary initiative was a review of South Africa's industrial strategy (Joffe et al., 1995). Key focus areas of the industrial strategy project were: markets and ownership structures; small and medium-sized enterprises and the conglomerates; technological and institutional capacities and human resource development and workplace organization.

Although this investigation into the development of an industrial strategy for South Africa focused narrowly on the manufacturing sector, the issues identified were also relevant to agriculture, mining and the services sectors. Many of the findings of this project related to competition issues, and in 1995 the new Department of Trade and Industry (DTI) started a three-year programme of consultation with competition experts and a broad range of stakeholders in South Africa to develop a new competition policy. The product of this extensive exercise was put forward in 1997, as DTI's *Guidelines for Competition Policy* (Government of South Africa, 1997) intended to stimulate discussion and debate on the role of competition policy in the restructuring of the economy.

Another complementary policy area that enjoyed much attention during the policy reform process was small business development. Between 1993 and 1994 an extensive empirical and theoretical study was conducted to identify key constraints to small business development in South Africa. A number of small business support initiatives were developed to actively promote small business development, with the expectation that small business would become an engine of growth and employment creation. These initiatives included financial schemes (loans or credit guarantees), skills support schemes and technology transfer schemes, among others.

The 1997 DTI *Guidelines for Competition Policy* considered the existing competition law of 1979 and found it wanting in a number of respects to address the challenges at hand. The 1979 Maintenance and Promotion of Competition Act did not contain any provisions related to vertical or conglomerate configurations or concentration of ownership. There were no pre-merger notification requirements. The 1979 Act contained no explicit prohibitions and the final yardstick for decisions was the 'public interest', which was not defined in the Act. The ad hoc and inconsistent decisions of the Competition Board were thus not unexpected. The Competition Board was appointed by the Minister of Trade and Industry, and a special court was to hear appeals, but never actually did hear any. A regulation issued by the Minister of Trade and Industry in 1984 declared some practices per se unlawful. These included resale price maintenance, horizontal collusion on price, terms or market share and bid rigging. There were, however, no prosecutions despite this regulation.

Effective implementation of a strong competition policy was viewed as an important tool to regulate private enterprise, given that the ANC's policy of nationalization, which had been espoused before to its election, had been abandoned, when the new government came to power. Specific goals of competition policy included the dilution of the high level of concentration of economic power, on the grounds that this was detrimental to balanced economic development. In particular, competition law was to reduce the domination of the economy by a white minority and to promote greater efficiency of the private sector. After a comprehensive policy process, which included debates within the National Economic Development and Labour Council (NEDLAC), a new competition law (the Competition Act No. 89 of 1998) was promulgated and became effective in September 1999. The Act provides for the establishment of three specific institutions to implement the law: a Competition Commission, a Competition Tribunal and a Competition Appeal Court.

The Competition Act incorporates features that reflect the unique challenges facing South Africa's economic development. It permits, and in certain cases requires, consideration of equity issues such as empowerment, employment and impact on small and medium enterprises. Enterprise development is thus an important focus for South Africa's new competition policy and law. Although equity considerations are explicitly incorporated into South Africa's competition law, political channels as a means of appealing these issues are not permitted. There is also no ministerial power to override the decisions of the competition agencies as there had been previously.

The introduction of South Africa's new competition policy and law took place within the broader context of a new industrial policy, a liberalized trade policy and revamped labour legislation in the second half of the 1990s. This was a new era in policy-making for economic transformation.

KEY FEATURES OF SOUTH AFRICA'S COMPETITION ACT

The Competition Act No. 89 of 1998 covers all economic activity in South Africa, and has extraterritorial reach to the extent that the Act applies to 'all economic activity within, or having an effect within, the Republic' (Government of South Africa, 1998). The nature and extent of this extraterritorial reach has been tested in one case thus far: the Botash case dealing with the effect of an American export cartel, exporting soda ash to Botswana (Government of South Africa, Competition Commission, 2003). Both Botswana and South Africa are members of the Southern African Customs Union (SACU); hence with a common external tariff, imports into Botswana can be expected to have an effect within South Africa.

South Africa is member of the Southern African Customs Union (SACU) and its members concluded a new customs union Agreement in 2002. This Agreement requires that all members of SACU have a competition policy and that they collaborate in the implementation of that policy. This new SACU Agreement and its competition policy provisions are important in the context of regional integration developments in Southern Africa. The countries of the customs union have a long history of economic integration (SACU is the oldest customs union in the world) and South African enterprises have extensive interests and operations in all the member countries. Recently, enterprises in the smaller SACU member states have raised complaints about the behaviour of South African enterprises in their countries, with requests for assistance via trade remedies. It may well be that this option is being sought because these countries do not have competition policy and implementing agencies and no regional competition policy or institutions exist either. This situation raises the issue of competition policy and enterprise development in the Southern African region, where only one member state currently has a competition law and implementing agencies. Without recourse to competition law remedies, enterprise development in the smaller countries could be adversely affected by the enterprises from South Africa.

Currently, South Africa is the only member of SACU that has an operational competition policy and law. Namibia passed a Competition Act in 2003, but has yet to establish the Namibian Competition Commission provided for in the Act. Both Swaziland and Botswana have draft competition laws and Lesotho has embarked on an economic mapping exercise and the development of an inventory of laws affecting competition.

The South African Competition Commission is an investigatory body to which competition complaints may be addressed. It also conducts preliminary investigations in merger impact assessments and makes recommendations to the Competition Tribunal. The Competition Tribunal is an adjudicatory body (or court of first instance) to which the Commission may refer complaints for further investigation and adjudication and which considers large merger transactions. The third institution is the Competition Appeal Court, which hears appeals arising from Tribunal decisions. This is a court dedicated to competition matters.

The overall purpose of the Competition Act is to promote and maintain competition, in order:

(a) to promote the efficiency, adaptability and development of the economy;
(b) to provide consumers with competitive prices and product choices;
(c) to promote employment and advance the social and economic welfare of South Africans;
(d) to expand opportunities for South African participation in world markets and recognize the role of foreign competition in the Republic;
(e) to ensure that small and medium-sized enterprises have an equitable opportunity to participate in the economy; and
(f) to promote a greater spread of ownership, in particular to increase the ownership stakes of historically disadvantaged persons. (Government of South Africa, 1998).

The Act's policy purpose focuses in the first instance on economic efficiency. South African competition law also explicitly includes public interest considerations, in the articulation of its purpose; it therefore attempts to balance efficiency concerns and the broader development priorities in the competition framework.

The focus on small and medium-sized enterprises is important against the background of the structure of the South African economy. High levels of concentration and the conglomerate structure of business in many sectors, from mining to manufacturing and services, are important challenges for small business development in South Africa, besides the common challenges that SMEs face more generally. The conglomerate structure of business in South Africa and the strong vertical linkages that exist in many industries can be effective barriers to entry for smaller enterprises.

The objective of promotion of a greater spread of ownership, especially regarding historically disadvantaged persons, reflects the concerns about the skewed distribution of income and wealth in South Africa. South Africa had for many decades one of the most unequal distributions of income in the world, with strong racial fault lines through the distribution. Greater spread of ownership and SME promotion are deemed to be important to ensure longer-term balanced and sustainable development.

The Act's preamble reverts to the political motivations that provided the rationale for the policy reform process of the new government. The particular problems facing competition law and its effective enforcement, including practices, some of which were promoted and supported by apartheid policies and laws, led to high levels of concentration of ownership and control, inequitable constraints on economic participation by the majority of South Africans and ineffective restraints on anti-competitive trade practices. This legacy is viewed through an equity lens, rather than an efficiency lens. In the 1979 competition legislation, public interest, although included in the Act, had not been defined. The new legislation articulates four pillars of the public interest. Perhaps the most distinctive pillar is empowering historically disadvantaged persons. The Competition Act, in this respect, echoes the focus in South Africa's Constitution on full and equal enjoyment of all rights and freedoms and enshrines the economic empowerment of black persons in South Africa in the Act.

Policy statements related to economic efficiency and consumer benefits provide for flexibility in application. References to adaptability and development of the economy extend beyond an interpretation of economic efficiency in a static welfare sense, to incorporation of dynamic considerations including market entry, enterprise mobility and innovation.

Consumer interests are also included in a broad sense; not only price is important, but consumer choice matters too. Thus, maintaining scope of choice may possibly be supported despite perhaps higher prices. A particular challenge emerges from the lack of consumer organization in South Africa. Consumers in South Africa (and this is also the case in many other developing countries) are generally not well informed of their rights and the potential to pursue complaints through the competition authorities and South Africa does not have specific consumer protection legislation. Advocacy is thus a key challenge for the South African competition authorities.

The Competition Act's rules draw on international experience; the rules on restrictive practices derive from the EU Treaty and the merger regulation is similar to that of Canada. Besides select per se prohibitions, in general, a violation of the Act is contingent upon demonstration of a net anti-competitive effect. Exemptions that provide a counter to the prohibitions contained in the Act also incorporate competition-plus issues. Exemptions that should be time-bound, may be granted for reasons that include the promotion of exports, promotion of SMEs or firms controlled by historically disadvantaged persons. The scope for exemptions is broad, suggesting that even per se prohibited acts may be condoned if they contribute to the identified exemption factors. A particular reason for consideration of an exemption application is 'ensuring economic stability' (Government of South Africa, 1998). The rationale for including this potentially extensive consideration was to facilitate ministerial input on industrial policy concerns or issues of national interest. Ministerial designation is not sufficient to ensure an exemption on such grounds; this has to be considered by the Competition Commission and it will decide if the statutory standard is met.

Merger control provisions are very detailed and public interest issues feature prominently in merger review. Specified merger thresholds will determine the process of notification and assessment. Large mergers are investigated by the Competition Commission, whose decision forms a rec- ommendation to the Competition Tribunal that may accept, reject or amend the Commission's decision. Small and intermediate mergers are investigated by the Commission and a decision is made, which may be appealed to the Tribunal. Decisions by the Tribunal in all cases may be appealed to the Appeal Court.

The merger evaluation process is clearly outlined in the Act. First it has to be established whether the merger is likely to substantially prevent or lessen competition (SLC test). Second, if it has been decided that the merger will lessen competition, then it must be established whether the merger will result in 'technological, efficiency or other pro-competitive gains' (Government of South Africa, 1998) that will outweigh the anti- competitive effects of the merger. Third, irrespective of the outcome of the evaluation of the competition impact of the merger, a public interest test has to be conducted. Thus, even though a merger may not have an adverse effect on competition, it still has to be reviewed on public interest grounds.

Explicit criteria to consider in the SLC test are included in the Act (Section 12A(2)); with these, however, a measure of flexibility remains. These criteria serve to some extent the purpose of general guidelines for the conduct of a merger assessment. They include barriers to entry, import competition, history of collusion, vertical integration and the 'failing enterprise' argument.

If the authority decides that the merger is likely to substantially prevent or lessen competition it must then assess whether the merger transaction will result in any efficiency gains. The efficiency test is therefore included as a defence for an anti-competitive merger transaction. The nature of the balance between the SLC test and the efficiency test poses significant chal- lenges to the authorities, in that a weigh-up of a competition compromise and efficiency benefits (both static and dynamic) has to be considered. It has been conceded that perhaps following the United States in bringing the efficiency test into the competition assessment, alongside other factors already included in the Act, may make the task of the authorities more manageable.

The public interest test is mandatory in all merger assessments. Section 12A(3) of the Competition Act specifies the public interest test:

(3) When determining whether a merger can or cannot be justified on public interest grounds, the Competition Commission or the Competition Tribunal must consider the effect that the merger will have on:

(a)   a particular industrial sector or region;
(b)   employment;
(c)   the ability of small businesses or firms controlled by historically disadvantaged persons to become competitive; or
(d)   the ability of national industries to compete in international markets. (Government of South Africa, 1998)

The public interest test in the South African Competition Act is distinctive for a number of reasons. First, the public interest test is explicitly included in the Act and also delineated very specifically in terms of the criteria above. This means that select public interest concerns enjoy focus in the context of competition assessments. Second, the test empowers the competition authorities to prohibit or allow a merger that does or does not, respectively, pass muster on the SLC test. Third, the competence to allow or disallow a merger on the basis of a public interest consideration is accorded to the competition authority, not any other minister or stakeholder representative. The Act does, however, require that the Minister of Trade and Industry (or another minister directly affected by the merger) be served a copy of the merger notification, so that they can plead the case before the competition authorities.

In the case of intermediate or large mergers, the primary acquiring enterprise and the primary target enterprise must provide a copy of the merger notice to any registered trade union that represents a substantial number of its employees, or the employees or their representatives if there are no registered trade unions. Any person, whether or not a party to the merger transaction, may submit any document or relevant information for consideration by the competition authorities. The Minister of Trade and Industry may participate in any intermediate or large merger as a participant to make representation on any public interest matter.

Although there has been criticism concerning the inclusion of public interest issues in the Competition Act, their inclusion has to be read in context. Major challenges to sustainable development in South Africa are employment creation and black economic empowerment. Explicit reference to these factors is thus to be expected in a significant area of policy and law such as competition and in some sense provides a balance of considerations in the challenge to develop a set of complementary policies and laws to facilitate enterprise development and the achievement of broader socioeconomic objectives.

Recognizing the importance of the interface between sector regulation and competition law, the Competition Act (as amended, 2000) specifies that the competition authorities and sector regulators have joint jurisdiction in relevant sectors. A Regulators' Forum is being established to implement this provision of the Act and makes the Competition Commission responsible to 'negotiate agreements with regulatory authorities to coordinate and harmonize the exercise of jurisdiction over competition matters' (Government of South Africa, 1998 (amended 2000)) within a specific sector or industry.

Thus far the Independent Communication Authority of South Africa (ICASA), the National Electricity Regulator (NER) and the Postal Regulator (PR) have concluded memoranda of agreement with the Competition Commission.

SUPPORTING ENTERPRISE DEVELOPMENT THROUGH COMPETITION POLICY

Substantively, the workloads of the Competition Commission and the Tribunal have overwhelmingly been concentrated on merger control. This distinguishes South Africa from developing and transition economies with new competition agencies and highlights the political concerns in South Africa about the high concentration of economic power. Through pre-notification and merger assessment, a demonstration effect, in the area of merger control, provides evidence of South Africa's new competition law's strong impact. While the explicit consideration of public interest concerns emphasizes their pervasive policy importance, checks and balances in the Competition Act ensure that decisions are transparent and void of direct political control.

It is useful to reflect on the experience of South Africa since the implementation of the new Competition Act. As regards merger control, competition law practitioners indicate that in the early days, merger notifications were mostly undertaken by lawyers (filling in required information in forms provided by the competition authorities). Now no merger filing would be complete without a detailed impact assessment. Lawyers and economists now work together in an interdisciplinary manner to assess the likely impact of the proposed transaction.

Competition law forms an important part of effective market governance. The rules of the market game, that include competition rules, can enhance market outcomes by promoting not only the achievement of efficiencies but also greater equity. To this extent South Africa's competition law is progressive in its explicit incorporation of public interest considerations; whereas even mature jurisdictions shy away from such potentially contentious territory.

With South Africa's history, the inclusion of public interest concerns makes good policy sense. The nature of the South African economy, its grossly unequal distribution of income and wealth and hence too its inequality of economic opportunity have to be addressed by a coherent set of policy initiatives. Thus, employment creation, black economic empowerment and small and medium-sized enterprise development are familiar objectives across a range of economic policies. A challenging question is to what extent different policies can impact on the promotion of small and medium-sized enterprises – what specifically can be the contribution of competition policy in this regard?

It may be quite obvious that, especially in the short term, direct industry support policies, such as the provision of credit or marketing support, may be more visibly effective in supporting SMEs. However, the contribution of competition policy, while in some cases being more indirect, can play an extremely important role in ensuring that SMEs not only get access to specific market opportunities but also do not fail because of anticompetitive practices.

Competition policy and the law that gives effect to this policy provide indispensable checks and balances to ensure that the market process works without being rigged by larger enterprises or enterprises that may have market power, which can be used to the disadvantage of other market participants. This does not mean that there should be no casualties of the market and the process of competition but competition should be fair and without prejudice.

The following merger transactions and the decisions of the competition authorities will illustrate the impact of public interest considerations in merger impact assessments. Specifically the cases will highlight the consideration of SME and empowerment concerns.

Pioneer Foods–SAD Holdings

Pioneer Foods has diverse interests in milling, baking, poultry, animal feeds and branded consumer goods. The merger transaction involves the purchase by Pioneer of all shares in South African Dried Fruit Holdings (SAD) and all of its subsidiaries. SAD has business interests in nuts, vinegar, dried flowers, dried fruit, wine and salads. This is a large merger transaction, and hence it was first reviewed by the Competition Commission and then referred to the Competition Tribunal for further investigation and approval.

Assessment of the relevant markets of the two parties indicated that there are only two markets with product overlap and hence relevance for the merger assessment. These are ready-to-eat (RTE) cereals, and jar vegetables (salads). The discussion here will focus on the former market, in which international brand leaders such as Kellogg's, as well as small home-based producers of RTE cereals for health-conscious consumers, participate. There are thus various drivers of competition in the RTE market. And it may be argued that a finer delineation of more than one market is necessary to assess effectively the impact of the proposed merger transaction.

The geographic market for RTE cereals is defined as the South African national market and there is limited import competition. This is because distribution and sales are primarily through supermarket chains that operate nationally. Market definition proved an interesting exercise; breakfast cereals comprise hot cereals and muesli products. If the cereal market is taken as a single market, including both hot cereals and muesli products, then Tiger Brands (which is not involved in the transaction) would be dominant. However, if branded cereals is defined as the relevant market, then Kellogg's is dominant. In the muesli market, taking a narrow market definition, then Nature's Source (which is a subsidiary of SAD, the primary target enterprise) is dominant.

The Competition Tribunal was persuaded that consumers display a high degree of substitutability especially among hot cereals and muesli products (the parties had submitted extensive price elasticity studies to indicate that the appropriate market definition was RTE cereals). Consumer demand was highly price elastic, and the cross-price elasticities indicated high degrees of product substitution.

It was concluded that even if muesli was defined as a separate 'niche' market, this market demonstrated very low barriers to entry. This was an important consideration because on the one hand large-scale producers faced significant barriers to entry while the barriers to small-scale producers were very low (many produced from home, and sold their products from specialist health shops or other non-retail chain outlets).

What became apparent to the Tribunal was that the small producers compete vigorously among themselves and very few grow to the extent that they can attempt to compete with the likes of Kellogg's or Pioneer Foods. An important issue in this case was the nature of interaction between large-scale producers and the supermarket chains. The retail food market in South Africa is an oligopolistic one, with a few large chains of retail supermarkets competing actively with one another. They provide a strong source of countervailing power to the power of large-scale producers of consumer food products, including breakfast foods. One of their strong bargaining chips is allocation of shelf space in supermarkets. The market leader is accorded prime space, followed by the house brand, then the number two player follows and other players after that. Competition is thus intense as retail chains and suppliers bargain on price and shelf space, for example.

Taking into account these dynamic drivers of competition in the RTE market, the parties to the transaction argued that it was reasonable to conclude that far from reducing competition in the RTE market, the proposed merger may be expected to increase the level of competition in the RTE market as Pioneer Foods' bargaining power vis à vis the retail chains is likely to be strengthened, and that Kellogg's, the market leader, is likely to face more substantial competition.

The conclusion of the Tribunal was that the merger would not harm small business prospects and the contestability of the RTE market would not be adversely affected by the merger. The merger was approved unconditionally. 'It is possible for small scale players to continue to enter the market by developing niche brands. The merger is not likely to adversely affect the potential of small scale or niche entrants to the market' (Government of South Africa, 2003), was the conclusion of the Tribunal.

This decision highlighted the fact that in some cases it may be possible to define the market not only in terms of product and geography but it may be necessary to consider size of enterprises. In this case the large enterprises (competitors of Kellogg's) can be said to operate in a market delineated from the market where small, niche (home) producers compete intensively with one another. It is quite unusual for small, niche producers to grow to the extent to where they migrate to the large enterprise market.

Bernina-Saskor Case

The Bernina-Saskor case (Government of South Africa, Competition Commission, 2002) arose from a complaint by an independent service provider alleging that Bernina-Saskor, the sole importer and supplier of Bernina sewing machine parts in South Africa, had instructed its franchisees not to provide the complainant with Bernina machine parts. The Commission concluded, and the respondent concurred, that the respondent had contravened the provisions of the Act (Section 8(d)(1)) in that they had required a supplier not to deal with a competitor and a consent order was concluded. In terms of the consent order, the instruction to franchisees was withdrawn immediately, and parts would be supplied to any customers. The machine parts would be used typically by small (often independent) enterprises repairing sewing machines. The restrictive practice was thus adversely affecting a niche market of small (even micro) service providers.

Ring Pharmacies Case

A group of 33 individually owned pharmacies (which had formed an association called Ring Pharmacies), are all small and medium-sized enterprises. Ring Pharmacies had been engaging in joint marketing initiatives to assist them to compete with pharmacy chains. They applied for an exemption so that they could continue to conduct joint marketing initiatives to enable them to compete with established chains of pharmacies.

In recent years, in South Africa, pharmacy chains have proliferated and the small individually owned pharmacy has become a rarity. The exemption was granted for five years to enable these SMEs to compete with the large chains. This decision recognizes the benefits of small, individually owned pharmacies, some of which may not have been targeted by the pharmacy chains as a result of their location and performance. The decision is thus proactive support for small enterprises to compete in a market that has experienced a new reconfiguration as the chains have become commonplace.

Economic empowerment of historically disadvantaged persons is a key policy objective. Empowerment is achieved through many initiatives including employment equity requirements. The role of competition policy in empowerment is illustrated in a case that highlighted very different interpretations of this public interest consideration by the Competition Commission and the Competition Tribunal.

Shell–Tepco Merger

The Shell–Tepco merger took place in the oil industry. This industry is a high-volume, low-margin, capital-intensive industry, and in South Africa also highly regulated. Price control, especially retail price maintenance, and import control are key features of the regulatory dispensation. Maximum prices are set for petrol (gas), diesel and paraffin, from which dealers may discount. Stakeholders in the industry and the Department of Minerals and Energy have set goals to achieve Black Economic Empowerment (BEE) in the industry. At the time of the merger, BEE in the oil industry was in its infancy, with BP being the leader in this regard. Shell was therefore very interested in this merger, which would provide it with an empowerment partner.

Shell South Africa (SA) manufactures and markets petroleum and petroleum products directly and indirectly through subsidiaries and franchise outlets in South Africa. A distinction is made between the retail and commercial markets. The retail market is business-to-business, which buys in bulk either on tender or contract or at negotiated prices. In the retail market, products are sold to consumers through retail franchise networks such as petrol stations. The geographic market for the commercial segment is national because of 'hospitality' agreements among oil companies in terms of which they swap products (with regulated specifications) at different locations determined by the location of the refineries and customers. This means that a commercial customer can go to any depot with which the contracting oil company has a hospitality agreement.

The geographic market for retail is subnational. Data was only, however, available at the magisterial district (local council) level, and hence this influenced the geographic market definition of the retail segment. Shell is one of several oil majors operating in South Africa. At the time of the merger transaction, Shell SA was the second largest national player in the retail diesel and commercial paraffin markets, the third largest player in the retail petrol market and the fourth largest national player in the commercial petrol market. Tepco by contrast was one of the smallest players in all relevant markets. Tepco is a wholly owned subsidiary of Thebe Investment Corporation. It markets and distributes petroleum and petroleum products as its main business.

An important consideration in this case was the role of government-induced regulation in the oil industry. Although the Department of Minerals and Energy has embarked on a process of managed liberalization, regulation still accounts for much of the distortion in the various markets in the industry. Another important consideration was that product specifications, specifically, are regulated. The relative product homogeneity facilitates substitution by consumers and thus enhances competition among suppliers. In the commercial market segment, where prices are not regulated, customers interviewed by the Tribunal indicated that they can negotiate prices with suppliers and this prevents the abuse of even a dominant position in a narrowly defined geographic market.

The merger passed the SLC text – no lessening of competition was anticipated in the relevant markets, which were defined as the marketing and distribution of petroleum products nationally in South Africa. However, the Commission conditionally recommended that the merger be approved, on the grounds that the merger would remove Tepco as an independent player in the petroleum industry and would inhibit the ability of a firm owned or controlled by historically disadvantaged individuals to become competitive. The conditions for approval were that Tepco should remain an independent company jointly controlled by Thebe and Shell and Tepco's brand should be maintained to ensure its independence. The first condition would require a restructuring of the deal that the parties had put together and neither wanted. Tepco indicated that it was experiencing structural difficulties and hence it wanted to be taken over by Shell – after the deal it would be owned and controlled by Shell.

The Tribunal criticized the Commission's recommendation as patronizing, indicating that empowerment is not 'further obliging firms controlled by historically disadvantaged persons to continue to exist on a life-support machine' (Government of South Africa, 2002). The second condition was viewed as linked to the first by the Tribunal and subjected to the same criticism – there was no reason to prolong the existence of a non-viable brand.

Tepco's locations were in high-risk markets that other suppliers were not prepared to supply. Thus, its exit from the market did not remove an effective competitor. The Tribunal emphasized that the parties are free to make whatever deal they chose – provided they meet the approval of the competition authorities.

The Tribunal overruled the Commission's recommendation and approved the merger unconditionally. One of the reasons for the Tribunal's decision was that Tepco could drain the financial resources of its parent company if it were forced to remain independent in the market. The conclusion to the Tribunal's decision is instructive:

> The role played by the competition authorities in defending even those aspects of the public interest listed in the Act is, at most, secondary to other statutory and regulatory instruments – in this case the Employment Equity Act, the Skills Development Act, and the (Empowerment) Charter itself spring to mind. The competition authorities, however well intentioned, are well advised not to pursue their public interest mandate in an over-zealous manner lest they damage precisely those interests that they ostensibly seek to protect. (www.comptrib.co.za)

This case raises very important considerations in the interpretation of the public interest in the context of a merger assessment. While public interest concerns are explicitly incorporated into the merger assessment process, it is recognized that they should be interpreted very cautiously and that the role of other policy initiatives in promoting those public interest objectives may be far more important that that of competition policy and law.

CONCLUSIONS

South Africa's experience in the development of its competition policy and law in the 1990s offers important lessons for other developing countries. First, the development of competition policy took place during a comprehensive policy reform programme. While this may not be feasible in other countries, it is important to note from this experience that due consideration for the policy synergies, perhaps among the collection of microeconomic policies such as trade, industrial, competition and labour market policies is important.

Second, a very important aspect of the development of competition policy and law is the building of a competition culture. In some developing countries economies are still in a transition from socialist-type or highly controlled economic systems. The private sector is an emerging one and the benefits of competition may not be appreciated or be obvious to all stakeholders in the economy. An inclusive process of discussion and education around competition issues may assist to develop a competition culture that will enhance the benefits of enforcement.

Even in South Africa, where a comprehensive policy process involved a broad spectrum of stakeholders, competition law practitioners indicate that it is sometimes difficult to obtain information from even large enterprises, for merger filings or investigation of competition complaints. The perception still seems to be that the implementation of competition law is a bureaucratic process, a hassle factor for business. The collaboration of competition champions (perhaps larger businesses) to extol the virtues of effective implementation of competition can play a role in this regard. In South Africa for example, South African Breweries, now a multinational beer producer, has a well-publicized compliance programme for managers and this has assisted in raising the profile of competition policy in the private sector. In merger regulation for example, trade unions are explicitly involved in the merger notification process. Thus competition policy becomes not only an issue for management but also for employees.

Third, South Africa's experience in implementing competition has highlighted the importance of capacity building. In South Africa, as in many other developing countries, there is not a long tradition of collaboration between lawyers and economists. Lawyers seldom study economics and economists are not likely to study law either. Competition policy and law requires an interdisciplinary approach, bringing lawyers and economists together. This is also a new area of study in South Africa, especially in the legal field, and this is probably similar in many developing countries.

A particular challenge as a result of the skills shortage has been the high rate of staff turnover at the Competition Commission. Commissioners with little more than a year's experience have become much sought after in legal firms and in the private sector. Capacity building should therefore be an ongoing exercise.

Fourth, the specific challenges faced in the South African case at the end of the apartheid era also hold important lessons for developing countries. Distortions by government regulation, high levels of concentration in ownership and control and vertically integrated conglomerate organizations were not conditions supportive of a strong competition culture and robust competition processes. This meant that the usual objective of competition policy to promote competition and economic efficiency was important, but at the same time, broader public interest objectives were also important. Public interest objectives mattered in the context of competition policy even though they were also to be pursued through other policy channels.

While public interest objectives are important, their introduction into competition policy and law has to be handled very carefully. South Africa's experience with its 1979 Maintenance and Promotion of Competition Act, offered clear lessons in this regard. The 1979 Act put the public interest as the final criterion against which competition decisions would be tested, but did not define the public interest. This led to ad hoc and conflicting case law and this was compounded by the political influence that could influence or override decisions by the Competition Board.

In the new Competition Act the public interest is explicitly articulated. Specifically four public interest pillars are identified and bounds are placed on the permissible recourse to public interest issues in competition cases. While it may be desirable to include public interest considerations explicitly to limit the scope of interpretation, care has to be taken both in the drafting of the law and in the implementation of that law. Caution must be exercised to ensure that decisions are credible and a consistent body of case law amplifies the letter of the law. Effective and consistent implementation of competition law is perhaps the most important advocacy tool in a developing country. There may be occasions where the promotion of public interest objectives will be better served by other policy interventions than competition policy and the competition authorities should be bold enough to hold back on such decisions (as was the case in the Shell–Tepco merger discussed earlier).

The unique South African history led to the delineation of four pillars of public interest: small and medium-sized enterprise development and black economic empowerment, employment, impact on a particular industry or region and the ability of national industries to compete in international markets. In the implementation of competition law thus far, it is in the case of merger control that employment, economic empowerment and small and medium-size enterprise development have featured most prominently. The ability of national industries to compete in international markets has not yet been considered key in any merger assessment.

In general, and specifically for developing countries, it is important not to overload the competition policy agenda. There are objectives (including in particular, public interest objectives) that can be more effectively achieved through other policy channels. Policy coordination and inter-policy consistency is critical, especially for developing countries that are facing the challenges of market development, with in some cases an emerging, rather than robust private sector, especially a small business sector. The number of public interest issues included in the competition policy agenda should therefore be strictly limited and effective implementation of the competition law synergies, with other policy initiatives supporting these public interest objectives, should be developed.

Although the public interest test in merger review is clearly specified, the Competition Tribunal has been cautious in its consideration of this test. This is the singular lesson for developing countries. If the credibility of the competition authority is to be built in the application of a public interest test then cautious application is recommended.

The South African experience with competition policy and law has also shown that despite resistance at the multilateral level to engage in negotiations to determine competition rules, it is not possible to avoid competition issues in bilateral negotiations. South Africa (and SACU) is currently negotiating a free trade agreement with the United States and competition policy is definitely on the agenda, as it is too in the negotiations with the European Free Trade Area (EFTA) to conclude a free trade agreement. It seems fair to say that such trade negotiations highlight the potential impact on domestic markets if competition policy does not exist.

The new generation trade agreements include trade-plus issues such as investment and the entry of new firms, perhaps large ones, may have serious effects on the nature and intensity of competition in developing country markets. The absence of competition policy and law could mean that domestic enterprises do not have any armour should the newcomers engage in anti-competitive practices. So while developing countries welcome and actively compete for foreign direct investment, they ought to ensure that competition policy and law is in place in order that competition is fair and enterprise development is facilitated not frustrated.

REFERENCES

Government of South Africa (1997) *The Evolution of Policy in SA: Proposed Guidelines for Competition Policy; a Framework for Competition, Competitiveness and Development*, www.compcom.co.za/aboutus/aboutus_evolution.asp? level= 2& desc=8.

Government of South Africa (1998), *Competition Act, No. 89*, Government Printer, Pretoria.

Government of South Africa (2001a), Competition Commission, *Annual Report 2001*.

Government of South Africa (2001b), Competition Tribunal, *Annual Report 2000/2001*.

Government of South Africa, Competition Commission (2003), Competition Tribunal, *Annual Report 2002/2003*.

Joffe, A., D. Kaplan, R. Kaplinsky and D. Lewis (1995), *Improving Manufacturing Performance in South Africa*, Cape Town: UCT Press.

Websites

www.compcom.co.za (Competition Commission)

www.comptrib.co.za (Competition Tribunal)

www.dti.gov.za (Department of Trade and Industry)

9. Competitive markets and competition policy in Indonesia

Efa Yonnedi

INTRODUCTION

Theoretical and empirical research reveals that the industrial sector in the Indonesian economy is highly concentrated (Hill, 1987; Bird, 1999). The World Bank in its 1994 and 1995 reports suggested that cartel practices occurred in some sectors such as cement, sugar processing, paper production, fertilizer distribution, rice and cloves. The view that the industrial market is highly concentrated is also well established amongst the general public particularly since the early 1990s, when it was obvious that the patrimonial nature of business–government relations had distorted economic policies, and there had been a complex interplay among key business players and the governments to impede the competitive process (Yonnedi, 2002).

Market structure and industrial concentration is an important issue in Indonesia because of the size of industrial sectors, the prevalent level of government protections and a traditional deep suspicion of large-scale enterprise (Hill, 1987). Industrial concentration is expected to remain high because government protection restrains competition from both domestic and international sources. Added to this there have been widespread views that big business contributed to undesirable market concentration, excessive diversification and lack of governance and transparency. An 'antibigness' can be traced to the early years of independence when President Sukarno nationalized a large part of the economy (Hill, 2000). The rise of the private sectors in Indonesia has been characterized by the emergence of *konglomerat* (conglomerate) and large-scale firms, which have received privileges from various protectionist policies.

Mainly in response to the oil prices crisis in the 1980s, the government embarked on various market opening policies, including trade and investment liberalization, deregulation and the privatization of state-owned enterprises. This brought about a long-term decline in market concentration (Hill, 1987; Bird, 1999; Pangestu et al., 2002). Moreover, the government enacted a competition law, referred to as the Law Banning Monopolistic Practices and Unhealthy Business Competition (hereafter 'the Competition Law') on 5 March 1999. The Competition Law demanded the establishment of a Business Competition Supervisory Commission (Komisi Pengawas Persaingan Usaha, KPPU). The inception of the KPPU was based on Presidential decree on 7 June 2000 and from this, KPPU had a mandate to implement the Competition Law and preserve a workable competitive market.

This chapter reviews the development of Indonesia's competition policy over the last three decades. Competition policy is defined as 'the set of policies and laws which ensure that competition in the market place is not restricted in such a way as to reduce economic welfare' (Motta, 2004, p. 30). The set of policies could be embodied in trade liberalization, industry deregulation and investment policies, privatization and competition law (Khemani and Dutz, 1996). These policies make use of market mechanisms to restructure the economy to achieve economic efficiency. The next section provides a very brief review of the Indonesian economy. The third section examines the level of industrial concentration in the manufacturing sector in Indonesia. The fourth reviews market-opening policies pursued by the government before and after the economic crisis of 1997. The fifth assesses the Competition Law and its implementation to date. The final section draws conclusions.

THE INDONESIAN ECONOMY

During the New Order between 1996 to 1998, Indonesia enjoyed sustained and rapid economic growth in which the Indonesian economy was long held up as a miracle economy and model of industrial policy – one of the 'newly industrialising economies' (NIEs) of Southeast Asia countries (World Bank, 1993). The average economic growth under the New Order was about 7 per cent and even during the 1990s (before the 1997 crash) economic growth had reached 7.5 per cent (Sjahrir, 1998, p. 53).

Not only did Indonesia enjoy a sustained and rapid economic growth, but it also succeeding in transforming its economy during the New Order. Table 9.1 shows the structural transformation of the Indonesian economy since the late 1960s up to 1990. During that time the dominance of the agriculture sector gave way to industry, trade and services sectors. There was also a switch from being a predominantly oil-financed economy to a non-oil-financed one.

During the 1980s and 1990s the manufacturing sector experienced extra-ordinary double digit growth and became the dominant sector within the

Table 9.1   Structural transformation of Indonesian economy, 1965–90

Structure	1965	1970	1980	1990
As percentage of GDP				
Openness				
• Total trade	14.0	22.2	46.8	54.7
• Non-oil exports	4.0	7.0	11.5	15.7
• Imports	7.5	10.6	15.5	26.3
Gross domestic investment	8.0	10.8	18.7	24.6
Gross national savings	7.9	9.5	32.8	26.3
Structure of output (%)				
• Agriculture	55.0	47.5	24.4	23.0
• Manufacturing	8.5	10.9	13.5	18.8
• Other industry	6.5	8.9	29.8	19.1
• Services	30.0	32.7	32.2	39.1
External debt	50.0	32.5	30.0	66.6
As percentage of exports				
Oil and gas exports	40.0	40.5	78.5	44.8
Debt service	11.0	6.0	13.9	27.3
Private investment as percentage of total	na	na	51.0	64.7

Source: Pangestu (1993, p. 101); na: not available.

Indonesian economy. Non-oil export revenues started to replace oil revenues from the 1980s. This rapid growth has been widely acknowledged as the source of employment creation. Fujita and James (1997) found that employment created by the export of light industries increased dramatically in absolute terms, far exceeding employment created by primary exports during 1980–90.

However, the economic miracle changed and became a never-ending crisis. Arriving unexpectedly, the economic crisis continued for almost seven years and the recovery path has been far from clear. The turmoil has weakened the confidence of investors and adversely affected the availability of credit. Sharp increases in commodity prices and changes in government policy towards fuel and rice subsidies have accompanied the financial chaos. In the two years following the financial crisis in 1997, Indonesia experienced negative economic growth of –13.2 per cent and –2.6 per cent respectively (ARIC, 2005). Prices spiralled upwards during these years. Estimates from the Central Bureau of Statistics (BPS) put annual inflation at about 75–80 per cent for 1998 (Beegle et al., 1999, p. 1). However, the average economic growth has improved to nearly 5 per cent in recent years.

COMPETITIVE MARKETS IN INDONESIA

This section examines industrial concentration, geographical distribution, ownership structure and the factors affecting market concentration in Indonesia.

Industrial Concentration

Drawing from Hill (1987, 1990), Aswicahyono, Bird and Hill (1996); Bird (1999) and Pangestu et al. (2002) the long-term pattern and structure of the manufacturing sector can be traced. Table 9.2 provides a summary of this research. It can be seen that different types of measures for market concentration show a consistent decline in industrial concentration between 1975–96. However, industrial concentration is still remarkably high by international standards even if it is compared with other developing countries (Hill, 1987).

One of the most recent papers examined the trend and level of industrial concentration in 67 Indonesian industries between 1975 and 1993 (Bird, 1999). Bird's study provides an assessment of the effect of market opening policies embraced during the 1980s in relation to industrial concentration. Bird divided industry concentration into quartile classes: 0–24 per cent, 25–49 per cent, 50–74 per cent and 75–100 per cent. Industries with a CR4 (four-firm concentration ratio) above 75 per cent are categorized as highly concentrated; those with a CR4 of 50–74 as moderately concentrated and those with a CR4 less than 50 per cent as having low concentration. Bird concluded that the simple average four-firm concentration ratios (CR4) in 67 manufacturing industries declined from 63.6 per cent in 1975 to 53.5 per cent in 1993 (Appendix 9.1). Industries that had CR4 between 75 and 100 per cent (high concentration industries) were 39.2 per cent of all manufacturing industries in 1975 and yet only 27.5 per cent in 1993. For the 67 industries, the CR4 unadjusted for trade was 53.3 per cent in 1993 whilst the adjusted four-firm concentration ratio was 41.1 per cent. Apparently Indonesia's manufacturing sector was becoming less concentrated on average during the period 1975–93.

Allowing for foreign trade reduces the concentration measure in most of the highly concentrated industries. Concentration is substantially lower after trade adjustment in carpets and rugs, wooden boxes and containers, paper products, structural clay products and shipbuilding.

Figure 9.1 shows the trends in industrial concentration in broad industry groups. The average manufacturing concentration has steadily declined during the period 1975–90 and slightly increased in the early 1990s. The early 1990s witnessed so-called 'reform fatigue', characterized by the slowness of deregulation. Even worse, non-transparent protection for vested interests was

Table 9.2 Previous research on market concentration in Indonesia

Author/Year	Period Coverage	Industry Coverage	Concentration Measures	Main Findings
Hill (1987)	1975–83		Four-firm concentration ratios (CR4)	• Seller concentration is high by developing countries standards • Highly concentrated in Jakarta and its neighbouring areas and East Java, accounting for 80% of national industrial output • Private (domestic) firms are important groups and steadily expanding
Aswicahyono et al. (1996)	1980–90		CR4, Herfindahl-Hirschman Index (HHI)	• A downward trend in concentration during the studied periods • Concentration fell more quickly in the most export-oriented industries e.g., textiles, garments and footwear, wood products
Bird (1999)	1975–93	67 industries	Unweighted and weighted CR4 (adjusting for international trade)	• Long-term decline in industrial concentration between 1975–93 • Using simple CR4 industrial concentration decline from 64% in 1975 to 54% in 1993 • Highly concentrated industries fell from 39% in 1975 to 27% in 1993 • Allowing for foreign trade reduces the average concentration ratios over time
Hill (1990)	1975–85	119 industries	CR4	• Probable reduction in concentration level (measured from the establishment)
Pangestu et al. (2002)	1975–96		CR4 and HHI	• Declining industrial concentration between 1975–95 • The decline in the prevalence of dominant firms • Market share mobility

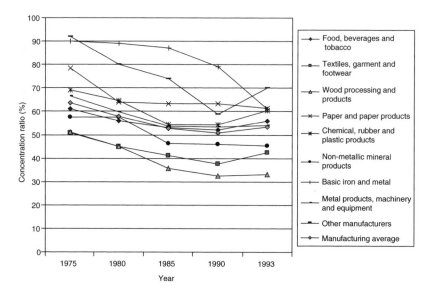

Source: Adopted from Bird (1999).

Figure 9.1 Concentration ratio trend, 1975–93

apparent in the sense of increases of tariffs, creation of monopolies, entry deterrence and price-setting practices (Pangestu et al., 2002). The most important examples are wheat flour, soybeans, garlic, cloves, milk, dairy products, automotive, cement and propylene. However, most of the industries were far less protected in 1993 than they were in 1975. Furthermore, paper and paper products, chemicals and plastics, the export-competing wood processing, textiles and garments sectors show a steady decline in concentration, and recorded among the lowest concentration levels in 1993. A considerable reduction also occurred in ice cream, cement, motor cycles and jewellery.

Many of the highly concentrated industries experienced some instability in their concentration levels. Between 1975 and 1993, cement, tyres, soap and detergents, chemical fertilizers and carpets and rug industries had experienced more than 10 per cent decline in their concentration levels. Conversely, white cigarette and wine sectors recorded a more than 15 per cent increase in concentration levels in the same period.

Geographical and Ownership Structure

In terms of geographical concentration, industrial location is 'heavily concentrated around Jakarta and in East Java' (Hill, 1987). The six most industrialized provinces, namely, Jakarta, East Java, West Java, Central Java, North Sumatera and South Sumatera, account for well over 80 per cent of industrial output (Hill, 1987).

Hill (1987) found that in 1975 and 1983, private firms were by far the most important group and their share has been expanding. Private firms contributed over half of manufacturing value-added and three-quarters of factory employment in 1983. Private sector firms dominated in consumer goods and labour-intensive industries such as kretek cigarettes, plywood, garments and textiles, most food products, spinning and rubber products.

In contrast, state enterprises played a dominant role in petroleum refining, sugar refining, fertilizers, cement and basic metal industries. Although state enterprises occupied a comparatively small number of industries, these industries are strategically important. The participation of the government in the manufacturing sector has been justified on the basis that they are 'agents of development', contributing to technology and increasing value-added.

The contribution of foreign investors in Indonesian manufacturing has been through equity investments, licensing agreements or other commercial agreements. For example, all domestic firms producing motor vehicles are under licence from overseas vehicle manufacturers (see Appendix 9.2). In 1983 there were 17 sizeable industries in which foreign investors contributed over 50 per cent of industry output (Hill, 1987).

According to Hill (1987, pp. 93–4) the role of private ownership in the manufacturing sector would require a cautious interpretation for a number of reasons. First, much of the very large-scale manufacturing is in state or foreign hands and often in the form of joint ventures between these two groups. Second, the largest incremental increase in shares has been in the private-foreign group, where output shares have almost doubled between 1975 and 1983. Third, industries excluded from Hill's study are large and predominantly state-owned. Finally, a significant degree of the private sector is closely interwoven with state officials through patron–client relationships.

Determinants of Industrial Concentration

High concentration ratios in the industrial sector can be theoretically attributed to economies of scale, anti-competitive conduct and government intervention (Hill, 1987). The first economy of scale is related to highly capital-intensive or highly product-differentiated industries such as fertilizers, cement, sheet glass, paper products, motor cycles, shipbuilding, noodles, white and clove cigarettes, malt beer, cosmetics and motor vehicles (see Figure 9.1). Second, highly concentrated industries such as wheat flour milling, malt beer, fertilizers and cement industries have had government constraints on domestic competition during the New Order (Bird, 1999). It is therefore likely that the combination of high import protection and high domestic concentration lessened competition in many Indonesian industries (Hill, 1987). The government with numerous regulations has restricted competition through trade and industry policies during the New Order.

Bird (1999) found that many of the concentrated industries in Indonesia are highly capital-intensive and require a large initial investment. An example of high concentration and low entry barriers is the Indonesian export-oriented industries. For these industries such as processed food, electronics and dry cell batteries, the CR4 has reached as high as 90 per cent. Logically, these industries have to compete internationally, and for this reason the scale of production needs to be high. The theory suggests that market concentration positively correlates with scale economies, absolute capital requirements and other barriers to entry. From this it can be expected that concentration would be higher in intermediate and capital goods industries than in consumer goods such as food and textiles. To some extent high concentration can also be associated with foreign ownership and state ownership. These two types of ownership share common structural characteristics such as high capital intensity, technology intensity and product differentiation.

INDONESIA'S COMPETITION POLICY FRAMEWORK

This section reviews the dynamics of competition policy in Indonesia leading to the enactment of the Competition Law in 1999. The section is mainly devoted to a review of the set of policies embraced by the government as part of its development strategies before the crash of 1997.

Market Opening Policies Before the Economic Crisis

The Indonesian experience with trade reforms and industrial deregulation has been varied over the years. Most often the major changes in the direction of trade and industrial policy have been linked to major political and economic crises in the country. Table 9.3 shows a diverse terrain of competing ideas or ideologies underpinning each policy promulgated by the government.

The major reforms have often been undertaken when an economic crisis occurred in the country. The period before the New Order, the so-called Guided Economy, was characterized as strongly inward-oriented. A large part of the economy was nationalized by President Sukarno and the state

Table 9.3   Trade and industry policy direction, 1958–97

Period and Major Economic and Political Crises	Policy Direction
Guided Economy (1958–65)	Strongly inward-oriented; nationalization; state-dominated economy; strict control over private domestic and foreign investment
New Order Rehabilitation and Stabilization (1967–73)	Moderately outward-oriented, beginning of ISI policy, liberalization of domestic and foreign investments; some rationalization of SOEs; rapid growth (1968–72); large volume of international aid and foreign investment
Oil boom (1974–81): sharp increase in oil price in 1973, second oil price increase in 1979, oil price is the principal of engine growth	Growing inward orientation; increasing ISI policy; increasing of trade barriers; regulatory and licensing regime increased; increasing share of public investment and SOE; growing restrictions on foreign and domestic investment
First external shock (1982–85): decline in oil prices, decline in primary commodity prices	Strongly inward-oriented; proliferation of non-tariff barriers; continued reliance on SOE and regulation of market economy
Second external shock (1986–88): sharp decline in oil prices and continued decline in primary commodity prices, yen appreciation, shock on external debt	Shift to outward-looking economy; deregulation of customs and imports, relaxation of foreign and domestic investment regulations, reduced reliance on SOE and public investment
Non-oil-led recovery (1988–97) – further oil price declined	Further shift to outward-oriented economy; deregulation extended to investment, finance, maritime and other areas; initial steps toward SOE privatization
The Asian Crisis of 1997–present	Further removal of trade and investment restrictions; Competition Law passed

Source: Adopted from the work of Aziz (1994), Hill (2000) and Nasution (2001), Aswicahyono and Hill (2002).

dominated the economy through strict controls over private domestic and foreign investment.

The second period was known as the New Order Rehabilitation and Stabilization phase. This was characterized by a mega political and economic crisis in the mid-1960s due to a collapse of the Old Order, which brought about the major economic crisis. The inflation rate was 595 per cent during this period. Between 1966 and 1970 the new government initiated rehabilitation and recovery policy measures. The government was concerned to control inflation, re-establish ties with international donor institutions and rehabilitate physical infrastructure through the introduction of orthodox monetary and fiscal policies. The government then welcomed foreign investment and gradually emulated liberal economic thinking. Import protection was reduced, though there was some upward adjustment in tariffs to stimulate domestic production of textiles in 1968. The 1967 Foreign Investment Law, and accompanying package of investment incentives, provided a 30-year guarantee against nationalization. As a result, a large volume of international aid and foreign investment flowed in and rapid growth occurred between 1968–72.

The next period from 1974 to 1981 witnessed rapid oil-financed growth. Some saw this era as a reversal from the liberalization of 1966–71. Although real gross domestic product (GDP) increased at an annual average rate of 7.7 per cent and in all years grew by at least 5 per cent, some policy distortions appeared. The regime became progressively inward-oriented, which led to an anti-export bias. The trade regime was biased by the growing controls on investment and finance in the form of investment licensing and credit allocation at subsidized interest rates. Backed up by revenue from the oil boom, investment came heavily from government in petro-chemicals and mining and other capital-intensive types of industries.

The fourth period saw oil prices fall, external debt rocket upwards and economic decline. This period also indicated the end of oil-financed growth. The policy responses came under the banner of a structural adjustment programme (1983–85). Tax, customs and bank reforms were introduced. The government cut back on expenditure, deferred and cancelled a number of large projects and devalued the rupiah in April 1983. However, trade and industrial policies became more inward-oriented and subject to more government intervention. Non-tariff barriers (NTBs), in the form of various import licensing, increased significantly during the 1983–86 period. In mid-1986, 43 per cent of the value of imports and 41 per cent of production were subject to import licensing (Pangestu, 1996). In 1986 the economy suffered a 34 per cent deterioration in the terms of trade and a jump in the debt–service ratio from 26 per cent in 1985 to 37 per cent in 1986 (Pangestu, 1996). In response to this crisis, the government embarked upon trade and regulatory reforms including; (1) the elimination of import licensing for 197 items accounting for 19 per cent of the value of imports, (2) a series of further trade reform packages to reduce NTBs, (3) easing investment licensing and relaxation of foreign investment restrictions. The removal of the NTBs brought down the percentage of imports and production under import licensing to 21 per cent and 29 per cent respectively by the end of 1988.

Two points can be made in relation to trade and industry policy and its association with industrial concentration throughout the New Order. First, trade and industrial policies were by and large directed towards influencing the pattern of industrialization through the protection of domestic industries. Indonesia adopted an import substitution strategy, beginning with final consumer goods and then moving to intermediate and capital goods. The regime was characterized by escalating protection through tariff and NTBs and high effective rate of protection, which biased against export production by imposing high costs on inputs using protection on export production, proliferation of administrative procedures and excessive government intervention. However, successive trade reforms from the mid-1980s through to 1996 did lead to greater import competition (Hill, 2002).

Second, as a consequence of the first point the major obstacles to fair and open competition was the government itself, which introduced a variety of regulations and restrictions on competition, including officially sanctioned cartels (as in the cement, plywood, paper and fertilizer industries), price controls (cement, sugar and rice marketing), entry controls (plywood manufacturing and retail trade), exclusive licensing (clove marketing and wheat flour milling), public sector dominance by government fiat (steel and fertilizer industries), ad hoc arrangements in favour of certain firms (preferential tax privileges accorded to the so-called 'national car' firm) and control and taxes on intra-country trade (Iqbal, 1995). Such policy-generated barriers to domestic competition were justified on the grounds of national interest, revenue-raising requirements, promoting infant industries and the distribution of 'essential' commodities (World Bank, 1996b, p. 45).

Apparently, the development of trade and industrial policy appears to confirm three guises of ideas underpinning development strategy: the dirigiste doctrine, the developmental state model and neo-classical ideas of development. Indonesia's dirigiste and developmental state model covers various interrelated elements such as import-substituting industrialization, sustained by the use of tariff and non-tariff barriers that protect domestic (infant) industries from international competition, extensive state intervention in financial and labour markets, significant reliance on state-owned enterprises and a predilection for detailed planning and regulation (Pangestu, 1994; Hill, 2000). 'Program Benteng' (Fortress Programme) during the Old Order was an important attempt to bring the economy under national control and was intended to support the indigenous majority. Since the country experienced colonization over a long period, it brought a perception that capitalism was associated with exploitation and colonialism. This led to a cynicism of liberal economic thinking and a suspicion of market forces and foreign investment. This interventionist or state-led development idea to some extent continued to exist when Suharto came into power, though Suharto's administration started to welcome foreign investors by introducing new foreign and domestic investment law. The New Order partly indicates a shift from a controlled to a market-based economic system.

The most significant investment deregulation policy to date is the June 1994 investment deregulation policy, which substantially diluted, if not altogether lifted, the mandatory divestment rule that had been a key principle of Indonesia's foreign investment policy since 1974. The approval of 100 per cent foreign ownership under the June 1994 investment deregulation package and the lifting of the mandatory divestment rule to minority ownership reflected a dramatic reversal of Indonesia's foreign investment policy. It made Indonesia's foreign investment policy more liberal than that of other East Asian countries.

Market Opening Policies After the Crisis

Further liberalization occurred after the economic crisis of 1997 when the government was forced to lift policy-generated barriers to domestic competition and trade as part of its initial assistance agreement with the IMF. As a consequence, tariff, import licensing and export restraints have been substantially reduced, exposing local businesses to more international competition in both import and export markets. Also, the commitment to the AFTA, GATT/WTO and APEC has forced the government to restructure import duties in the form of a tariff reduction schedule (Ministerial Decree of Finance No. 378/KMK.01/1996), where: (1) the import tariff of < 20 per cent in 1995 is gradually reduced up to a maximum of 5 per cent in 2000, and (2) the import tariff of > 20 per cent in 1995 is gradually reduced up to a maximum of 10 per cent in 2003, with an intermediate target of 20 per cent in 1998. As a consequence, the average rate of import tariffs was 9.34 per cent in 1998, 8.64 per cent in 1999 and 7.27 per cent in 2000.

Table 9.4 depicts the composition of the import tariff as a percentage of total tariff lines after the economic crisis of 1997. Import tariffs have been substantially reduced and are expected to provide a competitive environment for local firms in both import and export markets. In 2003, about 83 per cent of total tariff lines are under 10 per cent.

Various deregulation measures have been taken by the Indonesian government after the demise of the New Order regime. Similarly, the number of sectors closed to FDI has been steadily reduced until at present only a small number of activities are still closed to FDI. In view of the abrupt

Table 9.4   The composition of the import tariff as a percentage of total tariff lines

Tariff Rate (%)	1998	2000	2003
0–10	72.30	83.12	83.35
15–20	24.74	15.27	15.06
25–30	1.84	0.52	0.51
> 30	1.12	1.01	0.99
Total tariff lines	7212	7293	7540

Sources: Various LOIs (Letters of Intent) and Minister of Finance's Decree No. 96/KMK.01/2003.

depreciation of the rupiah, investment in export-oriented activities would likely become more profitable as these activities become more competitive. Policy initiatives have been focused on manufacturing and trade sectors that are expected to be the major contributor of growth. In short, in recent years there has been considerable progress in deregulating international trade. Import tariffs, licensing and export restraints have been substantially reduced and this environment is expected to provide competitive conditions for local firms in import and export markets. One important 'breakthrough' is the enactment of the Competition Law in 1999, which will be discussed in the next section.

COMPETITION LAW

There have been two competing ideas on whether or not to adopt a competition law in Indonesia. The first is the notion that the trade and investment regime would substitute for a specific competition law. This view has its root in arguments concerning the concentration problem in Indonesia's manufacturing sector originating from economies of scale, smallness of market and government intervention (Hill, 1987, 1990; Bird, 1999). Following this line of argument, then getting government economic policies right ought to mitigate the competition problems in Indonesia. Adopting more market opening policies such as trade and investment liberalization, deregulation and privatization of SOEs would achieve the objectives set for competition law.

In contrast, it has been argued that trade and investment policies are not 'sufficient' and a specific competition law would provide a complementary element to maintain a competitive market (Wie, 2002; Pangestu et al., 2002). In this respect, competition law is thought of as a means of last resort – a method of enforcing competition when other policies such as liberalization of trade and foreign direct investment (FDI) have not succeeded in making markets fully competitive. In other words, by preventing the creation of artificial barriers to entry and facilitating market access, a competition law complements and supports other market opening and competition-promoting policies (Khemani and Dutz, 1996).

Despite the arguments, there were two interrelated imperatives that led Indonesia to enact and implement the Competition Law passed in 1999. These included the crisis and subsequent policy conditionality imposed from 'outside' and the pattern of business–government relationships that have emerged before the crisis and have led to anti-competitive policies being pursued by the government.

First, the economic crisis of 1997 and 'policy conditionality' from outside triggered the government to adopt a variety of regulations and laws including an antitrust or competition law. It has been suggested that policy reforms almost always emerge in response to some form of crisis, whether it be economic or political. The crisis of 1997 ignited a national movement to reform in a more comprehensive way, including the area of competition policy. Crises, at the theoretical level, have 'the effect of shocking countries out of traditional policy patterns (old paradigms), disorganizing the interest groups that typically veto policy reforms and generating pressure for politicians to change policies that can be seen to have failed' (Williamson, 1994, p. 565). The Indonesian crisis was the worst in Asia – in terms of the size of currency depreciation, the negative growth rates and social dislocations – because the contagion process had been working strongly, not just in the economy but also in social and political lives. Another argument is that the condition for successful reform is strong external support both in the form of intellectual help and in the form of (conditional) foreign aid (Sachs, 1994, p. 503). Indonesia had these two factors: crisis and strong external help (conditionality). The enactment of the Competition Law in 1999 cannot be omitted from Indonesia's commitment under the IMF assistance programme, whereby Indonesia was required to pass a variety of laws and regulations and to remove the remaining trade and investment restrictions. Indonesia had to pass a competition law as can be seen from various letter of intents (LOIs) signed by the government of Indonesia as part of its commitments under IMF assistance. Competition law was therefore a response of both economic crises and policy conditionality influenced from 'outside'.

Second, it has been widely acknowledged that for several decades before the 1997 crisis there had been non-conducive business–government relations characterized by the economic rent-seeking between business figures and government. Crony capitalism was observed through decades of government support through the granting of exclusive licences to several key business players that were politically well connected to the government. There was little effective control from the government agencies. The legally sanctioned collusion and nepotistic practices were evident in uncompetitive bidding processes, cartels and vertically integrated operations long before the crisis of 1997. In this respect, competition was made unworkable by the government itself.

Accepting the premise that competition forces firms to improve their efficiency and their product quality and to innovate in order to win competition by offering low prices, more choices and high-quality products and services, people had first talked about 'competition law' in Indonesia since the early 1990s when technocrats, business people and the general public demanded the enactment of competition law to pursue such a competitive market and conducive business environment.

Indonesia's Competition Law was passed by Parliament on 5 March 1999 and subsequently followed by the instalment of KPPU. Indonesia's Competition Law was enacted as a response to quite different objectives and social and historical factors. The language used over the explicit objectives of Indonesia's Competition Law varies from incorporate 'economic welfare', 'consumer welfare', 'empowerment of small and medium-sized enterprises (SMEs)' and 'fairness and equity'. Article 3 of the Competition Law sets four objectives, namely: (1) to preserve the public interest and to improve national economic efficiency as a means to improve people's welfare, (2) to create a conducive business climate by regulating to ensure healthy business competition in order to maintain equal business opportunities for large, medium and small firms, (3) to prevent monopolistic practices and/or unhealthy business competition practices on the part of businesses and (4) to encourage effectiveness and efficiency in business activities.

The Law sets provisions on activities and agreements. It comprises several provisions on activities that are to be prohibited, including: maintaining a monopoly (Article 17) or a monopsony (Article 18); exercising market control – specifically through market blocking conduct by a monopolistic firm to deter entry by potential competitors (Articles 19, 20 and 21); conspiracy for example, where competitors agree in advance on which of them will submit the winning bid for a contract for which competitive bids are sought (Article 22); abuse of dominant position – a firm using its dominant position to deter entry by potential competitors (Article 25); interlocking directorship or cross-shareholdings among competing firms (Articles 26 and 27), mergers, consolidations and acquisitions (Article 28 and 29 of Law 5/1999).

Furthermore, the Competition Law contains several provisions on prohibited agreements, including oligopoly (Article 4), price fixing (Articles 5,

6, 7 and 8), market allocation (Article 9), boycotts (Article 10), cartels (Article 11), trust (Article 12), oligopsony (Article 13), vertical integration (Article 14), closed agreements (Article 15) and agreements with foreign parties that contain provisions likely to create a monopoly or introduce unhealthy business competition (Article 16).

The Competition Law also addresses several activities and agreements that are exempted from its provision. They are agreements related to intellectual property rights (Article 50b), the determination of technical standards for goods and services that do not restrain competition (Article 50c), research to improve the general living standards (Article 50e), activities of small-scale enterprises (Article 50h) and cooperative activities (Article 50i). Another important aspect of Indonesia's Competition Law is that it provides opportunities for the KPPU to review and provide advice on government policies that promote anti-competitive behaviour or inefficiency.

Basically the Competition Law includes provisions relating to both structure and conduct. It clearly appears to reflect the structural/concentration view of competition. For example, two articles of the Law set parameters for the KPPU to open investigations on firms holding a 50 per cent market share or two or three firms with a combined market share of 75 per cent for either abuse of dominant position or monopoly practices. Thus, Indonesia's Competition Law has been underpinned by the structural view of market concentration.

Problems of Indonesia's Competition Law?

The Competition Law has administrative sanctions that can be in the form of ordering the business to stop their anti-competitive actions or by fines ranging from around IDR1 billion to IDR25 billion. It is therefore viewed as a tool to reduce the economic power of conglomerates (big business). The operation of the Law has been challenged. First, many argue that the Law is open to different interpretations as a result of unclear goals between 'economic welfare' and protecting small and medium-sized enterprises. It has a serious lack of clarity concerning its objectives and confusion exists between objectives and the means to achieve them (Wie, 2002). For economists there is really one objective that is predominant, that is, to maintain and promote market competition as a means to achieve economic efficiency and thus improve the welfare of the general public. However, this might raise the question of what the legitimate goals of competition law should be. The social and political goals cannot be ignored in this respect. It is right that a competition law should have clear and simple goals that would reduce uncertainty in the business environment and complexity in implementation.

Second, Indonesia's Competition Law has placed more emphasis on a structural view of market concentration as the root of market failure, which may be detrimental to the consumer. The maximum market shares for monopolies (Article 17), monopsonies (Article 18), oligopolies (Article 14) and oligopsonies (Article 13) are clearly specified in the Competition Law (Wie, 2002). The KPPU, for example, will open investigations into firms holding 50 per cent market share or two or three firms with a combined market share of 75 per cent for either abuse of a dominant position or monopoly practices. For efficiency advocates however, the 'market structure view' fails to distinguish the market power resulting from firms operating efficiently or a government-granted privilege without a clear economic justification. The former was paramount in the case of Indonesia; the clove trading monopoly and national car policies controlled by Tommy Suharto (the youngest son of former President Suharto) are often-quoted examples.

Third, there are unnecessary and counter-productive exemptions from the provisions of the Law. Such kinds of exemptions may impede rather than promote competition. For example, by exempting the activities of small-scale enterprises and cooperatives will only send 'a green light' to SMEs and cooperatives to engage in anti-competitive behaviour at the expense of their peers. Although in line with the Constitution of 1945, the promotion of healthier competition in the market place should take into account the special needs of the SMEs and the need to better protect consumers with a view to promoting public welfare.

Fourth, the Law fails to confront the reality that the principal obstacle to competition in the past (during the New Order) has been more due to unnecessary government intervention in markets rather than the anti-competitive behaviour of private enterprises. As the general explanatory notes to the Competition Law point out, in the past 'the development of the private sector was adversely affected by various erroneous government policies that caused market distortions'. However, the law itself neglected this issue by not prohibiting government from introducing new barriers to domestic competition.

Implementation Issues

Having discussed the caveats of Indonesia's Competition Law, the complexity of the legal structure to implement the Law should not be underestimated. It is expensive to operate both in relation to the direct operating costs and those related to business compliance. There is a risk that the judicial system could be overloaded and bureaucratic resources could be diverted from more pressing needs. Hence concerns over the efficacy of regulation in the context of Indonesia appears to be a major issue for implementation.

The effectiveness of law enforcement may be undermined because of the nature of governance in Indonesia, which is characterized by collusive networks between business and government that allow rent-seeking, favouritism, corruption and nepotism. Past practices involved close dealings between government agencies and businesses, which favour many large firms. Since the KPPU is a part of a government agency, then it is also subject to political pressures, which may lead to abuse or subversion of public enforcement efforts. The general feeling is that the regulation could easily be captured by financial interests. The law cannot be easily enforced due to widespread resistance coming from bureaucrats and firms, which will see their positions of power, patronage, influence and control being threatened.

Another issue is that bureaucratic competency and capacity necessary to draft and implement a workable Competition Law is questionable in a weak governance context such as exists in Indonesia. Lack of institutional capacity and uncertainty over the perceived independence of the KPPU affect the effectiveness of KPPU in enforcing the Law. This lack of institutional capacity has also been complicated by the meagre budget provided to enforce the law.

An Early Observation of KPPU Activities

Established by the Presidential Decree No. 75/1999, the KPPU inherited the office accommodation and personnel of the Department of Industry and Trade. As mandated by Law No. 5/1999, the KPPU is an independent regulatory agency set up to investigate anti-competitive business practices and provide policy recommendations to the government concerning competition-related policy issues. The KPPU currently consists of 11 commissioners with a five-year term of office and a chance of reappointment for one additional term.

During its five years of activity, the KPPU has compiled and published annual reports and conducted special discussions on competition in specific industries. In addition to informing the public, several of its reports have investigated cases violating the Competition Law and others have instigated changes in laws or regulations for sectors in the economy designed to create more competitive conditions. Basically the KPPU can initiate inquiries/investigations based on the reported cases from the general public, its own monitoring and studies and expert advisers. The KPPU may also provide policy recommendations to the government on the competitive effects of specific anti-dumping actions and has done so in two cases (wheat flour and carbon black). Since its establishment the KPPU has received at least 86 reported cases from the general public and contributed to government policy reforms in various sectors (KPPU, 2002). Of 86 reported cases, 49 were received in a single year. The KPPU has also initiated four investigations based on its own observations. At the firm level, the Competition Law has been an important factor in devising organizational strategic strategies. Interviews with 27 senior managers in the telecommunications sector undertaken by the author in 2004 has confirmed this impression.

The KPPU has mostly investigated the reported cases categorized as tender conspiracies (collusion), cartel and closed agreements (KPPU, 2002). Table 9.5 shows the number and types of anti-competitive behaviours that have been investigated by the Commission in 2002. Most KPPU cases have been concerned with tender collusion involving state-owned enterprises or government agencies. However, there have been few cases that can be litigated due to lack of formal and 'hard evidence' (KPPU, 2002).

Tender collusions are not unique throughout Indonesian history and often cases have involved either the state budget-related transactions or the state's assets divestment programme. Sumitro Jojohadikusumo, an Indonesia's prominent economist, has indicated that the state budget has been corrupted about 30 per cent each year. However, ironically, 'activities relating to the tendering process of the state budget have not been easy to investigate owing to weak evidence or the difficulties of proving cases' (KPPU, 2002, p. 12).

Up to December 2002, nine reported cases have resulted in a decision (KPPU, 2002, Chapter 4). The first case investigated by the KPPU related to the tender collusion when PT Caltex Pacific Indonesia (CPI) announced the tender for pipes of a particular project. Initially all vendors could

Table 9.5   The reported cases from the public in 2002

Types of Activities and Agreements	Number
Tender collusions	27
Government policy	8
Cartels	1
Monopoly practices	1
Closed agreement	1
Abuse of dominance position	1
Market allocation	1
Other reported cases outside KPPU roles	9
Total	49

Source: KPPU (2002).

participate in the tender but later CPI changed its tender requirements so that all bidders had to offer both a high- and low-grade pipe requirement. The complaint originated from small suppliers who could not participate in the tender process to offer both grades and felt they were being treated unfairly. Also, CPI did not announce the tender openly through newspapers as required by law. The reports from the public suggested that there was collusion to determine the winner before the tender. The KPPU investigated the case and finally concluded that there was collusion among the bidders that violated Article 22 of Law No. 5/1999. However, there was a popular perception that CPI was not guilty as it changed its tender requirements in the response to a regulation set by the government. This reflected the lack of coordination and understanding between agencies and synchronization with government regulations.

The KPPU is facing at least two challenges in the process of its investigations. The first one relates to the 'misinformation effect'. In most of the cases there has been a propensity to report that anti-competitive behaviour has taken place, when in fact none existed. This has occurred when there has been an allegation concerning a violation towards competition that has not been grounded in 'solid' facts. One case investigated by the KPPU was the suspicious cartel occuring in the day old chick (DOC) industry. The case originated from a report from the private sector (a farmers' association). Five big players in the DOC industry were suspected of violating Article 11 of Law No. 5/1999, although the acquisition was not grounded in strong evidence. The KPPU initiated a public hearing and monitored the activity of the big five players. The KPPU continued its investigations and finally reached the decision that the big five were not proven to have engaged in anti-competitive behaviour. The production of industry is seasonal and its supply is relatively constant within one to two years. The suspicion of price fixing was not grounded in solid fact.

The second challenge for competition policy concerns 'equity vs. efficiency'. The KPPU is more concerned with 'equity considerations', specifically protecting small businesses rather than protecting the competitive process (Wie, 2002). This is arguably misguided in the sense that the law will not be able to achieve the objective of promoting and protecting open competition. For example, one of the earliest decisions of the KPPU was to stop Indomarco Primatama, an operator of the Indomaret mini-market retail chain, from expanding into locations where there were a large number of small traditional retailers (Wie, 2002, p. 336).

Last but not least, an effective functioning of the KPPU would in any event depend on many interrelated factors. Capacity building for investigators and commissioners who provide technical and administrative skills in handling cases is necessary, along with ensuring the independence of the

KPPU. The relative failure of antitrust law in Thailand is mostly associated with 'political and institutional' constraints that have damaged the independence of the competition agency (Round, 2002, p. 110).

CONCLUDING REMARKS

Indonesia is a new entrant into the field of competition law though it has embraced a set of policies towards workable competitive market conditions since the 1980s. The chapter has reviewed the development of competition policy in Indonesia during the last three decades. There has been a long-term decline in industrial concentration, in part a result of the government's wider competition policy. This was in spite of the restrictions on competition in Indonesia's market place that have been associated with a combination of government policies and basic industry characteristics.

Indonesia's competition policy was designed to respond to a range of different objectives and cannot be separated from its social and historical factors. Competition law, one modality of competition policy, was enacted as a response to growing demands from the general public, policy conditionality of the IMF and general public suspicions of big business as a result of the patron–client pattern of government–business relations.

The Indonesian Competition Law contains both structure-based and conduct-based provisions, which prohibit activities and agreements such as price fixing and market share agreements and on exclusive dealerships. It also has several provisions on vertical integration and various forms of price behaviour.

Criticisms of the recent Competition Law include a blurred objective, which leaves implementation open to various interpretations. There has also been a failure to distinguish between various types of monopoly, a tendency to prohibit certain activities and agreements between firms without a clear analysis of the underpinning economics involved, unnecessary and counter-productive exemptions from the provisions of the Law and a failure to address the reality that the competitive problems in the past were associated with unnecessary government intervention in the domestic markets. In the light of these outcomes, it may be necessary to amend the Law and clearly define its objectives and relevant provisions on prohibited activities, agreements and exemptions.

Implementation issues are the most difficult aspects of the regulatory framework in Indonesia. Concerns over 'regulatory capture', 'misinformation effects' and 'weak governance' can obstruct the efficacy of the Competition Law. Capacity building in the area of human resources, budget and technical and skill issues are a necessary condition. The investigations and decision of the KPPU have to be monitored to ensure that the KPPU implements the Competition Law in a competent and transparent manner in order to provide a healthy and predictable business environment.

REFERENCES

ARIC (2005), *ARIC Indicator*, http://www.aric.adb.org.cited 20 November 2005.

Aswicahyono, H. and H. Hill (2002), ' "Perspiration" Versus "Inspiration" in Asian Industrialisation: Indonesia Before the Crisis', *The Journal of Development Studies*, **38** (3), 138–63.

Aswicahyono, H.H., K. Bird and H. Hill (1996), 'What Happens to Industrial Structure When Countries Liberalise? Indonesia since the Mid-1980s', *The Journal of Development Studies*, **32** (3), 340–63.

Aziz, I.J. (1994), 'Indonesia', in J. Williamson (ed.), *The Political Economy of Policy Reform*, Washington, DC: Institute for International Economics, pp. 385–416.

Beegle, K., E. Frankenberg and D. Thomas (1999), 'Measuring change in Indonesia', *Labour and Population Program Working Paper Series*, 99–07, RAND, Santa Monica.

Bird, K. (1999), 'Concentration in Indonesian Manufacturing, 1975–93', *Bulletin of Indonesian Economic Studies*, **35** (1), April, 43–73.

Fujita, N. and W.E. James (1997), 'Employment Creation and Manufactured Exports in Indonesia, 1980–90', *Bulletin of Indonesian Economic Studies*, **33** (1), April, 103–15.

Hill, H. (1987), 'Concentration in Indonesian Manufacturing', *Bulletin of Indonesian Economic Studies*, **23** (2), August, 71–100.

Hill, H. (1990), 'Indonesia's industrial transformation: parts I and II', *Bulletin of Indonesian Economic Studies*, **25** (2), 79–120, **26** (3), 75–110.

Hill, H. (2000), *The Indonesian Economy*, UK: Cambridge University Press.

Khemani, R.S. and M.A. Dutz (1996), 'The Instruments of Competition Policy and their Relevance for Economic Development', *PSD Occasional Paper No. 26*, Washington, DC: The World Bank.

KPPU (2002), *Laporan Tahunan 2002 (Annual Report 2002)*, KPPU, Jakarta Ministerial Decree of Finance No. 378/KMK.01/1996.

Motta, M. (2004), *Competition Policy: Theory and Practice*, Cambridge University Press.

Nasution, A. (2001), 'Meltdown of the Indonesian Economy: Causes, Impacts, Responses, and Lessons', in A.L. Smith (ed.), *Gus Dur and the Indonesian Economy*, Singapore: Institute of Southeast Asian Studies (ISEAS), pp. 25–48.

Pangestu, M. (1993), 'The Role of the State and Economic Development in Indonesia', in M. Pangestu (ed.), *Economic Reform, Deregulation, and Privatization: The Indonesian Experience*, Jakarta: Centre for Strategic and International Studies, pp. 96–132.

Pangestu, M. (1994), 'Recent Economic Development', in R.H. McLeod (ed.), *Indonesia Assessment 1994*, Singapore: Institute of Southeast Asian Studies (ISEAS) and Canberra, Australia: ANU, pp. 75–110.

Pangestu, M. (1996), *Economic Reform, Deregulation and Privatization: The Indonesian Experience*, Jakarta: Centre for Strategic and International Studies (CSIS).

Pangestu, M., H. Aswicahyono, T. Anas and Dionisius Ardyanto (2002), 'The Evolution of Competition Policy in Indonesia', *Review of Industrial Organization*, **21**, 205–24.

Round, D.K. (2002), 'Editorial Introduction: Market Power in East Asian Economies; Its Origins, Effects and Treatments', *Review of Industrial Organization*, **21**, 107–12.

Sjahrir, (1998), *Krisis ekonomi menuju reformasi total*, Jakarta: Yayasan Obor Indonesia, Yayasan Padi dan Kapas.

Wie, K.T. (2002), 'Competition Policy in Indonesia and the New Anti-monopoly and Fair Competition Law', *Bulletin of Indonesian Economic Studies*, **38** (3), December, 331–42.

Williamson, J. (1994), 'In Search of a Manual for Technopols', in J. Williamson (ed.), *The Political Economy of Policy Reform*, Washington, DC: Institute for International Economics, pp. 11–28.

World Bank (1993), *The East Asian Miracle: Economic Growth and Public Policy*, World Bank.

Yonnedi, E. (2002), 'Before and After the Crisis: the Dynamics of Business–Government Relations in Indonesia', unpublished Masters thesis, Monash University, Australia.

APPENDIX 9.1   CHARACTERISTICS OF HIGHLY-CONCENTRATED INDUSTRIES

ISIC	Industry	Four-firm Concentration Ratio 1993 (%)		Ownership of Production 1993 (%)		Effective Rate of Protection 1995 (%)	Share of MVA* 1995 (%)	Relative Capital Intensity 1993 **	Forms of Regulatory Control
		Domestic	Trade-adjusted	Foreign	State				
31164	Wheat flour	100	100	0	0	−33	0.32	4.39	Entry, NTB, price, distribution
31310	Alcoholic liquors	100	n.a.	0	0	74	0	0.08	Entry, NTB
38430	Motor vehicles	100	100	50	0	600	3.92	4.39	Local content
39020	Musical instruments	98.6	87.8	98	0	75	0.16	1.41	NTB
31330	Malt beer	97.8	89.1	99	0	74	0.35	5.11	Entry, NTB
38440	Motor cycles	96.5	96.5	16	0	0	3.22	12.08	
31312	Wine	96.4	81.9	0	0	74	0.03	0.36	Entry, NTB
31171	Noodles	96.1	96	0	0	143	4.83	7.59	Monopoly, vertical integration
31122	Ice cream	95.2	95.2	0	0	85	0.02	0.39	
36220	Sheet glass	90.6	87.2	90	0	5	0.19	1.21	
31164	Processed vegs and fruits	89.8	79.2	0	0	−21	0.18	0.45	
36490	Structural clay products	89.5	32	0	12	53	0.02	0.52	
3111	Animal slaughtering	89	89	0	66	195	0.01	0.22	

Code	Product								Marketing
34190	Paper products	86.4	68.2	34	0.2	41	0.67	1.16	
39010	Jewellery	85.5	n.a.	13	0	−1	0.24	1.62	
33120	Wooden boxes	84.5	71.3	24	0.2	161	0.04	0.43	
36310	Cement	83	82	6	31	−12	1.52	2.89	Price, entry, distribution
36160	Kapok	81.8	n.a.	29	15	−6	0.13	1.02	
31420	Clove cigarettes	80.8	80.8	0	0	123	9.57	2.2	Clove monopoly, price, entry
35120	Chemical fertilizer	80.3	75.5	10	85	−19	2.07	2.84	Distribution, price, NTB
35222	Traditional medicine	80.3	80.3	5	0	−7	0.07	0.14	NTB
32140	Carpets and rugs	78.3	63.5	7	0	−6	0.11	1.6	
31260	Spices	77.6	n.a.	14.1	0	n.a.	0.08	0.51	
35232	Cosmetics	77.5	74.4	57	0	132	0.67	1.76	
35231	Soap and detergents	76	74.5	43	1	386	0.5	0.88	
35510	Tyres	75.8	73.4	44	0	600	0.82	1.15	Entry (lifted late 1980s)
38411	Shipbuilding	75.3	20.6	1	58	2	1.06	1.52	Import ban
31112	Processed meats	71.5	52.7	0.7	1.3	−1	0.03	0.31	
39030	Sports equipment	68.4	n.a.	60	0	3	0.07	0.31	
39060	Stationery etc.	64.6	40.3	4	0	n.a.	0.06	0.12	
31270	Food pastes	64.5	n.a.	72.7	0	n.a.	0.49	1.78	Local content
31121	Milk products	63.1	52.8	62	5.7	99	0.54	4.02	
38311	Storage batteries	62	53	58.8	0	3	0.24	1.58	

ISIC	Industry	Four-firm Concentration Ratio 1993 (%)		Ownership of Production 1993 (%)		Effective Rate of Protection 1995 (%)	Share of MVA* 1995 (%)	Relative Capital Intensity 1993 **	Forms of Regulatory Control
		Domestic	Trade-adjusted	Foreign	State				
37100	Steel and iron	61	48.9	23	41	−1	6.85	5.07	
38140	Metal containers	56	n.a.	36	0	175	0.34	0.47	
35130	Resins	51.2	16.6	3	47	−9	0.06	0.52	Distribution
35140	Pesticides	48.9	46	42	2	45	0.32	0.91	
38320	Electronics	43.3	5.8	49.7	12.6	81	1.62	0.78	
31340	Soft drinks	39.5	39	33	0.1	386	0.46	0.65	
32330	Leather products	38.7	36.9	60.1	0	7	0.34	0.32	
36110	Ceramics	37.8	28.2	25	2	41	0.91	0.63	
34120	Paper board products	34.8	27.5	16	0.4	41	0.69	1.07	
39040	Toys	34.4	n.a.	70	0	n.a.	0.23	0.13	
32400	Footwear	31.2	31	47	0.3	7	3.6	0.42	
31181	Sugar processing	20.7	19.4	0.3	74	55	1.6	0.56	Price, NTB, distribution
33113	Plywood	12.9	12	11	0.8	52	6.02	0.75	
	Average	53.5	41.1	22.5	9.4	23			

Notes:
* MVA: Manufacturing Value Added.
** Measured as the ratio of non-wage value-added per employee to the manufacturing average.
n.a. Not available.

Source: Bird (1999).

APPENDIX 9.2 OWNERSHIP SHARES BY INDUSTRY, 1975 AND 1983 (PERCENTAGE OF EACH INDUSTRY'S VALUE-ADDED)

Industry		1975				1983			
		G	P	F	G/F	G	P	F	G/F
311	Food	64	28	8	0	48	36	16	0
312	Manufacturing	8	71	10	11	7	69	24	0
313	Beverages	N	63	7	30	n	18	51	31
314	Tobacco	1	69	30	1	n	90	10	n
321	Textiles	14	66	18	2	9	63	27	1
322	Garments	N	100	n	0	n	97	3	0
323	Leather	7	91	2	0	29	71	0	0
324	Footwear	0	15	85	0	7	18	76	0
331	Wood products	6	69	26	0	3	77	19	n
332	Furniture	6	91	2	0	1	87	12	0
341	Paper products	37	38	25	0	26	51	24	0
342	Printing and publishing	37	52	5	7	14	75	2	10
351	Industrial chemicals	93	5	2	1	72	8	18	3
352	Other chemicals	4	45	50	1	3	34	61	2
355	Rubber products	34	15	51	0	5	74	22	0
356	Plastics products	N	86	14	0	0	71	29	0
361	Pottery	23	7	71	0	3	50	47	0
362	Glass	22	44	35	0	4	26	70	0
363	Cement	74	14	9	3	49	22	11	19
364	Structural clay products	3	97	1	0	8	92	0	0
369	Other non-metallic minerals	19	81	0	0	12	88	0	0
371	Basic metals	1	83	16	0	36	9	8	47
381	Fabricated metals	15	42	38	6	7	45	37	10
382	Machinery	57	26	10	8	23	34	32	11
383	Elec. machinery	6	51	35	8	3	40	54	4
384	Transport equipment	15	83	2	0	12	66	23	0
385	Professional & sci. eq.	0	100	0	0	0	100	0	0
390	Other	50	48	2	0	1	41	58	0
	Total	26	51	21	2	15	57	23	5

Notes:
G   Government.
P   Private (local).
F   Foreign.
G/F   Government/Foreign.

Source: Hill (1987).

APPENDIX 9.3   CONCENTRATION TRENDS IN BROAD INDUSTRY GROUPS

Sector	1975	1980	1985	1990	1993
Food, beverages and tobacco	61.0	55.8	52.9	52.1	55.9
Textiles, garment and footwear	50.7	44.9	41.1	37.6	42.5
Wood processing and products	51.1	45.1	35.6	32.4	33.2
Paper and paper products	78.5	63.9	63.3	63.2	61.5
Chemical, rubber and plastic products	69.2	64.7	54.4	54.5	60.5
Non-metallic mineral products	57.6	57.4	46.4	46.0	45.3
Basic iron and metal	90.0	89.0	87.0	79.0	61.0
Metal products, machinery and equipment	66.7	59.8	53.7	53.4	54.1
Other manufacturers	92.0	80.0	74.0	59.0	70.0
Manufacturing average	63.6	57.9	52.6	50.9	53.5

Source: Bird (1999), concentration is measured by unweighted average CR4.

10. Competition policy in Malaysia

Cassey Lee

INTRODUCTION

Competition policy became important in Malaysia following the regulatory reforms that accompanied the government's ambitious privatization programme. Sectoral regulation in the pre-privatization period involved mostly economic regulation and this was purely a matter of 'self-regulation' by the government. With privatization, new regulatory institutions and mechanisms have been established to regulate privatized entities. In the absence of a national competition policy or law, a sectoral approach to competition regulation was adopted. This approach to competition regulation has thus far been limited and ineffective.

The lack of a formal, comprehensive and coherent approach to competition regulation also resulted in the government's inability to deal with many competition-related issues that arise from its industrial policy and policy reforms in regulation and trade, as well as foreign direct investment (FDI). This chapter discusses the existing state of competition regulation in Malaysia and how it relates to some of the development problems of the country. The next section of this chapter provides the developmental and regulatory background for an evaluation of competition policy in Malaysia. This is followed by a discussion of policy reforms and competition-related problems in the country in the third section. A brief discussion of the impact of foreign competition on domestic development is provided in the fourth. The final section concludes.

THE NATIONAL CONTEXT

This section provides a discussion of the basic characteristics of the Malaysian economy as well as the developmental and regulatory context within which competition and competition policy in Malaysia ought to be evaluated.

Basic Characteristics of the Malaysian Economy

Malaysia is a relatively small developing country with a total population of around 24.5 million. The country's GDP was around RM355 billion in 2002. The country's GDP per capita at RM13 361 puts it in the company of middle-income countries. The country's economy is also very open. The country's trade intensity (ratio of total exports and imports to GDP) is around 2.3. Historically Malaysia has relied heavily on trade as a source of economic growth and development since its independence in 1957. The nature of the country's trade pattern has, however, undergone significant changes over the years. Malaysia has managed to transform itself from a major primary commodities exporter (in tin, rubber, oil palm) to a major manufacturing exporter. Today the country's manufacturing sector accounts for about 30 per cent of its gross domestic product and 76 per cent of its exports.

Development Policy in Malaysia

Growth with equity has long been the main objective of major economic policies in Malaysia. This emphasis on economic growth and wealth redistribution was essentially a response to racial riots that occurred in the country in May 1969. Following the racial riots, the government embarked on an extensive interventionist long-term development policy called the New Economic Policy (NEP).[1]

The NEP was implemented to eradicate poverty as well as redress the economic imbalance between the major races in the country. In the latter case, specific targets were set for ownership in the commercial and industrial sectors. This was achieved through many means, from outright purchase of equity by trustee companies (representing the Bumiputra [i.e., indigenous] community's interests) to licensing, quotas and government procurements. The implementation of NEP also marked the emergence of large state-owned enterprises (SOEs) to support wealth redistribution in the country.

Another example of the implementation of NEP is the enactment of the 1975 Industrial Coordination Act (ICA), which required manufacturing firms exceeding a given size threshold (e.g., 25 or more employees or paid up capital exceeding RM250 000) to apply for operating licences from the government. The use of the ICA to control entry into an industry was to ensure compliance with the NEP (in terms of ownership and employment).

By the early 1980s, the government embarked on another phase of interventionist policies through the promotion of heavy industry such as the national car project (Proton) and steel plant (Perwaja). The objective was economic diversification to enhance industrial linkages in the economy. Investments in these projects were accompanied by increases in import duties on both automobiles and steel. Not long after these policies were implemented, the severe recession in the mid-1980s brought about another major shift in government policy, this time in the form of privatization and economic liberalization.

The government's privatization policy, which had already begun by then, gained further momentum after the mid-1980s. The redistributive emphasis of the NEP remained an important element in the implementation of privatization. For example, the Privatization Guidelines stated that at least 30 per cent of the equity in privatized projects should be allocated to the Bumiputra community. Since the financial crisis of 1997/98, several projects that were privatized in the 1980s (but subsequently experienced substantial losses) have been renationalized. These have included two LRT systems in Kuala Lumpur (STAR and PUTRA), the national sewage system (IWK) and the national airline (MAS). Despite the extensive privatization that has taken place, regulatory reforms have lagged behind. Furthermore, the government continued to be a major shareholder (via vehicles such as Kazanah Nasional Berhad) of many of the privatized incumbent entities such as Telekom Malaysia Berhad and Tenaga Nasional Berhad.

Industry consolidation, involving the reduction of operators/firms via mergers, has also been an important feature of the economy since the financial crisis of 1997/98. This has mostly taken place in the financial sector (commercial banking, finance companies, brokerage houses, insurance companies), the communications and multimedia sector and, more recently, the plantation sector. These mergers have been undertaken with the objective of strengthening locally owned companies in anticipation of greater competition from foreign companies in lieu of the implementation of trade and investment liberalization measures under the country's WTO commitments.

Regulation and Competition in Malaysia

Since independence, the economic sectors in Malaysia have been regulated primarily at the sectoral level. Table 10.1 summarizes the current state of sectoral regulation in Malaysia. Economic regulation in these sectors mainly took the form of government control over entry conditions (via licences and permits) and in some sectors, prices. This sectoral approach to regulation has continued even after the implementation of a major privatization programme since the mid-1980s.

Table 10.1 Sectoral regulation in Malaysia

Sector	Regulatory Agency	Legislation	Type of Regulation
Distributive trade	Ministry of Domestic Trade and Consumer Affairs (MDTCA)	Consumer Protection Act 1999, Price Control Act 1946 and the Supply Control Act 1961	Prices of essential goods are regulated. No provision for competition regulation
Roads	Public roads are regulated by the Road Transport Department (Ministry of Transport)	Road Transport Act, 1987	Price regulation (toll rates) by the Ministry of Works
	Privatized roads are regulated by the Malaysian Highway Authority under the Ministry of Works		Commercial vehicle licensing (entry) by the Commercial Vehicle Licensing Board and the Ministry of Entrepreneurial Development
Railways	Railways Department (Ministry of Transport)	Railways Act 1991 and Railways (Successor Company) Act 1991	Price regulation (fare rates) by the Ministry of Transport
Ports	Corporatized ports are regulated by the respective Ports Commission (e.g., Johor Port Authority, Bintulu Port Authority, Klang Port Authority etc.)	Ports Authorities Act 1963, Ports Act (Privatization), 1990, and the various Port Commission Acts for each port	Price regulation by the port commission
	Federal ports are regulated by the Ministry of Transport		
Airports	Civil Aviation Department, Ministry of Transport	Civil Aviation Act, 1969; Landing, Parking and Housing, Passenger Services and Air Navigation Facility Charges (and) Regulations 1992	Price regulation by Ministry of Transport

Communications and multimedia	Communications and Multimedia Commission (CMC)	Communications and Multimedia Act 1998 (CMA)	Price regulation and Competition regulation – CMC advises the Ministry of Energy, Communications and Multimedia Entry is regulated via licensing
Electricity supply	Energy Commission	Energy Commission Act 2001, Electricity Supply Act 1990, Electricity Supply (Successor Company) Act 1990	Regulation of wholesale prices via agreements between IPPs and Tenaga Nasional (incumbent distributor company) Retail tariffs regulated by the Ministry of Energy, Communications and Multimedia
Water supply	Water Supply Department, Water Board, PWD	Water Supply Act and state legislation	For privatized suppliers prices are regulated through concession agreements

Source: Own compilation.

However, following privatization, new regulatory agencies were established in a few sectors such as ports, airports, energy, communications and multimedia. While economic regulation (e.g., entry, prices) continued to be the main focus of regulation in these sectors, the regulatory reforms in a few sectors have expanded the scope of economic regulation to include competition policy. These sectors include the communications and multimedia and the energy sectors. The relationship between economic regulation and competition is discussed in the remainder of this subsection.

The energy sector

The statement on competition by the Energy Commission in the Energy Commission Act 2001 is fairly general:

> to promote and safeguard competition and fair and efficient market conduct, or in the absence of a competitive market, to prevent the misuse of monopoly power or market power in respect of the generation, production, transmission, distribution and supply of electricity and the supply of gas though pipelines. (ECA 2001, p. 14)

At present competition regulation in the energy sector has not advanced beyond the above broad legal provision. The Energy Commission itself can be considered to be in a formative stage. It has not issued any specific guidelines on competition regulation in the sector. There seems to be a lack of urgency to implement competition regulation in this sector. This is partly because only the power generation segment has been liberalized and this segment is primarily regulated by the Ministry via contracts (between the incumbent distributor and independent power producers) and controls over tariffs.

The communications and multimedia sector

The Communications and Multimedia Act 1998 identifies more specific anti-competitive conduct that it considers illegal, such as collusion, rate fixing, market sharing, boycott of competitors and tying. The mechanism for competition regulation in the communications and multimedia sector is slightly more advanced than that in the energy sector. The Communications and Multimedia Commission has published three documents that serve as guidelines on competition regulation in the sector. These include the Guideline on Substantial Lessening of Competition (CMC, 2000a), the Guideline on Dominant Position in a Communications Market (CMC, 2000b) and the process for Assessing Allegations of Anti-competitive Conduct: An Information Paper (CMC, 2000c).

At present the CMC is experiencing difficulties in enforcing the competition policy elements in the CMA 1998. While it may be able to assess market structure elements (e.g., dominance), detecting anti-competitive conduct and acting upon it is difficult. This is partly compounded by the lack of capacity and experience in the CMC and the lack of any legal precedence in this area.

Transport sector

Competition in the transport sector is affected by regulations imposed under three ministries, namely the Ministry of Transport (MOT), the Ministry of Works (MOW) and the Ministry of Entrepreneur Development (MET). Overall, the MOT is the sector regulator and concentrates on transport infrastructure development (other than roads and highways) and their regulation. For example, port tariffs and airport tariffs are set by the Ministry with the advice of sectoral regulatory commissions. The MOW is responsible for regulating roads and highways including privatized ones (via the Malaysian Highway Authority). Tariffs for privatized roads are set by the MOW, often after consultation and approval at the Cabinet level.

The entry conditions in private commercial vehicle markets (such as commercial taxis, buses and trucks) are controlled by the MET via the Commercial Vehicle Licensing Board (CVLB), which is responsible for the issuance of licences in these markets. In some cases such as commercial buses and taxis, tariffs are set by the Ministry. Most of the prominent competition-related cases in recent years have occurred in the commercial vehicle market such as commercial buses and the trucking (haulage) industry.

Distributive trade

Distributive trade encompasses the retail and wholesale distribution sectors. The sector regulator is the Ministry of Domestic Trade and Consumers' Affairs (MDTCA). The Price Control Act 1946 empowers the Ministry to control and stabilize the prices of selected 'essential' goods (such as rice, sugar and poultry) in the country. The Ministry also controls entry conditions via the issuance of licences and permits in the distributive trade market such as petroleum retail distribution, supermarkets and hypermarkets. Recent examples of MDTCA's policy affecting competition includes restrictions on the issuance of hypermarket licences in major cities such as Kuala Lumpur, Johor Bahru and Penang and in towns with less than 350 000 population.[2] More recently the Ministry has also considered imposing quotas on goods displayed in supermarkets to ensure local products get adequate shelf space in such establishments.[3]

Mergers and acquisitions

The legal framework for the regulation of mergers and acquisition is provided by two statutes, namely, the Securities Commission Act 1993 (Part IV

Division 2) and the Malaysian Code on Take-Overs and Mergers 1998. The regulatory agency is the Securities Commission. These statutes were primarily enacted to protect investors' interest. There are no provisions in these statutes for the impact of M&As on competition. An important regulatory agency in the area of M&As is the Foreign Investment Committee (FIC) under the Economic Planning Unit in the Prime Minister's Department. Any M&A transaction involving foreign interests also need to get FIC approval. The FIC has guidelines limiting foreign equity participation in companies registered in Malaysia. The purpose of the FIC guidelines is to ensure that the pattern of ownership and control of private enterprises in the country is consistent with government policies. In the past, exemptions have been allowed for foreign direct investments that are export-oriented. In the wake of the financial crisis in 1997/98, the government also relaxed limits on foreign equity participation in Malaysian private enterprises. Even though the FIC guidelines focus on distributive issues, its implementation has effects on competition. Limits on foreign equity participation constrain the amount of resources that domestic firms can enlist from foreign investors to compete in the market.

Factors Affecting Intensity of Competition

A variety of factors affect the state of competition in Malaysia. These include economic regulation as well as the various development (e.g., NEP) and industrialization policies implemented by the government and discussed earlier. The possible impacts of these policies on competition are discussed below.

Economic regulation
Economic regulation is carried out extensively in all economic sectors in Malaysia. Price controls are imposed for the distribution of essential products (e.g., rice, sugar) to stabilize prices in the country. The tariffs for transport services such as taxi fares, bus fares and haulage rates are also controlled by the government. As most of the price controls are in the form of price ceilings, the impact of price controls depend on whether competition in these markets result in prices that are lower than the official price ceilings.

Entry regulation via issuance of licences continues to be an important instrument of economic regulation at the sectoral level in Malaysia. It has been an important instrument for undertaking wealth redistribution in the country. Entry regulation in Malaysia affects market structure directly. The effects of entry regulation on competition in the various sectors have been mixed. In some sectors liberal licensing approaches have resulted in highly competitive markets such as the domestic airline industry. In some instances price wars have occurred, for example in the haulage sector. In others the government have reduced the number of players, for example in the mobile telephony market from five firms to three through 3G licences.

Industrial policy

The Malaysian Government employs a number of instruments to further develop its economic sectors. Export-oriented industrial policies appear not to have raised competition-related issues probably because the goods produced are primarily exported. In contrast, import substitution strategies have raised issues related to market access, for example, in the auto motive sector industry in Malaysia. In anticipation of greater competition from foreign companies, the government has also taken proactive measures to consolidate various industries through mergers as in the financial sector.

Privatization and liberalization

The impact of privatization on competition has been a mixed one. In some sectors such as communications and multimedia, privatization was swiftly followed by liberalization, which increased the level of competition in the industry. In the power sector, competition did not increase, as only electricity generation was liberalized after the incumbent operator was privatized. In the sewerage sector, the incumbent continued to operate as a monopoly. In the airlines industry, the privatized incumbent operated as a monopoly in the domestic services sector until recently when competition intensified with the entry of a low budget carrier. Despite widespread privatization across many sectors, the government continued to hold a significant amount of shares in many of the major privatized entities such as Tenaga Nasional Berhad (power) and Telekom Malaysia Berhad (telecommunications). Table 10.2 summarizes some of the government's existing shareholdings in privatized entities via Kazanah Nasional Berhad, the investment arm of the government.

Supporting Evidence on Competition in Malaysia

The existing evidence on the state of competition in Malaysia has mostly been in the form of market concentration studies in the manufacturing sector. Studies on competition in the services sector have been neglected but there is some anecdotal evidence of competition-related cases in the sector. These are typically highly visible cases that have received attention from the media.

Table 10.2   Government's shareholding via Kazanah Nasional Berhad in selected privatized entities

Company	Sector	% held
Telekom Malaysia Berhad	Communications and multimedia	34.0
Malaysia Airports Holdings Berhad	Airports	23.5
PLUS Expressways Berhad	Road Transport – Highways	20.9
Projek Penyelenggaraan Lebuhraya Berhad	Road Transport – Highways	30.5
Tenaga Nasional Berhad	Power	35.6

Source: Malaysian Business (2004).

Quantitative evidence in the manufacturing sector

There has been a fair number of empirical studies on market concentration in the manufacturing sector in Malaysia. Table 10.3 summarizes the existing empirical findings on market concentration in this sector. Generally, the existing evidence indicates that many of the industries in Malaysia's manufacturing sector are relatively highly concentrated.

In terms of trends in market concentration, the available evidence is inconclusive. While Zainal Aznam and Phang (1993a) reported an increase in the overall concentration levels between 1979 and 2000, Nor Ghani et al. (2000) find an overall decrease during the 1985 to 1994 period. MDTCA (2003), on the other hand, indicates a slight increase in market concentration over the 1996 to 2000 period.

Most of the studies on market concentration in the manufacturing sector in Malaysia have focused on testing the Structure–Conduct–Performance (SCP) Hypothesis. The evidence on the importance of entry barriers appears to be fairly conclusive even though the type of entry barriers that matter may be subject to debate. The candidates for entry barriers include scale economies (Lall, 1979; Zainal Aznam and Phang, 1993b), capital intensity/requirement (Lall, 1979; Rugayah, 1992; Zainal Azman and Phang, 1993b; Bhattacharya, 2002 and MDTCA, 2003), advertising/product differentiation (Lall, 1979; Zainal Aznam and Phang, 1993; Bhattacharya, 2002).

A few of these studies have also attempted to ascertain the influence of imports, exports and FDI on competition. Generally the evidence here has also been very inconclusive. Rugayah (1992) found some evidence that exports and imports are related to market concentration but this has been refuted by Zainal Aznam and Phang (1993b) and MDTCA (2003). Lall (1979) found FDI to be an important determinant of market concentration but Rugayah (1992) found contrary evidence. There has also been an

Table 10.3   Market concentration studies in Malaysia, 1977–2004

Study	Sector Coverage	Period Coverage	Findings
Gan and Tham (1977)	Manufacturing	1968–71	Barriers to entry (scale economies, advertising) have significant influence on price-cost margins. Concentration is positively related to profitability
Gan (1978)	Manufacturing	1971	Concentration is related to profitability and this relationship is discontinuous
Lall (1979)	Manufacturing	1972	Barriers to entry (scale economies, capital requirements and product differentiation) are related to profitability. FDI is positively related to concentration. This impact is greater in the non-consumer industry
Rugayah (1992)	Manufacturing	1978–86	Price-cost margin is related to seller concentration, optimal plant size, minimal capital requirement, product differentiation competition from exports and imports and capital intensity. FDI is not related to profitability
Zainal Aznam and Phang (1993b)	Manufacturing	1979, 1985, 1990	Scale economies, capital intensity and advertising are related to concentration. Foreign presence (measured by ratio of output of foreign-controlled firm to total industry output) has some impact on market concentration. Entry of foreign-induced oligopolistic market structures through large firm size and product

Table 10.3   (continued)

Study	Sector Coverage	Period Coverage	Findings
			differentiation. Import competition and export opportunities are not related to market concentration
Nor Ghani et al. (2000)	Manufacturing	1985–94	Of the 132 industries surveyed, 12 showed increase in concentration, 53 showed decrease in concentration and 59 do not show any significant trends
Bhattacharya, M. (2002)	Manufacturing	1986, 1996	Capital intensity, advertising, and market size is related to market concentration
MDTCA (2003)	Manufacturing	1996, 1999, 2000	Efficient scale is related to market concentration. Firm size, capital intensity and export competition are not significantly related to concentration
Lee (2004)	Manufacturing	2000–01	The propensity to innovate is positively correlated to market concentration

Source: Own compilation.

attempt to link innovation to market structure in the manufacturing industry. Lee (2004) found innovation to be positively correlated with the level of market concentration.

Some anecdotal evidence in the services sector
There has been a dearth of studies on market concentration in the services sector. However, the government's intervention in consolidating the financial sector has clearly increased market concentration in this sector. Other non-tradeable sectors such as telecommunications have also witnessed M&As that have increased market concentration. While alternative modes of transport (such as LRT [Light Rail Transit]) were introduced in Kuala Lumpur, extensive consolidation (the phasing out of minibuses) has resulted in monopoly or duopoly markets in some urban bus routes. These

have had an impact on competition but their cases are not well documented. A few case studies of competition in the services sector that highlight some of competition-related issues in the sector are examined below.

(a) Market entry and competition: the MAS vs. AirAsia case   One of the more interesting cases of competition in the services sector has been the competition between Malaysian Airlines (MAS) and AirAsia. Before 2002 MAS was virtually a monopoly operator in the domestic airline market. With the entry of AirAsia the domestic airline market became more competitive. AirAsia offers no-frills domestic flights at low fares. MAS responded by introducing a new pricing scheme (Super Saver Scheme), which offers 50 per cent discounts for ten seats in every flight in response to competition from AirAsia. This is surprising since, only a year earlier in July 2001, the government had granted a request by MAS for an increase in the fares for domestic services within the Peninsular of Malaysia by about 52 per cent. AirAsia also responded to MAS's pricing strategy by offering lower fares in September 2002. Despite MAS's plea for government (Ministry of Transport) intervention to resolve the perceived 'price war', the government has maintained that the competition between the two firms is healthy. The MAS versus AirAsia case clearly highlights the impact of market entry on competition in the services sector.

(b) Regulation and competition: the Pangkor-Lumut ferry case   Another competition-related case in the services sector that has received widespread media attention is the Pangkor-Lumut ferry case. Ferry services between Lumut and the island of Pangkor are provided by two firms, namely the Pangkor-Lumut Express Feri Sdn Bhd (PLEF) and Pan Silver Ferry Sdn Bhd (PSF).[4] A price war erupted between the two firms in January 2003. As a result, the adult round trip ticket prices plunged from RM10 in December 2002 to as low as RM1 in July 2003. The ticket prices eventually stabilized at around RM4 until 20 October 2003 when ticket prices were increased from RM4 to RM10. There was an almost immediate public outcry following this price revision. An immediate response of the ferry operators to the public's complaint was to suspend the sale of monthly passes to frequent users of their services. The price increases were clearly an outcome of collusion between the two ferry operators to avert the adverse consequences of a protracted price war between them. Both firms had claimed that they incurred losses amounting to about RM10000 per month during the price war.

The government's response to the problem has been fairly haphazard. Following the public's complaints in October 2003, the Perak State Government attempted to negotiate with the ferry operators with the intention of persuading them to reduce their prices (RM7 was considered a reasonable price). This effort failed to resolve the problem. The State Government has indicated that it may seek the relevant ministry's intervention in the form of issuing more licences to create more competition. This case clearly highlights how the lack of regulatory oversight by the government could lead to anti-competitive conducts.

The case raises interesting issues about the potential links between regulation and competition. For example, it is not clear whether the pre-price-war prices (e.g., RM10) were outcomes of collusion that were subsequently unravelled by price undercutting by one of the firms. However, the price increases in October 2003 were clearly an outcome of the exercise of market power by the two colluding firms. It can be argued that a competition law that prohibits collusion (per se) would have been able to deal with this problem. Alternatively, in the absence of a competition law, the government could have opted to regulate the tariff. It is not even clear whether this later alternative is available to the government.[5]

(c) Liberalization and competition: the haulage industry case   An interesting case study that highlights the effect of market liberalization is the haulage industry. The haulage industry was liberalized in 1997 to increase its efficiency.[6] With the liberalization of the sector, the number of haulage firms increased from five in 1997 to around 60 firms in 2003. The incumbent five firms are members of the Container Hauliers Association of Malaysia (CHAM), which had a total number of six firms in 2003. Most of the new entrants (about 30 firms) have formed or joined another association, namely the Association of Malaysian Hauliers (AMH).

Following the continued entry of more new firms into the industry, a price war broke out in the industry in 2000. By 2003 container haulage rates had fallen between 20 to 40 per cent. In an effort to end the price war, the two industry associations met to agree to stop giving rebates (i.e., price cuts) to their customers with effect on 1 January 2004. Thus far the Commercial Vehicle Licensing Board (CVLB), the industry regulator, has not made any recent comments on the industry initiatives even though it sets price ceilings for the industry.

In the above case, entry liberalization in the haulage industry clearly precipitated price war in the industry. Industry associations, particularly the incumbent association, CHAM, have attempted to make a concerted effort to stop the price war. The total market share of both associations' members is fairly significant. The six CHAM members' market share in container haulage is about 55 per cent. It is probably too early to tell whether the industry associations' effort to stop the price war will work especially given the large numbers of firms involved. Furthermore, the continued practice by some firms of renting out their haulier permits to other companies and the illegal trucking of empty containers will continue to undermine the industry resolve to coordinate prices.

Since prices are regulated and the absence of a price war merely means prices are at par with the price ceiling set by CVLB, it is not clear whether the industry association's seemingly 'explicit collusion' can be construed as an anti-competitive conduct. Furthermore, the prevalence of lower prices in the industry calls into question the rationale or usefulness of regulating prices in the industry. Clearly, competition issues need to be addressed together with the issue of price regulation in industries such as the haulage industry.

REGULATORY, TRADE AND FDI POLICY REFORMS AND COMPETITION

Industrial policy plays an important role in economic planning and development competition in Malaysia. Regulation, trade and FDI policies are used to support the country's industrial policy. Competition issues often arise as an outcome of the interactions between these policies. In this section several case studies are discussed to explore these issues in greater detail.

Industrial Policy, Trade and Competition

(a) Industrial policy, trade liberalization and competition: AFTA and the national car industry

The national car company, Perusahaan Otomobil Nasional or Proton, was established in the early 1980s as a key component of Malaysia's heavy industrialization programme. From the onset of the project's implementation, the government tilted the playing field in the domestic car market in Proton's favour by exempting it from import duties on CKD (Complete, Knocked Down) kits. As a result, Proton was able to sell its cars at prices 20 to 30 per cent cheaper than comparable cars produced by other car assemblers in the country (Jomo, 2003). By the 1990s Proton had become the dominant car producer in the Malaysian Market.

Today about 75 per cent of vehicle sales are controlled by Proton (45 per cent) and the second national car company Perodua (30 per cent). This dominance was however, threatened by Malaysia's commitment under the ASEAN Free Trade Area (AFTA) agreement to reduce import duties to 20 per cent in 2005 and between 0 to 5 per cent in 2008.

The implementation of these trade liberalization commitments would seriously affect Proton's (and Perodua's) competitiveness vis-à-vis their competitors. The government's response in 2004 was to raise the excise duties to neutralize the reduction in import duty. The import duty on CKD passenger cars from ASEAN countries was reduced from 42–80 per cent to 25 per cent while excise duty was increased from 55 per cent to between 60–100 per cent. For CBUs (Completely Built Units) from ASEAN countries, the import duty was reduced from between 140–300 per cent to 70–190 per cent while excise duty was increased by between 60–100 per cent.

The above case illustrates how the impact of trade liberalization (e.g., via import tariff reduction) can be neutralized by the use of domestic policies (such as excise tax) by the government to support its industrial policy. In Malaysia's case, this strategy is probably an interim strategy aimed at buying some time for restructuring the national car industry. The restructuring for example, may take the form of a future joint venture with a major foreign car producer.

(b) Industrial policy, market entry and competition: the EON–Proton Edar case

Industrial policy may also create anti-competition problems. The recent case of EON versus Proton Edar illustrates this point. Cars produced by the national car company, Perusahaan Otomobil Nasional Berhad (Proton), have been traditionally distributed domestically by two firms, namely, Proton Edar Sdn Bhd (Proton Edar) and Edaran Otomobil Nasional Bhd (EON).[7]

EON was established in 1984 as the sole distributor of the national car (Proton Saga). The strategy adopted then was to separate the manufacturing activity from the distribution activity. Proton Edar was established in 1985 and it later evolved into a joint venture between DRB and Proton Berhad in 1993 to distribute Proton's cars (Proton Wira). Proton Edar became a wholly owned subsidiary of Proton in 2000 and subsequently began to distribute other Proton models (Wira, Perdana and Iswara) that were previously distributed by EON. In the same year, the ten-year distribution agreement between Proton and EON ended. A new dealership agreement has since not been concluded. These changes set the stage for further intensification of the rivalry between EON and Proton Edar to distribute Proton's cars.

Problems arose with the launching of a new Proton car, namely the Gen.2 on 8 February 2003. Not surprisingly, Proton chose to initially distribute Gen.2 solely through its wholly owned subsidiary Proton Edar. In addition, EON will have to obtain its supply of Gen.2 from Proton Edar. Proton has also argued that EON should restrict itself to selling 'a single brand in a single showroom', referring to EON's current practice of selling Proton's cars as well as that of Audi and Chevrolet.

Anti-competitive conduct is fairly obvious in the EON–Proton Edar case. There is a severe conflict of interest due to Proton's ownership of Proton Edar. It is in Proton's commercial interest to favour its own subsidiary Proton Edar against EON. This has manifested in Proton's conduct to vertically restrain EON's competitiveness by restricting its access to a new product. Worse, EON's only source of supply of the new product is now its rival, Proton Edar. Furthermore, Proton's insistence on 'a single brand in a single showroom' distribution policy is akin to market foreclosure to reduce inter-brand competition in the car market.

There was no government intervention at the initial stages of these controversies surrounding the EON–Proton Edar case. As the above debate became more public and acrimonious, the government did intervene to hasten both parties to sign a five-year dealership agreement on 2 March 2004. Part of the government ability to intervene in the above case is due to the fact that it is a major shareholder in both Proton and EON. The dealership agreement signed may contain elements that should go under competition policy scrutiny. One such clause is the requirement that EON allocates 70 per cent of its servicing capacity to Proton cars. This may be construed as the use of market power by the supplier firm (Proton) to force a buyer firm (EON) to limit the latter's ancillary services to other competing suppliers. This is an important issue given the importance of the ancillary services to the actual sale of the primary product (cars).

Industrial policy can also restrict competition via the promotion of strong vertically integrated structures. In the Proton case, this took the form of car production and distribution. The absence of a competition law obviously exacerbated these vertical restraint problems. If such a law had existed and if Proton was found to be guilty of anti-competitive conduct, it could have been forced to divest its distribution subsidiary. Furthermore, the government currently 'regulates' these companies via its substantial shareholdings in these companies. If the government were to divest its controlling shareholding in these companies, these companies would need to be regulated by competition laws.

(c) Industrial policy, regulation and competition: the steel industry case

Industrial policy can also create significant problems due the linkages of the targeted industry with other sectors. The steel industry in Malaysia is one such example. Aside from the car industry, Malaysia also focused on steel production as part of its heavy industrialization programme in the early 1980s. The two largest steel projects in Malaysia are Perwaja (producing billets) and Megasteel (producing hot-rolled coils, HRCs and cold-rolled coils, CRCs). After investing more than RM10 billion in Perwaja, the then loss-making firm was sold to a private company, Maju Group. Megasteel, in contrast, has always been a privately owned steel plant costing more than RM2.4 billion.

Both investments are protected from foreign competition through import duties and permits (administered by the Ministry of International Trade and Industry, MITI) and price regulation (set by the Ministry of Domestic Trade and Consumer Affairs, MDTCA). Rising demand for steel scrap (the basic raw material for making steel products) abroad since early 2003 had reduced the profit margin of local production of steel billets and bars for domestic consumption. As a result, steel supply for domestic consumption declined, leading to a sharp increase in steel prices. Domestic consumers of steel products such as the construction industry were severely affected. Concomitantly both Perwaja and Megasteel reported significant improvements in their financial performance.

The government responded to this problem by suspending for six months the import restrictions on steel billets and bars as well as exempting their raw materials from import duties. In addition, exports of steel were also restricted. The MDTCA was also directed to prepare a new pricing control scheme for domestic steel billets and bars in the form of an automatic price adjustment mechanism (APM). This new price mechanism is intended to provide incentives for steel production for domestic consumption.

The chain of events observed in the steel industry illustrates the complex interactions between industrial policy, competition and trade. In the above case the implementation of industrial policy (in the steel industry) via trade policy (import permits and duties) and regulation (price controls) resulted in adverse impacts on other sectors (construction and infrastructure). The temporary solution of liberalizing imports clearly increases competition between local and foreign steel producers. However, there is no indication that the government considers restricting exports as a temporary option, that is, until the APM is implemented. There is also no indication that industrial policy imperatives in the steel industry dominate those of other sectors in the longer run.

(d) FDI, regulation and competition: the hypermarket case

FDI has been an important source of capital in Malaysia's development. FDI continues to be regarded in a positive light in the manufacturing sector, partly because most manufacturing FDI is related to export activities. It provides capital, imported technology, generates employment and earns foreign exchange. FDI in the services sector also confers such benefits. However, when FDI in services may be related to the provision of services that compete with home-grown small businesses, such investments are seen to incur some social costs in the form of replacement of these small businesses. This argument is illustrated by the hypermarket case in Malaysia.

Since the establishment of the first hypermarket (Makro) in Malaysia in 1993, the sector has grown rapidly. Today there are some 22 hypermarkets in the urban conurbation of Klang Valley. Most of the well-established hypermarkets such as Carrefour (France), Tesco (United Kingdom), Giant (Hong Kong) and Makro (Netherlands) are foreign-owned. There have been significant concerns on the part of the government that hypermarkets compete with and can replace small neighbourhood retail (sundry) shops. The regulatory climate for FDI in the hypermarket business has changed from an accommodating one to a hostile one in the past two years. More stringent guidelines have been imposed over time such as higher population density preconditions (more than 350 000 persons), local product display requirements, stricter definition of hypermarkets (from 8000 sq. m to 5000 sq. m), and preliminary 'impact on sundry shops' surveys with a 3.5km radius, limits on operating hours (no 24-hour business) and limits on place of establishment (freeze on hypermarkets opening in Klang Valley, Penang and Johor Bahru). This adverse FDI environment culminated in the recent (20 April 2004) five-year freeze on the establishment of foreign-owned hypermarkets in Klang Valley, Penang and Johor Bahru. Interestingly, no reasons have been given by the Ministry responsible for regulating distributive trade (i.e., MDTCA).

The five-year ban on the establishment of foreign-owned hypermarkets in Klang Valley, Penang and Johor will clearly reduce the flow of FDI into the hypermarket sector. Discouraging hypermarket establishment may also delay restructuring of the retail trade sector that could enhance local upstream–downstream linkages as well as improve their productivity levels (Sieh, 2003). The differential treatment of foreign-owned versus locally owned hypermarkets also raises market access and competition issues in this sector. The consistency of such policies with the country's commitment under WTO-GATS is another issue.

As we have seen above, industrial policy, trade policy and FDI policy are intertwined. The neglect of addressing competition issues can substantially reduce the benefits of trade and FDI reforms that are geared towards enhancing industrial development. Lacking a coherent competition policy, the government is, in most instances, forced to rely on heavy-handed regulation to deal with such problems in an ad hoc manner. This approach is sometimes an outcome of the extensive shareholdings of the government in the economic sector. Clearly, the Malaysian government needs to adopt a more formal and coherent approach to dealing with competition issues to reap the full benefits of any reforms in trade and FDI policies. The next subsection provides some examples of what these benefits might look like.

The effects from Maximizing the Benefits of Policy Reforms

The benefits from policy reforms, whether regulatory, trade or FDI in nature, accrue to both consumers and producers. These benefits are discussed in the context of the above case studies:

(a) Consumers and users
In the context of the earlier discussion, consumers gain from lower prices, higher-quality products and greater variety of products. Trade liberalization in the form of tariff reductions on passenger vehicles such as those committed under AFTA would have meant Malaysians paying lower prices. Market liberalization such as those in the airlines sector could prompt competition between incumbent and new firms to the benefit of consumers. The same argument can be applied to hypermarkets. However, as the Pangkor-Lumut ferry case and the haulage case illustrate, competition issues could negate this benefit as operators collude to maintain high prices. The impact of policy reforms may extend beyond the sector to affect other sectors such as the case of the steel industry.

(b) Suppliers
Suppliers benefit from policy reforms in a different manner depending on the type and outcome of policy reforms. Trade liberalization may improve market access for foreign firms into countries such as Malaysia, provided other entry barriers such as excise taxes in the car industry are not raised to neutralize import tariff reductions. In the case of the steel industry, trade policy reforms both increase and decrease market access – import access is improved but exports are restrained. As the hypermarket case suggests, FDI-related investment promises ever more substantial long-run benefits – employment generation and restructuring of industry. These are, however, only forthcoming when competition issues such as discrimination between local and foreign hypermarkets are addressed.

CONCLUSIONS

Malaysia lacks a national competition law. Only two economic sectors have legal provisions for competition law but these have been relatively ineffectively enforced. Without such a law the government has not been able to establish a permanent institution that focuses solely on competition-related issues. Thus, international competition-policy-related issues are either not dealt with at all or they are discussed in ad hoc committees formed to address specific issues.

Due to the lack of a competition agency in Malaysia, the government has not taken a proactive interest in cross-border mergers that has gone under the scrutiny of competition authorities in the United States or Europe. In the Exxon-Mobil merger, the initiative to rationalize the gasoline distribution network has been taken by the companies concerned rather than being imposed by the government.

One of the most significant developments in international competition policy that has garnered significant interest amongst policy-makers in Malaysia has been the discussions, at the international level, on multilateral competition rules at the WTO. The Malaysian government's stance has been to seek deferment of this issue. This response has been influenced by the lack of a national competition law in Malaysia.

Overall, the impact of international competition policy on Malaysia's development appears to be minimal. This is foreseen to continue until either the international community makes significant progress on the discussions on multilateral competition rules or when Malaysia enacts a competition law.

NOTES

1. Even though the NEP (1971–90) was succeeded by other long-term development policies (such as the National Development Policy [NDP, 1991–2000]) these subsequent development policies continued to emphasize growth with equity. For more details of the NEP see Just Faaland et al. (2003).
2. The *STAR*, 'No Hypermarkets in Smaller Towns', 17 February 2004.
3. *New Straits Times*, 'Govt May Impose Quota on Goods Displayed in Supermarkets', 17 February 2004.
4. The information discussed in this case was compiled from: (1) *STAR*, 'Fare War Bleeds Ferry Operators', 25 October 2003; (2) *STAR*, 'Ferry Operator Seek Consensus', 3 November 2003; and (3) *New Straits Times*, 'Legal Advice Sought Over Fare Dispute', 17 December 2003.
5. For most ports, tariffs for ferry services operated by private companies are set by the port commission and/or the Ministry of Transport.
6. The information discussed in this case was compiled from: (1) *STAR*, 'Call to Stabilise Haulage Rates', 22 December 2003; (2) *New Straits Times*, 'Haulage Groups Agree to Stop Giving Rebates', 19 January 2004; and (3) *New Straits Times*, 'Smaller Hauliers on the Road to Overtaking Major Players', 4 February 2004.
7. The information discussed in this case was compiled from: (1) *STAR*, 'Officials Meet Cabinet over Distributorship', 12 February 2004; (2) *New Straits Times*, 'For EON, Proton Edar, It's Business Amid Talk of Rift', 17 February 2004; (3) *STAR*, 'Proton and EON Deny Report on Termination of Distribution Deal', 17 February 2004; (4) *STAR*, 'Mahaleel: EON Will Have to Wait for GEN.2',18 February 2004; (5) *New Straits Times*, 'EON Must Sell Gen.2 in Separate Showrooms, Says Proton CEO', 18 February 2004; (6) *New Straits Times*, 'Proton, EON Sign Five-year Super Dealership Agreement', 3 March 2004.

REFERENCES

Bhattacharya, M. (2002), 'Industrial Concentration and Competition in Malaysian Manufacturing', *Applied Economics*, 34, 2127–34.

CMC (Communications and Multimedia Commission) (2000a), 'Guideline on Substantial Lessening of Competition', Discussion Paper No. RG/SLC/1/00(1).

CMC (2000b), 'Guideline on Dominant Position in a Communications Market', Discussion Paper No. RG/DP/1/00(1).

CMC (2000c), 'Process for Assessing Allegations of Anti-competitive Conduct: An Information Paper', Information Paper No. IP/Competition/1/00(1).

Faaland, J., M. Mahathir and K. Jamaluddin (2003), *Malaysia's New Economic Policy: An Overview*, Kuala Lumpur: Utusan Publications.

Gan, W.B. (1978), 'The Relationship Between Market Concentration and Profitability in Malaysian Manufacturing', *Malaysian Economic Review*, **23** (1), 1–13.

Jomo, K.S. (2003), *M Way: Mahathir's Economic Legacy*, Kuala Lumpur: Forum.

Lall, Sanjaya (1979), 'Multinationals and Market Structure in an Open Developing Economy: The Case of Malaysia', *Weltwirtschaftliches Archiv*, **115** (2), 325–50.

Lee, Cassey (2004), 'Determinants of Innovation in the Malaysian Manufacturing Sector: An Econometric Analysis at the Firm Level', Centre on Regulation and Competition Working Paper No. 60, University of Manchester.

Malaysia (MDTCA) (2003), 'Study of Restrictive Business Practices and Their Effects on Malaysia's Competitive Dynamics', Ministry of Domestic Trade and Consumer Affairs (MDTCA).

Nor Ghani Md. Nor, Zulkifly Osman, Ahmad Zainuddin Abdullah and Chit Yit Jun (2000), 'Trends in the Malaysian Industrial Market Structure', *Journal Ekonomi Malaysia*, 34, 3–20.

Rugayah Mohamed (1992), 'Market Structure, Ownership and Profitability of Firms', Working Paper for ISIS–HIID Workshop.

Sieh, Mei-Ling (2003), 'Is WTO a Boon or a Bane for Shoppers and Retailers in Malaysia', Inaugural Lecture, University of Malaya.

Zainal Aznam Yusof and Phang Hooi Eng (1993a), 'Industrial Market Structure in Malaysia, 1979–1990', Working Paper No. 21, Bank Negara Malaysia.

Zainal Aznam Yusof and Phang Hooi Eng (1993b), 'Determinants of Industrial Market Structure in Malaysia, 1979–1990', Working Paper No. 22, Bank Negara Malaysia.

11. Competition policy and competitive markets in Bangladesh

Selim Raihan

INTRODUCTION

Over the last two decades Bangladesh has been pursuing extensive macroeconomic and microeconomic reforms. The aim of these reforms has been to develop and expand the private-sector-oriented market economy in the country and to improve the competitiveness of Bangladesh industry in the domestic and international market. Questions have been raised, however, over the effectiveness of these measures in promoting competition in the domestic market, especially in the context of the manufacturing industries. This point is particularly relevant when one considers that there is no formal 'competition policy' in Bangladesh. A wide range of policies and programmes do affect the competitive environment in the economy, including trade policy, industrial policy, exchange rate policy, monetary policy, fiscal policy and privatization. To a large extent these policies have been implemented as a part of an overall economic reform programme, namely, the Structural Adjustment Programme (SAP), which was initiated in 1987, and lending from the World Bank and the IMF.

Economic liberalization has been introduced in phases in Bangladesh. After Independence in 1971 the economy was highly restricted. Trade policy was characterized by high tariffs and non-tariff barriers and an overvalued exchange rate, which was supported by the import-substitution industrialization strategy of the government. This policy was pursued with the aim of improving the balance of payments and creating a protected domestic market for the manufacturing industries (Bhuyan and Rashid, 1993). The regime was also characterized by the dominance of the state sector over the private sector in the economy. The regime registered a major shift in the 1980s when a moderate liberalization was initiated in the areas of trade, industrial and exchange rate policies, and privatization of the state-owned enterprises. However, in the early 1990s, a large-scale liberalization of trade was implemented and industrial and exchange rate policies were designed to promote export-oriented industrialization in the economy.

This chapter examines the evolution of the policies and programmes that constitute an 'informal' competition policy in Bangladesh. It also evaluates the extent of competition in the Bangladesh manufacturing industries and attempts to explain the factors that influence domestic competition.

COMPETITION POLICY IN BANGLADESH

Competition policy refers to those policies pursued by the government that directly affect the behaviour of enterprises and the structure of industry, and the overall economic environment in general. Therefore, competition policy encompasses both the economic policies aimed at enhancing competition in the domestic market (i.e., trade and industrial polices, exchange rate policy, privatization, FDI policy and overall macroeconomic policies) and competition law designed to prevent anti-competitive business practices by firms and unnecessary government intervention in the economy. Bangladesh does not yet have a competition law, although a number of economic policies affect the competitive environment in the domestic market.

Trade Policy

In Bangladesh, three broad regimes of trade policy reforms can be defined: from 1972 to 1980 a regime of restricted trade; from 1980 to 1991 a regime of moderate trade liberalization; and from 1991 onwards a regime of rapid trade liberalization. During the first regime, trade, industrial and other associated policies were targeted towards developing an inward-looking economy. The broad objective of the policy regime was developing a pubic-sector-oriented economy, with the major emphasis placed on the leading and dominating role of the state. The expansion of the private sector was limited and restricted. In contrast, the second policy regime was characterized by moderate widespread reforms in all major areas of economic policy. Restrictions on trade were relaxed and different industrial policies were put in place to move the economy from an inward-looking to an outward-looking one. Significant privatization took place during this period. The pace of reforms accelerated and intensified during the third policy regime and, as such, became more open compared with the previous two regimes.

Trade policy in Bangladesh includes import and export policies. In Bangladesh several import and export policies have been put in place under these different trade policy regimes. The general picture of the changes in policies reflects the fact that Bangladesh has been moving away from a 'closed' to a more 'open' economy.

During the earlier trade regime, 1972–80, significant import controls were imposed. The major administrative instruments employed to implement the import policy during this regime were the foreign exchange allocation system and the import policy orders (IPOs). Under the IPOs, items were specified according to whether or not their importation was allowed, prohibited or required special authorization. The government relied upon import-licensing rather than tariffs and the exchange rate mechanism for the allocation of scarce foreign exchange among users. Except for some cases, licences were required for all other imports. The argument behind the import-licensing system was that such a system would ensure the allocation of foreign exchange to priority areas and protect vulnerable local industries from import competition. However, the system was subject to criticism for not being sufficiently flexible to ensure its smooth functioning under changing circumstances. Moreover, it was characterized by complexity, deficiency in administration, cumbersome foreign exchange budgeting procedures, poor inter-agency coordination, rigid allocation of licences and time-consuming procedures (Bhuyan and Rashid, 1993).

During the second regime, 1980–91, a moderate import liberalization took place. In 1984 a significant change was made in the import policy regime with the abolition of the import-licensing system and imports were permitted against letters of credit (L/C). Since 1986 there have been significant changes in the import procedures and in the IPOs with respect to their contents and structure. Whereas before 1986, the IPOs contained a lengthy Positive List of importables, in 1986 the Positive List was replaced by two lists, namely, the Negative List (for banned items) and the Restricted List (for items importable on fulfilment of certain prescribed conditions). Imports of any items outside the lists were allowed. These changes indicated a move towards import liberalization, since no restrictions were then imposed on the import of items that did not appear in the IPOs. With the aim of increasing stability and certainty in trade policy, two-yearly IPOs replaced the previous practice of issuing IPOs annually. Since 1990 the Negative and Restricted Lists of importables have been consolidated into one list, namely, the 'Consolidated List' (Ahmed, 2001).

The third regime, from 1991 onwards, represented a period of rapid import liberalization with considerable rationalization of tariff rates, in the form of lowering high tariff rates, reducing the number of rates and compressing tariff bands. As a result, average nominal rates of protection for all tradeables fell from 88.6 per cent in 1991 to 22.2 per cent in 1999. The import-weighted tariff also declined significantly during this period. Also, the dispersion in tariff rates has been reduced. As a result of the continued liberalization of the import regime, the number of tariff rates has been reduced from eight in 1993 to five in 2003 and the maximum tariff rate has been brought down from 350 per cent to 32.5 per cent during the same time.

The import-substitution strategy pursued until the mid-1990s was characterized by a high degree of anti-export bias. However, since 1985 several export policy reforms have been implemented, which have included trade, exchange rate, monetary and fiscal policy incentives, aimed at increasing the effective assistance to exports. A few sectors, especially ready-made garments (RMG), have been major beneficiaries of these reforms. Reforms have provided exporters with unrestricted and duty-free access to imported inputs, financial incentives in the form of easy access to credit and credit subsidies and various forms of fiscal incentives, such as rebates on income taxes and concessionary duties on imported capital machinery. The reforms have also aimed at strengthening the institutional framework for export promotion (Rahman, 2001). Major export promotion policies in Bangladesh have included the following:

- Export Performance Licensing (XPL)/Export Performance Benefit (XPB) Schemes. Until 1986, under the XPL Scheme, exporters of non-traditional products had been allocated import licences for specific products over and above their normal allotment. In 1986 the XPL Scheme was replaced by the XPB Scheme, which gave exporters an added benefit by allowing them to cash it in the secondary exchange market. However, the XPB scheme became redundant in 1992 as the dual exchange rate system was abolished in that year.
- Special Bonded Warehouse Scheme. This system was first introduced in 1978 for the RMG industry. This scheme exempts exporters from import taxes.
- Duty Drawback System. This system, introduced in 1983, targeted the RMG sector. This system has enabled exporters to clear imported inputs without actually paying any duty or sales taxes.
- Back-to-Back L/C System. The system introduced in 1987 allowed an exporter to import raw materials on a deferred payment basis, payments being effected out of the proceeds from exports.
- Cash Compensatory Scheme. Introduced in 1986, this scheme aimed at promoting backward linkages in the export sectors. This scheme has allowed exporters a cash assistance of certain percentages of their f.o.b. export value.
- Export Credit Guarantee Scheme. The scheme introduced in 1978 has provided exporters with credits at concessionary rates.
- Export Promotion Fund. This scheme has targeted exporters of new and non-traditional items by providing them with venture capital on easy terms and lower interest rates.

- Fiscal incentives. Various fiscal incentives such as rebates on income taxes and concessionary duties on imported raw materials and capital machinery have been given to exporters.
- Institutional development for export promotion. Established in 1977, the Export Promotion Bureau (EPB) has been a leading institution with the aim of promoting exports and designing plans and policies conducive to the private sector.

According to the government the aforementioned export promotion measures have been put in place with the aim of diversifying the export basket, improving the quality of exports, stimulating higher value-added exports and developing industries for backward linkages in Bangladesh (Ministry of Commerce, 1998). However, there has been some criticism that these measures are not consistent with other measures of trade liberalization undertaken in the economy. For example, Panagariya (1999) argues that export subsidies are not efficient and create distortion in the economy.

Industrial Policy

After independence in 1971, the government of Bangladesh nationalized all heavy industries, banks and insurance companies. As a result, by 1972 the nationalized units accounted for 92 per cent of the total fixed assets of the manufacturing sector in Bangladesh (Rahman, 1994). Private sector participation was severely restricted to the medium, small and cottage industries (Sobhan, 1990). In 1974 there were some revisions in the industrial policy through the relaxation of limits on private investment from 2.5 million taka to 30 million taka and by providing scope for domestic and foreign private investment.

After the change in political power in 1975 the government moved away from the nationalization programme and revised industrial policy with a view to facilitating a greater role for the private sector. Under the Industrial Investment Policy declared in December 1975, several significant changes were incorporated, which included increasing the private investment ceiling to 100 million taka, withdrawing restrictions on private sector participation in large-scale manufacturing, allowing direct foreign investment in the private sector and the reactivation of the Dhaka Stock Exchange (Rahman, 1994). Together with the denationalization and privatization process, the changing industrial policies led to a situation where by the end of 1970s, only 19 out of 144 industrial sub-sectors remained exclusive to the public sector. These changes led to a policy environment where the major thrust has been to support the growth of the private sector by amending the exclusive authority of the state in the economy.

During the 1980s the private sector development agenda became more prominent in industrial policies and emphasis was placed on a rapid expansion of the private sector in Bangladesh. This process was facilitated by the Structural Adjustment Programme (SAP), prescribed by the Bretton Woods Institutions, which was initiated in 1986 with a view to expanding the role of the private sector by relying more on market forces and downsizing the role of the public sector in economic activities. The New Industrial Policy (NIP) was put in place in 1982, and was further modified by the Revised Industrial Policy (RIP) in 1986. The thrust of these policies was to promote the agenda of private sector development and accelerate the process of privatization. These were accomplished through providing substantial incentives and opportunities for private investment. In addition, restrictions on foreign investments were further relaxed and in some cases removed. Several incentives were also provided for foreign investment. Steps were also taken to improve the performance of public enterprises. These included the restructuring of public enterprises, greater pricing flexibility, capital restructuring and the setting up of an improved performance appraisal system for public enterprises (Rahman, 1994).

The SAP was extensively and intensively implemented during the 1990s through various reform measures and these had also been reflected in the industrial policies during this period. The Industrial Policy of 1991, which was revised in 1992, re-emphasized the leading role of the private sector in the development of industries and clearly stated that the objective was to shift the role of the government from a 'regulatory' authority to a 'promotional' entity. Furthermore, emphasis was placed on encouraging domestic and foreign investment in the overall industrial development. This industrial policy also stressed the importance of developing export-oriented industries, creating forward and backward linkages and expanding efficient import-substituting industries in the economy. Apart from some reserved sectors, such as arms, ammunitions and other defence equipment and machinery, production of nuclear energy, forest plantation and mechanized extraction within the bounds of reserved forests and railways and air transportation (except air cargo and domestic air transportation), all other sectors had been made open for private investment. The industrial policy also allowed 100 per cent foreign direct investment (FDI), as well as joint ventures, both with a local private partner and with the public sector.

Further developments have been incorporated in the Industrial Policy of 1999, where private investment from local and foreign sources has been permitted in all sectors of the economy except four. These sectors are: (1) arms, ammunitions and other defence equipment and machinery; (2) production of nuclear energy; (3) security printing (currency notes) and minting; and (4) forest plantation and mechanized extraction within the bounds of reserve forests. Furthermore, private investment under Build–Operate–Own (BOO)/Build–Operate–Transfer (BOT) modalities has been encouraged in sectors such as (1) exploration and exploitation of oil, gas and other mineral resources, (2) power generation and distribution, (3) highways development including bridges and expressways, (4) port infrastructure development and operation of unbounded services, (5) transport facilities, (6) water treatment, distribution, sanitation and solid waste disposal, (7) industrial development zones, and (8) telecommunications.

Exchange Rate Policy

Until 1979 Bangladesh followed a system of fixed exchange rates under which the currency was substantially overvalued. During the 1970s only two major devaluations of the official exchange rate took place. First, immediately after independence in December 1971, Bangladesh devalued the currency by 58 per cent (but due to high inflation rates the value of the local currency deteriorated rapidly). Second, in May 1975 the currency was devalued with respect to the pound sterling by 85 per cent (Bhuyan and Rashid, 1993). The government also established the Wage Earners' Scheme (WES) in June 1974 and allowed a legal secondary exchange market to operate with the purpose of providing greater incentives to exporters and to give importers greater access to foreign exchange for the importation of raw materials.

In 1979 Bangladesh moved away from a fixed exchange rate system to a semi-flexible exchange rate system by pegging the value of taka to a basket of currencies of major trading partners (Bhuyan and Rashid, 1993). Since then the depreciation of the taka became more frequent with the purpose of enhancing the international competitiveness of exports. However, the depreciation measures were not sufficient enough to improve competitiveness and the taka remained overvalued during the 1980s.

Bangladesh maintained a dual market for foreign exchange during the 1980s. These included an official foreign exchange market and a secondary exchange market involving transactions of foreign exchange largely from remittances. This dual foreign exchange market allowed some exporters of non-traditional goods to receive a premium over and above the official exchange rate. However, with the aim of preventing the overvaluation of the exchange rate, the government had followed, since 1985, a policy of frequent adjustment of the nominal exchange rate to reflect changes in the currencies of the major trading partners relative to the US dollar. In 1992 the dual foreign exchange market was abolished and as a result, the official and the secondary exchange rates were merged. This helped to eliminate the informal market premium that had emerged due to the multiple exchange rates. It has been argued that the informal market premium acts as an implicit tax on trade, thus causing sub-optimal levels of both exports and imports (Ahammad, 1995).

Further to the move to a more flexible exchange rate, the government in 1994 accepted the International Monetary Fund Article VIII obligations, which required convertibility in the current account. The premise behind this move was based on the hope that it would create confidence in the Bangladesh currency, improve the management of the economy, facilitate international trade and support the process of trade liberalization. Several other measures, taken under the flexible exchange rate policy, included allowing exporters to retain a part of their foreign exchange earnings, increasing the amount of foreign exchange entitlements for business and travel, withdrawing the restrictions on non-residents' portfolio investment and allowing greater flexibility of authorized foreign exchange dealers.

The government persisted with a policy of flexible exchange rates during the late 1990s with a view to maintaining stability in the macroeconomy, ensuring competitiveness of exports in the international market and encouraging greater inflows of remittances. The official exchange rate had been regularly adjusted in response to the movements of the real effective exchange rate, changes in macroeconomic indicators, current account deficits and the developments in parallel markets. The taka has been made convertible for all transactions in the current account, with a view to linking the economy with international markets, particularly financial markets (Ahmed, 2001). Finally, the government introduced a floating exchange rate system in May 2003.

Monetary Policy

The principal objectives of the country's monetary policy have included regulating currency and reserves, managing the monetary and credit system, preserving the par value of the domestic currency, promoting and maintaining a high level of production, employment and real income, and fostering growth and development of the country's productive resources in the best national interest.

During the initial years after Independence, Bangladesh experienced a high level of inflation with an annual average rate close to 40 per cent. This high level of inflation hurt the low-income earners in both rural and urban areas (Ahmed, 1984). There were numerous factors that can be offered to explain high levels of inflation, such as the unprecedented rise in the prices of imported goods, the growth in money supply (as a result of high government expenditure in the post-war economy) and a series of external and domestic supply shocks (the international oil price rise in 1973 and severe droughts and floods in 1973 and 1974) (Hossain, 1996).

In 1975 the monetary policy changed direction, as Bangladesh entered into a standby arrangement with the IMF. With this change, the Bangladesh Bank (the Central Bank of Bangladesh) started to set short-term objectives for monetary policy in close collaboration with the government, through direct controls. Despite the controls both bank credit and the money supply continued to increase at high rates until the early 1980s. During the 1980s measures were undertaken to monitor credit and monetary expansion against the backdrop of the price situation and international reserve position. Several steps were put in place to achieve the targeted growth of domestic credit, and thereby the money supply, through imposing ceilings on credit to the government and the private sectors. However, due to the inefficiency of the financial system, these measures were unable to restrict the growth of broad money, which remained considerably high during the 1980s.

In 1989 the government adopted a comprehensive Financial Sector Reform Programme (FSRP). The Bangladesh Bank, at the beginning of 1990, started to move away from the use of direct quantitative monetary control to more indirect methods of monetary management. Although the fixing of targets continued to remain a centrepiece of policy, the way to achieve it began to change. Credit ceilings on individual banks and direct controls of interest rates were withdrawn. At the present time the money supply is regulated through indirect manipulation of reserve money instead of imposing credit ceilings. Major instruments of monetary control currently used by the Bangladesh Bank are the bank rate, open market operations, rediscount policy and the statutory reserve requirement.

Fiscal Policy

Fiscal policies in Bangladesh are aimed at ensuring macroeconomic stability of the economy, promoting economic growth and developing a mechanism for the equitable distribution of income. The main tools to achieve these objectives have been changes in public revenue, public expenditure and the management of public debt.

In the initial years after Independence, the reconstruction and rehabilitation work of the economy had a depressing effect on public savings. In spite of large inflows of foreign aid, the increasingly large financing gap became the main concern of the government. The situation was further aggravated by frequent internal and external shocks during the later years. As a result, government fiscal policies during the 1970s and 1980s were largely oriented towards rehabilitating the wartorn economy as well as stabilizing it from various shocks. Instead of making efforts to raise taxes, cutting expenditures and improving the performance of the public sector enterprise, the government became heavily dependent on foreign aid for financing development expenditure. This had gradually led to the development of a weak fiscal structure and poor fiscal management. The tax structure was highly inefficient, with more than 80 per cent of the total tax revenue coming from indirect taxes, amongst which taxes on imports contributed about 60 per cent. Since most imports were in the government sector and basic-need-oriented, it was hardly possible to increase import duties. On the other hand, despite higher production costs, prices of most public goods could not be rationalized due to socioeconomic considerations. These were kept low for social equity reasons. This resulted in inadequate cost recovery in the public sector.

In the early 1990s comprehensive steps were undertaken by the government to improve the country's fiscal front. The major target was to restrict the growth of current expenditure to a level below the growth of nominal GDP. In line with the Enhanced Structural Adjustment Facility (ESAF) of the IMF, a number of reforms were initiated, the most important of which was the introduction of the value-added tax (VAT) in July 1991. The VAT system, together with protection-neutral supplementary duties, largely replaced the earlier structure of differentiated sales taxes on imports and excise duties on domestic goods. Steps were taken to reduce interest rates on government savings instruments and subsidies for food and jute. A large number of public sector enterprises were denationalized through sales to the private sector. These reform measures resulted in an improvement in the fiscal situation of Bangladesh after 1990. As a result, the overall budget deficit came down to around 6 per cent of GDP in the late 1990s from an annual average level of 8.4 per cent during the 1980s.

Up to 1990, the fiscal deficit in Bangladesh had been primarily financed by foreign aid with little contribution from domestic resource mobilization. Since 1990 there has been a considerable shift in the composition of financing the budget deficit. Whereas in 1990 domestic sources could provide only 15 per cent of the total deficit, in 2000 the figure rose to 47 per cent. However, an absolute decline in the flow of external funds on concessionary terms has also contributed to this. Increased dependence on local funds has largely reduced the dependence on foreign aid for the implementation of the budgetary programme but this has also increased the risk of an additional burden of higher interest costs from domestic borrowing.

Privatization Programme

Bangladesh inherited a private-sector-dominated economy at the time of Independence in 1971. In 1972 the government nationalized about 92 per cent of the fixed assets in the industrial sector, mostly owned by the

Pakistanis (formally known as West Pakistanis) who abandoned them after Independence. Some large companies owned by Bangladeshis were also taken over by the government. However, denationalization started quickly in the mid-1970s. By 1975 some 120 small companies had been returned to their owners or were liquidated or privatized. Jute, textiles, sugar and 15 other sectors were reserved for government ownership. The New Industrial Policy of 1982 represented a major step forward for privatization in Bangladesh. The jute and textiles industries were partially denationalized. Under the New Industrial Policy of 1982, 222 state-owned enterprises (SOEs) were privatized.

In 1993, following a major review of the privatization programme funded by the Asian Development Bank, the Privatization Board was established. The Board was responsible for the implementation of the privatization programme of the government. The Privatization Board was entrusted with the overall responsibility of privatizing SOEs identified for privatization, whether small, large, profitable or non-profitable. The Privatization Board was composed of Members of Parliament, representatives of the private sector and professional groups.

The objectives of the privatization programme of the Bangladesh government, as stated by the Privatization Board, were as follows (Privatization Board, 1996):

- Improving the financial and operating positions of the SOEs by deploying resources competitively and efficiently. Poor performances of the dominant SOEs usually depress private sector growth. Privatization is a means of ensuring a more efficient development of the industrial and other economic sectors.
- Making Bangladesh attractive for investment by:
  - disposing of a large number of uncompetitive companies, which drain the funds for social development and make the country less competitive compared with other South and Southeast Asian countries and thus less attractive to foreign investors;
  - developing and strengthening domestic financial markets and attracting a larger base of foreign funds through large public offerings of the government's properties.
- Encouraging development of the private sector, which:
  - improves enterprise performance by competitive pressure;
  - strengthens market forces and competition, thereby increasing productivity and efficiency in the economy.
- Developing the capital markets by:
  - attracting foreign investors who are interested in investing in larger offerings and companies;

- building a wider ownership base and thus spreading the benefits of growth to broader layers of the population.
- Creating international business standards.

In June 1994 the government decided to further activate and strengthen the role of the private sector in trade and industry, with the intention of accelerating economic development. Accordingly the government adopted a privatization policy and laid down the detailed procedures to facilitate the process of privatization. The policy was aimed at relieving the financial and administrative burden of the government, improving efficiency and productivity, facilitating economic growth, reducing the size and presence of the public sector in the economy and help meeting the national economic goals. However, the pace of privatization became slow during the 1990s, and between 1991 and 1997, only 18 SOEs were privatized.

FDI Policy

Bangladesh has been pursuing a highly liberalized foreign direct investment (FDI) policy since the early 1990s. The Industrial Policy of 1999 aimed at encouraging domestic and foreign investments and promoting export-oriented industries. The Bangladesh government has been pursuing the policy of foreign investment actively. With respect to the investment incentives or export and import policies there are no major discriminations between the foreign and domestic private investors. The policy framework for foreign investment in Bangladesh is based on the Foreign Investment (Promotion and Protection) ACT, 1980, which provided for:

- non-discriminatory treatment between foreign and local investment;
- protection of foreign investment from exportation by the state; and
- ensured repatriation of proceeds from the sale of shares and profit.

Foreign investors have been provided with a wide range of liberal and attractive incentives in Bangladesh, which the government hails as the most liberal in Asia. These incentives include 100 per cent foreign ownership in most sectors, tax holidays, reduced import duties on capital machinery and spares, duty-free imports for 100 per cent export-oriented sectors and tax exemptions on technology remittance fees, on interest on foreign loans and on capital gains by portfolio investors. Though there have been few performance requirements, these have generally not been obstacles to the foreign investors. The 100 per cent export-oriented foreign investors have benefited from the system of customs bonded warehouses. Foreign investors have also been allowed to repatriate their profits freely, which has been supported by the full convertibility of the taka on the current account. Furthermore, foreign investment has been exempted from any prior approval, except registration with the Board of Investment.

Competition Law in Bangladesh

Bangladesh still lacks clearly spelled-out competition laws. Though there is no formal regulatory body in the country, the Ministry of Commerce is empowered to deal with monopoly practices by firms. There are some important sectors in the economy that exhibit the presence of significant monopoly practices. The major utility sectors such as electricity, gas, water supply, railway, airline (international) and fixed line telecommunications and a few manufacturing industries, such as fertilizers, are owned by the government and they predominantly enjoy monopoly power. The private sector on the other hand, is characterized by the absence of such monopoly. Nonetheless there is a view that most dominant suppliers in the private sector practice collusive arrangements and a few importers in the private sector dominate the market in many products. However, due to the lack of a clearly specified competition law these issues are still unexposed.

There are concerns that consumers' rights are not protected in Bangladesh because of the lack of an effective legal provision. Moreover, no legal entity is entrusted to watch over business practices of private firms. Although protecting the interest of consumers and at the same time overseeing business practices of private firms are not easy tasks. Consumers' interests should be protected in a way so that private enterprises do not feel an excessive regulatory burden.

The only 'competition law' that was promulgated in 1970 and is still valid in Bangladesh is the ordinance called Monopolies and Restrictive Trade Practices (Control and Prevention) Ordinance. Under the provisions of this ordinance, a regulatory body can take measures against undue concentration of economic power, growth of unreasonable monopoly power and unreasonable restrictive trade practices. The ordinance contains a statutory provision of establishing a regulatory body by the government consisting of not less than three members. The regulatory body has the power to make recommendations to the government, to the appropriate authority or officer for suitable government actions. The regulatory body can investigate the allegations of monopoly practices by the private firms and can issue judicial proceedings if required. There are also provisions for penalties and appeals under this ordinance. However, up until the present this ordinance has not been given any effect in Bangladesh.

COMPETITIVE MARKETS IN BANGLADESH MANUFACTURING INDUSTRIES

In Bangladesh there are concerns whether domestic markets for the manufacturing industries are competitive or not. There are various ways of examining the extent of competition in the manufacturing industries: such as through the calculation of the concentration ratios, the importance of the private sector in the economic activities, price-cost margins, import penetration ratios and export orientation ratios. Despite their limitations these indices have been widely used in the economic literature to evaluate the competitive regime of the manufacturing industries.

It is however important to note that there is no updated research on the extent of competition in the Bangladesh manufacturing industries. There is a lack of up to date survey data to construct indices, such as the three-firm and four-firm concentration ratios for different manufacturing sectors. Given these shortcomings, this chapter, using the available census data, has calculated indices for the share of the private sector in manufacturing activities, price-cost margins, sectoral import penetration ratios and sectoral export orientation ratios, which help in evaluating the extent of competition in the Bangladesh manufacturing industries.

Scope of the Private Sector in the Manufacturing Industries During the 1990s

One of the major aspects of the competitive regime is the importance of the private sector in the economic activities. It is generally believed that an increase in the private sector participation in the economy enhances the level of competition. The relative importance of the government and private sectors in Bangladesh manufacturing industries changed over time in favour of the private sector, mainly due to the policy of privatization. Under privatization and the denationalization programme the government encouraged the development and expansion of the private sector in the economy while retrenching the scope of the government sector.

Share of the private sector in the manufacturing gross output

One way of exploring the scope of the private sector is to examine the relative shares of the output of private sector manufacturing industries in total manufacturing output. This analysis identifies the sectors that are predominantly private-sector-oriented in terms of the contribution towards sectoral manufacturing output. Table 11.1 presents the relative shares of government, private and joint ventures in various manufacturing sectors at the 3-digit ISIC code levels (see also Appendix 11.1

Table 11.1 *Relative shares of government and private sectors in manufacturing gross output (in per cent)*

Sectors	1990			1994			1998		
	Govt.	Private	Jt. Venture	Govt.	Private	Jt. Venture	Govt.	Private	Jt. Venture
311+312	17.38	80.92	1.7	9.49	83.69	6.82	5.77	93.83	0.40
313	0.00	100.00	0.00	0.00	100.00	0.00	38.46	61.54	0.00
314	0.05	45.68	54.27	0.00	50.15	49.85	0.00	60.44	39.56
321+322	37.22	61.85	0.93	21.56	78.44	0.00	15.61	82.27	2.12
323	0.64	98.38	0.98	0.00	99.68	0.32	0.13	97.28	2.59
324	0.00	100.00	0.00	0.00	100.00	0.00	0.00	100.00	0.00
325	0.00	100.00	0.00	0.00	100.00	0.00	0.00	100.00	0.00
331	13.13	86.87	0.00	21.05	78.95	0.00	9.34	90.66	0.00
332	26.51	73.49	0.00	25.5	74.5	0.00	6.57	93.43	0.00
341	57.43	40.81	1.76	–	–	–	50.68	49.32	0.00
342	3.37	96.63	0.00	8.07	91.93	0.00	0.00	100.00	0.00
352	83.94	4.65	11.41	98.97	1.02	0.00	90.8	2.35	6.85
351+353	3.16	57.01	39.83	21.64	75.44	2.92	3.31	72.21	24.48
354	100.00	0.00	0.00	100	0.00	0.00	100.00	0.00	0.00
355	0.00	100.00	0.00	0.00	100	0.00	0.00	100.00	0.00
356	5.62	94.38	0.00	5.74	94.26	0.00	0.00	100.00	0.00
357	2.52	97.48	0.00	0.00	100.00	0.00	0.00	100.00	0.00
361	0.00	100.00	0.00	0.00	100.00	0.00	0.00	100.00	0.00
362	0.00	49.2	50.8	0.00	100.00	0.00	0.00	38.17	61.83
369	50.21	44.83	4.96	–	–	–	6.97	44.54	48.49
371	23.12	76.17	0.71	–	–	–	11.36	88.64	0.00
372	0.00	100.00	0.00	0.00	100.00	0.00	0.00	100.00	0.00
381+382	7.15	92.81	0.04	2.35	97.65	0.00	0.75	99.25	0.00
383	9.46	90.54	0.00	11.28	88.72	0.00	5.49	94.51	0.00
384	18.41	64.79	16.8	20.66	70.89	8.45	44.92	54.06	1.02
385	44.03	55.44	0.53	18.32	81.68	0.00	10.49	89.04	0.47
386+387	0.00	100.00	0.00	0.00	100.00	0.00	0.00	100.00	0.00
Total	23.95	69.02	7.03	10.82	82.58	6.6	9.44	83.49	7.07

at the end of the chapter for a list of the manufacturing sectors and their codes).

Table 11.1 suggests that during the 1990s there had been an increasing dominance of the private sector in terms of the share in gross output in most of the manufacturing sectors. In 1990 among the 27 manufacturing industries, the presence of government was prominent in the sectors, such as 321–322, 332, 341, 352, 354, 369, 394 and 385. The government had 80 per cent or more share in gross output in two sectors (352 and 354), between 50 and 79 per cent share in two sectors (341 and 369) and between 40 and 49 per cent share in one sector (385). In 1994 and subsequently in 1998, a gradual decline of the share of the government sector is observed.

The aggregate figures also indicate that the share of government sector in total manufacturing gross output significantly declined from 23.95 per cent in 1990 to 10.82 per cent in 1994, and it further came down to 9.44 per cent in 1998. On the other hand the share of the private sector increased from 69 per cent in 1990 to 82.58 per cent in 1994, and it further increased to 83.49 per cent in 1998. The share of joint ventures remained stable between 6 and 7 per cent during the 1990s.

Share of the private sector in manufacturing employment

Another way of exploring the scope of the private sector in the economy is by examining the relative shares of private sector employment in the manufacturing industries. Table 11.2 reports the calculated shares. It is generally found that the sectors with a high government share in manufacturing gross output are also the sectors with a high government share in manufacturing employment. The general trend is that during the 1990s the share of the government sector in manufacturing employment declined in these sectors, and hence the share of the private sector increased. It is also evident from Table 11.2 that in the case of aggregate manufacturing employment the share of government sector declined drastically, from 24.84 per cent in 1990 to 9.86 per cent in 1994, and it further came down to only 7.43 per cent in 1998. In 1998 the private sector alone accounted for 91.31 per cent of total manufacturing employment.

Share of the private sector in manufacturing fixed assets

Table 11.3 suggests that although in terms of gross output and employment the government sector did have low and declining shares in the 1990s, the share of the government sector in total manufacturing fixed assets was still quite high during that period. The share of the government sector in total manufacturing fixed assets was 59.82 per cent in 1990, which came down to 55.5 per cent in 1994, and further declined to 41 per cent in 1998. The aggregate share of the private sector in total manufacturing fixed assets was only 36 per cent in 1990. That share increased to 42.85 per cent in 1994, and in 1998 it further rose to 54.2 per cent. At the sectoral level it is found that the number of sectors with a high government share in manufacturing fixed assets is higher than the previous two cases (share in gross output and employment). The reason behind this is because of the fact that many of the large-scale capital-intensive manufacturing units are still in the government sector.

Price-cost Margins

It has been generally argued that higher price-cost margins represent higher monopoly profits, and therefore indicate higher market imperfections

Table 11.2   Relative shares of government and private sectors in manufacturing employment (in per cent)

Sectors	1990			1994			1998		
	Govt.	Private	Jt. Venture	Govt.	Private	Jt. Venture	Govt.	Private	Jt. Venture
311+312	23.75	75.42	0.83	14.23	84.81	0.96	11.05	88.87	0.08
313	0.00	100.00	0.00	0.00	100.00	0.00	31.75	68.25	0.00
314	0.15	82.52	17.33	0.00	96.21	3.79	0.00	98.67	1.33
321+322	37.52	62.28	0.20	20.22	79.78	0.00	19.76	79.68	0.56
323	0.73	97.53	1.74	0.00	100.00	0.00	0.21	97.91	1.88
324	0.00	100.00	0.00	0.00	100.00	0.00	0.00	100.00	0.00
325	0.00	100.00	0.00	0.00	100.00	0.00	0.00	100.00	0.00
331	6.27	93.73	0.00	8.58	91.42	0.00	2.38	97.62	0.00
332	17.88	82.12	0.00	32.77	67.23	0.00	5.47	94.53	0.00
341	57.85	39.28	2.87	–	–	–	59.92	40.08	0.00
342	7.17	92.83	0.00	6.09	93.91	0.00	0.00	100.00	0.00
352	5.87	71.57	22.56	4.72	92.32	2.96	4.22	88.39	7.39
351+353	73.74	19.67	6.59	93.18	6.82	0.00	79.54	12.71	7.75
354	100.00	0.00	0.00	100.00	0.00	0.00	100.00	0.00	0.00
355	0.00	100.00	0.00	0.00	100.00	0.00	0.00	100.00	0.00
356	9.58	90.42	0.00	0.00	100.00	0.00	0.00	100.00	0.00
357	3.85	96.15	0.00	0.00	100.00	0.00	0.00	100.00	0.00
361	0.00	100.00	0.00	0.00	100.00	0.00	0.00	100.00	0.00
362	0.00	73.92	26.08	0.00	100.00	0.00	0.00	64.08	35.92
369	4.09	95.32	0.59	0.00	100.00	0.00	0.63	98.86	0.51
371	31.50	66.08	2.42	–	–	–	13.02	86.98	0.00
372	0.00	100.00	0.00	0.00	100.00	0.00	0.00	100.00	0.00
381+382	3.13	96.78	0.09	2.60	97.40	0.00	4.07	95.93	0.00
383	12.44	87.56	0.00	0.00	100.00	0.00	9.81	90.19	0.00
384	14.18	75.44	10.38	2.57	87.81	9.62	3.49	93.84	2.67
385	64.72	33.99	1.29	35.78	64.22	0.00	14.93	81.89	3.18
386+387	0.00	100.00	0.00	0.00	100.00	0.00	0.00	100.00	0.00
Total	24.84	72.86	2.30	9.86	89.33	0.81	7.43	91.31	1.26

and lack of competition. The formula used to calculate the price-cost margins for the manufacturing sectors in Bangladesh is as follows: $PCM = (VA - LC)/O$, where, PCM is the price-cost margin, VA is the value of value-added in the manufacturing sector, LC is the labour cost and O is the value of output. The calculated price-cost margins for the 27 manufacturing sectors in Bangladesh for 1990, 1994 and 1998 are reported in Table 11.4.

It is found that some sectors did have high price-cost margins in 1990 (such as 313, 314, 325, 332, 351+353, 352, 354, 357, 361, 362, 369 and 385), and most of them continued to keep those high price-cost margins in 1994

Table 11.3   *Relative shares of government and private sectors in*
manufacturing fixed assets (in per cent)

Sectors	1990			1994			1998		
	Govt.	Private	Jt. Venture	Govt.	Private	Jt. Venture	Govt.	Private	Jt. Venture
311+312	25.65	72.57	1.78	25.72	71.32	2.96	7.53	92.34	0.13
313	0.00	100.00	0.00	0.00	100.00	0.00	17.58	82.42	0.00
314	0.28	52.74	46.98	0.00	66.72	33.28	0.00	36.20	63.80
321+322	34.82	59.98	5.20	–	–	–	40.70	55.84	3.46
323	6.70	91.72	1.58	0.00	99.92	0.08	4.43	91.89	3.68
324	0.00	100.00	0.00	0.00	100.00	0.00	0.00	100.00	0.00
325	0.00	100.00	0.00	0.00	100.00	0.00	0.00	100.00	0.00
331	30.64	69.36	0.00	15.06	84.94	0.00	4.58	95.42	0.00
332	11.62	88.38	0.00	39.40	60.60	0.00	11.78	88.22	0.00
341	71.98	27.11	0.91	0.00	100.00	0.00	66.72	33.28	0.00
342	0.54	99.46	0.00	3.60	96.40	0.00	0.00	100.00	0.00
352	2.67	66.01	31.32	4.38	86.78	8.84	1.21	78.42	20.37
351+353	97.58	1.39	1.03	99.82	0.18	0.00	97.24	0.38	2.38
354	100.00	0.00	0.00	100.00	0.00	0.00	100.00	00.0	0.00
355	0.00	100.00	0.00	0.00	100.00	0.00	0.00	100.00	0.00
356	0.72	99.28	0.00	0.00	100.00	0.00	0.00	100.00	0.00
357	2.17	97.83	0.00	0.00	100.00	0.00	0.00	100.00	0.00
361	0.00	100.00	0.00	0.00	100.00	0.00	0.00	100.00	0.00
362	0.00	52.61	47.39	0.00	100.00	0.00	0.00	9.78	90.22
369	77.51	17.64	4.85	–	–	–	18.70	73.73	7.57
371	68.07	31.57	0.36	–	–	–	59.03	40.97	0.00
372	0.00	100.00	0.00	0.00	100.00	0.00	0.00	100.00	0.00
381+382	37.35	62.56	0.09	0.00	100.00	0.00	0.22	99.78	0.00
383	39.37	60.63	0.00	0.00	100.00	0.00	7.72	92.28	0.00
384	20.33	58.68	20.99	–	–	–	3.45	96.11	0.44
385	32.51	56.13	11.36	95.67	4.33	0.00	58.21	39.65	2.14
386+387	0.00	100.00	0.00	0.00	100.00	0.00	0.00	100.00	0.00
Total	59.82	36.06	4.92	55.50	42.85	1.65	41.08	54.20	4.72

and 1998. In 1998 it also observed that price-cost margins have actually increased (such as for 313, 314, 325, 331, 352, 354, 357, 381–382 and 385), except for a few sectors where price-cost margins decreased compared with the figures in 1990 and 1994, and went below 30 per cent marks (such as for 332 and 385)

Sectoral Import Penetration Ratio

It is generally argued that foreign competition, as measured by the import penetration ratio, tends to promote competition in the manufacturing

Table 11.4   Price-cost margins in the manufacturing industries

Sectors	1990	1994	1998
311–312	0.15	0.31	0.16
313	0.38	0.37	0.57
314	0.61	0.71	0.71
321–322	0.05	0.34	0.18
323	0.18	0.22	0.15
324	0.14	0.14	0.08
325	0.35	0.24	0.54
331	0.17	0.14	0.35
332	0.35	0.15	0.15
341	0.19	0.22	0.15
342	0.23	0.29	0.18
351+353	0.37	0.52	0.37
352	0.38	0.73	0.51
354	0.42		0.75
355	0.10	0.19	0.25
356	0.23	0.40	0.15
357	0.34	0.41	0.43
361	0.40	− 0.22	0.34
362	0.44	0.30	0.32
369	0.33	0.74	0.19
371	0.09	0.57	0.31
372	0.15	0.79	0.08
381–382	0.16	0.41	0.48
383	0.24	0.22	0.15
384	0.25	0.69	0.61
385	0.34	0.42	0.28
386–387	0.17	0.45	0.25

sectors. The sectoral import penetration ratio is defined as the share of sectoral imports in sectoral available output (domestic output + imports). Thus, the sectoral import penetration ratio is equal to $m_{it}/(Y_{it} + m_{it})$, where, m_{it} is the imports in sector i at time t and Y_{it} is domestic output in sector i at time t. The figures are calculated for the years 1990, 1994 and 1998 at the 3-digit ISIC code level, and are reported in Table 11.5. The advantage with the sectoral import penetration ratio is that it considers import penetration at each sector, thus giving a better picture of foreign competition at the sectoral level as against the figures of import penetration for the economy as a whole.

Table 11.5 presents the calculated import penetration ratios for 27 manufacturing sectors in Bangladesh for three specific years during the

Table 11.5   Sectoral import penetration ratio (per cent)

Sectors	1990	1994	1998
311+312	22.02	17.32	24.19
313	29.27	10.56	1.60
314	1.88	1.04	0.60
321+322	29.47	43.15	50.09
323	0.50	1.91	1.74
324	0.13	0.56	0.31
325	0.44	4.08	1.07
331	7.94	9.83	24.34
332	1.19	0.95	6.89
341	22.60	53.71	49.16
342	12.61	12.36	12.10
351+353	47.27	62.29	61.57
352	12.78	20.05	16.61
354	93.84	–	93.05
355	54.66	74.81	66.06
356	68.87	69.19	78.37
357	64.69	69.85	71.57
361	1.22	3.75	10.01
362	53.66	85.03	57.86
369	58.12	44.22	41.61
371	38.47	32.51	49.84
372	99.49	99.19	99.77
381+382	50.88	62.84	35.82
383	93.68	97.76	98.41
384	49.38	58.60	35.24
385	46.08	27.08	44.95
386+387	97.35	97.68	98.47

1990s. It is evident from that table that in 1998 the sectors with high import penetration ratios (ratios 40 per cent or more) were 321–322, 341, 351+353, 354, 355, 356, 357, 362, 369, 371, 372, 383, 385 and 386–387. The general trend is that during the 1990s there has been an increase in sectoral import penetration ratios in most of the manufacturing sectors.

Sectoral Export Orientation Ratio

It has been argued that export orientation also captures the extent of 'openness' or increased foreign competition in a country, as in most of the developing countries the regimes of trade restrictions had been associated with

Table 11.6   Sectoral export orientation ratio (per cent)

Sectors	1990	1994	1998
311+312	8.27	8.38	8.30
313	2.37	0.50	1.71
314	0.80	0.15	0.47
321+322	32.90	37.24	72.47
323	104.00	71.67	83.75
324	67.62	70.45	33.47
325	2.97	14.63	7.07
331	4.85	38.99	50.22
332	0.00	0.04	0.04
341	0.01	0.05	0.69
342	0.50	0.10	0.03
351+353	4.82	16.53	12.08
352	0.56	0.42	0.14
354	–	–	44.90
355	0.00	0.43	0.00
356	0.00	0.03	0.13
357	0.33	2.11	83.98
361	8.84	14.27	41.19
362	0.57	0.00	0.79
369	0.00	0.02	0.01
371	0.04	0.01	0.09
372	0.00	51.98	2.81
381+382	2.04	7.20	2.40
383	66.38	100.0	100.0
384	0.69	4.22	3.02
385	0.72	0.75	3.85
386+387	15.24	100.0	100.0

high anti-export bias (Bhagwati, 1978; Krueger, 1978). The sectoral export orientation ratio is defined as the share of sectoral exports in sectoral output at the 3-digit ISIC code level. Therefore, sectoral export orientation ratio is equal to x_{it}/Y_{it}, where, x_{it} is exports from sector i at time t, and Y_{it} is sectoral output.

Table 11.6 presents the calculated export orientation ratios for the 27 manufacturing sectors in Bangladesh. It is found that in 1990 only four sectors (such as 323, 324, 354 and 383) were export-orientated sectors (exporting 40 per cent or higher of their output). But in 1998 this number increased to eight with the sectors, such as 321–322, 323, 331, 354, 357, 361, 383 and 386–387 exporting at least 40 per cent of their output. Export orientation in other sectors has remained minimal.

FACTORS INFLUENCING DOMESTIC COMPETITION IN BANGLADESH MANUFACTURING INDUSTRIES: A MODEL OF PRICE-COST MARGINS

Several factors can be identified that influence domestic competition in Bangladesh manufacturing industries. In this chapter the price-cost margin has been considered as an indicator of domestic competition. A multivariate panel econometric model has been built to explain the variation in the price-cost margin in Bangladesh manufacturing industries. The proposed model of price-cost margins is as follows:

$$PCM = \beta_0 + \beta_1(K/L) + \beta_2 MO + \beta_3 EO + \varepsilon$$

where the price-cost margin is a function of variables that reflect the competitiveness of the industry such as the import penetration ratio (MO) and the export orientation ratio (EO). Industries' capital–labour ratio (K/L) has been specified as a control variable in the model. Finally, ε is the error term.

The relationship between capital intensity and the price-cost margin is argued to be positive. It is generally argued that higher capital-intensive manufacturing firms tend to be more monopolistic. On the other hand, the labour-intensive firms tend to behave more competitively.

The relationship between import penetration and the price-cost margin is not well established. It has been argued by Urata (1984) that the relationship between import penetration and the price-cost margin can be negative if each domestic firm believes that the foreign firm does not react to its output change (Cournot behaviour). But the relationship can be positive if each domestic firm believes that only foreign firms react to maintain their market share (perfect collusion). However, import penetration does not have any impact on the price-cost margin if all domestic and foreign firms react to maintain their market share.

There are conflicting hypotheses on the relationship between export orientation and profitability (Caves, 1985). Export activities can help in promoting competitive power of the domestic industry by pressurizing the non-competitive sectors to behave in a competitive way. However, a domestic monopoly that is less exposed to import competition and has relatively lower cost may export at world prices and exploit market power in the domestic market (Yalchin, 2000).

Data Analysis: Non-stationary Panel Data and Panel Cointegration

The panel estimation of the model for price-cost margins in the context of Bangladesh manufacturing industries requires data for price-cost margins, fixed assets, labour input, sectoral import penetration ratios and sectoral export orientation ratios. Data for the first three variables have been calculated at the 3-digit ISIC (International Standard Industrial Classification) code level for 27 sectors with a time span of 22 years. Sources of data are the Census of Manufacturing Industries (CMI) of Bangladesh (various years) and World Bank (2001). The figures for the sectoral import penetration ratio and the sectoral export orientation ratio have been calculated from the data at the 3-digit level available from the CMI and World Bank (2001).

Since this study uses a panel database with a substantial time span (22 years), it is necessary to check the stationarity of the variables under consideration. It has been suggested that if there is a considerable longer time span in a panel dataset then the variables under consideration might be non-stationary and thus a simple OLS estimation may end up with spurious regression results (Kao, 1999; Kao, Chiang and Chen, 1999; McCoskey and Kao, 1999). The stationarity of the panel variables can be checked by applying panel unit root tests. The leading papers comprising testing for unit roots in panel regression models are those by Levin and Lin (1992, 1993); Im, Pesaran and Shin (1997); Harris and Tzavalis (1999); Maddala and Wu (1999); Hadri (2000) and Breitung (2000). In this study the Im, Pesaran and Shin (1997), known as IPS for short, panel unit root test is applied to check the stationarity of the variables under consideration. The IPS (1997) test is based on averaging individual ADF tests statistics when the error terms are serially correlated with the different serial correlation coefficients across cross-sectional units. The results of the IPS tests are reported in Table 11.7.

The test results of Table 11.7 suggest that for the variable ln*PCM*, the IPS (1997) tests are conclusive. Both the two tests of IPS (1997) confirm the

Table 11.7   Im, Pesaran and Shin (1997) unit root tests on levels of variables

Tests	ln*PCM*	ln(*K*/*L*)	ln*MO*	ln*EO*
IPS (1997)				
Without time trend	− 0.274	− 1.123	− 0.133	0.390
	(0.391)	(0.130)	(0.446)	(0.348)
With time trend	− 0.604	− 0.386	− 0.331	0.425
	(0.272)	(0.557)	(0.556)	(0.275)

Notes:
(a) *PCM* = price-cost margins, *K*/*L* = capital–labour ratio, *MO* = sectoral import penetration ratio, *EO* = sectoral export orientation ratio.
(b) The critical probabilities are reported in parentheses.

presence of unit roots. In the case of $\ln(K/L)$, two tests of IPS (1997) provide conclusive evidence in favour of the presence of unit roots. For $\ln MO$ and $\ln EO$, the IPS (1997) test results provide clear evidence of the presence of unit roots. It is therefore concluded that all the variables under consideration are non-stationary. The order of integration of the non-stationary variables is also checked by applying the IPS (1997) unit root test on the first difference of the variables. The order of integration of the non-stationary variables is important because if variables are of a different order of integration then special care is needed to find out the valid relationship among those variables. It is found that the variables are stationary on their first differences, that is, they are I(1).

When all the variables in the model are stationary then traditional methods can be used to estimate the model. If, however, at least one of the series turns out to be non-stationary then more care is needed. In this case, to infer the long-run relationships among the variables some form of co-integration analysis is required. Cointegration techniques in time-series analysis are well established. However, similar to the unit root tests in panel regression, cointegration tests in panel data are relatively new. The leading papers in panel cointegration tests are Kao and Chiang (1998); McCoskey and Kao, 1998); Kao (1999) and Pedroni (1995, 1999). The Kao (1999) tests for panel cointegration are applied to the models under consideration.

Kao (1999) explores the spurious panel regression model and examines the asymptotic properties of the least-squares dummy variable (LSDV) estimator. Kao presents residual-based tests for cointegration in panel data using the Dickey–Fuller (DF) and the augmented Dickey–Fuller (ADF) type tests, deriving the asymptotic distributions for the tests. Table 11.8 reports the results of the Kao (1999) cointegration tests for the regression model.

Table 11.8   Kao (1999) cointegration tests for the regression model

Tests	The Model
DF_ρ	$-7.75\ (0.000)$
DF_t	$-5.23\ (0.000)$
DF_ρ^*	$-17.83\ (0.000)$
DF_t^*	$-5.86\ (0.000)$
ADF	$-4.632\ (0.000)$

Notes:
(a) The null hypothesis is 'no cointegration'.
(b) The critical probabilities are reported in parentheses.
(c) Cointegration tests statistics are calculated through the residuals from the OLS estimation.

It appears that the test results for regression the model show conclusive evidence for rejecting the null hypotheses of 'no cointegration'. It is therefore concluded that the model is cointegrated.

Estimation of the Model

In panel econometrics, one convenient way of modelling the long-run and short-run effects, without imposing any restriction on the relationship between the short-run and long-run responses, is through the use of an 'unrestricted error correction mechanism' (UECM) model (Alogoskoufis and Smith, 1991; Banerjee et al., 1993; Reilly and Witt, 1996). The estimation results of the model are reported in Table 11.9.

It is evident from Table 11.9 that the coefficient on the error correction term ($\ln PCM_{it-1}$) has the correct sign, is highly significant and lower than 1 (in absolute value), thus confirming a valid representation of the error correction mechanism. The coefficient on the error correction term (ECT) suggests a rather slow adjustment to the long-run steady state relationship from any short-run deviation as 33 per cent of the disequilibrium errors are corrected within just one year.

It also appears from Table 11.9 that the short-run coefficients of all the explanatory variables (the first differences of the variables) are not

Table 11.9   Unrestricted error correction mechanism for the model

Dependent variable: $\Delta \ln PCM_{it}$	
Explanatory variables	Coefficients
Constant	-0.352^{***} (0.092)
$\ln PCM_{it-1}$	-0.330^{***} (0.034)
$\Delta \ln(K/L)_{it}$	0.026 (0.024)
$\ln(K/L)_{it-1}$	0.045^{**} (0.022)
$\Delta \ln MO_{it}$	-0.006 (0.008)
$\ln MO_{it-1}$	-0.012^{*} (0.023)
$\Delta \ln EO_{it}$	0.014 (0.016)
$\ln EO_{it-1}$	0.031^{*} (0.026)
Industry fixed effect, (χ^2, df = 47)	Yes (2.86^{**})
Time effect, (χ^2, df = 20)	Yes (85.85^{**})
R^2 (adjusted)	0.38
Observations	567

Notes:
(a) ***, ** and * indicate statistical significance at the 1, 5 and 10 per cent respectively.
(b) Hypotheses relating to fixed and time effects were tested using likelihood ratio tests.
(c) Figures in parentheses indicate standard errors.

statistically significant. However, the long-run coefficients on all the variables are statistically significant. To derive the value of the long-run coefficients for the variables the following formulation of the unrestricted error correction mechanism has been used:

$$LRC = -\frac{LAG}{ECT}$$

where LRC = long-run coefficient, LAG = coefficient on the lagged explanatory variable, and ECT = coefficient on the error correction term. Table 11.10 reports the estimated long-run elasticities of the model.

The results in Tables 11.9 and 11.10 suggest that in the short run the effect of capital intensity (the capital–labour ratio) on the price-cost margin is not statistically significant. However, in the long run the capital intensity exerts a positive impact on the price-cost margin, implying that the higher the capital intensity of the manufacturing firms the higher will be the price-cost margin and the lower will be the degree of competition. This suggests that capital-intensive firms tend to be more monopolistic, whereas the labour-intensive firms tend to be on more competitive markets.

The short-run impact of the sectoral import penetration ratio on the price-cost margin is negative but is not statistically significant. In the long run, however, the negative relationship between the sectoral import penetration ratio and the price-cost margin is statistically significant. This suggests that in the long run higher import penetration tends to reduce the price-cost margin in the Bangladesh manufacturing industries. This confirms the hypothesis that increased foreign competition tends to promote increased domestic competition.

With respect to the sectoral export orientation ratio it is observed that the short-run impact is not statistically significant. But interestingly, the long-run impact on the price-cost margin is positive and statistically significant. This finding suggests that in the long run the higher the degree of sectoral export orientation tends to increase the price-cost margin in the manufacturing industries in Bangladesh. One explanation behind such an apparent paradox could be that the export basket in Bangladesh is quite

Table 11.10 Long-run elasticities of the explanatory variables

Variables	Long-run Elasticities
K/L	0.136
MO	0.027
EO	0.093

narrowly based and one sector, the ready-made garment (RMG) sector, constitutes about 80 per cent of the total export earnings. The outstanding performance of the RMG sector is significantly facilitated by the quota and GSP facilities in the United States (US) and European Union (EU) markets, which did not in fact promote competition in this sector.

CONCLUSION

This chapter has reviewed various policies and programmes relating to competition policy in Bangladesh. It is observed that a range of policies have been put in place to promote competition in the economy but a formal competition law has not been enacted. The examination on the manufacturing industries shows that during the 1990s there was an expansion of the private sector and a contraction of the state sector in the economy. The panel econometric model on the price-cost margin in the manufacturing sector indicates that higher capital intensity has tended to reduce the degree of domestic competition in the long run. Furthermore, increased foreign competition, as measured by the import penetration ratio, has tended to increase the degree of domestic competition. But increased sectoral export orientation has tended to increase the price-cost margin in the long run.

REFERENCES

Ahammad, H. (1995), *Foreign Exchange and Trade Policy Issues in a Developing Country: The Case of Bangladesh*, Aldershot: Avebury.

Ahmed, S. (1984), 'Inflation in Bangladesh: Causes and Consequences', PhD dissertation, Boston University.

Ahmed, N. (2001), *Trade Liberalization in Bangladesh*, Dhaka: University Press Ltd.

Alogoskoufis, G. and R. Smith (1991), 'On Error-correction Models', *Journal of Economic Surveys*, **5**, 97–128.

Banerjee, A., J.J. Dolado, J.W. Galbraith and D.F. Hendry (1993), *Cointegration, Error-correction, and the Econometric Analysis of Non-stationary Data*, Oxford University Press.

Bhagwati, J. (1978), *Foreign Trade Regimes and Economic Development: Anatomy and Consequences of Exchange Control Regimes*, Cambridge, MA: Ballinger.

Bhuyan, A.R. and M.A. Rashid (1993), *Trade Regimes and Industrial Growth: A Case Study of Bangladesh*, Dhaka: Bureau of Economic Research, University of Dhaka.

Breitung, J. (2000), 'The Local Power of Some Unit Root Tests for Panel Data', *Advances in Econometrics*, **15**, 161–78.

Caves, R. (1985), 'International Trade and Industrial Organization: Problem Solved and Unsolved', *European Economic Review*, **28**, 377–95.

Hadri, K. (2000), 'Testing for Stationarity in Heterogeneous Panel Data', *Econometrics Journal*, **3** (2), 148–61.

Harris, R.D.F. and E. Tzavalis (1999), 'Inference for Unit Roots in Dynamic Panels where the Time Dimension is Fixed', *Journal of Econometrics*, **91**, 201–26.

Hossain, A. (1996), *Macroeconomic Issues and Policies: The Case of Bangladesh*, New Delhi: Sage Publications.

Im, K.S., M.H. Pesaran and Y. Shin (1997), 'Testing for Unit Roots in Heterogeneous Panels', mimeo, Department of Applied Economics, University of Cambridge.

Kao, C. (1999), 'Spurious Regression and Residual-based Tests for Cointegration in Panel Data', *Journal of Econometrics*, **90**, 1–44.

Kao, C. and M. Chiang (1998), 'On the Estimation and Inference of a Cointegrated Regression in Panel Data', mimeo, Center for Policy Research, Syracuse University.

Kao, C., M. Chiang and B. Chen (1999), 'International R&D Spillovers: An Application of Estimation and Inference in Panel Cointegration', *Oxford Bulletin of Economics and Statistics*, Special Issue, 691–709.

Krueger, A.O. (1978), *Foreign Trade Regimes and Economic Development: Liberalization Attempts and Consequences*, Cambridge, MA: Ballinger.

Levin, A. and C.F. Lin (1992), 'Unit Root Tests in Panel Data: Asymptotic and Finite Sample Properties', Department of Economics, University of California at San Diego, Discussion Paper No. 92–93 (revised 1993).

Levin, A. and C.F. Lin (1993), 'Unit Root Tests in Panel Data: New Results', Department of Economics, University of California at San Diego, Discussion Paper No. 93–56.

Maddala, G.S. and S. Wu (1999), 'A Comparative Study of Unit Root Tests with Panel Data and a New Simple Test', *Oxford Bulletin of Economics and Statistics*, Special Issue, 631–53.

McCoskey, S. and C. Kao (1998), 'A Residual-based Test of the Null of Cointegration in Panel Data', *Econometric Reviews*, **17**, 57–84.

McCoskey, S. and C. Kao (1999), 'Testing the Stability of a Production Function with Urbanization as a Shift Factor', *Oxford Bulletin of Economics and Statistics*, Special Issue, 671–90.

Ministry of Commerce (1998), *The Export Policy Order 1997–2002*, Dhaka, Bangladesh.

Panagariya, A. (1999), 'Evaluating the Case for Export Subsidies', mimeo, Department of Economics, University of Maryland, College Park.

Pedroni, P. (1995), 'Panel Cointegration: Asymptotic and Finite Sample Properties of Pooled Time Series Tests with an Application to the PPP Hypothesis', Indiana University Working Papers in Economics No. 95–013.

Pedroni, P. (1999), 'Critical Values for Cointegration Tests in Heterogeneous Panels with Multiple Regressors', *Oxford Bulletin of Economics and Statistics*, **61**, 663–78.

Privatization Board (1996), *Privatization Policy*, September, Dhaka.

Rahman, S.H. (1994), 'Trade and Industrialization in Bangladesh: An Assessment', in G.K. Helleiner (ed.), *Trade Policy and Industrialization in Turbulent Times*, London and New York: Routledge.

Rahman, S.M. (2001), 'A Computable General Equilibrium Analysis of Alternative Economic Policy Strategies for Agriculture in Bangladesh', unpublished PhD dissertation, University of Manchester.

Reilly, B. and R. Witt (1996), 'Crime, Deterrence, and Unemployment in England and Wales: An Empirical Analysis', *Bulletin of Economic Research*, **48**, 137–55.

Sobhan, R. (1990), 'The Political Economy of South Asian Economic Cooperation', *Bangladesh Journal of Political Economy*, **10** (1), 26–48.

Urata, S. (1984), 'Price-cost Margins and Imports in an Oligopolistic Market', *Economic Letters,* **15**, 139–44.

World Bank (2001), *Trade and Production Database*, World Bank, Washington.

Yalchin, C. (2000), 'Price-cost Margins and Trade Liberalization in the Turkish Manufacturing Industry: A Panel Data Analysis', mimeo.

APPENDIX 11.1 LIST OF THE MANUFACTURING SECTORS UNDER THE 3-DIGIT ISIC CODES

ISIC Code	Sectors
311–312	Food Manufacturing
313	Beverage Industries
314	Tobacco Manufacturing
321–322	Textile Manufacturing
323	Wearing Apparel
324	Leather and its Products
325	Footwear except Rubber
331	Wood and Cork Products
332	Furniture Manufacturing
341	Paper and its Products
342	Printing and Publishing
351 + 353	Drugs and Pharmaceuticals + Other Chemical Products
352	Industrial Chemicals
354	Petroleum Refining
355	Miscellaneous Petroleum Products
356	Rubber Products
357	Plastic Products
361	Pottery and Chinaware
362	Glass and its Products
369	Non-metallic Mineral Products
371	Iron and Steel Basic Industries
372	Non-ferrous Metal Industries
381–382	Fabricated Metal Products
383	Non-electrical Machinery
384	Electrical Machinery
385	Transport Equipment
386–387	Scientific, Precision etc. + Photographic, Optical Goods

Source: Census of Manufacturing Industries, Bangladesh Bureau of Statistics, Government of Bangladesh.

PART III

Competition and competitive advantage

12. The role of South African competition law in supporting SMEs

Kim Kampel

INTRODUCTION

The South African Competition Act No. 89 of 1998 reflects the government's aims to incorporate particular public interest policies that reflect the changing socioeconomic and political context within which the Act was promulgated. One of the Act's explicit purposes is to 'ensure that small and medium-sized enterprises have an equitable opportunity to participate in the economy'. Such policy considerations are embodied in certain provisions of the Act, which is interesting from the perspective of a developing country with a fledgling competition regime. Nearly five years on, it is useful to examine how the Act has fared.

The ultimate goal of any competition policy is to enhance consumer welfare. The premise is that markets are not competitive where it can be shown that prices increase or the choice of product or service available to the consumer is limited as a result of monopolistic conduct. However, the South African Act specifically mandates attention to small and medium-sized enterprises' (SME) interests. Therefore, South African competition law is in theory SME-friendly, insofar as it proclaims to protect SME interests by promoting access to markets as well as acknowledging their rights to participate in the economy. However, the enforcement of competition law may in reality sometimes be incompatible with SME interests. The difficulty is precisely that frequently the larger, integrated firm is more efficient than its SME counterpart. Large firms are able to leverage their relative strength in the market to source at lower cost and to achieve scale benefits that its smaller counterpart simply cannot match, thereby bringing down prices for consumers. Most sophisticated competition regimes adhere to a competition policy that protects competition itself (ensuring lower prices and greater product choice for consumers) at the expense of protecting individual competing firms, who may not be able to offer the lowest prices or widest choice. Whilst optimally, markets should ensure competitive prices and services, they also function properly if they eliminate inefficient players. But surely competitors, regardless of size, make up the fabric of competitive markets and therefore, they too deserve protection under competition law? This dichotomy is not always easy to understand and leads to misapplication of the Competition Act's provisions.

What this chapter seeks to do is to evaluate to what extent South African competition law assists SMEs, primarily by reference to those SME cases that have been dealt with by the competition authorities between 1999 and 2004. It describes the manner in which the South African Competition Act has been implemented and policy goals interpreted with regard to SMEs, including evaluating how efficiency-driven competition principles interface with SME considerations. Focus is placed on South African competition law's protection of SME interests vis-à-vis larger competitors engaging in anti-competitive conduct, rather than on SMEs as perpetrators of anti-competitive conduct. This chapter therefore serves as an internal review of SME-related provisions and procedures within the Competition Act and their application to real-life SME-initiated cases. Such an analysis is conducted with due consideration to the extent to which the competition authorities' task is complicated by certain structural market features, which frequently may create a hostile environment for SMEs. It will be shown that South African competition law by and large presents a competent model for a country emerging from a protected and distorted economic history. However as yet, competition and not small business interests have been the basis for the determination of decisions under South African competition law.

Ideally it would be beneficial to examine the impact of competition law on SMEs by measuring the long-term effects of the decisions of the competition authorities on SMEs that have been affected by them. This would involve longitudinal empirical assessments of growth in profitability, sales and employment. However, the competition authorities are too young and their decisions too fresh for this type of analysis to be done at this stage. Moreover, data collection is difficult, since the Competition Commission, which interacts to a greater extent with SMEs seeking to initiate complaints, has, at the date of writing, no formalized database dedicated to SME matters and much of the available information is confidential.

Definition of Small Business

Small businesses in South Africa vary in size across a broad spectrum and are characterized by a large informal sector. The National Small Business Act No. 102 of 1996 sets out an expansive definition of the South African small business sector, reflecting its stratified nature. SMEs are categorized as either survivalist; very small (or micro); or formal small and medium-sized entities, in accordance with various thresholds of turnover, assets and employee numbers (Berry et al., 2002). Micro firms have growth potential and involve the owner and family members or four employees at most and turnover is below R150 000. Formal small and medium-sized firms have five to 100 and 100 to 200 employees respectively, which are still owner managed. Turnover is between R2 to R25 million for small and between R4 to R50 million for medium-sized enterprises. SMEs in South African competition law are defined in accordance with this Act.[1]

The survivalist sector refers to the informal sector in South Africa and competition issues and therefore competition law is not within their immediate ambit of concern. Many of the cases that come before the competition authorities are brought by formal SME entities. Therefore, this chapter will focus on such formal micro, small and medium-sized enterprises.

SMEs AND THE COMPETITION ACT NO. 89 OF 1998

The South African Competition Act No. 89 of 1998 ('the Act') became operative in September 1999. The Act lists a plurality of goals, including, the promotion of efficiency, adaptability and the development of the economy; providing consumers with competitive prices and product choices; promoting employment and advancing social and economic welfare of South Africans; expanding opportunities for South African participation in world markets and recognizing the role of foreign competition in the Republic. Primarily therefore, the Competition Act seeks to maximize consumer welfare by efficiently allocating resources, whilst furthermore incorporating amongst its goals the furthering of certain socio-economic objectives (Whish, 2001). Two additional purposes of the Act point to the need to ensure that SMEs have an equitable opportunity to participate in the economy, and that there is a greater spread of ownership, in particular to increase the ownership stakes of historically disadvantaged persons. The latter is designed to cater for Black Economic Empowerment (BEE) companies and the former to SMEs. How these two sets of goals interact will be evident later on.

The New Act

The new Act No. 89 of 1998 was designed to cure the deficiencies of its predecessor, the Maintenance and Promotion of Competition Act of 1979, regarded by many as a blunt instrument against the monopolies it confronted. The Competition Act's attention to SME and other public interest considerations reflects the post-apartheid government's intention to remove or reduce the distorting effects of excessive economic concentration and corporate conglomeration, collusive practices and the abuse of economic power by firms in a dominant position. It was furthermore hoped that this policy would ensure that 'the participation of efficient small and medium-sized enterprises in the economy was not jeopardized by anti-competitive structures and conduct' (OECD, 2003, p. 6 citing Notice 1954).

The Act also reflects the culmination of a controversial and charged debate. When the new bill was being drafted, big business opposed using the new competition legislation for the attainment of broader socioeconomic interests. Their sentiments echoed an established school of thought that abhorred the idea of the Act incorporating social goals underpinning competition policy (Gal, 2004). Competition law purists have questioned whether it is the job of competition authorities to protect smaller players, or whether such a task is more effectively pursued by sector regulators, trade associations, or more appropriately, through enforcement of social legislation or application of industrial policies. However, small business proponents advocated that, in order for small business to be able to participate in the economy, the prevailing high levels of market concentration needed to be urgently addressed and that internal competition measures were needed to address the market power of monopolies. The drafters eventually managed to strike a balance between the views of these opposing camps. The new Act therefore bravely incorporates these competing interests.

South Africa has a unique economic history. Its exclusion from world markets for many years resulted in the development of an extremely protected economy during the earlier part of the twentieth century. Government concessions, including subsidized inputs in industries such as manufacturing and agriculture, together with strict market controls, high tariffs, low levels of foreign direct investment and high levels of government ownership, have over the years, contributed to the creation of a highly concentrated economy. This means that in many market sectors, a few large firms hold considerable market power (see Table 12.1), measured in terms of their share of the relevant market. The creation of statutory monopolies in utilities such as telecommunications has only served to heighten this restrictive and protected environment (OECD, 2003). Today high levels of market concentration, specifically in manufacturing, agriculture and mining, are still evident in various sectors of the South African economy.

Why do SMEs deserve special protection? First, the post-1994 government has committed itself to a small business strategy on the basis of the notion that small business will act as an impetus to growth within the

Table 12.1 *Proportion of market share accounted for by leading South*
African firms in various sectors

Industry/Sector	Number of Leading Firms	Approximate Market Share Commanded by Leading Firms
Paper	2	98%
Plastics	3	74%
Manufacture of wine and beer	2	80%
Iron and steel basic industries	3	73%
Sugar	2	50% +
Gold production	3	87%

Source: African Statistics (Pty) Ltd (2001), various Tribunal decisions.

economy. Furthermore, the economic context in South Africa has historically been hostile to small business. Several industries in South Africa have
been categorized as tight oligopolies, where several large firms dominate the
competitive landscape, typically producing a large portion of industry
output and protected by high entry barriers. Higher concentration levels,
whereby a few firms typically dominate most sectors, increase the likelihood of their potentially exerting their market power to the exclusion of
other, especially smaller competitors. Large firms may frequently control
access to raw materials or other strategic resources or, if vertically integrated, to more than one level of the supply chain. Smaller producers or
customers in South Africa often have no choice but to rely on such firms
for supply, especially in the context of a small developing economy, where
exchange rate fluctuations and other costs limit the viability of imports as
substitutes. A dominant firm's leverage in the market is often strategically
used to push SMEs out of the market in order to capture market share,
entrench market power and ultimately, drive prices up. Such exclusionary
tactics may be surreptitiously invoked, such as refusing to supply the SME
with vital inputs, manipulating pricing of such inputs or levying abnor-
mally low prices on their own products or those of a vertically integrated
subsidiary, in order to force smaller competitors out of business. Since
SMEs are highly susceptible to cash flow problems and lack economies of
scale, it does not take long before they are driven from the market.

In this market context, some South African SMEs are keenly aware of
the might of their larger rivals and of the risk that if they stepped into their
competitive terrain they could be wiped out in an instant. This awareness
in many instances drives SMEs to greater efficiencies, to either lower their
cost base or to innovate. They tend to niche themselves by differentiating a
product or targeting a specific market, which enables them to compete more

effectively. For instance, many SME family-run businesses rely on concessions granted by suppliers, based on sound, established relations built up over several years. In certain industries, relatively small firms are able to survive for extraordinarily long periods. This could be attributable to demand, technological conditions or a sector's unique craft characteristics being conducive to small firms establishing a product niche and a reliable customer base that enables them to remain competitive despite the relatively small scale of their operations.[2] A legitimate pro-competitive response, many would argue. However, in a highly concentrated market context, even efficient dynamic new firms will experience difficulty in breaking into the market while such market structures would also prevent existing viable firms from growing and expanding their market reach. For instance, in a highly concentrated retail sector, some SMEs cite bias against local products as a barrier to entry at the retail level.[3] Similarly, where SMEs niche themselves with respect to a particular market, and start producing favourable returns, larger firms may look on this market as potentially lucrative and engage in anti-competitive or exclusionary conduct in order to grab market share from the smaller firm. In some respects, merely the reputation of the market power of dominant, integrated competitors could well serve as a deterrent to entry or to innovation and growth for SMEs in respect of a particular market.

This explains why, in South Africa, accessing markets has been highlighted by many small business lobbyists and independent business proponents as the single biggest competitive challenge facing SMEs (Small Business Project, 1997). They have highlighted the prevalence of monopoly capitalism and wealth centralization in South Africa as an inhibitor of robust market rivalry that constrains growth in South Africa and have appealed to the competition authorities to address these issues. Precisely how this has been achieved under South African competition law in the context of a highly concentrated market is dealt with below.

The Interface Between BEE and SME Goals

SME interests are closely aligned with BEE interests under the Act. For instance, the public interest clauses under the merger provisions discussed in the next section specifically mandate the authorities to consider the merger transaction's effect on 'the ability of small and black-owned firms to be competitive'. Due to South Africa's unique political history, apartheid policies excluded the majority of the population from formal employment and economic activities, fuelling the growth of large white-owned businesses. Post-1994, the attention to SME enhancement is designed to compensate for the massive unemployment rate and the inability of the formal employment sector to absorb the unemployed. Indeed, the government has established an affirmative procurement strategy designed to assist SMEs owned by previously disadvantaged individuals. BEE therefore ranks high on the government agenda. Small business interests are closely aligned with promoting BEE since BEE business operations are frequently (though not always) small. Therefore in a competition context, more often than not, the two are conflated and expression is given to SME claims under the auspices of BEE claims.[4] However, the competition authorities will refrain from upholding a mere romantic public interest claim, where doing so would jeopardize precisely those interests they seek to protect.

In early 2002 the competition authorities dealt with a merger involving a major petroleum company (Shell) and a smaller retail outlet (Tepco) the division of a BEE holding company. The disposal of Tepco was criticized as selling out a BEE competitor to a dominant white-controlled firm. However, the smaller company was a failing firm, likely to exit the market in any event. Its holding company would acquire, in exchange for the sale, a significant minority share in Shell's marketing arm. The Commission in fact recommended that the Tribunal give greater credence to public interest issues and impose conditions on the merger, which would entail ensuring that control of Tepco remained in the hands of historically disadvantaged persons, and that the Tepco brand remain in the market. On appeal, the Tribunal, in approving the merger unconditionally, considered that the holding company's sale of its troublesome asset was a commercially prudent decision and one that ultimately would benefit black economic empowerment since it enabled them to usefully deploy the capital into other BEE ventures.

PROVISIONS OF THE COMPETITION ACT AS THEY RELATE TO SMEs

SMEs and Merger Control

The bulk of the substantive work carried out by the competition authorities is devoted to addressing mergers and practices prohibited in terms of the Competition Act. All mergers above a defined threshold must be notified to the competition authorities. The thresholds for parties to notify mergers, set by the Minister of Trade and Industry, are determined by the total assets or turnover of merging parties.

Small firms are more likely to be encouraged to enter a market if the possibility of merger provides a financial cushion in the event of failure (Bjork, 1978). Moreover, the ability to merge provides the small, successful firm with the opportunity to sell out to a larger firm and re-channel the proceeds into other ventures.[5] In recognition of this, the merger process under South African law has been made more flexible vis-à-vis those small transactions that are required to be notified. In response to various criticisms, recent amendments to the Act raised the thresholds for small mergers to be notified to the Commission from R5 million to R30 million of turnover or assets for the target firm. Notification for those small mergers that do qualify is now voluntary, alternatively the Commission may require notification within six months of the parties implementing the merger, but only if it feels that the merger has anti-competitive consequences. This means that smaller firms who are acquired by a larger firm no longer face stiff notification fees and long investigative time periods. These amendments enable cash-strapped SMEs relying on the investment of larger companies to grow and therefore compete equitably in the market. Alternatively, they can use the funds to deploy into another SME venture. This flexibility is important in a context where the government seeks to encourage SME growth and transition up the ranks of the formal sector.

When larger companies merge, structural changes may occur in a market that consolidates market power in a particular sector in the hands of the merged entity, often to the exclusion of other smaller competitors. Under the merger provisions, the Act sets out an array of factors to determine whether competition in the market will be 'prevented or substantially lessened' and therefore whether the merger should be prohibited, approved or approved with conditions. A unique feature of the Act is the encapsulation of SME interests under the public interest mandate in the merger provisions of the Act. Under this provision, the authorities must consider whether the merger can or cannot be justified on substantial public interest grounds. In other words, the public interest clauses of the Act dictate that the competition authorities are empowered to assess mergers on the basis of various 'non-efficiency' arguments. These include: the transaction's effect on employment; on a particular industrial sector; on the ability of small and black-owned firms to be competitive; and finally, on the ability of South African business to be competitive internationally. To date no transaction has been determined on grounds of public interest alone. The competition authorities have never permitted an anti-competitive merger transaction because of its positive impact on public interest and they have never prohibited a pro-competitive transaction because of its negative impact on the public interest.

Despite the fact that public interest grounds have not determined any particular merger, several mergers, decided on purely competition grounds, did pay homage to SME interests through the imposition of conditions in their favour. For instance, in one such merger, conditions were imposed, though not on the basis of the public interest provisions of the Act, but rather on competition grounds, which had the effect of benefiting small business.[6] The merger concerned two dominant retailers in the furniture industry. The target firm supported a wide range of small, local independent manufacturers of furniture and bedding, while the acquiring firm purchased its furniture and bedding predominantly from a dominant furniture manufacturer.[7] The concern was that the merged entity would divert furniture purchases from the independent suppliers to the large furniture manufacturer, thereby leading to the demise of the independents. In this way, the merger would increase concentration in the furniture manufacturing sector and thereby increase barriers to entry into the retail sector. Approximately 12 to 15 independent furniture manufacturers intervened to voice these concerns. The Tribunal ultimately approved the merger on condition that the merged firm continued to purchase from independent furniture manufacturers in the same proportion as they had before the merger for a period of time. The order applied generally to independents and not merely to those that intervened.[8]

Similarly, in a merger between a large fast-moving consumer group and a retail convenience store chain, the Tribunal imposed conditions on its approval of the merger, which had the effect of ensuring a level playing field for the franchisees (small businesses) being acquired.[9] In order to address the concern about potential competitive asymmetries and discrimination between competing franchisees, the condition stipulated that the acquiring firm conclude new franchise agreements with all its franchisees.

Incorporation of public interest considerations into a merger evaluation ensures the transparency and inclusiveness of the whole process vis-à-vis SMEs. All three competition institutions – the Competition Commission, Competition Tribunal and Competition Appeal Court – are completely independent of any political authority. The Minister of Trade and Industry has a right to make representations on public interest grounds only as a party to merger proceedings. Therefore, the competition authorities answer only to the Competition Act and the Constitution, free of any ministerial override or veto. Holding a single competition authority responsible for the entire evaluation, as opposed to deferring the public interest aspect of decision-making to another political authority, ensures that the competition authorities are empowered to influence proactively and give effect to SME and other public interest considerations in a tangible and expedient way.

SMEs and Prohibited Practices

In a relatively small, highly concentrated economy, enforcement of the prohibited practice provisions of the Act under Chapter 2 is one area where the Act has the potential to assist those SMEs aggrieved by anti-competitive practices by larger firms. Prohibited practices refer to those substantive infringements of competition law perpetrated by large powerful companies.[10] Typically the victims are smaller competitors or SMEs. They are prosecuted either as restrictive agreements, which have the effect of substantially preventing or lessening competition in a market (Sections 4 and 5) or as abuses of a dominant position including exclusionary acts and price discrimination (Sections 8 and 9). Subsequent comment on the Act has remarked that the price discrimination provision signals to small business that the Act caters to their interests.[11]

SMEs are themselves unlikely to be the perpetrators of restrictive practices or abusers of dominance. The Minister of Trade and Industry has set a de minimis threshold of R5 million in turnover or assets, below which abuse of dominance prohibitions do not apply, in order to ensure that small firms will not be considered dominant in small markets (OECD, 2003). However, in instances where SMEs themselves may potentially infringe the Act, they are afforded immunity from prosecution under the exemption provisions of the Act. If a group of SMEs feels any agreement or practice it engages in might amount to a prohibited practice, it can apply for an exemption from being scrutinized, on the grounds that the objective of the practice is to promote the ability of small businesses or firms controlled by previously disadvantaged persons to become competitive. This would arise for instance where many SMEs collaborate to form a buying group in order to garner bulk discounts. In one matter an association of individually owned pharmacies were exempted from the Act and permitted to advertise and market jointly in order to compete with the larger chains. Under normal circumstances, such an association would have been outlawed in terms of the section prohibiting competitors combining to fix price or other trading condition. The joint marketing effort, however, had the effect of boosting the group's growth, persuading the Commission to extend the exemption for another five years. In practice however, such concessions are rarely sought from the competition authorities. There are heavy exemption fees involved.

The 'abuse of dominance' provisions, a subset of the prohibited practice provisions, were envisaged by the drafters of the Act as being an important means for smaller competitors to challenge the abusive conduct of their larger, unscrupulous rivals. Section 7 of the Act sets out thresholds in terms of which a firm is either dominant or presumed to be dominant or has market power, depending on its percentage market share in a particular market. Competition law recognizes in these provisions the need to check the abusive market power of unconstrained monopolists. Specifically, they outlaw a range of exclusionary acts that are most likely to be perpetrated vis-à-vis SMEs or smaller market participants as existing firms or new entrants seeking access to markets. Depending on which type of prohibited practice it invokes, an SME must either prove that competition in a specifically defined market will be 'substantially prevented or lessened', alternatively that a dominant firm is abusing its position in that market.

HOW ARE SME RIGHTS PURSUED UNDER COMPETITION LAW?

Some of the procedural protections, though benefiting complainants at large, have built in concessions that are designed to also assist smaller competitors and SMEs.

Complaints

Alleged infringements of the Act may be brought at the behest of the Commission, or the SME-complainant itself by means of invoking the complaint procedures of the Act. The Commission, being the investigative body, is obliged to investigate all the complaints it receives. Much like a prosecutor in criminal proceedings, it will represent a complainant's interests by bringing meritorious complaints before the Tribunal for hearing and adjudication. This is important since it means an SME complainant would be saved from incurring the costs of going it alone. Though a complaint may be rejected for lack of merit by the Commission (non-referred), the complainant still has an opportunity to pursue its complaint at the Tribunal, by initiating its own independent claim and pursuing the litigation process independently.

Interim Relief Applications

Most contraventions (of the Act) have an immediately adverse effect on SMEs, stifling their ability to compete fairly or gain access to markets. Complaints investigated by the Commission may take up to a year. The Act provides for complainants to apply for interim relief to the Tribunal directly, pending finalization of the investigation by the Commission. Interim relief applications in theory, would require less stringent proof than would be the case when the final complaint referral is heard. Since private complainants can bring these applications to the Tribunal, they can potentially afford SMEs more expedient redress. However, as discussed later, these applications carry their own risks and are frequently not deemed by SMEs to be worthwhile.

Settlements Procedures

Settlement agreements or consent orders are a valuable means for complainants to achieve redress from a larger rival who is prepared to negotiate to avoid further cost, embarrassment and the inconvenience of enforcement procedures. Such agreements are negotiated at the Commission level and then endorsed by the Tribunal after a brief hearing. This has proved to be successful – a large proportion of complaints are settled. For instance, between 2000 and 2001, at least six consent orders involving SMEs were negotiated between the parties and endorsed by the Tribunal. Inducement on larger players to settle is therefore a valuable potential means by which the Act can assist to level the playing fields for SMEs. Therefore, settlement agreements enable tangible benefits to flow to SMEs as a by-product of direct enforcement of the Act.

HOW SUCCESSFUL HAVE SMEs BEEN?

Analysis of SME-Related Prohibited Practice Cases

At this stage it is important to draw a distinction between those cases lodged with the Commission for investigation and those that were proceeded with to the adjudication stage before the Tribunal.

SME complaints lodged at Commission

Most of the prohibited practice complaints lodged with the Commission are by small businesses (Lebelo, 2001). In 2000, 61 per cent of the total complaints received by the Commission related to abuse of dominance claims (Competition Commission, 2000, *Annual Report*). In 2001, the Commission reported that 72 per cent of the prohibited practice cases filed with it were by SMEs (Competition Commission, 2001, *Annual Report*). Anecdotal evidence from Commission officials indicates that this was also the case between 2002 and 2003. The Commission has remarked that this high percentage of SME cases is indicative of the non-regulatory barriers that small firms face and the need to regulate the conduct of dominant firms in South Africa.[12]

SME complaints prosecuted at Tribunal

Since all meritorious prohibited practice cases must be adjudicated by the Tribunal, it is possible to glean the number of successful SME-related matters referred by the Commission to the Tribunal, from Tribunal records. Accordingly, those cases initiated by SMEs and heard by the Tribunal on the merits over the last four years are examined below.

Table 12.2   Prohibited practices adjudicated before Tribunal, 1999–2004

	Prohibited Practices Cases Granted	Prohibited Practices Cases Refused	Total
SME-initiated prohibited practices	5	4	9
Non-SME-initiated prohibited practices	1	4	5
Total	6	8	14

Source: Data extracted from Competition Tribunal website and *Annual Reports*.

What is apparent is that in proportion to the number of complaints lodged by SMEs at the Commission there have been relatively few complaints involving SMEs successfully prosecuted either by SMEs directly, or on their behalf by the Competition Commission before the Tribunal.[13] Though Table 12.2 reflects that figures of prohibited practices referred to the Tribunal generally are low, it must be recalled that SME cases comprise the majority of complaints lodged at the Commission. Many SME complaints do not ever reach the Tribunal for adjudication, the majority are non-referred by the Commission for lack of merit or withdrawn. In 2002, approximately 14 per cent of the complaints received by the Commission for investigation involved SMEs, historically disadvantaged individuals (HDIs) or BEE entities. The Commission itself acknowledged that this figure in respect of SME complaints was low. Table 12.3 reflects a breakdown of successful SME enforcement actions adjudicated by the Tribunal by section and type.

In five years there were two successful complaint referrals brought before the Competition Tribunal, and both were initiated by SMEs. However, both complaints were prosecuted by the Competition Commission in response to a complaint lodged. No complaint has been successfully prosecuted before the Tribunal by an SME directly. As far as interim relief goes, three out of 12 applications were granted in favour of SMEs. As with direct complaint referrals, interim relief applications are brought by applicants directly, therefore are funded and enforced by them without the help of the Commission. In the next section we deal with why the prosecution rate for SMEs for direct complaint referrals and interim relief applications is low.

Of significance is that of the five prohibited practices successfully prosecuted by SMEs before the Tribunal, two restrictive practices succeeded on the basis of outright prohibitions (one complaint and one interim relief matter). Outright prohibitions are regarded as blatant competition

Table 12.3   Types of successful SME prohibited practice cases before Tribunal

Matter	Nature of Proceeding	Section of Act Infringed	Description of Anti-competitive Conduct	Sector
South African Raisins and Other v. *SAD Holdings Limited*	Interim relief	Section 8(d)(i)	Inducing supplier or customer not to deal with competitor	Agriculture
Cancun Trading No. 24 CC v. *Seven-Eleven Corp SA*	Interim relief	Section 5(2) – outright prohibition	Resale price maintenance – outright prohibition	Retail convenience
JJP Bezuidenhout v. *Patensie Sitrus Beherend Bpk*	Interim relief	Section 8(d)(i)	Inducing supplier or customer not to deal with competitor	Agriculture
Competition Commission v. *Patensie Beherend Bpk*	Complaint referral	Section 8(d)(i)	Inducing supplier or customer not to deal with competitor	Agriculture
Competition Commission v. *Federal Mogul Aftermarket*	Complaint referral	Section 5(2) – outright prohibition	Resale price maintenance – outright prohibition	Motor vehicle parts

Source: Competition Tribunal Records.

transgressions, such as price fixing, resale price maintenance and market division. SMEs more readily succeeded in these cases because in such cases, experience has shown that the anti-competitive effects of this type of conduct are so well-established, the Act does not require the complainant to actually prove a substantial prevention or lessening of competition in a market.

An example of the type of conduct that infringed one of the categories of outright prohibitions of the Act was evident in an interim relief case in the retail convenience store market. A group of SME franchisees succeeded in their complaint that the dominant franchisor was engaged in minimum resale price maintenance, in other words, engaging in conduct that obliged the franchisees to sell their merchandise at minimum prices set by it.[14] The effect was to severely constrain the ability of franchisees to compete in the relevant market on the basis of price. The offending franchisor was heavily fined as a result.

The other category of prohibited practice in respect of which SMEs typically succeed, are on the basis of the respondents abusing their dominant position. All of these dealt with infringements of Section 8(d)(i), namely, conduct that induced a supplier or customer not to deal with a competitor, which falls under the category of exclusionary conduct. Again, the overall number of abuse of dominance cases successfully prosecuted by SMEs in the competition authorities' five-year history is relatively few, especially in view of the proportionately high number of abuse of dominance cases lodged with the Commission. One would expect more prosecutions under Chapter 2 of the Act generally, specifically because the Act was legislated to deal with the rigours of a highly concentrated market structure.

WHY ARE SO FEW SME CASES REFERRED OR PURSUED TO FINALITY?

Practical Constraints

First, considerable resources, specifically those of the Commission, are expended on sifting out claims that simply cannot be sustained under the Competition Act. The Commission's resources are typically very stretched due to the volume of notifications received. SMEs usually cannot afford to wait the prescribed year for the Competition Commission to investigate the complaint. Some SMEs complain that there is a culture at the Commission that does not fully appreciate their need for rapid responses. Though they can apply for interim relief, Commission officials interviewed confirmed that despite the fact that SME cases almost always entail the real likelihood of the SME exiting the market pending finalization of the investigation, there is a huge discrepancy between the number of SME cases they investigate and those in respect of which interim relief is applied for by SMEs.

Second, SMEs decline to approach the Tribunal for interim relief due to the spectre of an adverse costs order against the SME if the matter is ultimately dismissed by the Tribunal. Alternatively, if the matter is proceeded with as a full-blown complaint, all too frequently SMEs lack sufficient resources to employ sophisticated senior counsel or to pursue the matter to the adjudication stage and it is later withdrawn. The unattractiveness of pursuing a lengthy process that might not yield anything besides prohibitively high legal costs is a significant deterrent for SMEs. A well-resourced legal team can extend matters for years on end, expending huge amounts, sums that SMEs can simply not sustain. Therefore, most SMEs, in the absence of a certain outcome, display an unwillingness to commit the requisite funds to pursue the matter to finality.

Third, despite the existence of an informal structure and prosecutorial authority to support interest groups, this has not been the practical effect.[15] Intimidatory tactics are common, it is not unknown for large companies to boycott an SME's business as a direct result of their pursuing a complaint against them, or even as a result of their giving evidence against them. The upshot is that there have only been a handful of occasions on which SME groups have intervened or participated in merger or prohibited practice hearings before the Tribunal. In fact, there has been more representation by labour and empowerment groupings than by SMEs. This could also be attributable to the fact that SMEs are simply not informed of the merger in time to make representations. Several SMEs have indicated that they only heard about the proceedings after the fact, frequently in the press. The competition authorities are therefore disadvantaged by not having the benefit of first-hand marketplace information from independent trade associations to gain a true reflection of the dynamics of a particular marketplace.

Moreover, legal practitioners take centre stage, largely due to affluent larger companies. Competition law is regarded as highly specialized and SMEs are frequently unable to find legal representatives prepared to undertake a complex competition law case. Those existing legal specialists, who usually act for large corporates, charge fees unaffordable for SMEs. The inaccessibility is exacerbated by the lack of transparency around the procedural and substantive issues required to prosecute SME complaints successfully under the Act.

Lack of Merit

Where they are aware of the existence of the Act, many SMEs lack practical knowledge as to how the substantive provisions of the Act can be implemented. What is clear is that most SMEs share a consistent ignorance and paucity of familiarity and understanding of the competition authorities, their role and how the Act's procedures could be invoked to protect them. In particular, SME complainants frequently misunderstand the requirements of proof necessary to sustain a claim of anti-competitive conduct. Even if a larger player is perpetrating an anti-competitive practice against an SME, defective or incomplete filings ensure the case is thrown out. SMEs frequently frame their complaint as a commercial claim, based on personal or pecuniary harm suffered and neglect to focus on injury to competition in general. That is why civil, commercial disputes are often brought under the guise of competition complaints. Similarly, where they rely on abuse of dominance claims, SMEs frequently fall short of proving either dominance or fail to build up a sufficient case to establish abusive conduct. In the South African context many firms may be dominant in most sectors, but not all of them will be abusing their dominance, therefore these claims are difficult for an SME to prove and are treated with circumspection by the competition authorities. Large companies sometimes simply prefer to deal with similarly large customers or suppliers who are able to provide the requisite volumes to make doing business worthwhile. This phenomenon is perhaps more accentuated in South Africa as a result of the existence of highly concentrated market sectors

Competition cases involve complex legal and economic arguments and are difficult to understand unless legally represented. Since many complaints of alleged anti-competitive conduct entail severe repercussions, including large fines and associated civil claims, stringent evidence must be produced to support allegations of anti-competitive conduct. This is because the competition authorities are cognizant to adopt a hard line against the Act being invoked frivolously, as a bargaining or pressure tactic by disgruntled competitors seeking to obtain undeserved concessions from larger rivals, which would impede the normal competitive workings of the market. They strive, as all new competition authorities do, for uniformity and certainty of legal rules in order to establish their legitimacy and consolidate a body of jurisprudence. Furthermore, adherence to legal rules is seen as crucial in order to bring certainty to business. Since inter-firm rivalry is generally beneficial to the consumer, it is not always easy to distinguish exclusionary conduct from beneficial competition, and businesses need to know where they transcend this line.

The Tension Between Competition Law and SME Interests

Complaints relying on those sections of the Act where the SME must prove a substantial prevention or lessening of competition in a particular market are rarely successfully invoked by SMEs. In any defined market an SME will typically hold a market share of 10 per cent or less, therefore there is unlikely to be a substantial prevention or lessening of competition if the SME exits the market.

The failure by SMEs to frame cases properly before the competition authorities reflects a fundamental tension between competing policy goals: protecting the consumer from high prices and limited product choice versus protecting the SME from competitors acting anti-competitively towards them. The competition authorities consistently look to discern a general anti-competitive effect on consumer welfare generally and not only in relation to one SME or group of SMEs. The mandated attention to SME interests in the Act creates a dilemma for competition law, of which class of rights to protect at the expense of the other. Large firms have a real cost advantage over small firms, which allows them to charge lower prices. Efficiency considerations are firmly entrenched in many of the Act's provisions because the Department of Trade & Industry believed that a competition law focused on economic efficiency and applied by politically independent bodies was appropriate for South Africa's well-developed industrial and service sectors (OECD report, 2003, p. 9). This means that certain classes of anti-competitive conduct can be 'offset' if the respondent firm can prove any technology, efficiency or other pro-competitive gain outweighing the anti-competitive effect of that conduct.[16] In other words, large integrated firms can legitimate their alleged anti-competitive conduct on the basis of so-called efficiency claims, because efficiency necessarily entails lower prices and consumer welfare is enhanced.

The application of this approach was illustrated in a recent case in the cigarette distribution industry. In 2002 a group of 11 cigarette wholesalers who distributed cigarettes on behalf of the dominant cigarette producer in the country, British American Tobacco (BAT) applied for interim relief against BAT. BAT held 93 per cent of the market, its nearest rival held only 4.6 per cent. The SME distributors complained that in attempting to implement a new distribution agreement, BAT was making it impossible for them, as small traders, to remain and compete in the market. They alleged that insofar as BAT excluded the applicants from expanding in the market, it was abusing its dominant position. The Tribunal dismissed the application because, amongst other reasons, the distributors were not viable in any event and it was not clear that the new system would lead to a greater reduction of distributors than would the old system. Even if it would, evidence on how much the market would be foreclosed as a result was lacking. BAT (the dominant firm) was not proved to be engaging in an exclusionary strategy.[17] In its judgement the Tribunal remarked that whilst markets function properly if they ensure competitive prices and services, they also function properly if they eliminate inefficient players.

SUCCESSFUL SME CASES

Does that mean that SMEs are always denied relief if a larger competitor can prove efficiencies? What about those innovative SMEs that have the potential to generate greater cost savings and efficiencies who are frequently intimidated out of the market or simply denied entry to it by their rivals' anti-competitive conduct? Such firms are clearly not free-riders, nor inefficient, indeed it is these innovative and differentiated small firms that need to be protected from monopolistic heavyweights, in the event of the latter engaging in deliberate anti-competitive tactics to attempt to eliminate them or completely bar their entry into the market.

There have been cases where pure competition principles and small business interests have converged. These are cases where the particular conduct resulted in both consumer welfare being undermined, whilst at the same time being exclusionary of competitors. Though responding parties almost always attempt to justify anti-competitive conduct on the basis of efficiency benefits, the competition authorities have been alive to the prospect of the efficiency defence being misappropriated as a justification for monopolization. In fact, in several decisions, the Competition Tribunal has recognized that the possibility exists that large dominant firms are disincentivized from becoming more efficient, specifically because of an absence of competition in their particular sector. For instance, in 2002, a complaint was successfully pursued by a citrus farmer against the local packing and distribution company, Patensie (a former cooperative reconstituted into a company), of which the complainant farmer was a member. The case broadly concerned the interests of the entire value chain throughout the farming community, many of whom can be defined as SMEs in terms of the Act. The Tribunal found that Patensie, through the provisions of its Articles of Association, was abusing its dominant position in the market for the packing and marketing of citrus fruit in the particular local region. Patensie's Articles of Association clearly provided that the members were obliged to deliver their entire output to Patensie for the purposes of packing and marketing. In other words, Patensie required its customers (who were also its members) to deal with it or conversely, 'not to deal with a competitor', namely other packing houses in the district, who offered more competitive terms. The offending Articles were declared invalid.

This case clearly shared the strong exclusionary effect that the dominant firm's conduct had on the particular market. Interestingly, another case concerning the agricultural market also dealt with an inducement by a dominant raisin processor, on certain 'grapes-for-raisins' producers not to deliver their raisin production to the complainant raisin processor. This was condemned also on the basis that it was exclusionary of other competitors in the market. What is significant is that the Tribunal in this case dispelled the dominant firm's efficiency claims, commenting that the efficiency claims of the dominant firm had to be shown to be particularly strong to offset the efficiency loss resulting from its anti-competitive conduct.

What seems clear is that those cases where SMEs have more readily succeeded are where the SME can show that a dominant firm's conduct is part of a blatant, overarching strategy to exclude it and other competitors from the market. Alternatively, they may succeed on the basis of those outright prohibitions or 'per se' abuses, where the SME need not prove a substantial lessening of competition in the market.

CONCLUSIONS

Competition law can only facilitate access to markets, but once there South African SMEs still confront many obstacles, due to the legacy of an enduringly concentrated market structure. A prevailing culture of dominance where abusive conduct is accepted as normal business practice still endures. Certainly the low volume of abuse of dominance cases before the competition authorities suggest that this might be the case. Relaxation of market structures will evolve as big business adjusts to market liberalization and the inevitable relinquishing of power.

Notwithstanding these structural problems, the competition authorities are sufficiently empowered by the Act to accommodate concessions for SMEs and to interpret the goals of the Act in such a way as to develop a unique SME-related jurisprudence. Though many strict competition advocates might not approve of these policy goals, their incorporation in the Act serve to steer the minds of the competition authorities towards SME interests, which enable them to be consistently mindful of and conscientious to the needs of smaller competitors. Where SME concerns have been aligned with Black Economic Empowerment goals, they have a better opportunity of being advanced. However, the challenge remains to continue to make a concerted effort to avoid painting competition decisions with public interest idealisms, where they are without substance, or risk sacrificing the legitimacy of the Act's goals.

By imposing merger conditions that have created a fair and level playing field for independent SMEs, as well as by outlawing exclusionary conduct, the competition authorities have protected the integrity of the competitive process and aimed to lower entry barriers. However, thus far the South African competition authorities have applied an orthodox competition-focused approach. No decision has been taken solely in deference to small business concerns.

In South Africa, the effect of abusive market conduct on small firms' ability to compete is less discernable and often disguised by monopolistic firms. It is precisely because the history of monopolistic conduct in South Africa is so subtle, yet pervasive and entrenched, that SME claims of exclusion and harm will have to be rigorously interrogated by the competition authorities in the future. The question of where the line is drawn between abusive conduct and healthy competition will need to be addressed on a case by case basis in the context of each particular market sector. Therefore, while the Competition Act provides the architecture for protecting small business interests, the extent to which the competition authorities will specifically give effect to these issues will play out over time, as the competition authorities are challenged to test the limits of the Act in protecting innovative, differentiated SMEs in their own right.

NOTES

1. See Chapter 1, Section 1, Sub-section (xxxii) of the Competition Act.
2. *Bidvest and Paragon* Competition Tribunal, Case No. 56/LM/Oct01. In a merger in the stationery supplies market, it emerged that sub-contracting enabled small players to win large contracts and then to sub-contract components of the contract to other players.
3. As in the case of the Fume cosmetic group, see article entitled 'Fume Foray into Retail', *Business Day*, 10 October 2002.
4. Various sections of the Act, notably Section 12A (3)(c), the public interest provision in mergers, contain a unitary reference to BEE and SME considerations. Similarly, the Competition Commission's brochure guide for small business incorporates black business, and states that small and black business stand to benefit from the application of the Act through: 'investigations of practices prohibited by the Act; merger control and the granting or refusing of exemption applications'.
5. Two mergers where this has occurred is *Pioneer Foods (Pty) Ltd and SAD Holdings Limited*, Case No. 23/LM/Apr 02 and *Shell South Africa (Pty) Ltd and Tepco Petroleum (Pty) Ltd*, Case No. 66/LM/Oct01.
6. See *J D Group Limited and Profurn Limited*, Case No. 60/LM/Aug 02. In this case, competition concerns arose out of the vertical integration issues arising from the merger.
7. Though in the Tribunal decision the view is expressed that the independent manufacturers were not SMEs but previously disadvantaged individuals, it seems that many of them would fall into the strict definition of a small business. In any event, subsequent discussion around this case has regarded these independent manufacturers as small business entities.
8. Note this case was overturned by the Competition Appeal Court in September 2003. The CAC ordered that all conditions imposed on the merger by the Tribunal be set aside. Perhaps if this had been decided on public interest grounds, the CAC would not have overturned it so readily. Competition officials have commented that this should not be viewed as a setback to small business interests: 'Suppliers No Longer Protected in JD merger', Colin Anthony, *Real Business Supplement, Business Day*, October 2003. Subsequent to this case, similar conditions were imposed in favour of independent furniture manufacturers in another merger between a dominant furniture manufacturer and its subsidiary that supplies it with MDF and chipboard inputs. Once again, the smaller manufacturers voiced their concerns. This decision has not to date been released by the Tribunal.
9. *Fluxrab Investments No. 58(Pty) Ltd and Seven Eleven Africa (Pty) Ltd*, Case No. 44/LM/Aug 03.
10. Unlike in the merger provisions of the Act, there is no express provision for SMEs or other public interest groups with respect to the prohibited practice provisions, nevertheless these sections were designed with such interest groups in mind.
11. With respect to price discrimination, South Africa follows US legislation, the Robinson-Patman Act 1936 and Clayton Act 1914. Reekie (1999) comments that the main purpose

was to prevent powerful retailers from obtaining undue favours from their suppliers relative to SME traders. This section has to date not been successfully invoked by SMEs
under SA competition law. However, a case alleging price discrimination by a large supplier vis-à-vis its customer, a small business, has been dealt with by the Competition
Tribunal.

12. The absence of comprehensive data with respect to SME complaints lodged with the
Commission does not allow one to assess whether prohibited practices are being perpetrated against SMEs in specific sectors or not.

13. Of course this could well reflect that the number of complaints lodged are frivolous but
the fact that so many are lodged does serve as some indication that there is a need for
competition protection in the first place. Anecdotal evidence from smaller competitors
would confirm this.

14. *Cancun Trading No. 24 CC and Seven-Eleven Corp SA*, Case No. 18/IR/Dec99.

15. The Act provides for interested parties (including SME and other public interest stakeholders) to appear before the Tribunal by applying to participate to make representations
in hearings into mergers and restrictive practices, where they feel their interests are likely
to be (materially) affected; Section 53 of the Act and Tribunal Rule 46. In the *Cancun
Trading* case mentioned above, 13 complainants, all franchisees of the respondent made
a joint submission.

16. Specifically, in restrictive horizontal or vertical practice claims, with respect to certain
classes of exclusionary acts under abuse of dominance.

17. The distributors also relied on the allegation of resale price maintenance, namely, that
BAT was forcing them to resell their goods at the same price to retailers as the wholesale
price that they paid. The Tribunal held that there was no evidence of resale price maintenance since there was nothing to prevent the distributors from discounting the wholesale price.

REFERENCES

Anthony, C. (2003), 'Suppliers No Long Protected in JD Merger', *Real Business
Supplement, Business Day Newspaper*.

Berry, A. et al. (2002), 'The Economics of SME in South Africa', *Trade and
Industrial Policy Strategies*, 1–39.

Bjork, R.H. (1978), *The Antitrust Paradox. A Policy at War with Itself*, New York:
The Free Press.

Competition Commission (2000–03), *Annual Reports*, Pretoria.

Competition Tribunal (2000–03), *Annual Reports*, Pretoria.

Gal, M. (2004), 'The Ecology of Antitrust: Preconditions for Competition Law
Enforcement in Developing Countries', in *Competition, Competitiveness and
Development from Developing Countries*, UNCTAD, New York and Geneva:
United Nations.

Lebelo, S. (2001), Country Report on the Institutional Framework Governing the
Competition Regime in South Africa, *Corporate Strategy and Industrial
Development Research Project*, School of Economic and Business Sciences, WITS.

OECD (2003), OECD Forum on Competition Peer Review, 2003, *Competition Law
and Policy in South Africa*, Paris: OECD.

Reekie, D. (1999), 'The Competition Act, 1998: An Economic Perspective', *South
African Journal of Economics*, **67** (2), 257–88.

Small Business Project (1997), 'Competitive Markets – an Imperative for Small
Business Growth', *SME Alert*, 2, 4 November, Johannesburg.

South Africa Parliament (1998), *The Competition Act No. 89 of 1998*, Pretoria, Government Printer.

Whish, R. (2001), *Competition Law*, Fourth Edition, Bath: The Bath Press.

13. Globalization and competition in the South African wine industry

Joachim Ewert and Jeffrey Henderson

INTRODUCTION

In studying the relation between global markets and agricultural industries and the consequences the processes involved have for inequality and poverty, the South African wine industry highlights many of the key issues in need of analytic and policy attention. Among these issues the questions of racial and class divisions within the industry, the implications of government competition and regulatory policies and the problems (for producer companies and workers) of being absorbed into the global value chains of oligopolistic retailers, are evident (Henderson, 2002). This chapter discusses these and cognate matters and briefly indicates some of the policy conclusions that seem relevant not only for this industry and for South Africa, but perhaps also for other export-oriented agricultural and agricultural processing industries elsewhere in the developing world.

THE CHALLENGE

In its most recent policy papers the South African wine industry defines the major challenge as 'creating a vibrant, united, non-racial and prosperous South African Wine Industry' (SAWB, 2003). While it acknowledges the significant progress made over the last decade or so, not least of which is a tenfold increase in exports, it admits that it still has a considerable way to go towards greater 'competitiveness, sustainability and equity'.

In a significant passage the SAWB's (2003) Wine Industry Plan (WIP) admits

> that while there has been some progress in poverty alleviation in South Africa, this has largely been the result of progress in urban areas. Farm workers remain one of the poorest and most marginal groups in South African society and are the poorest in terms of wage employment in the formal sector. The wine industry must ensure that this categorization does not apply to its profile. (SAWB, 2003, pp. 22–3)

The statement echoes the findings of a research team that investigated the feasibility of a statutory minimum wage for South African agriculture: 'Our main conclusion. . . is that the circumstances of farm workers justify the introduction of a minimum wage . . .'. Using a 'capability' measure of poverty, the report stressed that 'improvement . . . [also] requires invest-ment in nutrition, education, health etc.' (CRLS, 2001). Although farm workers in the Western Cape (where most of the wine industry is situated) were generally better off than in other provinces, their condition still neces-sitated a statutory minimum wage, albeit at the highest of a four-tier wage (CRLS, 2001, p. xiv). In the end the Department of Labour set a two-tier wage, with most of the magisterial districts in the Western Cape falling into the top category.

Despite widespread poverty in the rural Western Cape, the WIP does not highlight 'poverty alleviation' as an explicit objective. Instead 'socioeco-nomic transformation' 'de-racialization' and 'economic empowerment' is to be achieved through 'equitable access to resources, business opportuni-ties, markets and decision-making [along the full value chain] by histori-cally disadvantaged and economically marginalized South Africans'. The report recognizes that the challenge is not made any easier in the face of 'large inequalities and entry barriers . . . and the relative slow progress to redress these characteristics since 1994'. Nevertheless, the SAWB thinks that its objectives can be attained through

> the strengthening of representation of the previously excluded, the institutional integration of . . . these groups into industry level decision making processes; and a targeted approach to open up access to business and economic growth opportunities and social upliftment . . . [F]ocus [is] on the most disadvantaged participants rather than on old or new elites. (SAWB, 2003)

Nice words, but there is no reason to believe that it will turn out this way. Only time will tell. Already there are ominous signs.

OBSTACLES IN THE WAY OF 'EMPOWERMENT' AND THE ALLEVIATION OF POVERTY

A striking feature of both the Vision 2020 and WIP policy papers is their voluntarist and normative, not to say ideological nature. A lot of space is spent on what should or is going to be done (i.e., objectives) in the way of transformation. However, there is little analysis of the current state of the industry and the formidable structural obstacles that stand in the way of change. While not insurmountable, obstacles to market access, brand development, redistribution and the problems generated indirectly by oligopolistic retailers, need to be faced head on if viable strategies are to be forged.

Our analysis of these obstacles focuses on three interlinked transitions, which, it is held, are central to the understanding of wine industry reorganization and its implications for livelihoods on the ground. These are first, the process of local industry deregulation and restructuring; second, the increasing integration of the local industry into international markets and value chains; and third, the legislative changes that have accompanied democracy in South Africa. These transitions, it will be argued, have had complex, mutually overlapping and reinforcing effects. On the one hand the industry has seen lateral expansion and an impressive, sustained rise of exports. On the other hand many cooperative wine cellars and their members have found it very difficult to re-gear themselves away from the industry's historic orientation towards bulk wine production and to face up to the 'quality revolution' and the demands of supermarket wine retailers. Power is shifting downstream, away from primary producers to processors, marketers.

This has had uneven and complex implications upstream for farm-based livelihoods. On the one hand the changed environment encourages farmers to go beyond management strategies based on cheap, expendable and low wage labour: improved wages, higher levels of training and modernized management approaches are required, not only by law but by the imperatives of survival in an increasingly competitive sector. Farm managers have, however, stopped short of the wholesale modernization of the employment relationship. The selective introduction of elements of 'modern' organization and the partial compliance with labour legislation has resulted in a wide range of hybrid formations – strategies that rely simultaneously on elements of both traditional paternalist and modern capitalist management approaches. But not all workers have benefited from this. Across the board, and perhaps particularly on estate and private cellars in the vanguard of globalization, the 'triple transition' has accelerated and deepened trends towards the rationalization of labour.

On the farmed landscapes of the Western Cape, a deepening divide is therefore taking shape. The shrinking core of workers who manage to hold on to permanent employment, though often still living on the farm and caught in the web of paternalism, are on the whole net beneficiaries from these changes. Increasingly their permanent status, improved skills, better pay, housing and other benefits set them apart from the seasonal, casual and contract workers: a rural lumpenproletariat, often residing in rural, peri-urban or metropolitan shanty towns. These trends look hard to ameliorate let alone to reverse. Unless agricultural employment is supplemented by economic growth, state support for competitiveness and pro-poor welfare strategies, peripheral workers will be doomed to scrabble for a precarious existence on the margins of the Cape wine lands.

THE WORLD WINE MARKET: A TOUGH PLAYING FIELD

One of the most noticeable features of the South African wine industry between 1917 and the mid-1990s was its elaborate regulatory system, presided over by the KWV. Planting quotas, minimum prices and mechanisms of 'surplus removal' decisively shaped the dominant features of the South African wine industry for the greater part of the twentieth century (Ewert, 2003).

At the level of primary production an important part was played by the cooperative cellars that came to dominate wine production. Most of these implemented a 'pool system' in terms of which grapes of a particular cultivar were sold in bulk, with farmers being paid according to the number of tons delivered and the selling price realized for the pool as a whole. An important objective of every cooperative was to realize the highest possible financial return ('payouts') for its members. Co-ops were also linked closely to the networks of white power in the rural Western Cape. Rural civil society in the farming areas of the Western Cape was dominated by the white landed settler elite. Formal institutions such as the National Party and the Broederbond obviously played a key role, but as important were the informal networks of filiation and affiliation between key settler families – and the way these networks allowed political control of agro-institutions (du Toit, 2003).

From early on, this system was marked by a high degree of downstream concentration and integration. Farmers and their cooperatives sold most of their wine in bulk to the KWV and other producing wholesalers. Although they were guaranteed a minimum price, periodic surplus production and a limited domestic market continued to favour the wholesalers well into the 1990s. In addition, the distilling industry – buoyed by South Africa's distinctive brandy market – played an unusually important role. Not only did it help with the removal of surplus wine but the producing wholesalers on whom cooperatives so heavily depended came to see distilling as the place where the real money was to be made: one author described the South African wine industry as 'a vast distillery draining a partly subsidised annual wine lake' (Robinson, 1999, p. 648).

Given its history the industry has been facing novel and important challenges since the late 1980s. These challenges need to be very clearly understood. It is a truism in the South African wine industry that 'the future' lies in re-orienting production away from bulk wine and developing the ability to produce for the 'quality' market (Spies, 2001a). Like most truisms it is in equal parts fundamentally correct and seriously oversimplified. Wine is never just wine, grapes are never just grapes, and the implications of 'the demand for quality' differ from context to context. The global alcoholic beverage market is fragmented and complex and the markets for South African wines and wine grapes are no exception.

Three linked trends in the international alcoholic beverage market and its commodity systems have played a particularly important role. First, the global beverage industry has increasingly come under pressure, partly because of the global economic downturn and partly because of increasing health concerns among consumers. Second, the wine market has been increasingly affected by the growth of supermarket wine retailers, which have fundamentally changed the way in which wine is consumed and marketed. This is closely linked to the third trend, which is the increasing prominence in the premium and super premium wine market of branded wines, promising to deliver not only quality but also consistency.

Together these trends have meant that wine markets have been characterized by increasingly divergent price trends. Low-priced blended table wines have poor prospects in a world where consumption has fallen by a quarter since 1982. In France and Italy – the bastions of working class wine drinking – consumption has halved in the past 30 years. At the same time there is a global trend towards buying better quality wines (Rachman, 1999). While wine sales at lower price points have remained stagnant, higher price points have shown buoyant growth. At the turn of the new century the most lucrative price bracket was at over £4 sterling in Britain and $7 in the United States. In the latter market, wines selling at more than $7 account for only 22 per cent of sales by volume, but almost 50 per cent of revenues. As *The Economist* put it in a recent survey of the international wine industry: '[T]he message is clear: the best place is at the upper end of the market, where growth is fastest and margins are fattest' (Rachman, 1999, p. 111).

The most important international wine market is Western Europe, where 70 per cent of the world's wines are still made and consumed. Within this region Britain is particularly important for premium wine exporters. Unlike the parochial market of France, where imports command less than 5 per cent of premium wine consumption, Britain is the fourth largest wine market and world's biggest importer of wine – and supermarket retailers are particularly prominent here. Supermarkets distribute over 60 per cent of all wine consumed in the United Kingdom (Rachman, 1999, p. 111). The main beneficiary of this trend has been Australia, which has pioneered the industrialization of premium branded wine production; while France has traditionally had the biggest share of the British market, Australia's share of the UK wine market has risen from 8 per cent to 15 per cent between 1993 and 1999, while seven of the top selling wine brands in the United Kingdom in 2001 were Australian.

South African wines have also made important inroads into international markets. Wine exports grew to 210 million litres in 2002 – up from 50.7 million litres in 1994. Exports accounted for 33.5 per cent of 'good wine' (i.e., table wine) production, compared with just 14.6 per cent in 1995. In addition, 61.5 million litres of bulk wine were exported. Total export value for wines in 2001 was about R4.5 billion. Approximately 50 per cent of bottled wine exports are to the United Kingdom, 21 per cent to the Netherlands, 9 per cent to Scandinavia and 6.5 per cent to Germany – together accounting for more than 85 per cent of South Africa's wine exports (VinPro, 2004, p. 20). In 2002 South Africa was the fastest-growing wine country exporting to the United Kingdom. For the first time the country had a brand listed in the top five wines retailed in the United Kingdom with 'Kumala' at number four.

This growth has contradictory implications for wine makers. The most important buyers of South African wine in Britain are the oligopolistically organized supermarket chains. Of these, Tesco, Asda-Walmart, Morrison-Safeway and J. Sainsbury are by far the largest, though Waitrose and the Co-op also have significant market shares. To land a sales contract with one of them is a much sought-after prize in the Western Cape wine lands (especially for cooperative cellars). But while these new markets mean new opportunities, they also mean tougher bargaining. Supermarkets have stringent purchasing practices. They impose strict phytosanitary and technical requirements on suppliers and they work consistently to force down prices. Applying practices typical of their branded food and drink retailing in general (see GPN, 2003) they, for instance, charge 'rents' for shelf space and position and pass on the profit/loss associated with temporary product 'promotions' to their suppliers rather than absorbing these themselves. While Tesco is often regarded as the most problematic of the British supermarkets in this sense, only Waitrose and the Co-op seem to escape the criticism of South African wine industry personnel. It is no coincidence that Waitrose and the Co-op have parent companies (the John Lewis Partnership and the Co-operative Wholesale Society respectively) with strong historical commitments to corporate social responsibility and ethical trading.

For producers who cannot conform to the threshold requirements indicated above, there is a risk of being left out of this market altogether. For would-be entrants into the South African wine industry (black-owned companies, for instance), such threshold and purchasing practices represent formidable obstacles indeed.

So although South African growers and cellars are starting to learn the rules of the 'new competition', life is not going to get easier. Competition between wine producing countries and between individual producers is bound to intensify. Much will depend on the ability to establish 'branded' wines that stand out from the rest. This requires not only the ability to make good wine but also the ability to deliver consistency and volume at the same time. To build a brand in the United Kingdom for instance, requires the ability to bring 3–6 million litres to the market per year and to support it through strong advertising and an efficient logistical supply operation (Loubster, 2001, p. 36). Very few cellars can achieve this on their own.

These trends are particularly significant given that the most important growth opportunities for South African wine remain in these overseas markets. In the context of the South African beverage industry as a whole, wine has done relatively well and the market for table wines and lower end premium wines blended in bulk – wines such as Distell's mass-market leaders 'Graca', 'Paarl Perlé' and 'Autumn Harvest Crackling' – has remained healthy. These markets however, show scant opportunity for growth. And more to the point, there is very little money in them for grape growers. Bulk wines after all, can now be sourced internationally and even South African stalwarts such as 'Tassenberg' include wine made from Argentinean grapes.

Survival is not made any easier by the fact that globalization is a two-way street. In 2002 South Africa imported approximately 31 million litres of 'natural wine', compared with approximately 216 million litres of exports (SAWIS, 2003, p. 26). While most of the imported premium wines remain unaffordable for all but the wealthiest section of South African society, it is the import of bulk blending and distilling wine that is impacting the most on South African cooperative wineries, many of whom came to rely on the product for the greater part of their existence. As a result these growers and cellars were often poorly prepared for the new environment to which they awoke in the mid-1990s. At that stage less than 20 per cent of South Africa's good wine production qualified for the 'HP' price category. Also the industry had become almost exclusively oriented towards the domestic market. Having neither the know-how nor the confidence to compete in Europe on a big scale, the industry found it difficult to venture into foreign domains. This is especially true for the cooperative sector.

AFTER DEREGULATION: CONCENTRATION AND DIVERSIFICATION

The second important dimension of change is local industry de- and re-regulation. Starting in 1988, deregulation was a practical fact two years before the coming to power of the ANC. One year later sanctions were lifted. Since then the South African wine industry has been in a process of major flux. Political transition has removed the privileged status of the wine industry and farmers' lobbies. The measures that protected farmers from competitive pressures have been removed and old alliances have been cracked by new opportunities and new markets. The wine grape commodity system is being restructured in complex and contradictory ways – with significant consequences for growers.

First, traditional industry power relations are being reshaped by processes of globalization, deregulation and legislative change. Moves to amend liquor legislation have signalled to the producing wholesalers that their competitive stranglehold over retail would no longer be tolerated (Hoe, 1998, p. 79) – while the increasing importance of local supermarket wine retailing is causing a rethink in 'trade' strategy anyway. Consolidation in the international drinks industry – particularly through the merger of Grandmet and Guinness to form of industry giant Diageo – has called into question many of the historic arrangements around distribution rights for international liquor brands (*Financial Mail*, 15 December 2000, pp. 30–32). South Africa's producing wholesalers, for many years the biggest frogs in a very small pond, are themselves increasingly vulnerable to international and local competitive pressure.

Two distinct trends seem to be taking shape. On the one hand there are clear moves toward concentration and integration, for example, the merger of Distillers and Stellenbosch Farmers Winery to form Distell, South Africa's second-largest alcoholic beverage company and the alliance between Stellenbosch Vineyards and Australian-based BRL Hardy. Although the Distell merger was challenged before the Competition Tribunal, the latter gave it the green light. Distell now controls more than 70 per cent of all brandy sales and 60 per cent of the total production of premium wine and spirits. Opinion is divided about the creation of this new giant. Some – notably Seagrams South Africa and Bulmers – have argued that it will exercise an unhealthy domination in the wine sector, squeezing out competition and stifling innovation. Distell portrays itself as a company poised to enter decisively into the global market, there to compete with Gallo, Southcorp, Diageo and the real giants of the wine world. Sixty percent of Distell's shares are controlled by the combined holding of Rembrandt and KWV. While the shareholders may be happy, others were less fortunate. Two thousand people lost their jobs in the wake of the merger (du Toit, 2003).

At the same time there is significant diversification, with an increase in the numbers of independent wine makers and cellars. Private cellars and independent labels are proliferating.[1] Their number has increased from 105 in 1998 to 266 in 2002. The increase in private cellars is the result of estates de-listing, in order to have more freedom in the sourcing of grapes and cooperative cellars that have transformed themselves into private companies. Producing wholesalers have increased from five in 1998 to 13 in 2002.

Since 1998 indeed, the number of cooperatives has fallen from 69 to 50. Of those that have 'disappeared' two have gone bankrupt while the others have undergone mergers and/or changed into companies. If the survivors want to escape the more pessimistic scenario, more may be forced to pool their resources. In 2000, a study of 28 cooperative and former cooperative cellars showed that only five had retained their traditional cooperative structure. All others were in a process of transformation – with regard to both their internal and their external organization (Martin, 2001).

The implications of these shifts are complex and uneven but together they seem to signal an important shift in the power relations between growers, cellars and retailers. One particularly important development is the coming into being of a complex new internal market in both wine and grapes. With the development of new branded premium wines (e.g., 'Arniston Bay' and 'Two Oceans') that are not linked to particular vineyards, cellars that can produce premium wine according to desired specifications have a wider range of possible buyers for their products than before. Similarly, there is a much more dynamic market for wine grapes. A part of both these markets are driven simply by quality and price but many brand owners, cellars and growers also tend to prefer entering into medium- and long-term relationships in order to avoid uncertainty.[2] Increasingly, staying in these relationships depends on the ability to produce grapes and/or wines that conform to 'quality' and other standards specified by the buyer.

The result is a complex and shifting new strategic terrain. Cellars are exploring a wide range of different routes through trial and error and incremental changes. Some co-ops have chosen to remain in a medium- to long-term contractual relationship with domestic producing wholesalers, while others have embarked on their own marketing and sales. Nevertheless, four years ago, 70 per cent of production was still sold in bulk – mainly to domestic wholesalers but also to overseas buyers (Martin, 2001). Only a handful of cooperatives did their own marketing and sales. They were only exporting an average of 5 per cent of their output. Although some headway has been made in co-ops' effort to gain more independence from the wholesalers, it remains difficult. Two years ago the manager of one former cooperative estimated that it costs R1 million to establish a 'brand'.[3] In addition one needs the necessary volumes, an effective supply chain and the international marketing network – all things difficult to achieve for cooperatives, not to say 'new farmers'.

None of these shifts are easily accomplished. New and emerging sales strategies often require or presuppose organizational changes. The transition from mass to 'quality' production entails shifting power relations in grower–cellar relationships at district level, and brings power struggles between co-op management and growers that are not always easily resolved. It is often hard to 'engineer' the transition – particularly in a context where recalcitrant members can veto changes that challenge established practices.

For 'new farmers' the issue is not whether they should take the side of the pro-change faction amongst co-op members or not. For them it is extremely difficult to become a member in the first place. Not only are land and establishment costs extremely high, but would-be members also have to pay an entrance fee (a so-called 'delivery right'), which can run into hundreds of thousands of rand. To set up one's own cellar involves millions. As a result a more feasible option for 'new farmers' may be a kind of 'outgrower' relation with a private cellar or producing wholesaler, such as is operating in Olifantsriver region. Farm worker equity schemes are another possibility but they have their own difficulties as we shall see below.

ENTER THE STATE: ATTEMPTS AT 'EMPOWERMENT'

The third important dimension of change relates to national democratization. Again, the periodization of this shift is complex. Moves to bring farm workers into the fold of modern industrial relations started before 1994 with the basic Conditions of Employment Act 1993, but the coming into power of an ANC government deepened and accelerated these trends. A veritable slew of legislation was passed, providing for a wide range of labour, social and land rights, ranging from basic conditions of labour in 1993 to the promulgation of minimum wages in 2003.[4] A paternalist state has stepped in to push back the paternalist authority of the farmer and has created new limits to farmers' control over workers' lives.[5] These changes seriously challenge the legal and formal underpinnings of traditional farm paternalism.

But challenging paternalism is not the same as replacing it. There is evidence that many farmers are reluctant to comply with labour legislation, if not downright hostile to it (Kleinbooi and Hall, 2001). Most farmers comply with the main provisions of the BCEA (e.g., hours of work, leave and holiday provisions) but some are reluctant to implement the UIF, the EEA and the SDA (Sunde and Kleinbooi, 1999) (see note 4 for definition of these abbreviations). However, most of farmer anger and opposition is reserved for ESTA – the Extension of Security of Tenure Act, which gives farm workers the right to keep on living in the farm cottage even after they have been retrenched or reached retirement age. Nevertheless, enforcement by the state is weak and as a result, many farm workers have lost their permanent jobs and housing on the farm since the Act was introduced. Given the state's track record, it remains to be seen whether the enforcement of the minimum wages is going to be any better. Weaknesses in the legislation, a small inspectorate, huge caseloads and a shortage of conciliation commissioners compound the problem. Although labour law has significantly disrupted the institutional order of paternalist labour management, it has not decisively transformed it. The state is far away and lacks the ability to enforce its own laws. Farm workers find that insisting on their rights can be a dangerous strategy and know that maintaining patronage relationships may be as important. The result on the ground is a complex palimpsest in which labour relationships are simultaneously governed both by the formal codes of legislation and by the personal relationships and implicit contracts of paternalist practices (Flensted-Jensen, 2002).

In addition farmers are changing the nature of the battleground. Though labour law has curtailed their power, they have retained the ability to restructure their business on their own terms. This results in trends that could make labour law irrelevant in important sectors – and that poses important challenges to traditional forms of worker organization.

FARMERS' RESPONSES AND IMPLICATIONS FOR WORKERS

How growers are affected by these changes depends partly on how they are located within the agro-commodity system. Not everyone is well positioned to take advantage of the growing market for premium and export wines. One important obstacle is geography: generally speaking, wine grape farmers in the hotter regions face serious disadvantages in trying to break into the quality market. A second factor is the historical bias in existing plantings toward high yielding cultivars unsuitable for the production of quality wines.

Nevertheless, approximately 50 per cent of all vineyards have been replanted since the early 1990s. Most of the new plantings involve the so-called 'noble' varieties, that is, Cabernet Sauvignon, Merlot, Pinotage, Shiraz, Sauvignon Blanc and Chardonnay. In 2002, noble cultivars represented 40.5 per cent of all plantings, compared with only 13.8 per cent in 1991. Red wine production increased from 10.9 per cent of all grapes pressed in 1992 to 21 per cent in 2002.

The conversion has come at a price, not only in the form of land and establishment costs but also in the guise of more labour-intensive vineyard practices required by 'quality production'. Better quality grapes require more precise pruning techniques, careful 'suckering' and canopy and crop control. This means higher labour costs. There are more problems. The unleashing of market forces among grape growers and the revival of the tendency to 'plant after the price', reintroduces important elements of instability. During the late 1990s when red wine grapes were in short supply, farmers could command good prices for quality Shiraz and Cabernet Sauvignon grapes. As more and more farmers join the bandwagon, those prices are sure to drop. Increasingly, growers of wine grapes are at the mercy of those further downstream in the value chain. Though high margins will be possible for some, many growers will face tightening quality, 'ethical' and phytosanitary standards, increasing pressure on their margins and increasing levels of risk.

This has important consequences for workers. Unlike grape growers in the EU for instance, South African wine farmers receive no subsidies and have to absorb the higher labour costs themselves. Little wonder that many farmers are reacting angrily to the state's attempts to intervene in labour affairs on 'their' farm. Minimum wages in particular caused huge protests in certain quarters of the organized farming lobby (*Die Burger*, 14 May 2003). However, formal protest is not the farmers' most significant response. Facing a sustained challenge to their power as employers and feeling increasing competitive pressures, many farmers seem to be opting for the one measure that is still within their power: restructuring their businesses. Many seem to be resorting to casualization, externalization and contractualization, deepening an already segmented labour market and further deepening the divide between 'winners' and 'losers'.

In the first years after democratization, evidence on employment trends seemed mixed. While the initial post-sanction years still recorded an increase in aggregate employment, this trend may have started to change in the late 1990s. In 1997 both industry figures and academic research recorded an increase over the previous four years. While industry figures cited a 7 per cent increase, a survey of 104 farms in 1997, revealed a 5 per cent rise in permanent employment. In 1997 farmers also estimated that 'their' permanent labour force would grow by an additional 3 per cent until the year 2002. The same estimate was made for casual labour (Ewert ct al., 1998). The trends in wine were backed up by Agricultural Census figures (1996), which showed that the Western Cape together with Mpumalanga, were the only provinces to show an increase in agricultural employment. The fact that agriculture in both provinces was inserted into the export sector played a major part.

Trends may have started shifting however. The above-mentioned survey was done in 1997, shortly after the restructuring of the cooperatives sector had begun in all earnest (i.e., in 1995–96) and during a huge upsurge in new plantings. Four years later however, another survey of 77 wine, fruit and vegetable farms in six districts of the Western Cape suggested an uneven but noticeable trend away from permanent farm employment (du Toit and Ally, 2004). These trends were more pronounced on deciduous fruit-growing farms but they were still present on wine farms. Almost 60 per cent of farms in the survey (and more than 54 per cent of wine farms) had reduced the size of the permanent labour force in the previous three years and on almost half (and 41 per cent of the wine farms sampled), management indicated plans to reduce permanent labour in future. For the most part, jobs were not being replaced by machines but by casual labour, with strong shifts towards the use of labour contractors and casual workers and a distinct trend towards the use of women workers (du Toit and Ally, 2004, pp. 15–16; see also Kritzinger, Barrientos and Rossouw, 2004).

In addition, significant numbers of white farmers seemed to be walking away from the 'social responsibility' functions they have traditionally been held to have in terms of paternalist ideology. Key here was the withdrawal from the provision of housing to farm workers. Some 57 per cent of farmers reported having at least one empty house on the farm, with this figure reaching 83 per cent in some districts. Less than a quarter of respondents indicated that they planned to continue renovating existing housing stock and almost a third of farmers (32 per cent of the whole sample, and 33 per cent of wine farmers) were considering abandoning their 'traditional' housing function altogether (du Toit and Ally, 2004, p. 22).

The increasing employment of casual labour is paralleled by the rising introduction of mechanical grape harvesters. Grape harvesters represent important advantages for farmers. Not only do they represent a significant reduction in labour costs – one machine may replace as many at 70 workers per 12 hour shift[6] – but they also offer important quality advantages, enabling farmers to harvest quickly when sugar levels are right or at night to make sure grapes are cool. In 1995 a total of 95 machines were recorded for the whole industry. A year later this figure already stood at 144 – an increase of 52 per cent. In the 1997 survey of 104 farms, 36 per cent of producers made use of mechanical harvesters (Ewert et al., 1998). Diffusion may have slowed down but there is no reason to believe that it has come to a halt.

Increasing levels of casualization and externalization have serious consequences for rural livelihoods. Asset poverty means that poor households in the new peri-urban settlements around Western Cape towns in the farming districts lack direct access to land and the other resources required for either household food production or independent entrepreneurial activity. Unemployment is rife and in many regions and rural towns, livelihoods are cobbled together from state welfare grants and cash from seasonal and casual employment. In the rural Western Cape that means farm work. The move off-farm does not end the dependence on the agro-food sector and in the winelands, the 8–12-week vintage period presents a crucial window for supplementing cash incomes. Women, young people and new migrants are particularly insecure in the search for work. On any given day there are many more work seekers than the farmer needs. In scenes reminiscent of the book *Grapes of Wrath* by John Steinbeck, the farmer or their superviser can pick and choose amongst those clambering to get onto the lorry for a day's wages. Under these circumstances casuals are unlikely candidates for unions – not as ordinary paid-up members, let alone the vanguard.

PROSPECTS FOR EQUITABLE CHANGE

Trade Unions and Rural Social Movements

The structural changes in the wine industry affect the prospects for equitable change and the likely impact of interventions aimed at improving livelihoods on the ground. Most obvious of these is the prospect of trade unionism shifting – or at least challenging – power relations between employers and workers. Again legal change has had limited effects. Legal 'industrial' action on the part of farm workers first became a possibility with the passing of the 1994 Agricultural Labour Act; since this act was replaced by the 1995 Labour Relations Act, farm workers have the explicit right to strike and access to mediation services.[7] But unionization in most parts of the rural Western Cape has been rather slow and piecemeal.[8]

Part of the reason lies in farmer opposition – organized agriculture has vehemently resisted central bargaining in the industry, forcing unions to fight for recognition farm by farm. Here unions are on unfavourable terrain: not only are resources stretched by distance, isolation and the poverty of their organizational base, but they are also up against the legacy of paternalism itself.

But that is not the whole story. Trade union strategies themselves may be ill-suited to agricultural organizing. Farm workers draw upon their previous historic traditions of resistance; but these traditions are very unlike the overt, adversarial, confrontational discourse of factory unionism. Rather they rely on the 'weapons of the weak', operating within the framework of the paternalist moral universe itself, relying on individual appeals, consensual negotiations and the avoidance of the appearance of open conflict

(Scott, 1985). These tactics are often dismissed as evidence of servility or compliance by organizations drawing on urban political traditions. These dismissals are based on a failure to understand the complex art of making claims and securing demands in a context where the networks of white power are so tightly woven and where the previous employer acts as the reference for the next job application (see for example, Flensted-Jensen, 2002). The point is not simply that flirting with the unions – and becoming marked as a 'troublemaker' – would seriously impair a worker's re-employment prospects: it is also that prospects for union organization remain slender as long as they tend to replace, rather than draw upon, the already existing cultural repertoire and traditions of farm workers' resistance and agency.

While genuine worker representation is vital in the contestation of on-farm power relations, it is unlikely to be secured through the export to the farms of the Fordist models of trade union organization developed in South Africa's urban workplaces (du Toit and Ewert, 2002). If workers and unions want to make headway, the focus of organization needs to shift beyond the ranks of permanent, full-time on-farm and mostly male workers and greater priority has to be placed on organizing the African and female workers who are so much more predominant in the seasonal and externalized labour force. Not only are these workers more vulnerable but their priorities differ significantly and in gendered ways from those of permanent workers (Barrientos and Kritzinger, 2002). In addition, as Andries du Toit has argued, it will be hard to organize these workers effectively if an artificial divide is made between their specifically farm-labour-related problems and all the other serious difficulties with rural service delivery and infrastructure provision that dwellers in rural informal settlements will experience (du Toit, 2000).

Equity Share Schemes

Much more ambiguous than trade unionism as a possible intervention into the power relations between workers and farmers are farm worker equity share schemes (FWES). Apart from perennial problems like the high cost of arable land and the lack of cashflow (VinPro, 2004, pp. 41–2), it can be argued that these schemes do not represent a radical break with the traditions of the past: indeed, they bear many resemblances to the innovations of 'neo-paternalist' initiatives like the Rural Foundation and in their emphasis on the convergence of the interests of management and workers, may be argued to involve a radicalization or extension of some of the most fundamental elements of paternalist ideology. They can however, bring significant benefits to farm workers in the longer run and, to the extent that they turn management decision-making itself into a contested terrain, may contain significant opportunities for changes to the highly authoritarian, racially hierarchical management practices of traditional paternalism. Ultimately however, they will tend to work mostly to the benefit of the small core of on-farm workers, and even when they are so designed as to minimize differences between permanent and seasonal workers, their overall impact is likely to be the deepening of the division between the 'insiders' and the 'outsiders'.

Industry Initiatives

Perhaps most ill-defined of all are the prospects for equitable change arising out of formal industry transformation. Here a key question is the extent to which industry leadership can give the process any direction at all. In the years immediately after transformation, the KWV's initial response to democratization was to attempt to avoid government's grasp simply by privatizing itself. When it finally abandoned this course of action after two years of legal wrangling, it seems to have settled on trying to ensure that what change happens, happens on its terms. The South African Wine Industry Trust (SAWIT), set up by the KWV in terms of its out of court settlement with the then Minister of Land Affairs and Agriculture, has manifestly failed to implement its obligations to ensure the development and empowerment of farm workers. Devco, the arm of SAWIT charged with supporting 'new farmers' and the 'upliftment' of farm workers has spent only a fraction of its funding and was by March 2004 being accused of violating its terms of reference (*Sunday Times* [South Africa] 29 February 2004). Nevertheless, towards the end of June 2004 it was announced that a long-awaited empowerment deal had been struck between the KWV and a 'broad-based consortium' of black business people, professionals, trade unions and 'non-profit organizations' (*Die Burger*, 28 July 2004). In terms of the agreement, the consortium would acquire a 25.1 per cent share in KWV. It would be partly funded by SAWIT's DEVCO arm.

Although KWV and the beneficiaries hailed the deal as an historical act, it has come in for criticism from various quarters. Some critics point out that a large chunk of DEVCO money is going to a single project, whereas the funds are earmarked for empowerment in the industry at large (*Die Burger*, 28 July 2004). Equally serious is the criticism of a conflict of interest. Members of the SAWIT executive are said to be amongst the beneficiaries. At the same time it is not clear how much the unions, NGOs and ordinary workers will benefit, if at all.

Meanwhile the framework for debating change in the industry was set by 'Vision 2020', a 'strategic study' commissioned by Winetech in 1999. This

resulted in the announcement in June 2000 of a 'strategic agenda' dominated by the need to 'achieve international competitiveness' and the
imperative to 'shift to a . . . market-driven industry', 'terroir-based production', 'total value chain management' and so forth. The document also
contained the customary references to 'human development', 'social
responsibility', 'affirmative action' and 'broadening the base of economic
participation' (Winetech, 2000).

Vision 2020 played a key ideological and political role, providing a legiti-
mating framework for the continuation of processes of deregulation and
restructuring that were already under way. And in this it seems to have been
moderately successful, if one credits its authors' insistence that there was
widespread buy-in by cooperative cellar management during 2020's 'road
show' in 2000. As a strategic document however, it had significant limitations. It tended to avoid dealing at all with the trade-offs, costs and choices
involved in balancing the various imperatives it identified. Neither the
'agenda' nor the reports that go with it (Spies, 2001a, 2001b) provide any
clue as to how economic participation is to be broadened or how rural
livelihoods can be created and sustained.

These tensions and questions will become increasingly hard to avoid in
2004 and after. In October 2002, the KWV created the South African Wine
and Brandy Company, a corporatist body with a council divided into four
'chambers' ('producers' [i.e., growers], 'cellars', 'labour' and the 'trade') but
still heavily staffed by representatives of the old establishment. At a conference on Black Economic Empowerment in the South African Wine
Industry at the end of October 2003, it announced a 'Wine Industry Plan'
broadly based on Vision 2020 – a plan that was in principle accepted by the
Minister of Agriculture. This set the scene for the development of a Black
Economic Empowerment Charter for the Wine Industry. Quite aside from
the cloud hanging over the heavily compromised SAWIT, any such charter
faces the challenge of balancing and reconciling numerous different
agendas – not least being very different models of what 'Black Economic
Empowerment' could be. The expectations of middle-class Black South
Africans who hope to buy into opportunities to share the profits of the
industry will have to be balanced against the demands of those arguing that
workers should be included in broad-based empowerment.

Although land ownership is among the most difficult and least attractive
segments of the value chain to buy into, the SAWB in conjunction with
VinPro and Nedbank, has just produced a policy paper on land reform in the
wine industry. It takes full cognizance of the high entry barriers and 'classi-
cal' pitfalls of equity share schemes. At the same time it puts on the table a
number of different land reform models that it deems viable – given that
certain conditions (including 'donor funding') are satisfied (VinPro, 2004).

While much in Vision 2020 and SAWB policy papers makes sense, the more difficult part is putting it into practice. The SAWB leadership may know where it wants to go but evidence suggests that awareness of the WIP amongst the rank and file wine farmers is very low. Also the institutional instruments may be in place but why should the average grape grower, already reeling under cost pressures, go along with it? Clearly, incentives are needed. According to WIP, funding will come 'from industry sources and levies, government provisions, international donors, . . . investors' and SAWIT (SAWB, 2003, p. v). However, whether the EU for instance, will assist with more funding over and above the R114 million promised in terms of EU–SA trade agreement remains to be seen. As it stands the R114 million are going into the KWV empowerment deal.

Incentives or not, the government could possibly use 'sticks' to make farmers and cellars buy into transformation and 'empowerment'. For instance, a clause in the Liquor Act gives government the power to withdraw the licence of a cellar that appears to drag its feet on this issue. However, the state will probably think twice, lest it wants more unemployment on its hands.

Thus, without much in the way of either 'carrots' or 'sticks', it seems unlikely that either the WIP or the BEE charter will produce much in the way of concrete results for poor people living in the Cape wine lands.

CONCLUSIONS

Deregulation, legal reform and global integration in the South African wine industry has brought about the 'deep' restructuring of the labour force into a smaller, permanent core and a growing, casual periphery. For this core of permanent workers, the 'quality revolution' has brought the upskilling of work – as well as increased opportunities to share in the value they create. Increasingly however, this improvement goes hand in hand with the loss of permanent work and greater vulnerability for many others. It is improbable that these trends will be challenged by industry transformation and 'Black Empowerment', which are likely to continue to be shaped by the interests of those who already have a stake in the industry.

These trends pose an important challenge to those concerned about the livelihoods, living conditions and interests of farm workers, both nationally and internationally. These issues can not be satisfactorily addressed within the terms of the frameworks of analysis and the meta-narratives that structure policy debates. These frameworks are unduly focused on farm workers' identity as workers and the strategies aiming to address their problems are overly situated within the problematic of employment and workplace transformation. Important though continued growth, workplace change and employment are, they offer only limited scope for addressing farm workers' interests.

The perspective needs to be broadened to include global value chains, state support for greater international competitiveness, pro-poor policies, the building of social capital in the wine lands and equity other than the redistribution of land. Additionally, attempts need to be made to strengthen significantly the commitments of foreign supermarket chains to ethical trading (perhaps through the tax system) and restricting their oligopolistically derived capacities to force down prices to the detriment, ultimately, of the poor.

NOTES

1. In 2002 the structure of the industry was as follows: 4501 primary producers (i.e., grape growers), 50 cooperative cellars, 92 estates, eight producing wholesalers (personal communication, Debbie Wait, SAWIS, 8 May 2002). The most important producing wholesalers today are: Distell, Guinness UDW, Douglas Green Bellingham, Edward Snell and Co., Jonkheer Boerewynmakery, Mooiuitsig Wynkelders and KWV. All these, except KWV, are represented by CWSI. One of the biggest international liquor firms, Pernod Ricard, may soon join the CWSI (personal communication, Marike de Kock, Cape Wine and Spirits Institute [CWSI], 3 June 2003).
2. Interviews with Distell officials, November and December 2001.
3. Personal communication, MD of Simonsvlei cellar, February 2002.
4. The most important pieces of legislation applicable to farm workers are: the Basic Conditions of Employment Act, 1998 (the BCEA); the Occupational Health and Safety Act of 1993 (OHSA); the Compensation for Occupational Injuries and Diseases Act of 1993 (COIDA); the Labour Relations Act No. 66 of 1995 (the LRA); the Employment Equity Act No. 55 of 1998 (the EEA); the Skills Development Act and Skills Development Levies Act (the SDA and the SDLA); the Extension of Security of Tenure Act No. 62 of 1997 (ESTA); the Unemployment Insurance Act (UIF); the Sectoral Determination 8: Farm Worker Sector: the Determination sets two categories of minimum wages, viz. R800 p.m. or R4.10 per hour (for those working 27 hours or less per week) in 'Areas A' and R650 p.m. or R3.33 per hour in 'Areas B'. The Determination came into effect on the 1 March 2003 and is valid until 29 February 2004. The rates may then be increased.
5. Dismissals for instance, are no longer simply a matter of farmers' prerogative. Statistics for the Commission for Conciliation, Mediation and Arbitration, Western Cape, show that of the 4801 disputes heard by CCMA commissioners in Western Cape agriculture between November 1996 and October 2003, 67 per cent were unfair dismissal disputes, followed by 'matters of mutual interest' (7.9 per cent), 'unfair labour practices' (6.2 per cent) and 'organizational rights' (3.5 per cent). Statistics supplied by Anthea Edwards, CCMA head office, Johannesburg, 6 October 2003.
6. Personal communication, Johan Botha, vineyard manager, Fairview Cellar, Paarl, 28 May 2003.
7. The services are provided by the Commission for Conciliation, Mediation and Arbitration (CCMA) – a kind of industrial relations 'fire brigade' designed for the speedy resolution of disputes, including those in agriculture.
8. Precise figures are very hard to come by, given the fragile and fluctuating fortunes of unions in the wine sector. Most observers agree however, that they do not exceed 10 per cent of the permanent labour force (i.e., between 5000–6000 members). Two unions, the

Food and Allied Workers Union (FAWU) and the National Union of Food, Wine and Beverage Workers of South Africa, claim a combined total of 3000 signed up members at the cellars of wholesalers represented by CWSI and KWV. Both these unions, plus SAPAAWU (SA Agricultural, Plantation & Allied Workers Union) and eight smaller unions claim to have members at private, estate and cooperative cellars and at farm level. However, no reliable figures are available. This also goes for the so-called Farm Workers Association. Interestingly the General Secretary of the Association is the former MD of the now defunct Rural Foundation, Ockie Bosman. They claim substantial support amongst farm workers, but do not sign up or register members.

REFERENCES

Barrientos, S. and A. Kritzinger (2002), 'Global Value Chains and Poverty: The Case of Contract Labour in South African Fruit', Paper to the Conference on Globalisation, Growth and (In-)equality, Centre for the Study of Globalisation and Regionalisation, University of Warwick.

CRLS (2001), *The Determination of Employment Conditions in South African Agriculture*, report to the Department of Labour, South African Government. Centre for Rural Legal Studies and National Institute of Economic Policy.

du Toit, A. (2000), 'Room for Manoeuvre: "Globalisation", "Modernisation" and Equitable Change in the Western Cape's Deciduous Fruit Industry', Paper to the Xth World Rural Sociology Conference, Rio de Janeiro, Brazil (July/August).

du Toit, A. (2003), 'Hunger in the Valley of Fruitfulness: Globalization, "Social Exclusion" and Chronic Poverty in Ceres, South Africa', Paper to the Conference on Staying Poor: Chronic Poverty and Development Policy, University of Manchester (April) (www.chronicpoverty.org).

du Toit, A. and F. Ally (2004), *The Externalization and Casualization of Farm Labour in the Western Cape*, Belville: PLAAS/CRLS.

du Toit, A. and J. Ewert (2002), 'Myths of globalisation: private regulation and farm worker livelihoods on Western Cape farms', *Transformation*, **50**, 77–104.

Ewert, J. (2003), 'Co-operatives to Companies: The South African Wine Industry in the Face of Globalization', in R. Almas and G. Lawrence (eds), *Globalization, Localization and Sustainable Livelihoods*, Aldershot: Ashgate.

Ewert, J. et al. (1998), *State and Market, Labour and Land*, Research Report, Departments of Sociology and Agricultural Economics, University of Stellenbosch.

Flensted-Jensen, M. (2002), 'Law, Power and the Political Process: A Study of the Ambiguities of Land Reform Legislation in the Western Cape Province in South Africa', unpublished Masters thesis, University of Aarhus.

GPN (2003), 'The Internationalisation/Globalisation of Retailing: Towards a Geographical Research Agenda', Working Paper, 8, School of Geography, University of Manchester.

Henderson, J. (2002), 'Globalisation on the Ground: Global Production Networks, Competition, Regulation and Economic Development', Working Paper, Centre on Regulation and Competition, University of Manchester.

Hoe, S.A. (1998), 'Brou vorder met sy nuwe fofus', *Finansies & Tegniek*, 26 June.

Kleinbooi, K. and R. Hall (2001), 'Employment Trends in Western Cape Agriculture', Paper to the Conference on International Agricultural Trade and Rural Livelihoods, Somerset West, South Africa (October).

Kritzinger, A., S. Barrientos and H. Rossouw (2004), 'Global Production and Flexible Employment in South African Horticulture: Experiences of Contract Workers in Fruit Exports', *Sociologia Ruralis*, **44** (1), 17–39.

Loubster, S.S. (2001), *The Wine Business: A Strategic Marketing Framework*, Stellenbosch: Winetech.

Martin, C. (2001), 'Les Coopératives dans le Secteur Viticole Sud-Africain', unpublished Masters thesis, CNEARC, Montpellier.

Rachman, G. (1999), 'The Globe in a Glass: A Survey of Wine', *The Economist*, 8 December, 97–115.

Robinson, J. (1999), *The Oxford Companion to Wine*, Oxford: Oxford University Press.

SAWB (2003), *Wine Industry Plan*, Stellenbosch: South African Wine and Brandy Company.

SAWIS (2003), *Wynbedryfstatistiek*, 27.

Scott, J.C. (1985), *Weapons of the Weak*, New Haven: Yale University Press.

Spies, P.H. (2001a), *Strategic Outline of the South African Wine Industry*, Stellenbosch: Winetech.

Spies, P.H. (2001b), *Option Analysis and Scenarios for the South African Wine Industry*, Stellenbosch: Winetech.

Sunde, J. and K. Kleinbooi (1999), *Promoting Equitable and Sustainable Development for Women Farm Workers in the Western Cape*, Stellenbosch: Centre for Rural Legal Studies.

VinPro (2004), *Land Reform in the Wine Industry: The Wine Producer Programme*, Stellenbosch: VinPro.

Winetech (2000), 'Strategic Agenda for Discussion by Study Groups', mimeo, Stellenbosch: Winetech (June).

14. Foreign competition and growth: Bangladesh manufacturing industries

Selim Raihan

INTRODUCTION

The relationship between increased foreign competition (or trade liberalization) and economic growth is a controversial issue. Trade liberalization has been one of the major policy reforms in the developing countries for the last two decades. Whilst there is an apparent consensus that the effects of increased foreign competition on economic performance are likely to be positive, the evidence to support this is far from conclusive. On the one hand, the theories on the relationship between opening up the economy and growth are not clear and on the other hand, there are marked differences in the methodologies and correspondingly the findings of the empirical research on the foreign competition–growth nexus. Macro-level studies tend to concentrate on the cross-country variation in growth performance and link this to variations in the level of trade liberalization. Single-country macro studies largely assess the impact of trade liberalization on growth performance over time. There is a vast literature that explores the impact of reform at the sectoral level. The study presented in this chapter is an empirical investigation of foreign competition on the manufacturing sector in Bangladesh. It seeks to find out whether or not an increase in foreign competition affects the output of the manufacturing sector in Bangladesh between 1977–98.

Most of the empirical research in this context has used firm-level data in a panel framework and often fails to use a long enough time span to incorporate both the pre- and post-trade liberalization period. Furthermore, most of the empirical studies on trade liberalization and competition appear to date back to the 1980s and early 1990s and as a consequence they use outmoded econometric techniques. Recent developments include panel unit root tests and panel cointegration tests, which suggest that if there is a considerable longer time span in a panel dataset then the variables under consideration might be non-stationary and thus a simple OLS estimation may end up with spurious regression results (Kao, 1999; Kao, Chiang and Chen, 1999; McCoskey and Kao, 1999).

FOREIGN COMPETITION AND GROWTH

Theoretical models addressing trade reform have tended to end up with different policy conclusions that largely result from the different assumptions on which the models have been derived (Tybout, 2000). Assumptions have differed in relation to the degree of market imperfections. In the main, two classes of models have been used. Static models have tended to look at the ways in which domestic firms respond to the competitive pressures that they face, to the size of the market within which they operate, and to changes in scale economies and 'X-efficiency' after trade liberalization (Helpman and Krugman, 1985; Grossman, 1992).

The 'X-efficiency' argument suggests that trade protection reduces industrial sector efficiency (Tybout, 1991, 1992). It is argued that in markets with barriers to entry, lack of exposure to foreign competition allows domestic producers to exercise monopoly power and, therefore, enjoy 'super-normal' profits. This acts as a disincentive for firms to achieve 'scale efficiency', and to get the maximum possible output from their inputs. When an economy is exposed to greater international competition, domestic industries are forced to respond to this challenge by adopting new technologies with the aim of reducing X-inefficiency. Thus the argument for 'X-efficiency' views export expansion and import liberalization as being helpful for enhancing competition and inducing greater efficiency, which paves the way for a better economic performance (Nishimizu and Robinson, 1983). The argument of increasing returns also postulates that free trade widens the market, which helps to reduce production costs. Kaldor (1967) attributed this to the presence of scale economies.

In contrast, dynamic models have attempted to explain technology acquisition and productivity change after trade liberalization (Rodrik, 1988, 1992; Miyagiwa and Yuka, 1995). Rodrik (1988) formulates a framework in which the representative firm's rate of catch-up to international productivity levels depends positively on its market share. It is argued that trade reforms would likely accelerate the transition to state-of-the-art technologies among exportables and decelerate the process among import-competing sectors. It is also argued that one-way domestic producers can compete is through choice of techniques. Hence producers could tacitly collude when protected from foreign competition by failing to modernize their plants, and trade liberalization may induce defection from the collusive equilibrium.

A variety of approaches have been used to test empirically the theoretical propositions raised by these models. Tybout (2000) provides a useful survey of this literature. The results obtained from these empirical exercises vary considerably. Some studies report a positive impact of increased foreign competition on economic performance in the manufacturing sector, while other studies reveal a negative impact or no association. Nishimizu and Robinson (1983), for example, examine the impact of trade regimes on sectoral total factor productivity (TFP) growth for Korea, Turkey, Yugoslavia and Japan. Their study finds that import-substitution regimes seem to be negatively correlated with a change in TFP whereas export-expansion regimes are positively correlated with a change in TFP. The study by Krueger and Tuncer (1982) on Turkey provides strong support for the efficiency gains to be derived from liberalization and concludes that periods of greater liberalization have coincided with periods of faster growth in total factor productivity. Parallel conclusions have also been reached by Condon, Corbo and de Melo (1985) for Chile, Page (1980) for India and Pitt and Lee (1981) for the Indonesian weaving industry. Furthermore, more recent studies such as Harrison (1994), Tybout and Westbrook (1995), Pavcnik (2002) and Fernandes (2003) have also observed productivity increases following trade liberalization in the Ivory Coast, Mexico, Chile and Columbia.

In contrast, Tybout, de Melo and Corbo (1991) find no evidence of increased productivity following liberalization in Chile. Tsao (1985) also finds that productivity growth during the period of liberalization in the 1970s is negligible or negative in some sectors of manufacturing in Singapore. Pack (1988) reports that comparisons of total factor productivity growth among countries pursuing different international trade orientations do not reveal systematic differences in productivity growth in manufacturing. After reviewing studies based on within-country temporal correlations, Pack (1988) and Havrylyshyn (1990) both conclude that there is no strong evidence linking productivity and openness.

The upshot of the above discussion points to the fact that, barring differences in methodological approaches and coverage, there is little consensus on the impact of increased foreign competition on economic performance and productivity growth. The link is therefore clearly an empirical issue. With the aim of adding to the growing evidence on this theme, this study explores the foreign-competition–growth-productivity nexus in the context of Bangladesh manufacturing industries.

TRADE LIBERALIZATION IN BANGLADESH

After a period of restricted trade regime until the mid-1970s Bangladesh initiated a more liberalized trade regime. The period of restricted trade regime was characterized by inward-looking policies of creating an import-substituting industrial base through a protective domestic environment, conserving foreign exchange, maintaining a stable balance of payment and a dominant role for the public sector in almost every aspect of the economy. However, this regime has been criticized on grounds of its inefficient allocation of resources, rent-seeking activities, anti-export bias, development of an incompetent industrial structure, slow growth of the economy and problems with balance of payments. Under structural adjustment programmes, more open, liberal, export-orientated and private-sector-based policies were put in place. The programmes were targeted towards reforms in different aspects of the economy including fiscal, financial, trade and industrial policy reforms; public resource management; privatization and institutional and sectoral reforms (Mujeri and Khondker, 2004).

The pace and extent of trade liberalization accelerated during the late 1980s and early 1990s when more comprehensive programmes of stabilization and economic reforms were put in place under the structural adjustment programmes prescribed by the World Bank and the IMF. The structural adjustment programmes were initiated in 1987 and implemented through the Structural Adjustment Facility (SAF) and the Enhanced Structural Adjustment Facility (ESAF) of the IMF and the World Bank (see Sobhan, 1991 and Mujeri, Shahabuddin and Ahmed, 1993 for a detailed discussion).

In Bangladesh, trade liberalization programmes and associated economic reforms during the 1980s and 1990s significantly liberalized external trade and foreign exchange. Following the implementation of these reforms there has been rationalization and simplification of the trade regime in Bangladesh, with significant lowering of tariff rates, phasing out of the quantitative restrictions, simplification of the import procedures, introduction of tax reforms and the introduction of various export promotion measures. The major changes due to the reforms are summarized as follows:

- Import procedures were simplified and the number of tariff bands was reduced significantly. Twenty-four slabs of import duty rates set in the 1980s were replaced with only four slabs in 2000.
- In 1992 the highest customs duty rate was 350 per cent. It was reduced to 37.5 per cent in 2000. The unweighted average tariff rate declined to 22 per cent in 1999 from 114 per cent in 1989, while the

import-weighted average tariff rate declined to 19 per cent from 114 per cent over the same period. Import taxes such as development surcharges, regulatory duties and sales taxes were abolished in 1991. It is however important to note that despite reductions in many tariffs, total tariffs still remain high by international standards since, in addition to customs duty, several other taxes are levied upon imports such as value-added tax, supplementary duty, infrastructure development surcharges and licence fees.

- There has been a significant reduction in the number of commodities under quantitative restrictions. In 1987 the number of commodities under the four-digit code subject to quantitative restrictions was 550, which declined to 124 under the Import Policy of 1997–2002. The decline in quantitative restriction is also manifested in the fact that whereas in 1992, about 12 per cent of around 10 000 tariff lines were subject to quantitative restrictions, in 1999 it came down to less than 4 per cent. The restriction was also relaxed in the later years and at present less than 0.5 per cent of imports, mainly in the textile category, are subject to quantitative restrictions.

- There has been a move towards a more market-determined exchange rate. The policy of multiple exchange rates was replaced by a unified exchange rate in 1992 and the domestic currency (taka) was pegged to a currency-weighted basket. Since 1992 a policy of creeping devaluation has been followed to maintain exchange rate flexibility and export competitiveness. The currency was made convertible for all current account transactions. Finally, in 2003 Bangladesh initiated a fully flexible exchange rate system.

- Under the export-oriented industrialization strategy, different export promotion measures were put in place with the aim of diversifying the export basket, improving the quality of exports, stimulating higher value-added exports and developing industries for backward linkages. The export-promoting measures undertaken were: special bonded warehouse facilities, the establishment of export-processing zones, a duty drawback scheme, a rebate on insurance premiums, an income tax rebate, an export-credit guarantee scheme, incentives for exporting non-traditional industrial products, an export promotion fund, value-added tax refunds, tax holidays and retaining foreign exchange from export earnings.

Overall, it could be concluded that during the 1990s the trade regime in Bangladesh became significantly more open compared with the earlier period and exposed the manufacturing sector to considerably increased foreign competition.

ANALYTICAL FRAMEWORK

The use of a production function approach to examine the relationship between foreign competition and growth relationship is popular among researchers. The advantages with this approach are twofold: (1) relevant factors can be controlled for in the analysis, which helps in finding the key variables in the relationship being examined; (2) the production function approach identifies the sources of growth, which are central to the neo-classical model of Solow (1956). The Solow model considers three sources of growth: the accumulation of physical capital, the growth of labour force and the growth of total factor productivity. We can therefore start with a simple neo-classical production function to estimate the basic Solow-type sources of growth and then we can incorporate various measures of foreign competition in the original model to examine whether the variables representing foreign competition turn out to be statistically significant or not.

We start with a Cobb-Douglas production function. In a panel framework, the production function is defined for each sector and each year;

$$Y_{it} = A_{it}K_{it}^{\beta_i}L_{it}^{\gamma_i} \tag{14.1}$$

where Y_{it} is real valued-added for sector i in time period t, K_{it} is the capital stock and L_{it} is the number of workers. A_{it} is the technology specified in the model. Technology includes both a possible intercept and trend term:

$$A_{it} = e^{\alpha_i + \delta_i t + \varepsilon_{it}} \tag{14.2}$$

Taking the natural log of (14.1) forms the following model:

$$\ln Y_{it} = \alpha_i + \delta_i t + \beta_i \ln K_{it} + \gamma_i \ln L_{it} + \varepsilon_{it} \tag{14.3}$$

To verify the link between foreign competition and growth, the model (14.1) can be extended further by including some measures of foreign competition. The underlying hypothesis of such inclusion is that apart from the Solow-type basic sources of growth, the measures of foreign competition may have a significant influence on growth. Such inclusion of foreign competition variables results in:

$$Y_{it} = A_{it}K_{it}^{\beta_i}L_{it}^{\gamma_i}\Gamma_{it}^{\theta_i} \tag{14.4}$$

where Y, A, K, L are defined earlier and Γ represents measures of foreign competition. With the help of (14.2) and the natural logarithm of (14.4), the final equation to be estimated becomes:

$$\ln Y_{it} = \alpha_i + \delta_i t + \beta_i \ln K_{it} + \gamma_i \ln L_{it} + \theta_i \ln \Gamma_{it} + \varepsilon_{it} \qquad (14.5)$$

As Harrison (1996) points out, the inclusion of trade liberalization or foreign competition measures in the production function is consequently a test of their impact on technological change – growth in output after controlling for other factors of production. It is also important to note that in line with the arguments made by Harrison (1994) that the assumption of constant returns to scale may lead to biased estimates of traditional productivity residuals, the models specified in equations (14.3) and (14.5) make no restrictions on returns to scale. Therefore, the sum of input coefficients in (14.3) and (14.5) need not add up to unity.

The organization of the rest of this chapter is as follows. First, the variables used in this research and sources of the data of these variables are described. Second, different panel unit root tests of the models under consideration are applied. Third, different panel cointegration tests of the models under consideration are applied. Fourth, estimation results for the models incorporating various indicators of foreign competition are reported. Finally, the implications of the estimation results are discussed.

DATA ON VARIABLES

The panel estimation of the production function requires data for value-added, capital stock and labour. Data for the manufacturing sector in Bangladesh is available at the three-digit ISIC (International Standard Industrial Classification) code level for 27 sectors with a time span of 22 years (a list of manufacturing industries at the three-digit ISIC code level is reported in Appendix 14.1). Sources of data are the Census of Manufacturing Industries (CMI) of Bangladesh (various years) and World Bank (2001). The data for fixed assets reported in the CMIs has been treated as data on capital stock. Data on employment for workers has been treated as data on the labour force.

In this study five measures of foreign competition have been used. The first two measures are time-series variables for the economy as a whole, that is, import penetration of consumer goods (defined as the import of consumer goods as a percentage of total imports for the economy as a whole) and the implicit nominal tariff (defined as import duties as a percentage of total imports for the economy as a whole). It is argued that the import penetration of consumer goods might be a better indicator of foreign competition in a country-specific context since under trade restrictions, imports of consumer goods are restricted the most (Andriamananjara and Nash, 1997). It is also observable from Figure 14.1 that the ratio of imports of

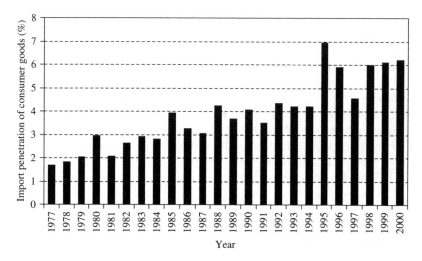

Source: Bangladesh Bureau of Statistics (various years).

Figure 14.1   Trend in the import penetration of consumer goods

consumer goods as a percentage of total imports was less than 2 per cent in the late 1970s and increased to 6 per cent in the late 1990s. This first indicator of foreign competition is called *OPEN1*. The source of data for *OPEN1* is the author's own estimates based on the data from the Bangladesh Bureau of Statistics (various years).

The second measure of foreign competition is the implicit nominal tariff rate. It is often argued that the implicit nominal tariff is a 'more reliable' measure of foreign competition in comparison to the average tariff. As Figure 14.2 suggests, the implicit nominal tariff was nearly as high as 20 per cent in the late 1970s but fell to 12 per cent in the late 1990s. It is also observable that since 1992 (the year of massive trade liberalization in Bangladesh) there has been a sharp decline in the ratio. This indicator is referred to as *OPEN2*. The source of data for *OPEN2* is the author's estimates based on the data from the NBR (2001).

It is however important to note some caveats regarding the use of these two measures of foreign competition. Both variables are single time-series variables and their use in panel regression assumes that they have the same magnitude of effects across different manufacturing sectors. This assumption may seem to be too rigid, although the inclusion of single time-series variables in panel regression analysis is not uncommon (see, for example, Iscan, 1998).

This is why two other measures of foreign competition are considered. The data for these measures are panel in nature. The first of these is the

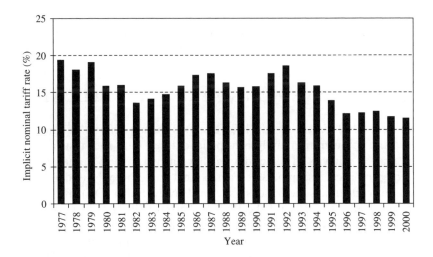

Source: World Bank (2001).

Figure 14.2 Trend in the implicit nominal tariff rate

sectoral import penetration ratio, defined as sectoral imports as a percentage of sectoral available output (sectoral output plus imports) at the three-digit ISIC code level. Thus, the sectoral import penetration ratio $= m_{it}/Y_{it} + m_{it}$, where, m_{it} is the import in sector i at time t and Y_{it} is the output in sector i at time t. The advantage with the sectoral import penetration variable is that it considers import penetration in each sector, thus provides a better picture of foreign competition at the micro-level compared with import penetration for the economy as a whole. The sectoral import penetration ratio is referred to as *OPEN3*. The sources of data for *OPEN3* are the CMIs and World Bank (2001).

The second of the two panel variables is the sectoral export-orientation ratio defined as sectoral exports as a percentage of sectoral output at the three-digit ISIC code level. Thus, the sectoral export-orientation ratio $= x_{it}/Y_{it}$, where x_{it} is export from sector i at time t and Y_{it} is sectoral output. The sectoral export orientation ratio helps in understanding the export and growth nexus. It is also argued by many that export orientation captures the extent of foreign competition in a country since in most developing countries trade restrictions had been associated with a high anti-export bias (Bhagwati, 1978; Krueger, 1978). The fourth measure of foreign competition is called *OPEN4*. The sources of data for *OPEN4* are the CMIs and World Bank (2001).

The final indicator of foreign competition is *OPEN5*, used as a dummy variable. This variable takes on two values: zero for the pre-trade liberalization period (period before 1992) and one for the post-trade liberalization period (period after 1992). All variables in the analysis are expressed in real terms by using appropriate sectoral deflators.

DATA ANALYSIS: NON-STATIONARY PANEL DATA

A recent development in panel regression is the application of unit root tests and cointegration analysis in panel dataset. Unit root tests and cointegration analysis in panel dataset have increasingly become popular among empirical researchers. It is agreed that the commonly used unit root tests in single time-series analysis such as Dickey–Fuller (DF), augmented Dickey–Fuller (ADF) and the Phillips–Perron (PP) tests lack power in identifying unit roots, and the use of panel data unit root tests is one way of increasing the power of unit root tests based on a single time series (Frankel and Rose, 1996; Macdonald, 1996; Oh, 1996; Wu, 1996; Maddala and Wu, 1999). The leading papers on testing for unit roots in panel dataset are by Levin and Lin (1992, 1993); Im, Pesaran and Shin (IPS) (1997); Harris and Tzavalis (1999); Maddala and Wu (1999); Hadri (2000) and Breitung (2000).

The stationarity of the variables is initially checked. Out of the seven variables (In Y, InK, InL, In$OPEN1$, In$OPEN2$, In$OPEN3$, In$OPEN4$), five variables (In Y, InK, InL, In$OPEN2$, In$OPEN4$) are panel in nature and the rest (In$OPEN1$, In$OPEN2$) are single time-series variables. For the two single time-series variables only the IPS (1997) tests are applied as this is simply an ADF test of single time series averaged over the number of cross-section units. All estimation and testing is done in GAUSS 3.0 using the package NPT 1.3 (NPT 1.3 is developed by Chiang and Kao, 2000) and COINT 2.0 and in PCGIVE.

Levin and Lin (1992, 1993)

The pioneer work in panel unit root tests was undertaken by Levin and Lin (1992, 1993). Levin and Lin (1992) developed several models and checked the null hypothesis of unit roots. In each of the models limiting distributions are as $N \to \infty$ and $T \to \infty$. The procedures of the models are summarized in Table 14.1.

For Models 1 to 4, Levin and Lin (1992) show that

(a) $T\sqrt{N}\hat{\rho} \Rightarrow N(0, 2)$
(b) $t_{\rho = 0} \Rightarrow N(0,1)$

Table 14.1 Levin and Lin unit root test models

Model 1	$\Delta y_{it} = \rho\, y_{it-1} + \varepsilon_{it}$	$H_0: \rho = 0$	without intercept and time trend
Model 2	$\Delta y_{it} = \rho\, y_{it-1} + \alpha_0 + \varepsilon_{it}$	$H_0: \rho = 0$	with intercept and no time trend
Model 3	$\Delta y_{it} = \rho\, y_{it-1} + \alpha_0 + \delta_t + \varepsilon_{it}$	$H_0: \rho = 0,$ $\delta = 0$	with intercept and time trend
Model 4	$\Delta y_{it} = \rho\, y_{it-1} + \theta_t + \varepsilon_{it}$	$H_0: \rho = 0$	without intercept and time trend but with time-specific effect
Model 5	$\Delta y_{it} = \rho y_{it-1} + \alpha_i + \varepsilon_{it}$	$H_0: \rho = 0,$ $\alpha_i = 0$ for all i	without intercept and time trend but with individual specific effect
Model 6	$\Delta y_{it} = \rho\, y_{it-1} + \alpha_i + \delta_i\, t + \varepsilon_{it}$	$H_0: \rho = 0,$ $\alpha_i = 0$ for all i, $\delta_i = 0$ for all i	without intercept and time trend but with individual specific effect and individual time trend
Model 7	$\Delta y_{it} = \rho\, y_{it-1} + \varepsilon_{it}$	$H_0: \rho = 0$	without intercept and time trend but correlation across time trend

For Model 5, if $\sqrt{N}/T \to 0$, then

(a) $T\sqrt{N}\hat{\rho} + 3\sqrt{N} \Rightarrow N(0, 10.2)$

(b) $\sqrt{1.25}t_{\rho = 0} + \sqrt{1.875N} \Rightarrow N\left(0, \dfrac{645}{112}\right)$

In Model 6, both the intercept and the time trend vary with individuals, and in Model 7 serial correlation is assumed.

Banerjee (1999) identifies the Levin and Lin analysis as the first formal demonstration of the correction and standardization factors required in order for the unit root estimators to have Gaussian distribution in the limit.

Levin and Lin (1993) also provide an important extension to the unit root test, which is designed to take care of the problem of heteroscedasticity and autocorrelation. This is achieved by subtracting cross-section averages from the data to eliminate the influence of the aggregate effects, and by applying the augmented Dickey–Fuller (ADF) test to each individual series and normalizing the disturbances. The proposed models in Table 14.2 are as follows:

Competition and competitive advantage

Table 14.2   Levin and Lin extended unit root test models

Model 1 $\Delta y_{it} = \rho_i y_{it-1} + \sum_{j=1}^{p_i} \theta_{ij} \Delta y_{it-j} + \varepsilon_{it}$ $H_0 : \rho = 0$ without individual specific effect and individual time trend

Model 2 $\Delta y_{it} = \alpha_i + \rho_i y_{it-1} + \sum_{j=1}^{p_i} \theta_{ij} \Delta y_{it-j} + \varepsilon_{it}$ $H_0 : \rho = 0$, $\alpha_i = 0$ for all i with individual specific effect and without individual time trend

Model 3 $\Delta y_{it} = \alpha_i + \delta_i t + \rho_i y_{it-1} + \sum_{j=1}^{p_i} \theta_{ij} \Delta y_{it-j} + \varepsilon_{it}$ $H_0 : \rho = 0$, $\alpha_i = 0$ for all i, $\delta_i = 0$ for all i with individual specific effect and individual time trend

---

The aforementioned models are estimated by regressing first Δy_{it} and then y_{it-1} on the remaining variables in the models (in this case in Models 2 and 3). Suppose, the residuals from these two regressions are $\hat{e}_{it}$ and $\hat{V}_{i,t-1}$ respectively. The regression of

$$\hat{e}_{it} \,\text{on}\, \hat{V}_{it-1}:$$

$$\hat{e}_{it} = \rho_i \hat{V}_{it-1} + \varepsilon_{it}$$

gives $\hat{\rho}_i$ from the ith cross-section. Because of the heteroscedasticity in ε_{it} Levin and Lin suggest the following normalization to control it:

$$\hat{\sigma}_{e_i}^2 = \frac{1}{T - p_i - 1} \sum_{t=p_i+2}^{T} (\hat{e}_{it} - \hat{\rho}_i \hat{V}_{it-1})^2,$$

$$\tilde{e}_{it} = \frac{\hat{e}_{it}}{\hat{\sigma}_i},$$

$$\tilde{V}_{it-1} = \frac{\hat{V}_{it-1}}{\hat{\sigma}_{e_i}}$$

It is assumed that $\tilde{e}_{it}$ will be individually and independently distributed for all i.

The long-run variance of y_i is estimated by:

$$\hat{\sigma}_{y_i}^2 = \frac{1}{T-1} \sum_{t=2}^{T} \Delta y_{it}^2 + 2 \sum_{L=1}^{\bar{K}} w_{\bar{K}L} \left(\frac{1}{T-1} \sum_{t=L+2}^{T} \Delta y_{it} \Delta y_{it-L} \right)$$

where $\bar{K}$ is the lag truncation and $w_{\bar{K}L}$ is the lag window.

The next step is to estimate the ratio of long-run to short-run standard deviation for each individual series and then calculate the average ratio for the panel as:

$$\hat{S}_{NT} = \frac{1}{N} \sum_{i=1}^{N} \frac{\hat{\sigma}_{y_i}}{\hat{\sigma}_{e_i}}$$

Finally, the following panel regression is estimated by using all i and t:

$$\tilde{e}_{it} = \rho \tilde{V}_{it-1} + \tilde{\varepsilon}_{it}$$

The resulting t-statistic is

$$t_{\rho=0} = \frac{\hat{\rho}}{RSE(\hat{\rho})}$$

where,

$$RSE(\hat{\rho}) = \hat{\sigma}_{\varepsilon} \left[\sum_{i=1}^{N} \sum_{t=2+p_i}^{T} \hat{V}_{it-1}^2 \right]^{-1/2}$$

$$\hat{\sigma}_{\varepsilon}^2 = \frac{1}{N\tilde{T}} \sum_{i=1}^{N} \sum_{t=2+p_i}^{T} (\tilde{e}_{it} - \hat{\rho} \tilde{V}_{it-1})^2$$

$$\tilde{T} = T - p - 1 \text{ and}$$

$$\bar{p} = \frac{1}{N} \sum_{i=1}^{N} p_i$$

is the average lag length used in the individual ADF regression.

Since the test statistic is not centred around zero, the Levin and Lin statistic is an adjusted t-statistic:

$$t_{\rho}^* = \frac{t_{\rho=0} - N\tilde{T}\hat{S}_{NT}\hat{\sigma}_{\varepsilon}^{-2}RSE(\hat{\rho})\mu_{\tilde{T}}^*}{\sigma_{\tilde{T}}^*}$$

where $\sigma_{\tilde{T}}^*$ and $\sigma_{\tilde{T}}^*$ are the mean and the standard deviation adjustment terms that are obtained from Monte Carlo simulation and tabulated in Levin and Lin (1993). Under the following null hypothesis:

$$H_0 : \rho = 0$$

the panel test statistic t_ρ^* has the property that as $T, N \to \infty$

$$t_\rho^* \Rightarrow N(0,1)$$

Maddala and Wu (1999) point out that the major problem with the Levin and Lin test is the fact that ρ is the same for all observations. Thus if ρ_i is denoted by the value of ρ for the ith cross-section unit, then according to the Levin–Lin test the null and alternative hypotheses are the following:

$$H_0 : \rho_1 = \rho_2 = \ldots\ldots\ldots = \rho_N = \rho = 0$$

$$H_1 : \rho_1 = \rho_2 = \ldots\ldots\ldots = \rho_N = \rho < 0$$

It is however pointed out by Maddala and Wu (1999) that the null makes sense under some circumstances but the alternative is too strong to be held in any interesting empirical cases:

> For example, in testing the convergence hypothesis in growth models, one can formulate the null as implying that none of the economies under study converges and thus $\rho = 0$ for all countries. But it does not make any sense to assume that all the countries will converge at the same rate if they do converge. (Maddala and Wu, 1999, 635)

The results of the Levin and Lin (LL) unit root tests (1992, 1993) are reported in Table 14.3. It can be noted that since the two variables In*OPEN1* and In*OPEN2* are single time-series variables we do not apply Levin and Lin on these two variables.

With respect to value-added (ln Y) it is found from Table 14.3 that results are mixed with LL (1992) and LL (1993). Two out of the seven LL (1992) tests and one out of the three LL (1993) tests show unit roots. In the case of capital stock (ln$K$), three out of seven LL (1992) tests and one out of the three LL (1993) tests show unit roots. While considering labour force (ln$L$), the LL (1992) and LL (1993) tests are inconclusive: two out of seven LL (1992) tests and one out of the three LL (1993) tests show unit roots. In the case of both ln*OPEN3* and ln*OPEN4*, LL (1992) and LL (1993) tests produce similar inconclusive results.

It appears from the exercise that the Levin and Lin (1992 and 1993) tests do not provide conclusive evidence in determining whether the variables under consideration are stationary or not. Other panel unit tests are therefore applied to check stationarity of these variables.

Table 14.3 *Levin and Lin (1992, 1993) unit root tests on levels of variables*

Tests	ln Y	ln K	ln L	ln OPEN1	ln OPEN2	ln OPEN3	ln OPEN4
LL (1992)							
Without intercept and time trend	0.355	0.051	0.045	—	—	−0.677	−0.422
	(0.387)	(0.479)	(0.531)			(0.211)	(0.332)
With intercept and no time trend	−3.091	−5.803	−3.073	—	—	−3.650	−8.238
	(0.001)	(0.000)	(0.001)			(0.000)	(0.000)
With intercept and time trend	−3.023	−5.60	−2.873	—	—	−3.641	−8.116
	(0.001)	(0.000)	(0.002)			(0.000)	(0.000)
Without intercept and time trend but with time-specific effect	−7.042	−9.88	−8.586	—	—	−3.385	−9.886
	(0.000)	(0.000)	(0.000)			(0.000)	(0.000)
Without intercept and time trend but with individual specific effect	−1.279	−0.772	0.599	—	—	−0.768	−0.530
	(0.150)	(0.434)	(0.274)			(0.445)	(0.410)
Without intercept and time trend but with individual specific effect and individual time trend	−4.309	−10.287	−7.596	—	—	−6.897	−11.482
	(0.000)	(0.000)	(0.000)			(0.000)	(0.000)
Without intercept and time trend but with correlation across time trend	77.838	1.136	271.92	—	—	−92.549	340.476
	(0.000)	(0.132)	(0.000)			(0.000)	(0.000)
LL (1993)							
Without individual specific effect and individual time trend	−0.747	−0.352	−1.208	—	—	0.758	1.22
	(0.240)	(0.362)	(0.113)			(0.332)	(0.109)
With individual specific effect and without individual time trend	32.779	29.849	49.486	—	—	74.447	53.614
	(0.000)	(0.000)	(0.000)			(0.000)	(0.000)
With individual specific effect and individual time trend	197.666	106.935	178.582	—	—	181.858	289.35
	(0.000)	(0.000)	(0.000)			(0.000)	(0.000)

Notes:
(a) *OPEN1* = import penetration ratio of consumer goods; *OPEN2* = implicit nominal tariff rate; *OPEN3* = sectoral import penetration ratio; *OPEN4* = sectoral export-orientation ratio.
(b) The critical probabilities are reported in parentheses.

Im, Pesaran and Shin (1997)

In contrast to the Levin–Lin tests, Im, Pesaran and Shin (1997), subsequently referred to as IPS, allow for a heterogeneous coefficient of y_{it-1}. IPS (1997) propose two tests: the first one is based on averaging individual ADF test statistics when error terms are serially correlated with different serial correlation coefficients across cross-sectional units; and the second one is the use of the group-mean Lagrange Multiplier (LM) statistic. The following ADF regressions are estimated:

$$\Delta y_{it} = \rho_i y_{it-1} + \sum_{j=1}^{\rho_i} \theta_{ij} \Delta y_{it-j} + \alpha_i + \varepsilon_{it}, t = 1, 2, \dots T$$

to test the null, $H_0 : \rho_i = 0$ for all i against the alternatives, $H_1 : \rho_i < 0$, for at least one i.

The group-mean t-bar statistic is given by:

$$\psi_{\hat{T}} = \frac{\sqrt{N}\left\{ \bar{t}_{NT} - N^{-1} \sum_{i=1}^{N} E[t_{iT}(P_i,0)|\rho_i = 0] \right\}}{\sqrt{N^{-1} \sum_{i=1}^{N} Var[t_{iT}(p_i,0)|\rho_i = 0]}}$$

Where

$$\bar{t}_{NT} = N^{-1} \sum_{i=1}^{N} t_{iT}(p_i,\theta_i),$$

and $t_{iT}(p_i,\theta_i)$ is the individual t-statistic for testing $\rho_i = 0$ for all i. IPS (1997) tabulated the values of $E[t_{iT}(P_i, 0)|\rho_i = 0]$ and $Var[t_{iT}(p_i, 0)|\rho_i = 0]$ in their paper.

On the other hand, to derive the LM-statistic first define:

$$\overline{LM}_{NT} = N^{-1} \sum_{i=1}^{N} LM_{iT}(p_i, \theta_i)$$

where $\theta_i = (\theta_{i1}, \theta_{i2}, \dots, \theta_{ip_i})'$ and $LM_{i,T}(p_i, \theta_i)$ is the individual LM-statistic for testing $\rho_i = 0$. Then the standardized LM-bar statistic is given by:

$$\psi_{\overline{LM}} = \frac{\sqrt{N}\left\{ \overline{LM}_{NT} - N^{-1} \sum_{i=1}^{N} E[LM_{iT}(p_i, 0)|\rho_i = 0] \right\}}{\sqrt{N^{-1} \sum_{i=1}^{N} Var[LM_{iT}(p_i, 0)|\rho_i = 0]}}$$

IPS (1997) tabulated the values of $E[LM_{iT}(p_i, 0)|\rho_i = 0]$ and $Var[LM_{iT}(p_i, 0)|\rho_i = 0]$ in their paper. It is also shown that under $H_0 : \rho_i = 0$ for all i,

$$\psi_{\overline{LM}} \Rightarrow N(0,1)$$

as $T, N \to \infty$ and $N/T \to k$ where k is a finite positive constant.

The IPS (1997) test has however, been criticized by Maddala and Wu (1999) for not being able to test the unit root in an unbalanced panel.

The results of the IPS tests are reported in Table 14.4. The IPS (1997) tests for two single time-series variables $\ln OPEN1$ and $\ln OPEN2$ are reported because, as mentioned earlier, IPS (1997) tests are nothing but ADF tests of single time series averaged over the number of cross-section units.

The test results of Table 14.4 suggest that for the variable $\ln Y$, IPS (1997) and IPS LM (1997) tests are conclusive. The two tests of IPS (1997) confirm the presence of unit roots and again the two tests of IPS LM (1997) also show unit roots. In the case of $\ln K$, two tests of IPS (1997) show the presence of unit roots, while IPS LM (1997) shows unit roots in only one of the two tests. While considering $\ln L$, both IPS (1997) and IPS LM (1997) tests provide conclusive evidence in favour of the presence of unit roots. For

Table 14.4   *Im, Pesaran and Shin (1997) unit root tests on levels of variables*

Tests	$\ln Y$	$\ln K$	$\ln L$	$\ln$ OPEN1	$\ln$ OPEN2	$\ln$ OPEN3	$\ln$ OPEN4
IPS (1997)							
Without time	−0.274	−1.123	0.813	−0.133	0.390	−1.037	−0.257
trend	(0.391)	(0.130)	(0.334)	(0.446)	(0.348)	(0.149)	(0.401)
With time	−0.604	−0.386	−0.380	−0.331	0.425	−0.978	−0.942
trend	(0.272)	(0.557)	(0.541)	(0.556)	(0.275)	(0.163)	(0.189)
IPS LM (1997)							
Without time	−1.041	−0.985	−0.548	–	–	−0.101	−0.423
trend	(0.197)	(0.253)	(0.327)			(0.125)	(0.363)
With time	−0.587	2.726	−0.285	–	–	−0.846	−0.879
trend	(0.324)	(0.011)	(0.483)			(0.355)	(0.163)

Notes:
(a) *OPEN1* = import penetration ratio of consumer goods; *OPEN2* = implicit nominal tariff rate; *OPEN3* = sectoral import penetration ratio; *OPEN4* = sectoral export-orientation ratio.
(b) The critical probabilities are reported in parentheses.

ln*OPEN1* and ln*OPEN2* the IPS (1997) test results provide clear evidence of the presence of unit roots. In the case of ln*OPEN3*, both IPS (1997) and IPS LM (1997) tests confirm the presence of unit roots. For the variable ln*OPEN4* it is also found that both IPS (1997) and the IPS LM (1997) tests are conclusive in detecting unit roots.

Harris and Tzavalis (1999)

Assuming that the time dimension of the panel is fixed, Harris and Tzavalis (1999) develop similar asymptotic unit root tests for first-order autoregressive panel data models. They show that the limiting distributions of the test statistics are normal. The assumption concerning the fixed time dimension allows for the analytical expression for the moments of the distributions. In their models, similarity with respect to the initial conditions of the data-generating process is achieved by including fixed-effect dummy variables in the regression model. On the other hand, similarity with respect to fixed effects in the data-generating process is achieved by including a linear deterministic trend for each individual unit of the panel. The authors also argue that when fixed effects or individual trends are included as regressors the least squares estimator of the autoregressive parameter is inconsistent and thus the test statistics must be appropriately adjusted. They also suggest, with the help of Monte Carlo evidence, that their proposed tests have an empirical size that is very close to the nominal 5 per cent level and substantially more power than the corresponding unit root tests for the single time-series case. The corresponding models are in Table 14.5 below.

The results of the Harris and Tzavalis (1999) tests are reported in Table 14.6. The Harris and Tzavalis test on ln*OPEN1* and ln*OPEN2* are not applied as these two variables are single time-series variables. It is evident from Table 14.6 that for all the variables under consideration, two out of three Harris and Tzavalis tests show unit roots.

Table 14.5   Harris and Tzavalis unit root test models

Model 1	$\Delta y_{it} = \psi y_{it-1} + v_{it}$	H_0: $\rho = 0$	without intercept and time trend
Model 2	$\Delta y_{it} = \alpha_i \psi y_{it-1} + v_{it}$	H_0: $\rho = 0$, $\alpha_i = 0$ for all i	with intercept and without time trend
Model 3	$\Delta y_{it} = \alpha_i + \beta_i t + \psi y_{it-1} + v_{it}$	H_0: $\rho = 0$, $\alpha_i = 0$ for all i, $\beta_i = 0$ for all i	with intercept and time trend

Table 14.6   Unit root tests on levels of variables

Tests	ln Y	ln K	ln L	ln OPEN1	ln OPEN2	ln OPEN3	ln OPEN4
Without intercept and time trend	0.396 (0.346)	0.024 (0.490)	0.572 (0.283)	–	–	−0.822 (0.210)	−1.160 (0.140)
With intercept and without time trend	−0.771 (0.238)	−0.478 (0.440)	−0.650 (0.257)	–	–	−0.253 (0.487)	−0.386 (0.487)
With intercept and time trend	−17.960 (0.000)	−17.903 (0.000)	−18.050 (0.000)	–	–	−17.285 (0.000)	−17.974 (0.000)

Notes:
(a) *OPEN1* = import penetration ratio of consumer goods; *OPEN2* = implicit nominal tariff rate; *OPEN3* = sectoral import penetration ratio; *OPEN4* = sectoral export-orientation ratio.
(b) The critical probabilities are reported in parentheses.

A Recapitulation of the Unit Root Test Results

The various unit root tests mentioned above produced mixed results in detecting unit roots. It has been seen that the Levin and Lin (1992, 1993) tests are not conclusive whereas the IPS (1997) tests and the Harris and Tzavalis (1999) tests are largely conclusive. It is generally considered that the IPS (1997) tests and the Harris and Tzavalis (1999) tests are more powerful in detecting unit roots in panel dataset than the Levin and Lin (1992 and 1993) tests. This study relies on the IPS (1997) and the Harris and Tzavalis (1999) tests and therefore it can be concluded that all our variables are non-stationary in their levels.

Unit Roots on First Differences of Variables

A basic question is how to check the order of integration of these non-stationary variables. The order of integration of the non-stationary variables is important because if variables are of a different order of integration then special care is needed to find out the valid relationship among those variables. In simple terms, if a series has to be differenced d times in order to get a stationary series, then it is integrated of order d or I(d). Table 14.7 reports the results of the unit root tests of the seven non-stationary variables in their first differences. It is clearly evident from Table 14.7 that all

Table 14.7 Unit root tests on first differences of variables

Tests	$\Delta \ln Y$	$\Delta \ln K$	$\Delta \ln L$	$\Delta \ln OPEN1$	$\Delta \ln OPEN2$	$\Delta \ln OPEN3$	$\Delta \ln OPEN4$
LL (1992)							
Without intercept and time trend	−26.621 (0.000)	−33.444 (0.000)	−29.930 (0.000)	—	—	−32.427 (0.000)	−33.386 (0.000)
With intercept and no time trend	−26.915 (0.000)	−33.962 (0.000)	−31.033 (0.000)	—	—	−32.466 (0.000)	−33.478 (0.000)
With intercept and time trend	−26.901 (0.000)	−33.961 (0.000)	−31.033 (0.000)	—	—	−32.421 (0.000)	−33.475 (0.000)
Without intercept and time trend but with time-specific effect	−24.207 (0.000)	−28.512 (0.000)	−25.470 (0.000)	—	—	−27.475 (0.000)	−26.603 (0.000)
Without intercept and time trend but with individual specific effect	−23.810 (0.000)	−31.563 (0.000)	−28.577 (0.000)	—	—	−29.132 (0.000)	−30.517 (0.000)
Without intercept and time trend but with individual specific effect and individual time trend	−22.956 (0.000)	−31.623 (0.000)	−28.048 (0.000)	—	—	−28.814 (0.000)	−30.434 (0.000)
Without intercept and time trend but with correlation across time trend	−317.29 (0.000)	— 645.921 (0.000)	−345.990 (0.000)	—	—	−624.987 (0.000)	−580.089 (0.000)
LL (1993)							
Without individual specific effect and individual time trend	85.446 (0.000)	86.237 (0.000)	−170.590 (0.000)	—	—	76.952 (0.000)	86.368 (0.000)

With individual specific effect and without individual time trend	147.305 (0.000)	144.511 (0.000)	236.317 (0.000)	—	—	188.344 (0.000)	248.597 (0.000)
With individual specific effect and individual time trend	232.073 (0.000)	308.097 (0.000)	396.117 (0.000)	—	—	299.158 (0.000)	359.610 (0.000)
IPS (1997)							
Without time trend	-13.577 (0.000)	-14.459 (0.000)	-11.969 (0.000)	-27.659 (0.000)	-4.543 (0.000)	-14.796 (0.000)	-17.777 (0.000)
With time trend	-10.666 (0.000)	-11.745 (0.000)	-8.577 (0.000)	-27.710 (0.000)	-5.324 (0.000)	-12.250 (0.000)	-15.797 (0.000)
IPS LM (1997)							
Without time trend	-9.847 (0.000)	-15.767 (0.000)	-8.532 (0.000)	—	—	-11.214 (0.000)	-18.721 (0.000)
With time trend	-7.568 (0.000)	-10.115 (0.000)	-5.410 (0.000)	—	—	-9.012 (0.000)	-12.218 (0.000)
HT (1999)							
Without intercept and time trend	-84.277 (0.000)	100.363 (0.000)	-94.253 (0.000)	—	—	-94.249 (0.000)	-1008.10 (0.000)
With intercept and without time trend	-37.572 (0.000)	-45.178 (0.000)	-43.165 (0.000)	—	—	-41.234 (0.000)	-44.124 (0.000)
With intercept and time trend	-21.839 (0.000)	-26.895 (0.000)	-25.512 (0.000)	—	—	-24.697 (0.000)	-26.088 (0.000)

Notes:
(a) OPEN1 = import penetration ratio of consumer goods; OPEN2 = implicit nominal tariff rate; OPEN3 = sectoral import penetration ratio; OPEN4 = sectoral export-orientation ratio.
(b) The critical probabilities are reported in parentheses.

the tests unanimously reject the null hypotheses of unit roots of the variables on their first differences. It can therefore be argued that all the seven variables are I(1), that is, they are non-stationary on their levels but stationary on their first differences.

Some Other Panel Unit Root Tests

The Maddala and Wu (1999) test allows for a unit root test in an unbalanced panel. Breitung (2000) indicates the losses of power due to bias correction terms in the Levin–Lin (1993) test and a detrending bias in IPS (1997). Breitung suggests a new test without bias correction. Hadri (2000) proposes a test based on the null of stationarity against the alternative of unit roots in panel data with individual error over t to the case of heterogeneous and serially correlated errors over t.

PANEL COINTEGRATION TESTS

When all the variables in the model are stationary then traditional methods can be used to estimate the model. If however, at least one of the series turn out to be non-stationary then more care is needed. In this case, to make inferences concerning the long-run relationships between the variables, some form of cointegration technique is required. Cointegration techniques in time-series analysis are popular and well established. However, like the unit root tests in panel regressions, cointegration tests in panel data are relatively new. The leading papers in panel cointegration tests are Pedroni (1995, 1999); Kao and Chiang (1998); McCoskey and Kao (1998) and Kao (1999). Here only the Kao (1999) and Pedroni (1995, 1999) tests for panel cointegration are discussed.

Kao Tests (1999)

Kao (1999) explores the spurious panel regression model and examines the asymptotic properties of the least-squares dummy variable (LSDV) estimator. Kao shows that the LSDV estimator in the case of spurious regression in panel data is consistent, but the t-statistics diverge. The probability that the t-statistics will be 'wrong' goes to one as N and $T \to \infty$. This obviously gives improper inferences about the regression coefficients and has implications for the null distribution of the cointegration test. The null hypothesis of this test is 'no cointegration'.

Kao presents the residual-based tests for cointegration in panel data using the Dickey–Fuller (DF) and the augmented Dickey–Fuller (ADF) type tests, deriving the asymptotic distributions for the tests. The procedure for the tests is as follows:

Let the regression model be:

$$y_{it} = x'_{it}\beta + z'_{it}\gamma + e_{it}$$

and the estimated residuals:

$$\hat{e}_{it} = \rho\hat{e}_{it-1} + v_{it},$$

where

$$e_{it} = \tilde{y}_{it} - \tilde{x}'_{it}\ddot{\beta},$$

$$\tilde{y}_{it} = x_{it} - \sum_{s=1}^{T} h(t, s)y_{is},$$

and,

$$\tilde{x}_{it} = x_{it} - \sum_{s=1}^{T} h(t, s)x_{is}$$

In order to test the null hypothesis of no cointegration, the null is written as:

$$H_0 : \rho = 1$$

The OLS estimate of ρ and the t-statistics are given as:

$$\hat{\rho} = \frac{\displaystyle\sum_{i=1}^{N}\sum_{t=2}^{T} \hat{e}_{it}\hat{e}_{it-1}}{\displaystyle\sum_{i=1}^{N}\sum_{t=2}^{T} \hat{e}_{it}^2}$$

and,

$$t_\rho = \frac{(\hat{\rho} - 1)\sqrt{\displaystyle\sum_{i=1}^{N}\sum_{t=2}^{I} \hat{e}_{it-1}}}{S_e}$$

where,

$$s_e^2 = \frac{1}{NT}\sum_{i=1}^{N}\sum_{t=2}^{T} (\hat{e}_{it} - \hat{\rho}\hat{e}_{it-1})^2$$

Assuming $z_{it} = \{\mu_i\}$, Kao proposes following four DF type tests:

$$DF_\rho = \frac{\sqrt{N}T(\hat\rho - 1) + 3\sqrt{N}}{\sqrt{10.2}},$$

$$DF_t = \sqrt{1.25}t_\rho + \sqrt{1.875N},$$

$$DF_\rho^* = \frac{\sqrt{N}T(\hat\rho - 1) + \dfrac{3\sqrt{N}\hat\sigma_v^2}{\hat\sigma_{0v}^2}}{\sqrt{3 + \dfrac{36\hat\sigma_v^4}{5\hat\sigma_{0v}^4}}}, \quad \text{and}$$

$$DF_t^* = \frac{t_\rho + \dfrac{\sqrt{6N}\hat\sigma_v}{2\hat\sigma_{0v}}}{\sqrt{\dfrac{\hat\sigma_{0v}^2}{2\hat\sigma_v^2} + \dfrac{3\hat\sigma_v^2}{10\hat\sigma_{0v}^2}}}$$

The proposed DF_ρ and DF_t are based on the strong exogeneity of the regressors and errors. On the other hand, DF_ρ^* and DF_t^* are for checking cointegration assuming an endogenous relationship between regressors and errors.

The ADF test statistic is derived by running the following regression:

$$\hat{e}_{it} = \rho\hat{e}_{it-1} + \sum_{j=1}^{p}\vartheta_j\Delta\hat{e}_{it-j} + v_{itp}$$

With $H_0 : \rho = 1$ the ADF test statistic is constructed as:

$$ADF = \frac{t_{ADF} + \dfrac{\sqrt{6N}\hat\sigma_v}{2\hat\sigma_{0v}}}{\sqrt{\dfrac{\hat\sigma_{0v}^2}{2\hat\sigma_v^2} + \dfrac{3\hat\sigma_v^2}{10\hat\sigma_{0v}^2}}}$$

where t_{ADF} is the t-statistic of ρ in the aforementioned ADF regression. Kao shows that the asymptotic distributions of DF_ρ, DF_t, DF_ρ^*, DF_t^* and ADF converge to a standard normal distribution $N(0, 1)$ by the sequential limit theory.

Table 14.8 reports the results of the Kao (1999) cointegration tests for different regression models. Column 2 shows the results using the original model without incorporating any of the foreign competition measures. On

Table 14.8   Kao (1999) cointegration tests for different models

Tests	Original model	Original model includes OPEN1	Original model includes OPEN2	Original model includes OPEN3	Original model includes OPEN4
DF_ρ	-7.75	-7.75	-7.75	-7.75	-7.87
	(0.000)	(0.000)	(0.000)	(0.000)	(0.000)
DF_t	-5.23	-4.88	-5.23	-4.83	-5.30
	(0.000)	(0.000)	(0.000)	(0.000)	(0.000)
DF_ρ^*	-17.83	-17.83	-17.84	-18.10	-17.95
	(0.000)	(0.000)	(0.000)	(0.000)	(0.000)
DF_t^*	-5.86	-5.61	-5.86	-5.53	-5.92
	(0.000)	(0.000)	(0.000)	(0.000)	(0.000)
ADF	-4.632	-4.63	-4.63	-4.61	-4.76
	(0.000)	(0.000)	(0.000)	(0.000)	(0.000)

Notes:
(a) $OPEN1$ = import penetration ratio of consumer goods; $OPEN2$ = implicit nominal tariff rate; $OPEN3$ = sectoral import penetration ratio; $OPEN4$ = sectoral export-orientation ratio.
(b) The critical probabilities are reported in parentheses.
(c) Cointegration tests statistics are calculated through the residuals from the OLS estimation.

the other hand, columns 3 to 6 report the results for models incorporating different measures of foreign competition.

While considering the original model, all the Kao (1999) tests provide conclusive evidence of cointegration. The test results for the model incorporating $OPEN1$, again show conclusive evidence for rejecting the null hypotheses of 'no cointegration'. All the test results for the model incorporating $OPEN2$ show cointegration. Again, all the Kao test results for the model incorporating $OPEN3$ suggest cointegration. Finally, all tests of Kao (1999) tests show clear evidence of rejecting the null hypotheses of 'no cointegration' for the model incorporating $OPEN4$.

Pedroni Tests (1995)

Pedroni (1995) deals with the residual-based tests for cointegration and spurious regression, allowing for different assumptions on the homogeneity and heterogeneity of the panel data. Pedroni's model allows for different intercepts (fixed effects), different slopes, endogenous regressors and heterogeneous long-run variance–covariance matrices. Pedroni also derives the asymptotic distributions of the tests proposed. The null of Pedroni's tests is 'no cointegration'. Pedroni studies the special case of homogeneous cointegrating vectors and shows that the residual-based tests for the null of 'no cointegration' have distributions that are asymptotically equivalent to 'raw' panel unit root tests if the regressors of the model are exogenous.

Pedroni (1995) proposes a pooled Phillips–Perron-type test. Under the null hypothesis of 'no cointegration', the panel autoregressive coefficient estimator, $\hat{\rho}_{NT}$, can be constructed as follows:

$$\hat{\rho}_{NT} - 1 = \frac{\sum_{i=1}^{N}\sum_{t=2}^{T}(\hat{e}_{it-1}\Delta\hat{e}_{it} - \hat{\lambda}_i)}{\sum_{i=1}^{N}\sum_{t=2}^{T}\hat{e}_{it-1}^2}$$

where $\hat{\lambda}_i$ refers to a scalar equivalent to the correlation matrix and corrects for any correlation effects. Thus Pedroni (1995) suggests the limiting distribution of the following two statistics:

$$PC_1 = T\sqrt{N}(\hat{\rho}_{NT} - 1)/\sqrt{2} \Rightarrow N(0,1)$$

$$PC_2 = \sqrt{NT(T-1)}(\hat{\rho}_{NT} - 1)/\sqrt{2} \Rightarrow N(0,1)$$

Pedroni later extends and revises his cointegration tests in which he derives seven explicit tests for cointegration in panel data under various different settings (see Pedroni, 1995, 1999). The results of Pedroni (1995) tests are reported in Table 14.9.

It is evident from Table 14.9 that the results of the two test statistics of Pedroni (1995) tests provide clear evidence of cointegration for all the models under consideration.

Pedroni Tests (1999)

The main focus of the Pedroni (1999) test is on providing the appropriate critical values for seven panel cointegration tests. Important features of these seven tests are that these tests (1) allow for multiple regressors, (2) allow for the fixed effects to differ across members of the panel, (3) allow for the cointegrating vector to differ across members of the panel (under H_1), (4) allow for heterogeneity in the errors across cross-section units. For all seven tests discussed in this chapter the null and alternative hypotheses are:

H_0: For each member of the panel the variables are not cointegrated.
H_1: For each member of the panel there exists a single cointegrating vector (which is not necessarily the same for each member of the panel).

Table 14.9   Pedroni (1995) cointegration tests for different models

Tests	Original model	Original model includes OPEN1	Original model includes OPEN2	Original model includes OPEN3	Original model includes OPEN4
PC_1	− 27.86	− 27.86	− 27.86	− 27.86	− 27.74
	(0.000)	(0.000)	(0.000)	(0.000)	(0.000)
PC_2	− 27.21	− 27.21	− 27.21	− 27.21	− 27.10
	(0.000)	(0.000)	(0.000)	(0.000)	(0.000)

Notes:
(a) $OPEN1$ = import penetration ratio of consumer goods; $OPEN2$ = implicit nominal tariff rate; $OPEN3$ = sectoral import penetration ratio; $OPEN4$ = sectoral export-orientation ratio.
(b) The critical probabilities are reported in parentheses.
(c) Cointegration tests statistics are calculated through the residuals from the OLS estimation.

The cointegration tests are based on the following panel regression model:

$$Y_{it} = \alpha_i + \delta_{it} + \sum_{m=1}^{M} \beta_{mi} X_{mit} + e_{it}$$

The first four tests are based on pooling along the 'within' dimension (pools the autoregressive coefficients across different members of the panel for the unit root tests on the estimated residuals). These four tests impose a common value for the autoregressive root under the alternative hypothesis.

Test 1: the panel *v*-statistic:

$$T^2 N^{3/2} Z_{\hat{v}NT} \equiv T^2 N^{3/2} \left(\sum_{i=1}^{N} \sum_{t=1}^{T} \hat{L}_{11i}^{-2} \hat{e}_{it-1}^2 \right)^{-1}$$

Test 2: the panel ρ-statistic:

$$T \sqrt{N} Z_{\hat{\rho} NT} \equiv T \sqrt{N} \left(\sum_{i=1}^{N} \sum_{t=1}^{T} \hat{L}_{11i}^{-2} \hat{e}_{it-1}^2 \right)^{-1} \sum_{i=1}^{N} \sum_{t=1}^{T} \hat{L}_{11i}^{-2} (\hat{e}_{it-1} \Delta\hat{e}_{it} - \hat{\lambda}_i)$$

Test 3: the panel t-statistic (non-parametric):

$$Z_{t NT} \equiv \left(\tilde{\sigma}_{NT}^2 \sum_{i=1}^{N} \sum_{t=1}^{T} \hat{L}_{11i}^{-2} \hat{e}_{it-1}^2 \right)^{-1/2} \sum_{i=1}^{N} \sum_{t=1}^{T} \hat{L}_{11i}^{-2} (\hat{e}_{it-1} \Delta\hat{e}_{it} - \hat{\lambda}_i)$$

Test 4: the panel t-statistic (parametric):

$$Z_{tNT}^* \equiv \left(\tilde{s}_{NT}^{*2} \sum_{i=1}^{N} \sum_{t=1}^{T} \hat{L}_{11i}^{-2} \, \hat{e}_{it-1}^{*2} \right)^{-1/2} \sum_{i=1}^{N} \sum_{t=1}^{T} \hat{L}_{11i}^{-2} \, (\hat{e}_{it-1}^* \, \Delta \hat{e}_{it}^*)$$

Finally, three tests are based on pooling along the 'between' dimension (averages the autoregressive coefficients for each member of the panel for the unit root tests on the estimated residuals). Unlike Tests 1 through to 4, the remaining three tests do not impose a common value for the autoregressive root under the alternative hypothesis.

Test 5: the group ρ-statistic:

$$T N^{-1/2} \, \tilde{Z}_{\hat{\rho}NT-1} \equiv TN^{-1/2} \sum_{i=1}^{N} \left(\sum_{t=1}^{T} \hat{e}_{it-1}^2 \right)^{-1} \sum_{t=1}^{T} (\hat{e}_{it-1} \, \Delta \hat{e}_{it} - \hat{\lambda}_i)$$

Test 6: the group t-statistic (non-parametric):

$$N^{-1/2} \tilde{Z}_{t\,NT-1} \equiv N^{-1/2} \sum_{i=1}^{N} \left(\hat{\sigma}_i^2 \sum_{t=1}^{T} \hat{e}_{it-1}^2 \right)^{-1/2} \sum_{t=1}^{T} (\hat{e}_{it-1} \, \Delta \hat{e}_{it} - \hat{\lambda}_i)$$

Test 7: the group t-statistic (parametric):

$$N^{-1/2} \, \tilde{Z}_{tNT}^* \equiv N^{-1/2} \sum_{i=1}^{N} \left(\sum_{t=1}^{T} \hat{s}_i^{*2} \, \hat{e}_{it-1}^{*2} \right)^{-1/2} \sum_{t=1}^{T} (\hat{e}_{it-1}^* \, \Delta \hat{e}_{it}^*)$$

One of the advantages with these tests is that they allow heterogeneity in the cointegrating vector, which is important because imposing homogeneity can often lead to concluding falsely that there is no cointegration. Moreover, allowing for multiple regressors is important since most cointegrating relationships are not simple binary relationships. Furthermore, allowing for heterogeneous autoregressive coefficients in the unit root under H_0 and H_1 is an important and desirable feature of this work (Tests 5 through to 7).

The results of the seven Pedroni (1999) tests are presented in Table 14.10. While considering the original model only for three cases of Pedroni (1999): panel v-statistic (without intercept and trend), panel ρ-statistic (without intercept and trend) and panel t-statistic: non-parametric (with both intercept and trend) the null hypotheses of 'no cointegration' cannot

Table 14.10   Pedroni (1999) cointegration tests for different models

Tests	Original model	Original model includes OPEN1	Original model includes OPEN2	Original model includes OPEN3	Original model includes OPEN4
I. Panel υ-statistic					
Without intercept and	−0.62	−1.97	−2.04	−3.18	−2.18
trends	(0.267)	(0.024)	(0.020)	(0.000)	(0.014)
With intercepts but	−2.97	−3.93	−4.00	−5.09	−4.13
without trends	(0.001)	(0.000)	(0.000)	(0.000)	(0.000)
With both intercepts	−6.26	−6.88	−6.95	−7.90	−7.06
and trends	(0.000)	(0.000)	(0.000)	(0.000)	(0.000)
II. Panel ρ-statistic					
Without intercept and	−1.50	0.88	0.64	1.11	0.67
trends	(0.065)	(0.187)	(0.259)	(0.132)	(0.249)
With intercepts but	0.53	2.69	2.43	2.92	2.46
without trends	(0.296)	(0.000)	(0.000)	(0.001)	(0.006)
With both intercepts	3.43	5.12	4.87	5.35	4.96
and trends	(0.000)	(0.000)	(0.000)	(0.000)	(0.000)
III. Panel t-statistic (non-parametric)					
Without intercept and	−3.44	−1.33	−1.69	−0.86	−1.77
trends	(0.000)	(0.090)	(0.045)	(0.193)	(0.037)
With intercepts but	−1.64	0.69	0.27	1.25	0.17
without trends	(0.049)	(0.243)	(0.392)	(0.105)	(0.429)
With both intercepts	0.99	3.26	2.76	3.90	2.65
and trends	(0.159)	(0.000)	(0.002)	(0.000)	(0.003)
IV. Panel t-statistic (parametric)					
Without intercept and	−85.64	−89.18	−95.61	−115.72	−103.44
trends	(0.000)	(0.000)	(0.000)	(0.000)	(0.000)
With intercepts but	−106.12	−102.92	−110.53	−134.32	−119.76
without trends	(0.000)	(0.000)	(0.000)	(0.000)	(0.000)
With both intercepts	−122.51	−117.04	−125.85	−153.41	−136.47
and trends	(0.000)	(0.000)	(0.000)	(0.000)	(0.000)
V. Group ρ-statistic					
Without intercept and	0.03	2.74	−2.74	2.74	−2.67
trends	(0.487)	(0.003)	(0.003)	(0.003)	(0.003)
With intercepts but	2.23	4.46	4.46	4.46	4.39
without trends	(0.012)	(0.000)	(0.000)	(0.000)	(0.000)
With both intercepts	4.78	6.47	6.47	6.47	6.40
and trends	(0.000)	(0.000)	(0.000)	(0.000)	(0.000)
VI. Group t-statistic (non-parametric)					
Without intercept and	−13.24	−13.24	−13.24	−13.24	−13.21
trends	(0.000)	(0.000)	(0.000)	(0.000)	(0.000)
With intercepts but	−13.24	−13.24	−13.24	−13.24	−13.21
without trends	(0.000)	(0.000)	(0.000)	(0.000)	(0.000)

Table 14.10   (continued)

Tests	Original model	Original model includes OPEN1	Original model includes OPEN2	Original model includes OPEN3	Original model includes OPEN4
With both intercepts	− 13.24	− 13.24	− 13.24	− 13.24	− 13.21
and trends	(0.000)	(0.000)	(0.000)	(0.000)	(0.000)
VII. Group t-statistics (parametric)					
Without intercept and	− 4.02	− 1.17	− 1.17	− 1.17	− 1.19
trends	(0.000)	(0.119)	(0.119)	(0.119)	(0.115)
With intercepts but	− 1.07	1.43	1.43	1.43	1.41
without trends	(0.141)	(0.075)	(0.075)	(0.075)	(0.078)
With both intercepts	1.78	3.95	3.95	3.95	3.93
and trends	(0.036)	(0.000)	(0.000)	(0.000)	(0.000)

Notes:
(a) *OPEN1* = import penetration ratio of consumer goods; *OPEN2* = implicit nominal tariff rate; *OPEN3* = sectoral import penetration ratio; *OPEN4* = sectoral export-orientation ratio.
(b) The critical probabilities are reported in parentheses.
(c) Cointegration tests statistics are calculated through the residuals from the OLS estimation.

be rejected. The remaining 18 cases of Pedroni (1999) tests can reject the null of 'no cointegration'. For the model incorporating *OPEN1*, in all except three cases of Pedroni (1999) tests (panel ρ-statistic, without intercept and trend; panel t-statistic: non-parametric, with intercept and trend; and group t-statistic: parametric: without intercept and trend) the null hypotheses of 'no cointegration' can be rejected. Again, for the model incorporating *OPEN2*, all the tests of Pedroni (1999) except three cases (panel ρ-statistic: without intercept and trend; panel t-statistic: non-parametric, with intercept but without trend; and group t-statistic: parametric, without intercept and trend) show cointegration. The test results for the model incorporating *OPEN3*, except four cases (panel ρ-statistic: without intercept and trend; panel t-statistic: non-parametric, without intercept and trend; and group t-statistic: parametric, without intercept and trend), the remaining 17 tests show clear evidence of cointegration. The test results corresponding to the model incorporating *OPEN4*, except three cases (panel ρ-statistic: without intercept and trend; panel t-statistic: non-parametric, with intercept but without trend; and group t-statistic: parametric, without intercept and trend), all other remaining tests show clear evidence of rejecting the null hypotheses of 'no cointegration'.

A Recapitulation of the Panel Cointegration Test Results?

The results of all Kao (1999) tests suggest that all five models are cointegrated. Again the test results of Pedroni (1995) tests indicate clear evidence of cointegration. In the case of Pedroni (1999) tests it is found that, except for a few cases, all the test results show cointegration for the five models under consideration. It can therefore be argued that all five models are cointegrated.

ESTIMATION TECHNIQUES

There are various ways of estimating the models with panel dataset. Different estimation methods possess merits and demerits. Given the purpose of the present research, the models can be run as an unrestricted error correction mechanism because it permits the separation of short-run and long-run effects. In order to check the potential endogeneity problem, models can be run using GMM, FM and DOLS methods. The intention is clear. If the signs, values and significance of the coefficients on the variables of interest are consistent across different methods of estimation then it can be argued that the estimation results are robust and non-sensitive to the estimation methods.

Unrestricted Error Correction Mechanism

In time-series econometrics, one convenient way of modelling the long-run and short-run effects, without imposing any restriction on the relationship between short-run and long-run responses, is through the use of an unrestricted error correction mechanism (UECM) model (Alogoskoufis and Smith, 1991; Banerjee et al., 1993). Hendry (1980) emphasized the importance of 'general to specific modelling' and in this context the UECM can be interpreted as a re-parameterization of the general 'autoregressive distributed lag' (ADL) or 'dynamic linear regression' (DLR) models. Reilly and Witt (1996) apply UECM in the context of a panel regression. In a panel framework, for two variables y and x, the first order DLR is:

$$y_{it} = a_{0i} + b_{0i}x_{it} + b_{1i}x_{it-1} + a_{1i}y_{it-1} + \varepsilon_{it}$$

where ε_{it} is a white noise residual. The aforementioned equation can be written as:

$$\Delta y_{it} = \alpha_{0i} + \beta_{0i}\Delta x_{it} + \beta_{1i}x_{it-1} + \alpha_{1i}y_{it-1} + \varepsilon_{it}$$

where $a_{0i} = \alpha_{0i}, b_{0i} = \beta_{0i}, \alpha_{1i} = a_{1i} - 1, \beta_{1i} = (b_{0i} + b_{1i})$, or

$$\Delta y_{it} = \beta_{0i} \Delta x_{it} - \lambda(y_{it-1} - \psi_{1i} x_{it-1} - \psi_{0i}) + \varepsilon_{it}$$

where $\lambda = -\alpha_{1i}, \psi_{1i} = \beta_{1i}/\alpha_{1i} = (b_{0i} + b_{1i})/(1 - a_{1i}), \psi_{0i} = \alpha_{0i}/\alpha_{1i}$.

This definition of the UECM imposes no restriction on the DLR, but is in terms of different parameters, which can be given an economic interpretation as impact effects (short-run) β_{0i}, a scalar adjustment coefficient, λ, and long-run effects Ψ_{1i}. The latter are interpreted as the parameters of an equilibrium relationship about which economic theory is informative.

It is, however, important to note that the estimates obtained from such a model could suffer from potential endogeneity problem of the variable and the inclusion of fixed effects may bias the coefficient on the lagged dependent variable (Hsiao, 1986).

The estimation results are reported for the original model without any foreign competition measure. Table 14.11 concerns the estimation results using the unrestricted error correction mechanism (UECM).

It is evident from Table 14.11 that the coefficient on the error correction term $(\ln Y_{it-1})$ is correctly signed, highly significant and lower than one (in absolute value), thus confirming a valid representation of the unrestricted

Table 14.11   Unrestricted error correction mechanism for the original model

Dependent Variable: $\Delta \ln Y_{it}$	Coefficients
Explanatory variables	
Constant	-0.294 (0.61)
$\ln Y_{it-1}$	-0.347*** (0.06)
$\Delta \ln K_{it}$	0.142*** (0.04)
$\Delta \ln L_{it}$	0.337*** (0.11)
$\ln K_{it-1}$	0.107*** (0.03)
$\ln L_{it-1}$	0.209** (0.09)
Industry fixed effect χ^2(df $= 47$)	Yes 5593***
Time effect χ^2(df $= 20$)	Yes 346.1***
R^2 (adjusted)	0.36
Observations	567

Notes:
(a) *** and ** indicate statistical significance at the 1 and 5 per cent levels respectively.
(b) Hypotheses relating to fixed and time effects were tested using likelihood ratio tests.
(c) Figures in parentheses indicate standard errors.

Table 14.12   Long-run elasticities of the production function

Variables	Long-run Elasticities
K	0.308
L	0.602

error correction mechanism. The coefficient on the error correction term (ECT) suggests a rapid adjustment to the long-run steady state relationship from any short-run deviation, as 34 per cent of the disequilibrium errors are corrected within just one year.

Short-run coefficients of both capital and labour (the first differences of *K* and *L*) are positive and highly significant. On the other hand, to derive the long-run coefficients for *K* and *L* the method described earlier is used. Table 14.12 reports the estimated long-run elasticities.

The results of the empirical estimation of the production function of the manufacturing sector in Bangladesh reported in Tables 14.11 and 14.12 on the whole are satisfactory. The production function estimates suggest that the long-run elasticity of labour is higher than that of capital, which is plausible given the characteristics of labour-abundant and capital-scarce countries like Bangladesh.

Does Increased Foreign Competition Make any Difference?

The analysis turns to an examination of whether or not foreign competition has had an impact on the growth of value-added in the manufacturing sector in Bangladesh. Columns 2 to 6 of Table 14.13 present the results for the unrestricted error correction mechanism for different models incorporating different foreign competition indicators.

Column 2 of Table 14.13 reports the estimation results of the model incorporating *OPEN1*. It is important to note that there is no change in the signs and significance of the coefficients on ECT, Δ*K*, Δ*L* and lagged ln*K* and ln*L* due to the inclusion of *OPEN1*. The short-run coefficient on *OPEN1* is negative, suggesting a possible negative impact on growth in the short run. However, a negative relationship is not supported by statistical significance. On the other hand, the long-run coefficient is positive, suggesting the possibility of a positive long-run relationship between foreign competition (through increased import penetration of consumer goods) and growth. But again such a relationship is not statistically significant. It can therefore be concluded that *OPEN1* fails to exert any significant impact on the growth of value-added in the manufacturing sector in Bangladesh both in the short and long run.

Table 14.13 *Foreign competition measures in the growth models: estimations using UECM*

Explanatory variables	Dependent Variable: $\Delta \ln Y_{it}$				
	Model includes OPEN1	Model includes OPEN2	Model includes OPEN3	Model includes OPEN4	Model includes OPEN5
Constant	0.611	−0.294	−0.137	0.256	−0.294
	(0.44)	(0.61)	(0.53)	(0.52)	(0.61)
$\ln Y_{it-1}$	−0.347***	−0.337***	−0.335***	−0.337***	−0.347***
	(0.06)	(0.06)	(0.07)	(0.05)	(0.06)
$\Delta \ln K_{it}$	0.142***	0.145***	0.116***	0.148***	0.142***
	(0.04)	(0.04)	(0.03)	(0.04)	(0.04)
$\Delta \ln L_{it}$	0.337***	0.335***	0.275***	0.317***	0.337***
	(0.11)	(0.11)	(0.08)	(0.101)	(0.11)
$\ln K_{it-1}$	0.107***	0.109***	0.088***	0.106***	0.107***
	(0.03)	(0.08)	(0.02)	(0.03)	(0.03)
$\ln L_{it-1}$	0.209**	0.206**	0.193**	0.198**	0.209**
	(0.09)	(0.09)	(0.08)	(0.08)	(0.09)
$\Delta \ln OPEN1_{it}$	−0.374	—	—	—	—
	(0.40)				
$\ln OPEN1_{it-1}$	0.061	—	—	—	—
	(0.14)				
$\Delta \ln OPEN2_{it}$	—	−0.002	—	—	—
		(0.02)			
$\ln OPEN2_{it-1}$	—	−0.365	—	—	—
		(0.24)			

	(1)	(2)	(3)	(4)	(5)
$\Delta \ln OPEN3_{it}$	—	—	−0.194*** (0.03)	—	—
$\ln OPEN3_{it-1}$	—	—	−0.137** (0.05)	—	—
$\Delta \ln OPEN4_{it}$	—	—	—	0.041 (0.01)	—
$\ln OPEN4_{it-1}$	—	—	—	0.005 (0.01)	—
$OPEN5$	—	—	—	—	−0.157* (0.09)
Industry fixed effect	Yes	Yes	Yes	Yes	Yes
χ^2(df = 47)	3453***	5103***	2180***	1164***	8244***
Time effect	Yes	Yes	Yes	Yes	Yes
χ^2(df = 20)	344.6***	320.1***	264.6***	516.2***	336.8***
R^2 (adjusted)	0.36	0.36	0.38	0.38	0.37
Observations	567	567	567	567	567

Notes:
(a) $OPEN1$ = import penetration ratio; $OPEN2$ = implicit nominal tariff rate; $OPEN3$ = sectoral import penetration ratio; $OPEN4$ = sectoral export-orientation ratio; $OPEN5$ = a dummy variable, which takes 0 and 1 values for pre- and post-liberalization periods respectively.

(b) ***, ** and * indicate statistical significance at the 1, 5 and 10 per cent levels respectively.
(c) Hypotheses relating to fixed and time effects were tested using likelihood ratio tests.
(d) Figures in parentheses indicate standard errors.

The third column of Table 14.13 shows the estimation results for *OPEN2* in the original model. Again, the inclusion of *OPEN2* does not change the signs and significance of original variables in the model. Both the short-run and long-run coefficients on *OPEN2* are negatively signed, suggesting the possibility of a negative impact on growth due to the increase in the implicit tariff rate, both in the short and long run. But such relationships are not established on grounds of statistical significance. It can therefore be concluded that there is no statistically significant association between the implicit nominal tariff rate and the growth of value-added in the manufacturing sector in Bangladesh.

The fourth column of Table 14.13 concerns the estimation results of the model incorporating *OPEN3*. It is also observed that the signs and significance of the original variables in the model are unaffected due to the inclusion of *OPEN3* in the original model. The short-run coefficient on *OPEN3* is negative and highly significant. The value of the coefficient is also high (0.19). This suggests that in the short run a 1 per cent increase in the sectoral import penetration ratio causes a 0.19 per cent decline in the growth rate of value-added in the manufacturing sector. On the other hand, the long-run coefficient is also negative and highly significant, which leads to the conclusion that there is a valid long-run negative relationship between the sectoral import penetration ratio and the growth of value-added in the manufacturing sector. The estimated long-run coefficient is high (0.40), suggesting a 0.40 per cent reduction in growth due to a 1 per cent increase in the sectoral import penetration ratio in the long run.

The fifth column of Table 14.13 reports the estimation results of the model incorporating *OPEN4*. Again the inclusion of *OPEN4* does not change the signs and significance of the original variables in the model. Both the short-run and long-run coefficients on *OPEN4* are positive but statistically insignificant, suggesting that there is no impact of sectoral export orientation on the growth of manufacturing value-added.

The sixth and final column of Table 14.13 presents the estimation results for *OPEN5*. *OPEN5* is a dummy variable to capture the differences in growth of value-added in the manufacturing sector between the pre- and post-trade liberalization period. It is evident that the coefficient on *OPEN5* is negative and significant at the 10 per cent level. This suggests that during the post-liberalization period there has been a decrease in the growth of manufacturing value-added in Bangladesh. This suggests that the period of trade liberalization in Bangladesh has exerted a negative impact on the growth of manufacturing value-added.

Estimation of the Models by using GMM, FM and DOLS Methods

One important point to mention is there might be a potential endogeneity problem associated with the indicators of foreign competition in the models, which arguably might have biased the results. It is likely that the growth of value-added could lead to increased or decreased imports and exports and thus could influence such indicators as *OPEN1, OPEN3* and *OPEN4*. It is therefore a valid question to ask whether or not the results are free from endogeneity bias. The endogenity problem is checked by estimating all five models in a GMM, FM and DOLS estimation framework.

GMM estimation
One way of tackling the endogeneity problem and the fixed effect bias is to use an instrumental variable approach and in this regard, the GMM estimation technique (see Arellano and Bond, 1991) of the following type is widely used.

Suppose $\phi = [\phi_1 \phi_2]'$ and $\xi = [\xi_1, \xi_2, \xi_3, \xi_t]'$. Then the one-step GMM estimator of the coefficient vector $\beta = [\phi, \xi, \alpha]'$ is given by:

$$\hat{\beta} = [X'Z(\hat{\Omega})^{-1}X'Z]^{-1}X'Z(\hat{\Omega})^{-1}Z'Y,$$

where $Y_1 = [\Delta y_{it}, \ldots, \Delta y_{Nt}]'$ and $X_t = [\Delta x_{it}, \ldots, \Delta x_{Nt}]'$ and Z_t is a set of instrumental variables.

A consistent estimator of Ω is:

$$\hat{\Omega}_{rv} = \sum_{i=1}^{N} (Z'_{it} H Z_{it}), \quad t = r, v$$

where N is the number of cross-sections, H is a $(t-2)$ square matrix which has twos in the main diagonal, minus ones in the first subdiagonals and zeros otherwise.

The advantage with the GMM-based regression is that it is free of sector-specific fixed effects as it is operated on first differences. However, the significant limitation is that applying first difference removes the long-run information. Most economic theory is stated as a long-term relationship between variables in level form and not as a first-difference form (Gujarati, 1998).

The results of the one-step GMM estimation of the five models are reported in Table 14.14.

It is clearly evident from Table 14.14 that the estimation results using the GMM method are consistent with that of UECM reported in Table 14.13. The variables *OPEN1, OPEN2* and *OPEN4* appear to have insignificant

Competition and competitive advantage

Table 14.14   One-step GMM estimation of the models

Explanatory variables	Dependent Variable: $\Delta\ln Y_{it}$				
	Model includes *OPEN1*	Model includes *OPEN2*	Model includes *OPEN3*	Model includes *OPEN4*	Model includes *OPEN5*
Constant	0.049	0.115	0.062	0.008	0.09
	(0.04)	(0.08)	(0.04)	(0.04)	(0.11)
$\Delta\ln Y_{it-1}$	0.449***	0.449***	0.403***	0.447***	0.413***
	(0.08)	(0.08)	(0.07)	(0.08)	(0.07)
$\Delta\ln K_{it}$	0.146***	0.144***	0.125***	0.139***	0.151***
	(0.04)	(0.03)	(0.04)	(0.04)	(0.05)
$\Delta\ln L_{it}$	0.240***	0.221***	0.252***	0.285***	0.253***
	(0.07)	(0.06)	(0.08)	(0.08)	(0.06)
$\Delta\ln OPEN1_{it}$	− 0.014	–	–	–	–
	(0.06)				
$\Delta\ln OPEN2_{it}$	–	− 1.28	–	–	–
		(0.34)			
$\Delta\ln OPEN3_{it}$	–	–	− 0.201***	–	–
			(0.03)		
$\Delta\ln OPEN4_{it}$	–	–	–	0.035	–
				(0.01)	
OPEN5	–	–	–	–	− 0.117**
					(0.05)
Industry fixed	Yes	Yes	Yes	Yes	Yes
effect χ^2(df = 46)	539.7***	201.8***	857***	412.2***	373.4***
Time effect	Yes	Yes	Yes	Yes	Yes
χ^2(df = 20)	260.2***	185.8***	267.5***	618.5**	274.9***
Serial correlation	− 1.5	− 1.4	− 1.1	− 1.2	− 1.1
N (0,1)					
Sargan statistics	487.2	493.2	583.8	520.3	429.6
χ^2(df = 836)					
Observations	540	540	540	540	540

Notes:
(a) *OPEN1* = import penetration ratio of consumer goods; *OPEN2* = implicit nominal tariff rate; *OPEN3* = sectoral import penetration ratio; *OPEN4* = sectoral export-orientation ratio, *OPEN5* = a dummy variable, which takes 0 and 1 values for pre- and post-liberalization periods respectively.
(b) *** and ** indicate statistical significance at 1 and 5 per cent levels respectively.
(c) Hypotheses relating to fixed and time effects were tested using likelihood ratio tests.
(d) Figures in parentheses indicate standard errors.

impact on growth rate of value-added in the manufacturing sector in Bangladesh. On the other hand, the remaining two indicators of foreign competition, *OPEN3* and *OPEN5*, have negative and significant impact on the growth rate on manufacturing value-added. The diagnostic tests of all the models do not provide any evidence against model specifications, suggesting in general that all the models perform reasonably well in all specifications.

Fully modified OLS method

Pedroni (1996) proposes a fully modified (FM) OLS estimator for hetero-geneous panel data. With the purpose of removing the nuisance par-ameters, the FM estimator corrects the dependent variable using the long-run covariance matrices and then applies a simple OLS estimation method to the corrected variables. The proposed FM estimator is given by:

$$\hat{\beta}_{FM} = \left[\sum_{i=1}^{N} \sum_{t=1}^{T} (x_{it} - \bar{x}_i)(x_{it} - \bar{x}_i)' \right]^{-1} \left\{ \sum_{i=1}^{N} \left[\sum_{t=1}^{T} (x_{it} - \bar{x}_i)\hat{y}_{it}^+ - T\hat{\Delta}_{\varepsilon u}^+ \right] \right\}$$

where $\hat{y}_{it}^+$ is the dependent variable corrected for endogeneity. Table 14.15 reports the estimation results.

Table 14.15 suggests that three indicators of foreign competition (*OPEN1*, *OPEN2* and *OPEN4*) are not statistically significant in regression models. On the other hand, *OPEN3* and *OPEN5* register a negative and significant impact on the growth of manufacturing value-added. It is however important to note that the value of the coefficient for *OPEN3* in the FM estimation is lower than the long-run elasticity of *OPEN3* (0.40) estimated by the UECM in Table 14.13.

Dynamic OLS method

Kao and Chiang (1998) however, point out that the FM estimator could, in some cases, be inferior to the OLS because of the failure to avoid the poten-tial problem of estimating the nuisance parameter. Also, it is argued that the FM estimator is complicated by the dependence of the correction term upon preliminary estimation (i.e., OLS), which may be biased in finite samples (Kao et al., 1999). Kao and Chiang (1998) therefore propose the use of a dynamic OLS (DOLS), as it differs from the FM estimation in that the DOLS does not require any initial estimation and any non-parametric cor-rection. The DOLS estimator includes both lag and lead terms to correct the nuisance parameter with a view to obtaining coefficient estimates with nice limiting distribution properties. The DOLS estimator is given by:

$$y_{it} = \alpha_i + x_{it}'\beta + \sum_{j=-q}^{q} c_{ij}\Delta x_{it+j} + v_{it}$$

Kao et al. (1999) however, acknowledge the fact that there is a major difficulty with using the DOLS because of the problem of choosing the appropriate lag and leads. The results of DOLS estimations are reported in Table 14.16.

Competition and competitive advantage

Table 14.15 *Model estimation results using FM estimator*

	Dependent Variable: $\ln Y_{it}$				
Explanatory variables	Model includes OPEN1	Model includes OPEN2	Model includes OPEN3	Model includes OPEN4	Model includes OPEN5
$\ln K_{it}$	0.313***	0.369***	0.368***	0.319***	0.362***
	(4.93)	(5.78)	(7.06)	(5.04)	(5.55)
$\ln L_{it}$	0.493***	0.463***	0.442***	0.492***	0.475***
	(10.74)	(9.78)	(11.47)	(10.62)	(10.51)
$\ln OPEN1_{it}$	−0.057	–	–	–	–
	(−0.42)				
$\ln OPEN2_{it}$	–	0.07	–	–	–
		(0.31)			
$\ln OPEN3_{it}$	–	–	−0.134***	–	–
			(−3.87)		
$\ln OPEN4_{it}$	–	–	–	0.066	–
				(−0.45)	
OPEN5	–	–	–	–	−0.117***
					(−2.60)
R^2	0.47	0.48	0.55	0.49	0.49
Observations	594	594	594	594	594

Notes:
(a) *OPEN1* = import penetration ratio of consumer goods; *OPEN2* = implicit nominal tariff rate; *OPEN3* = sectoral import penetration ratio; *OPEN4* = sectoral export-orientation ratio; *OPEN5* = a dummy variable, which takes 0 and 1 values for pre- and post-liberalization periods respectively.
(b) All regressions include unreported, industry-specific and time-specific constants.
(c) *** indicates statistical significance at 1 per cent level.
(d) Figures in parentheses indicate t-statistics.

It appears from Table 14.16 that only under the DOLS estimation framework does the first indicator of foreign competition (*OPEN1*) turn out to have a significant and negative impact on the growth of manufacturing value-added. Two indicators (*OPEN2* and *OPEN4*) are again not statistically significant. On the other hand, *OPEN3* and *OPEN5* exhibit a negative and significant impact on the growth of manufacturing value-added. As in the case of FM estimation, the value of the coefficients on *OPEN3* in DOLS estimation is lower than the long-run elasticity of *OPEN3* (0.40) estimated by UECM in Table 14.13.

The above exercises show that on the basis of the signs and significance of the coefficients the GMM, FM and DOLS estimation results are largely consistent with the UECM estimation results reported in Table 14.13.

Table 14.16   Model estimation results using DOLS estimator

	Dependent Variable: $\ln Y_{it}$				
Explanatory variables	Model includes *OPEN1*	Model includes *OPEN2*	Model includes *OPEN3*	Model includes *OPEN4*	Model includes *OPEN5*
$\ln K_{it}$	0.356***	0.339***	0.286***	0.362***	0.359***
	(4.80)	(4.55)	(4.71)	(4.91)	(4.71)
$\ln L_{it}$	0.492***	0.493***	0.498***	0.488***	0.491***
	(9.17)	(8.92)	(11.09)	(9.02)	(9.28)
$\ln OPEN1_{it}$	− 0.041*	−	−	−	−
	(2.69)				
$\ln OPEN2_{it}$	−	− 0.146	−	−	−
		(−0.51)			
$\ln OPEN3_{it}$	−	−	− 0.129***	−	−
			(− 3.19)		
$\ln OPEN4_{it}$	−	−	−	0.086	−
				(−0.69)	−
OPEN5	−	−	−	−	− 0.105**
					(− 1.99)
R^2	0.64	0.74	0.77	0.75	0.63
Observations	594	594	594	594	594

Notes:
(a) *OPEN1* = import penetration ratio of consumer goods; *OPEN2* = implicit nominal tariff rate; *OPEN3* = sectoral import penetration ratio; *OPEN4* = sectoral export-orientation ratio; *OPEN5* = a dummy variable, which takes 0 and 1 values for pre- and post-liberalization periods respectively.
(b) All regressions include unreported, industry-specific and time-specific constants.
(c) ***, ** and * indicate statistical significance at 1, 5 and 10 per cent levels respectively.
(d) Figures in parentheses indicate t-statistics.

Foreign Competition and TFP Growth

TFP growth is usually defined as the residual part of the growth equation (Hwang, 2003). From an empirical point of view it is given by the estimated constant – the deterministic component of TFP – plus the error term – the stochastic component of TFP that results from estimating the production function (Beddies, 1999). In a panel framework, in addition to the afore-mentioned components, the individual sector-specific constants and the time constants are also added to the TFP growth estimation. TFP growth can be defined as:

$$\ln TFP_{it} = \ln Y_{it} - \beta \ln K_{it} - \gamma \ln L_{it}$$

Below, a simple OLS method is used to estimate the TFP equation in order to get a panel dataset of TFP growth. Before estimating the foreign competition and TFP growth relationship, the unit root of the TFP growth series is checked, as well as the cointegration of the different models incorporating foreign competition. Table 14.17 reports the results for unit root tests. Only the IPS (1997) tests are applied to check for unit roots.

Table 14.17   Unit root tests for TFP

Tests	ln*TFP*	Δln*TFP*
IPS (1997)		
Without time trend	0.873 (0.351)	-2.777 (0.000)
With time trend	1.102 (0.141)	-3.240 (0.000)
IPS LM (1997)		
Without time trend	1.032 (0.163)	-3.785 (0.000)
With time trend	0.886 (0.375)	-4.582 (0.000)

Note: The critical probabilities are reported in parentheses.

It is clearly evident from Table 14.17 that ln*TFP* is non-stationary on level but stationary on first difference. Both the IPS (1997) and the IPS LM (1997) tests provide conclusive evidence in support of this statement. It can be concluded that ln*TFP* is I(1).

The results of the cointegration tests of different models of the foreign competition–TFP growth nexus are reported in Table 14.18. Here only the Kao (1999) tests are applied. The results of Table 14.18 suggest that all four models are cointegrated.

It appears from Table 14.19 that all the five models incorporating five indicators of foreign competition on the error correction terms (ECT) are correctly signed, highly significant and less than one in absolute value. Therefore, all five models exhibit a valid representation of the error correction mechanism. It is also evident from the table that *OPEN1* does not have any significant impact on TFP growth in the short run. However, it has a negative and statistically significant impact in the long run. Our second indicator of foreign competition, *OPEN2*, does not have a significant impact on TFP growth either in the short or long run. On the other hand, it appears that *OPEN3* does have a highly significant and negative impact on TFP growth in the short and long run. The fourth indicator of foreign competition, *OPEN4*, shows positive but insignificant impact both in the short and long run. The final foreign competition indicator, *OPEN5*, has a

Table 14.18 Cointegration tests for TFP

Tests	Model includes *OPEN1*	Model includes *OPEN2*	Model includes *OPEN3*	Model includes *OPEN4*
Kao (1999)				
DF_ρ	− 10.669	− 10.643	− 10.675	− 10.611
	(0.000)	(0.000)	(0.000)	(0.000)
DF_t	− 6.943	− 7.973	− 8.197	− 8.032
	(0.000)	(0.000)	(0.000)	(0.000)
DF_ρ^*	− 21.585	− 21.384	− 21.486	− 21.394
	(0.000)	(0.000)	(0.000)	(0.000)
DF_t^*	− 7.288	− 8.078	− 8.229	− 8.122
	(0.000)	(0.000)	(0.000)	(0.000)
ADF	− 5.407	− 5.423	− 5.413	− 5.419
	(0.000)	(0.000)	(0.000)	(0.000)

Notes:
(a) *OPEN1* = import penetration ratio of consumer goods; *OPEN2* = implicit nominal tariff rate; *OPEN3* = sectoral import penetration ratio; *OPEN4* = sectoral export-orientation ratio.
(b) The critical probabilities are reported in parentheses.
(c) Cointegration tests statistics are calculated through the residuals from the OLS estimation

Table 14.19 UECM model estimation for TFP

	Dependent Variable $\Delta \ln TFP_{it}$				
Explanatory variables	Model includes *OPEN1*	Model includes *OPEN2*	Model includes *OPEN3*	Model includes *OPEN4*	Model includes *OPEN5*
Constant	0.341	− 0.193	1.101***	0.216***	0.250***
	(0.54)	(0.31)	(0.33)	(0.79)	(0.07)
$\ln TFP_{it-1}$	− 0.419***	− 0.401***	− 0.523***	− 0.416***	− 0.419***
	(0.06)	(0.05)	(0.08)	(0.07)	(0.07)
$\Delta \ln OPEN1$	− 0.339	–	–	–	–
	(0.23)				
$\ln OPEN1_{it-1}$	− 0.063*	–	–	–	–
	(0.22)				
$\Delta \ln OPEN2$	–	− 0.005	–	–	–
		(0.12)			
$\ln OPEN2_{it-1}$	–	− 0.423	–	–	–
		(0.44)			
$\Delta \ln OPEN3$	–	–	− 0.305***	–	–
			(0.05)		

Table 14.19   (continued)

	Dependent Variable $\Delta \ln TFP_{it}$				
Explanatory variables	Model includes OPEN1	Model includes OPEN2	Model includes OPEN3	Model includes OPEN4	Model includes OPEN5
$\ln OPEN3_{it-1}$	–	–	–0.207*** (0.03)	–	–
$\Delta \ln OPEN4$	–	–	–	0.041 (0.09)	–
$\ln OPEN4_{it-1}$	–	–	–	0.015 (0.01)	–
OPEN5	–	–	–	–	–0.341*** (0.10)
Industry fixed effect χ^2(df = 47)	Yes 1696***	Yes 1990***	Yes 2143***	Yes 15.38***	Yes 2140***
Time effect χ^2(df = 20)	Yes 519.7***	Yes 757***	Yes 163.9***	Yes 511.1***	Yes 752.8***
R^2 (adjusted)	0.33	0.32	0.41	0.35	0.34
Observations	567	567	567	567	567

Notes:
(a) *OPEN1* = import penetration ratio of consumer goods; *OPEN2* = implicit nominal tariff rate; *OPEN3* = sectoral import penetration ratio, *OPEN4* = sectoral export-orientation ratio; *OPEN5* = a dummy variable, which takes 0 and 1 values for pre- and post-liberalization periods respectively.
(b) *** indicates statistical significance at 1 per cent level.
(c) Hypotheses relating to fixed and time effects were tested using likelihood ratio tests.
(d) Figures in parentheses indicate standard errors.

negative and statistically significant coefficient, suggesting that there is negative TFP growth during the post-trade liberalization period.

CONCLUSIONS

This chapter has attempted to contribute to the empirical understanding of the foreign competition–growth nexus by focusing research on the manu-facturing sector in Bangladesh. A panel database on the manufacturing sector in Bangladesh at the three-digit ISIC code level covering 27 sectors with a time span of 22 years (1977–98) has been used (see Appendix 14.1). Five indicators of foreign competition: import penetration of consumer goods, implicit nominal tariff, sectoral import penetration ratio, sectoral export-orientation ratio and a time dummy variable for trade liberalization have been examined. A production function framework was used for the analysis and various panel unit root tests were compiled to check the stationarity of the variables. It appears that all the variables in the panel dataset are non-stationary. Different panel cointegration tests were also applied to check for cointegration of the different models and it was found that all the estimation models are cointegrated. Four estimation techniques, the unrestricted error correction mechanism (UECM), the dynamic OLS (DOLS), the fully modified (FM) and the GMM techniques were used to estimate the various models. The results were largely consistent across different estimation techniques.

The results of the exercises presented in this chapter suggest that the relationship between foreign competition and output growth in Bangladesh manufacturing industries is ambiguous. Import penetration of consumer goods shows a negative association, though it is not statistically significant under UECM, GMM and FM estimation methods. However, the relationship is negative and significant only under the DOLS estimation. On the other hand, the implicit nominal tariff shows a positive but insignificant association under all the estimation techniques. In the case of sectoral import penetration, the relationship is negative and statistically significant under all the estimation techniques although it is positive but statistically insignificant for all the estimation methods in the case of sectoral export orientation. Finally, the dummy variables, under all four estimation methods, are negative and significant, suggesting a negative impact on growth during the post-trade liberalization period. The impact of five foreign competition measures on total factor productivity (TFP) in Bangladesh manufacturing industries was also examined and the results are again ambiguous. Three indicators, the import penetration of consumer goods, the sectoral import penetration ratio and the dummy variable appear to have a negative impact on total factor productivity growth, whereas the two remaining indicators, the implicit nominal tariff and the sectoral import penetration ratio exhibit a negative and positive impact on TFP growth respectively, though these relationships are not statistically significant.

The negative influence of the sectoral import penetration on sectoral value-added growth is an empirical finding in the context of Bangladesh economy. The major reason behind such a negative association is the fact that the increased level of competition was followed by significant trade liberalization during the 1990s and most of the import-competing sectors shrunk and suffered from declining value-added growth. This was not compensated by increasing growth in the non-import-competing sectors, that is, the export-oriented sectors. As a result, the manufacturing sector suffered from declining growth in value-added. This implies that most of the import-competing sectors in Bangladesh, though exposed to a significant rise in foreign competition, are still not mature enough to cope with this changing environment.

The insignificant impact of sectoral export orientation on the sectoral value-added growth is also an interesting finding in the context of Bangladesh. Two reasons can be given. First, ready-made garments (RMG) became the leading export earning sector in the 1990s and at present RMG exports constitute more than 85 per cent of total export earnings. But over the last 20 years there has been little variation in this sector as it is almost 100 per cent export-oriented and therefore is likely to have an insignificant impact on the value-added growth in the manufacturing sector. Second, the other few export-oriented sectors apart from the RMG, such as jute products, tea and leather did not perform well during the period under consideration. In fact, some of these sectors suffered from declining growth, which had a negative impact on the manufacturing value-added growth. Some of the sectors export an insignificant proportion of their total output, and as a result the positive externality effects expected from export growth do not really transmit to generate increased sectoral value-added growth in the manufacturing industries.

REFERENCES

Alogoskoufis, G. and R. Smith (1991), 'On Error-correction Models', *Journal of Economic Surveys*, **5**, 97–128.
Andriamananjara, S. and J. Nash (1997), 'Have Trade Policy Reforms Led to Greater Openness in Developing Countries?', Policy Research Working Paper 1730, Washington DC: The World Bank.
Banerjee, A. (1999), 'Panel Data Unit Roots and Cointegration: An Overview', *Oxford Bulletin of Economics and Statistics*, Special Issue.
Banerjee, A., J.J. Dolado, J.W. Galbraith and D.F. Hendry (1993), *Cointegration, Error-correction and the Econometric Analysis of Non-stationary Data*, Oxford University Press.
Beddies, C. (1999), 'Investment, Capital Accumulation and Growth: Some Evidence from the Gambia 1964–98', IMF Working Papers, 99/117, International Monetary Fund.
Bhagwati, J.N. (1978), *Protectionism*, London and Cambridge, MA: MIT Press.
Breitung, J. (2000), 'The Local Power of Some Unit Root Tests for Panel Data', *Advances in Econometrics*, 15, 161–78.
Chiang, M.-H. and C. Kao (2000), 'Non-stationary Panel Time Series Using NPT 1.3 – A User Guide', mimeo, National Cheng-Kung University and Syracuse University.
Condon, T., V. Corbo and J. de Melo (1985), 'Productivity Growth, External Shocks and Capital Inflow in Chile 1977–81: A General Equilibrium Analysis', *The Journal of Policy Modeling*, 329–406.
Fernandes, A. (2003), 'Trade Policy, Trade Volumes and Plant Level Productivity in Colombian Manufacturing Industries', mimeo, Washington DC: The World Bank.
Frankel, J.A. and A.K. Rose (1996), 'A Panel Project on Purchasing Power Parity:

Mean Reversion Between and Within Countries', *Journal of International Economics*, **40**, 209–24.

Grossman, G. (ed.) (1992), *Imperfect Competition and International Trade*, Cambridge, MA: MIT Press.

Gujarati, D.N. (1998), *Essentials of Econometrics*, New York and London: McGraw-Hill.

Hadri, K. (2000), 'Testing for Stationarity in Heterogeneous Panel Data', *Econometrics Journal*, **3** (2), 148–61.

Harris, R.D.F. and E. Tzavalis (1999), 'Inference for Unit Roots in Dynamic Panels where the Time Dimension is Fixed', *Journal of Econometrics*, **91**, 201–26.

Harrison, A. (1994), 'Productivity, Imperfect Competition and Trade Reform: Theory and Evidence', *Journal of International Economics*, **36**, 53–73.

Harrison, A. (1996), 'Openness and Growth. A Time-series, Cross-country Analysis for Developing Countries', *Journal of Development Economics*, **48**, 419–47.

Havrylyshyn, O. (1990), 'Trade Policy and Productivity Gains in Developing Countries: A Survey of the Literature', *The World Bank Research Observer*, **5** (1), 1–24.

Helpman, E. and P. Krugman (1985), *Market Structure and Foreign Trade: Increasing Returns, Imperfect Competition and the International Economy*, Cambridge, MA: MIT Press.

Hendry, D. (1980), 'Econometrics: Alchemy or Science', *Econometrica*, **47**, 403.

Hsiao, C. (1986), *Analysis of Panel Data*, Cambridge University Press.

Hwang, A.R. (2003), 'Exports, Returns to Scale, and Total Factor Productivity: The Case of Taiwanese Manufacturing Industries', *Review of Economic Development*, **7**, 204–16, May.

Im, K.S., M.H. Pesaran and Y. Shin (1997), 'Testing for Unit Roots in Heterogeneous Panels', mimeo, Department of Applied Economics, University of Cambridge.

Iscan, T. (1998), 'Trade Liberalisation and Productivity: A Panel Study of the Mexican Manufacturing Industry', *The Journal of Development Studies*, **34** (5), 123–48.

Kaldor, N. (1967), *Strategic Factors in Economic Development*, New York: W.F. Humphrey Press.

Kao, C. (1999), 'Spurious Regression and Residual-based Tests for Cointegration in Panel Data', *Journal of Econometrics*, **90**, 1–44.

Kao, C. and M. Chiang (1998), 'On the Estimation and Inference of a Cointegrated Regression in Panel Data', mimeo, Center for Policy Research, Syracuse University.

Kao, C., M. Chiang and B. Chen (1999), 'International R&D Spillovers: An Application of Estimation and Inference in Panel Cointegration', *Oxford Bulletin of Economics and Statistics*, Special Issue, 691–709.

Krueger, A.O. (1978), *Foreign Trade Regimes and Economic Development: Liberalization Attempts and Consequences*, Cambridge, MA: Ballinger [for the] National Bureau of Economic Research.

Krueger, A.O. and B. Tuncer (1982), 'An Empirical Test of the Infant Industry Argument', *World Bank Reprint Series*, No. 284, December.

Levin, A. and C.F. Lin (1992), 'Unit Root Tests in Panel Data: Asymptotic and Finite Sample Properties', Department of Economics, University of California at San Diego, Discussion Paper No. 92–93 (revised 1993).

Levin, A. and C.F. Lin (1993), 'Unit Root Tests in Panel Data: New Results', Department of Economics, University of California at San Diego, Discussion Paper No. 93–56.

Maddala, G.S. and S. Wu (1999), 'A Comparative Study of Unit Root Tests with Panel Data and a New Simple Test', *Oxford Bulletin of Economics and Statistics*, Special Issue, 631–53.

MacDonald, R. (1996), 'Panel Unit Root Test and Real Exchange Rates', *Economic Letters*, **50**, 7–11.

McCoskey, S. and C. Kao (1998), 'A Residual-based Test of the Null of Cointegration in Panel Data', *Econometric Reviews*, **17**, 57–84.

McCoskey, S. and C. Kao (1999), 'Testing the Stability of a Production Function with Urbanization as a Shift Factor', *Oxford Bulletin of Economics and Statistics*, Special Issue, 671–90.

Miyagiwa, K. and O. Yuka (1995), 'Closing the Technology Gap Under Protection', *American Economic Review*, **85** (4), 755–70.

Mujeri, M.K. and B.H. Khondker (2004), 'Globalization–Poverty Interactions in Bangladesh: What Policy Implications Can We Draw?', in M. Bussolo and J.I. Round (eds), *Globalization and Poverty: Channels and Policies*, Routledge.

Mujeri, M.K., Q. Shahabuddin and S. Ahmed (1993), 'Macroeconomic Performance, Structural Adjustments and Equity: A Framework for Analysis for Macro-Micro Transmission Mechanisms in Bangladesh', in *Monitoring and Poverty in Bangladesh: Report on the Framework Project*, Centre on Integrated Rural Development for Asia and the Pacific, Dhaka.

National Board of Revenue (NBR) (2001), *Annual Report*, Dhaka: Government of Bangladesh.

Nishimizu, M. and S. Robinson (1983), 'Trade Policies and Productivity Change in Semi-industrialized Countries', Development Research Paper, Washington DC: The World Bank.

Oh, K.Y. (1996), 'Purchasing Power Parity and Unit Root Tests Using Panel Data', *Journal of International Money and Finance*, **15**, 405–18.

Pack, H. (1988), 'Industrialization and Trade', in H. Chenery and T.N. Srinivasan (eds), *Handbook of Development Economics, Vol. I*, B.V. Elsevier Science Publishers.

Page, J.M., Jr. (1980), 'Technical Efficiency and Economic Performance: Some Evidence from Ghana', *Oxford Economic Papers*, **32**, 19–39.

Pavcnik, N. (2002), 'Trade Liberalization, Exit and Productivity Improvements: Evidence from Chilean Plans', *The Review of Economic Studies*, **69**, 238.

Pedroni, P. (1995), 'Panel Cointegration: Asymptotic and Finite Sample Properties of Pooled Time Series Tests with an Application to the PPP Hypothesis', Indiana University Working Papers in Economics No. 95–013.

Pedroni, P. (1996), 'Fully Modified OLS for Heterogeneous Cointegrated Panels and the Case of Purchasing Power Parity', Indiana University Working Papers in Economics No. 96–020.

Pedroni, P. (1999), 'Critical Values for Cointegration Tests in Heterogeneous Panels with Multiple Regressors', *Oxford Bulletin of Economics and Statistics*, **61**, 663–78.

Pitt, M. and L. Lee (1981), 'The Measurement and Sources of Technical Inefficiency in the Indonesian Weaving Industry', *Journal of Development Economics*, **9**, 43–54.

Reilly, B. and R. Witt (1996), 'Crime, Deterrence, and Unemployment in England and Wales: An Empirical Analysis', *Bulletin of Economic Research*, **48**, 137–55.

Rodrik, D. (1988), 'Imperfect Competition, Scale Economies and Trade Policy in

Developing Countries', in R. Baldwin (ed.), *Trade Policy Industrialization and Development: New Perspectives*, Oxford: Clarendon Press.

Rodrik, D. (1992), 'Closing the Productivity Gap: Does Trade Liberalization Really Help?', in G. Helleiner (ed.), *Trade Policy and Industrialization in Turbulent Times*, Routledge.

Sobhan, R. (ed.) (1991), *Structural Adjustment Policies in the Third World: Design and Experience*, Dhaka: University Press Limited.

Solow, R.M. (1956), 'A Contribution to the Theory of Economic Growth', *Quarterly Journal of Economics*, **70**, 65–94.

Tsao, Y. (1985), 'Growth Without Productivity: Singapore Manufacturing in the 1970s', *Journal of Development Economics*, **18**, 25–38.

Tybout J. (1991), 'Researching the Trade Productivity Link: New Directions', World Bank Policy, Research and External Affairs Working Papers, WPS 638.

Tybout J. (1992), 'Linking Trade and Productivity: New Research Directions', *World Bank Economic Review*, **6** (2), 189–212.

Tybout, J. (2000), 'Manufacturing Firms in Developing Countries: How Well Do They Do, and Why?', *Journal of Economic Literature*, **38**, 11–44.

Tybout, J. and M. Westbrook (1995), 'Trade Liberalization and the Dimensions of Efficiency Change in the Mexican Manufacturing Industries', *Journal of International Economics*, **39**, 53–78.

Tybout, J., J. de Melo and V. Corbo (1991), 'The Effects of Trade Reforms on Scale and Technical Efficiency', *Journal of International Economics*, **31**, 231–50.

World Bank (2001), *Trade and Production Database*, Washington: World Bank.

Wu, Y. (1996), 'Are Real Exchange Rates Stationary? Evidence from a Panel Data Test', *Journal of Money, Credit and Banking*, **28**, 54–63.

APPENDIX 14.1   LIST OF THE MANUFACTURING SECTORS UNDER THE THREE-DIGIT ISIC CODE

ISIC Code	Sectors
311–312	Food Manufacturing
313	Beverage Industries
314	Tobacco Manufacturing
321–322	Textile Manufacturing
323	Wearing Apparel
324	Leather and its Products
325	Footwear except Rubber
331	Wood and Cork Products
332	Furniture Manufacturing
341	Paper and its Products
342	Printing and Publishing
351 + 353	Drugs and Pharmaceuticals + Other Chemical Products
352	Industrial Chemicals
354	Petroleum Refining
355	Miscellaneous Petroleum Products
356	Rubber Products
357	Plastic Products
361	Pottery and Chinaware
362	Glass and its Products
369	Non-metallic Mineral Products
371	Iron and Steel Basic Industries
372	Non-ferrous Metal Industries
381–382	Fabricated Metal Products
383	Non-electrical Machinery
384	Electrical Machinery
385	Transport Equipment
386–387	Scientific, Precision etc. + Photographic, Optical Goods

Source: Census of Manufacturing Industries, Bangladesh Bureau of Statistics, Government of Bangladesh.

15. Domestic competition and technological and trade competitiveness*

Yuichiro Uchida and Paul Cook

INTRODUCTION

In recent years both theoretical and empirical research has emphasized the productive and dynamic efficiency gains from competition (Baily and Gersbach, 1995; Nickell, 1996). Productive or technical efficiency is linked to productivity-enhancing innovations, which contribute to greater dynamic efficiency in the longer run. The role of competition in improving enterprise efficiency emanates through the incentives provided by the disciplining effect of market competition. This effect induces enterprises to introduce cost-reducing improvements in production and speed up innovation and technological progress. Competition also works through a process of selection, in which weaker enterprises give way or are replaced by more efficient ones, although the strength of competition between enterprises is not just a function of the behaviour between enterprises but also of the external environment in which they compete, the state of infrastructure, legal framework and the effectiveness of the financial system (Carlin and Seabright, 2001).

In this dynamic setting, competition from new entrants in the market that experiment with new technologies become the driving force for innovation and in turn market incumbents are forced to innovate for their survival (Dasgupta and Stiglitz, 1980). It is argued that in industries characterized by rapid technological change, as, for example, in the telecommunications sector, competition for the market through standard-setting innovations is likely to be more significant than cost-reducing static efficiency (Ahn, 2002). The examination of the empirical link between competition and dynamic efficiency has tended to concentrate on the relationship between market

* Reprinted from the *Quarterly Review of Economics and Finance*, **45**, Uchida, Y. and Cook, P., 'The effects of competition on technological and trade competitiveness', 258–83, 2005, with permission from Elsevier.

structure and technical change. Empirical studies have often focused on the relationship between the size of an enterprise or the market power of an enterprise and the propensity to innovate, based largely on economies of scale provided by size and the size of profit mark-ups inducing research and development expenditure. This has translated into a spate of studies measuring the association between market structure and innovation, either as an input such as R&D expenditures or as an output from innovation activity through an assessment of the number of patents. Market power or the degree of domestic competition is usually measured by a statistical measure of concentration involving output or employment shares of the largest enterprises in a market, or price-cost margins of enterprises used as a gauge to the degree of monopolistic pricing. Import penetration, expressed as the ratio of imports to domestic production, is typically used to measure the extent of foreign competition.

Nevertheless, these are imperfect measures of the real extent and dynamic character of the competition process and their use is primarily determined by the relative ease with which data can be obtained compared with other approaches that might more accurately capture the intensity of competition. Carlin, Haskel and Seabright (2001), drawing on the World Bank/EBRD business environment survey, find that as measures of the short-term, market structure, market power and behavioural measures of competition are broadly consistent with one another and provide useful information on the general state of competition. Difficulties also arise in the interpretation to be placed on high and low degrees of market concentration. Vigorous competition is likely to eliminate less efficient enterprises and contribute to increased market concentration while at the same time signalling that competition is working well (Metcalfe, 1993; Aghion and Schankerman, 2000).

It is also widely accepted that a contributory factor to success in trade relates to the inherent advantages of specialization (Krugman, 1994). This can be rationalized from the perspective of neo-classical trade theory, emphasizing factor endowments as an element in a country's comparative advantage and as argued by new trade theorists, to the scope for specialization that emerges from opportunities to exploit increasing returns to scale. In turn, it is argued that a country's technological capability and specialization reflect its trade specialization and influence the export competitiveness of enterprises within a country. The analysis of a country's trade pattern over time therefore, reveals its technological specialization and changes in its specialization. This is a particularly neo-Schumpeterian explanation that links national systems of innovation to the sector structure of export performance (Narula and Wakelin, 1995). Indeed, the neo-Schumpeterian view indicates that international trade specialization, as a measure of competitiveness, is the outcome of country- and sector-specific learning processes relating to technological capability. The mechanism linking the two leads to a stability of trade specialization, in which trade patterns are likely to be stable and changes in the pattern of technological specialization are cumulative or path-dependent (Uchida and Cook, 2005).

The purpose of this chapter is twofold. First, to examine changes in technological and trade competitiveness and explore the relationship between them in a range of countries. Second, to analyse the relationship between domestic competition and changes in technological and trade competitiveness. The analysis is confined to three advanced industrialized countries: Germany, Japan and the United States, and six developing countries: Hong Kong, South Korea, Singapore, Argentina, Brazil and Mexico.

The next section discusses the methods and data used to derive indices of competitiveness and the approach adopted to examine the relationship between trade and technological competitiveness. Two indices are calculated, which measure technological and trade comparative advantage to be used as a proxy for competitiveness on a country and an industry basis. A measure of market competition is also derived based on market concentration. The third section analyses the patterns of trade and technological comparative advantage for each country and on an industry basis. The fourth examines the relationship between changes in trade and technological competitiveness and the role played by domestic competition. The fifth section provides an analysis of the relationship between changes in the level of domestic competition and technological and trade competitiveness. The final section draws conclusions.

METHODOLOGY AND DATA

Two indices measuring technological and trade comparative advantage were calculated as a proxy for competitiveness with respect to technology and trade. These indices were calculated for four periods: 1978–82, 1983–87, 1988–92 and 1993–97 and analysed on a country and industry basis.

Data was obtained from the National Bureau of Economic Research (NBER) US Patent Citations (USPC) (Hall, Jaffe and Tratjenberg, 2001) and the United Nations Commodity Trade Series (SITC, Revision 2, 3-digit level). A concordance table was developed since the data series for technology and trade have been compiled on the basis of different industrial categories. Using the concordance table, data has been rearranged into 29 manufacturing industries based on the International Standard Industrial Classification (ISIC).

Competition and competitive advantage

The indices relating to revealed comparative advantage (RCA) for trade (Balassa, 1965) and technological comparative advantage (TCA) were calculated as follows:

$$RCA = \frac{X_{ij}/\sum_i X_{ij}}{\sum_j X_{ij}/\sum_i \sum_j X_{ij}} \qquad (15.1)$$

where X_{ij} is the value of exports of sector j from country i.

$$TCA = \frac{P_{ij}/\sum_i P_{ij}}{\sum_j P_{ij}/\sum_i \sum_j P_{ij}} \qquad (15.2)$$

where P_{ij} is the number of patents of country i in sector j.

The range of each index value lies between zero and positive infinity. If the index equals unity, the share of the country i's exports or patents in industry j is identical to its share of exports or patents in all industries. If the index value is greater than unity, it indicates that a country has a relative export or technological competitive advantage in industry j. If it is less than unity, the respective competitiveness with respect to trade and technology for each country in a given industry is weak.

Two cautionary notes are warranted regarding the derivation and use of the index for TCA. First, in the past, many empirical studies collected patent counts based on the grant year but as Hall, Jaffe and Tratjenberg (2001) have pointed out, counts ought to be based on the year of application. The reasoning for this is that there is likely to be a time lag (possibly one to three years) between the granting of a patent and its application owing to bureaucratic delay. As a result, the use of patent counts based on the grant year introduces unnecessary measurement errors into the analysis. Second, Cantwell (1993) has argued that TCA indices are likely to suffer from so-called small number problems. It is reckoned that a minimum of 1000 patent counts distributed across 30 sectors or industries are necessary to generate statistically satisfactory normally distributed indices.

Seeking a solution to the normality problem associated with RCA and TCA indices has proved troublesome, in particular with the latter. The most commonly used method for RCA has been the logarithmic transformation of an RCA index (Soete and Verspagen, 1994). However, a TCA index has often resulted in values of zero owing to zero patent counts and in this case the log transformation could not be applied. Fagerberg (1994) arbitrarily added a small integer, 0.1, to the logarithmic formula (ln(TCA + 0.1)) in order to resolve the zero value problem for TCA and also to improve the normality problem, although it had no statistical foundation. Laursen and Engedal (1995) have developed symmetric RCA and TCA indices (hereafter, SRCA and STCA, respectively) to deal with the zero count problem as well as normality. These indices have an economic advantage in that they put the same weight to the changes below and above unity and appear to be the best ones to improve the normality problem (Dalum, Laursen and Villumsen, 1996). Since most East Asian and Latin American developing countries fail to produce a sufficient number of patents, the possibility of adverse effects has been minimized by transforming the indices into SRCA and STCA indices by the following formulae:

$$SRCA_t = \frac{RCA_t - 1}{RCA_t + 1},$$ (15.3)

$$STCA_t = \frac{TCA_t - 1}{TCA_t + 1}.$$ (15.4)

Accordingly each value for SRCA or STCA ranges from –1 to 1.

In order to measure the level of domestic competition, Herfindahl–Hirschman (HHI) indices were calculated using enterprise-level sales data on a country and an industry basis from 1980 to 1997. Data was obtained from Thomson One Banker Analytics. The sales data available for enterprises varied according to country. In some cases data was not available for earlier periods. Specifically data was available for 29 enterprises for Argentina (1993–97), 106 for Brazil (1987–97), 490 for Germany (1980–97), 201 for Hong Kong (1990–97), 1591 for Japan (1980–97), 227 for South Korea (1988–97), 56 for Mexico (1987–97), 138 for Singapore (1990–97), and 2413 for the United States (1980–97).

Herfindahl–Hirschman indices have been calculated as follows:

$$HHI = \sum_{i=1}^{it} (MS_i)^2,$$ (15.5)

where MS is the market share of the ith enterprise, $i = 1. . .n$. Note that the above HHI formula is often multiplied by 10000. In this study, this multiplication was omitted for simplicity and to enable a straightforward comparison the HHI was inverted and transformed into a logarithm using the following formula: $Ln(1/HHI)$.

Thomson One Banker Analytics categorizes enterprises based on the Standard Industrial Classification (SIC), and re-categorizing these into more detailed categories is virtually impossible since a number of enterprises engage in various activities that spread across different industrial categories. As a result, the study developed a further concordance table based on the SIC, to analyse the correlation between competition and the changes in technological and trade competitiveness. These industries have been rearranged into 19 industrial categories (see Table 15.1).

ANALYSIS OF TECHNOLOGICAL AND TRADE COMPETITIVENESS

This section analyses the changes in technological and trade competitiveness in the nine countries between the initial five-year period and the last five-year period of the dataset, namely 1978–82 and 1993–97. The analysis compares the movement of industries in each economy, shown in Figures 15.1–15.3, between the two periods. Each graph is divided into four quadrants at the point (0, 0), and STCA indices are plotted on the x-axis and corresponding SRCA indices on the y-axis. The industries in the upper right quadrant possess both technological and trade comparative advantage. Those in the lower right quadrant have technological comparative advantage without trade comparative advantage. The upper left quadrant shows the industries that do not have technological comparative advantage but possess trade comparative advantage. Finally, industries in the lower left quadrant hold no advantage with respect to trade or technology.

In the case of the advanced economies, as shown in Figure 15.1, it is apparent that there is very little movement between quadrants. Some exceptions are observed for the United States. The agricultural chemical industry (8) moved from the upper left to the upper right quadrant gaining both trade and technological advantage. There was also some movement in the case of toiletries (6), computers (20) and instruments (27). In general the results confirm the findings of a number of earlier empirical studies that technological and trade competitiveness in the advanced countries exhibits a cumulative or path-dependent pattern.

As for the East Asian developing economies the transformation of technological and trade competitiveness is far more evident. This is vividly revealed in Figure 15.2. Although Hong Kong's transformation pattern more or less resembles those observed in the advanced economies, the noticeable difference is the movement from the right to the left quadrants. The electronics (22) and instruments (27) industries moved from the upper right to the upper left quadrant, losing their technological advantage while retaining trade advantage, and computers (20) moved from the lower right to the lower left, losing both trade and technological advantage. Thus it may appear that Hong Kong has been losing its technological capabilities in the relatively high-tech industries. South Korea's transformation pattern is quite different. Here high-tech industries moved from the upper left

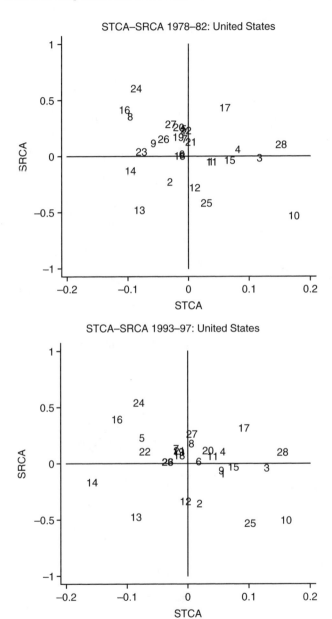

*Figure 15.1   Relationship between technology and trade: advanced
countries*

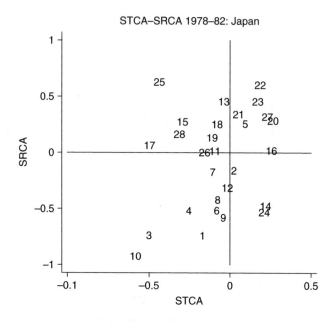

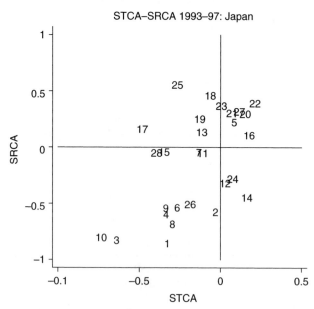

Figure 15.1   (continued)

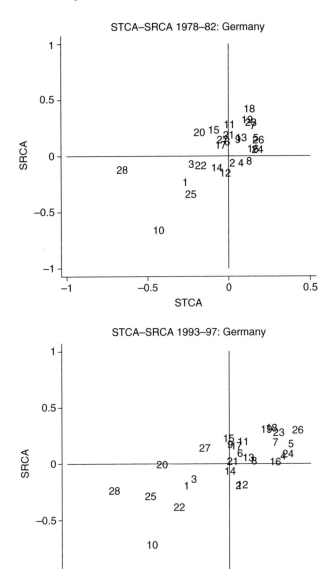

Figure 15.1 (continued)

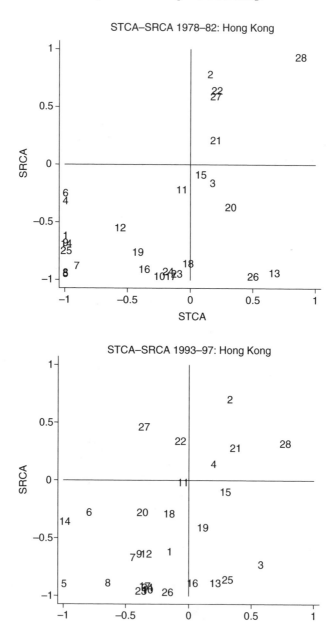

Figure 15.2   Relationship between technology and trade: East Asia

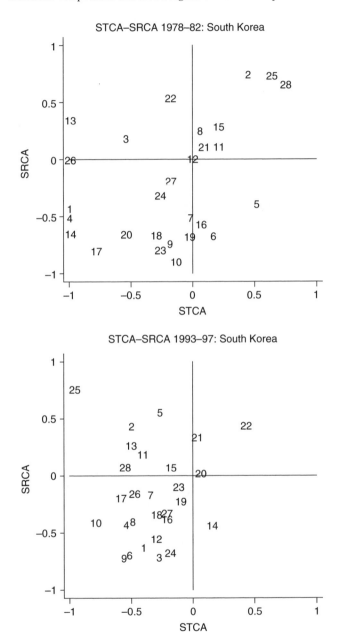

Figure 15.2   (continued)

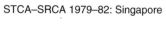

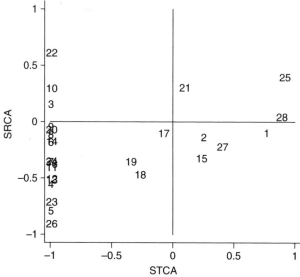

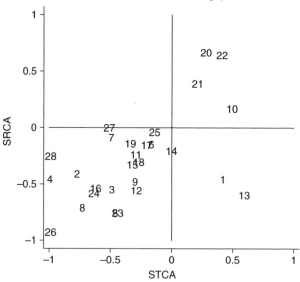

Figure 15.2   (continued)

(electronics (22)) and from the lower left (computers (20)) to the upper right quadrant gaining both technological and trade competitiveness in the last period. In contrast most of the traditionally well-established industries, such as textiles (2), shipbuilding (25) and toys (28), moved from the upper right to the upper left quadrant, losing their technological advantage but retaining their trade competitiveness. A similar but more rapid transformation can also be found in Singapore where high-tech industries, computers (20) and electronics (22), appear in the upper right quadrant in the last period. The decline of traditionally established Singaporean industries, shipbuilding (25) and toys (28), has been more rapid than in South Korea and these industries now possess no technological or trade advantages.

More moderate transformations are observed in Latin America, as shown in Figure 15.3. In Argentina toiletries (6), agricultural chemicals (8), motor vehicles (23) and shipbuilding (25) gained both technological and trade advantage in the later period. Brazil maintained a relatively stable pattern of technological and trade advantage although a few industries such as wood (3), stone (12) and non-ferrous products (14) gained trade and technological advantage. It is noticeable that in both Argentina and Brazil the relatively high-tech industries, such as computers (20) and electronics (22), failed to achieve both technological and trade advantage.

In contrast to Argentina and Brazil, Mexico's transformation pattern is more unique. While only one industry, engines (16), appeared in the upper right quadrant, eight industries, including plastic materials (5), drugs (9), electricals (21), electronics (22), motor vehicles (23), aircraft parts (24) and railroads (26), moved from the lower left to the upper left quadrant, indicating the establishment of trade advantage without any corresponding technological advantage. This conspicuous transformation is likely to have resulted from the effects of the North American Free Trade Agreement (NAFTA) or the relocation of assembly-type activities from the United States and other advanced countries to the northern part of Mexico.

In summary, as all three figures have shown, a total of 19 industries moved to the upper right quadrant between the two periods. These included 11 industries moving from the upper left to the upper right quadrant. These were toiletries (6), agricultural chemicals (8), computers (20) and instruments (27) in the United States; toiletries (6) in Germany; electronics (22) in South Korea; petroleum products (10) and electronics (22) in Singapore; toiletries (6) and shipbuilding (25) in Argentina; and stone (12) in Brazil. As for other cases, five industries moved from the lower right to the upper right quadrant: plastic products (11) in the United States; agricultural chemicals (8) in Germany; agricultural chemicals (8) in Argentina; wood (3) and non-ferrous products (14) in Brazil. The remaining three industries moved directly from the lower left to the upper right. These were paper

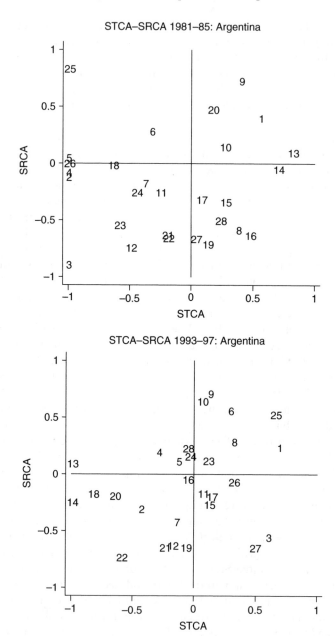

Figure 15.3 Relationship between technology and trade: Latin America

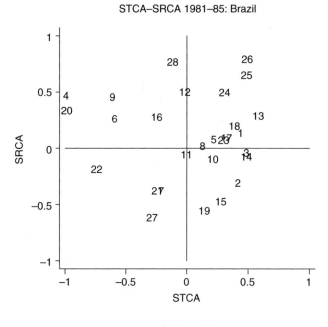

STCA–SRCA 1981–85: Brazil

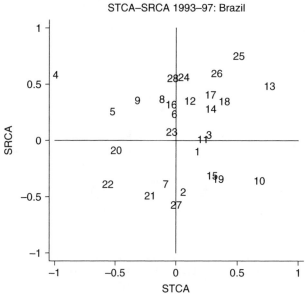

STCA–SRCA 1993–97: Brazil

Figure 15.3   (continued)

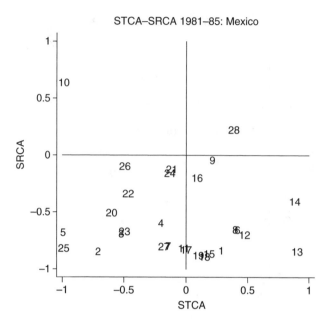

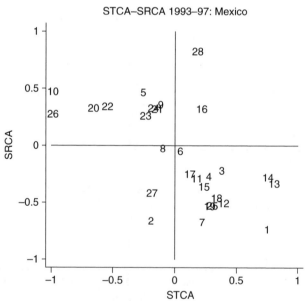

Figure 15.3 (continued)

products (4) in Hong Kong; computers (20) in Singapore; and motor vehicles (23) in Argentina.

It can be observed that, as far as the advanced countries are concerned, the pattern of technological and trade competitiveness can be considered to be cumulative or path-dependent. With respect to the East Asian economies, the transformation of competitiveness is more evident and rapid, particularly in the cases of South Korea and Singapore. In these latter two countries the transformation is characterized by changes in the industrial structure, from relatively low-tech and labour-intensive industries to relatively high-tech industries. In Hong Kong it appears that some of the high-tech industries are losing their technological capabilities. In the Latin American countries, a contrast between Mexico and the others is observed. While the transformation is moderate in Argentina and Brazil, in Mexico a number of industries have gained trade competitiveness without a corresponding competitive advantage with respect to technology.

On the whole, the majority of industries, irrespective of the level of development of the countries of their origin, established both technological and trade competitiveness initially by maintaining trade advantage without a corresponding advantage in technology. This appears to have been achieved through a process of learning by doing, linked to an exposure to international competition. Interestingly, even the high-tech industries in the United States, such as the computer (20) and instrument industries (27) followed this pattern, moving from the upper left to the upper right quadrant. This sequence may cast some doubt on the notion that the evolution of these industries can be explained purely in terms of a technological push, which would see industries moving from the lower left or lower right quadrant to the upper right segment.

DOMESTIC COMPETITION AND TRADE AND TECHNOLOGICAL COMPETITIVENESS

This section investigates the relationship between the changes in trade and technological comparative advantage and the role played by domestic competition. Figure 15.4 shows the level of domestic competition in the manufacturing sector on a country basis. The United States and Japan have the highest levels of domestic competition among the countries surveyed and the former appears to have an increased level of competition since the early 1990s. In contrast, possibly owing to reunification, the level of domestic competition in Germany has been falling since the early 1990s. As a result, in 1997 Germany's competition level, measured in terms of industrial concentration, was lower than Singapore's and almost the same as

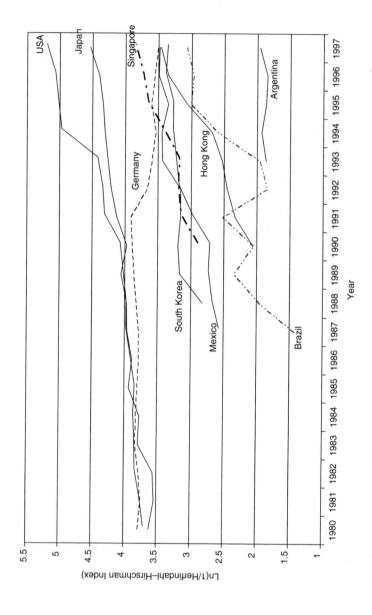

Figure 15.4   Levels of domestic competition in the manufacturing sector

Hong Kong's and South Korea's. South Korea gradually increased the level of domestic competition over time while domestic competition in Singapore only began to accelerate in the early 1990s. A similar trend can be observed for the level of domestic competition in Mexico. The most substantial increase in the level of domestic competition is found in Hong Kong and to a lesser extent in Brazil. Argentina's level of domestic competition remains far lower than the other economies.

Figure 15.5 shows the changes in the share of manufacturing exports used as a proxy for international competitiveness in the manufacturing sector. Not surprisingly the advanced economies have a higher share in manufacturing exports, suggesting that their international competitiveness is equally as high. Among these economies, the United States has been reinforcing its competitiveness since the early 1990s while Germany and Japan have been losing their competitiveness. Hong Kong and South Korea followed a similar trend with one another up until the late 1980s but since then, Hong Kong has increased its competitiveness. Singapore has lagged behind Hong Kong and South Korea in this respect until the late 1980s. Mexico started to catch up with East Asian economies in the early 1990s and its share was close to that of Singapore in 1997. In contrast, Argentina and Brazil have been maintaining stable and lower levels of international competitiveness throughout the period.

Similarly, RCA indices themselves convey information on international competitiveness. Accordingly, it can be inferred that higher values for RCA indices also point to higher levels of international competitiveness in those industries. While the earlier analysis emphasized the significance of learning by doing in relation to the movement of industries from the upper left to the upper right quadrant, this movement undoubtedly captures the crucial role played by the exposure to international markets and the resulting competitive pressures that are likely to have facilitated technological development.

In the analysis so far the role played by domestic competition in explaining changes in technological and trade competitive advantage has not been tackled. The remainder of this section therefore, focuses on the relationship between domestic competition and trade and technology. The coefficients of variation for the HHI indices, measuring domestic competition on an industry basis for our sample countries, are shown in Table 15.1.

It is apparent that there are no obvious industry-specific characteristics with respect to changes in domestic competition, except for the food industry. Here relatively high levels of changes in domestic competition are observed, possibly reflecting the relative ease of entry into this particular market. National or regional differences however, are more prominent than industry-specific ones. In the advanced economies, changes in the level of

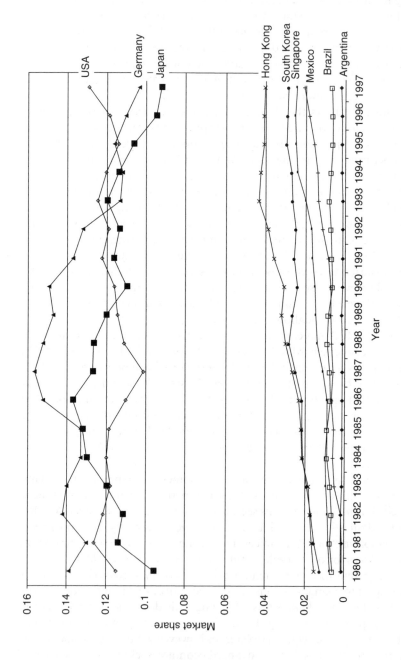

Figure 15.5 Levels of international competitiveness

Table 15.1 *Domestic competition: coefficients of variation (standard deviation/mean)*

Industry	Germany	Japan	USA	H. Kong	Korea	Singapore	Argentina	Brazil	Mexico
20. Food	0.56	0.30	0.11	0.48	0.91	0.22	0.20	0.61	0.56
21. Tobacco	na	na	0.04	na	na	0.0:	na	na	na
22. Textiles	0.11	0.21	0.34	0.45	0.95	na	na	0.45	0.05
23. Apparel	0.45	0.09	0.47	0.60	0.12	0.0:	na	0.45	na
24. Wood	0.52	0.48	0.07	0.50	na	na	na	0.09	na
25. Furniture	0.34	0.50	0.16	0.25	na	na	na	na	na
26. Paper	0.38	0.15	0.11	0.59	0.24	0.27	na	0.26	0.18
27. Printing	0.10	0.34	0.24	0.48	0.24	0.26	na	na	0.02
28. Chemicals	0.14	0.19	0.24	0.34	0.76	0.36	0.22	0.56	0.17
29. Petroleum	0.03	0.30	0.06	0.29	0.25	0.00	0.23	0.05	na
30. Plastics	0.20	0.36	0.06	0.12	0.31	0.61	0.35	0.54	0.34
31. Leather	0.27	0.11	0.11	0.36	0.22	na	na	0.06	na
32. Stone	0.20	0.27	0.14	0.15	0.48	0.23	0.13	0.48	0.44
33. Pri. Metals	0.09	0.13	0.30	0.39	0.37	0.15	0.22	0.50	0.31
34. Fab. Metals	0.24	0.49	0.43	0.70	0.48	0.50	0.08	0.41	0.31
35. Machinery	na	0.21	0.24	0.56	0.77	0.48	na	0.32	0.23
36. Electronics	0.12	0.24	0.24	0.67	0.60	0.43	na	0.34	0.23
37. Transport	0.09	0.15	0.09	0.27	0.56	0.41	0.33	0.72	0.68
38. Instruments	0.07	0.17	0.11	0.59	0.33	0.40	0.05	na	na

Note: Industrial category is according to ISIC.

domestic competition are higher in the relatively low-tech industries, such as textiles, apparel, wood and furniture, than in the medium and high-tech industries. In contrast, changes in competition are higher in the latter categories of industries for East Asia, as, for example, in fabricated metals, machinery, electronics and instrument industries. An interesting picture emerges in Latin America where the transport sector has higher levels of changes in domestic competition compared with other industries in the country.

To examine these characteristics further, Figure 15.6 shows the changes in the level of domestic competition between the first year when data are available (first bar for each industry) and 1997 (second bar) on an industry basis for each economy. The market concentration criteria used by the United States Department of Justice (1997), is applied to our analysis, where a Herfindahl–Hirschman index (HHI) less than 0.1 indicates a low concentration of the market concerned, while values between 0.1 and 0.18 signify moderate concentration and those greater than 0.18 indicate that the market is highly concentrated.

Among the advanced economies, it is apparent that domestic enterprises in almost all industries in the United States are operating in relatively competitive domestic markets. There are exceptions, for example the tobacco (21) industry, followed by the petroleum product (29) industry. Similarly, Japanese enterprises operate in highly competitive domestic markets, except for apparel (23), paper (26) and leather (31). In contrast, the levels of domestic competition for German industries are lower than those in the United States and Japan. Only four industries, foods (20), apparel (23), wood (24) and chemicals (28), had either high or moderately competitive markets in 1997 according to the criteria specified above.

As for the East Asian economies, Hong Kong had low levels of competition in domestic markets for all industries in the late 1980s. In less than ten years however, almost all industries had increased their level of competition and several had highly or moderately competitive markets. In particular, electronics (36), apparel (23) and industrial machinery (35) have significantly increased the level of competition in their markets. Similarly, South Korea had relatively highly concentrated markets in the initial period. In less than ten years however, almost all industries reduced their market concentration, particularly in textiles (22), food (20) and chemicals (28). In Singapore, while several industries maintained relatively concentrated domestic markets, some industries, such as plastics (30), industrial machinery (35) and electronics (36), noticeably increased levels of competition in their markets over time.

All industries in Argentina continue to have highly concentrated markets. In two industries, petroleum products (29) and plastics (30),

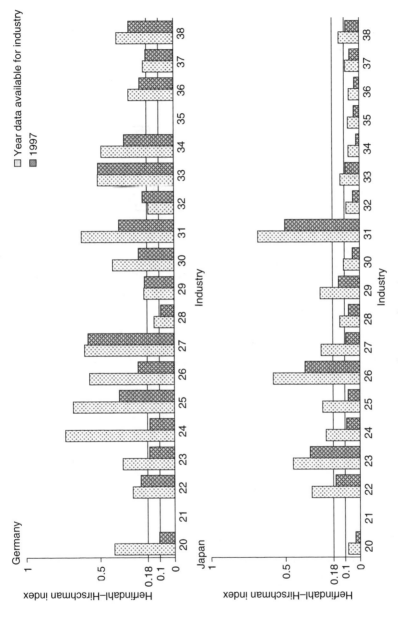

Figure 15.6 Changes in domestic competition in the manufacturing sector

353

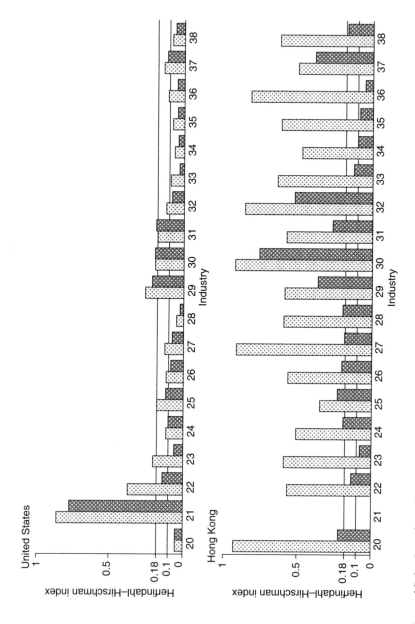

Figure 15.6 (continued)

354

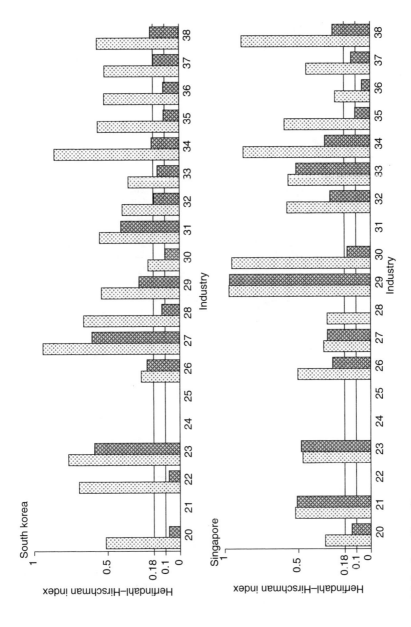

Figure 15.6 (continued)

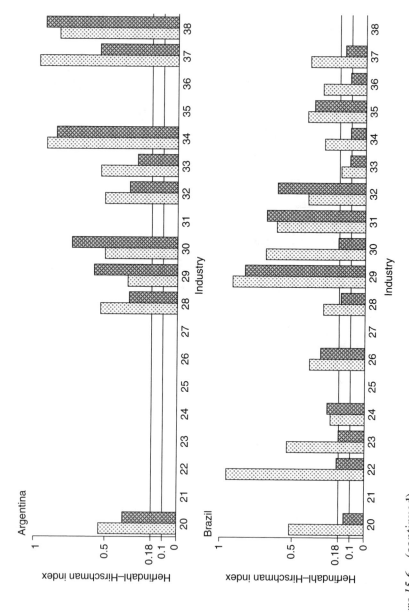

Figure 15.6 (continued)

356

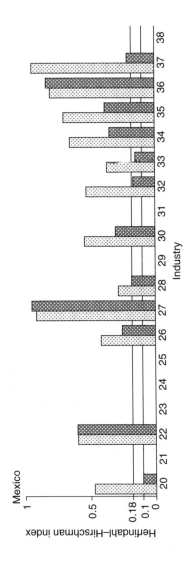

Figure 15.6 (continued)

market concentration has increased over time. The patterns for competition exhibited in Brazil and in Mexico are, more or less, similar to each other. Several industries reduced their market concentration while others maintained or increased it. In Brazil, food (20), chemicals (28), primary metals (33), fabricated metals (34), electronics (36) and transport equipment (37) had either highly or moderately competitive markets in 1997. In Mexico, by 1997, industries such as food (20), transport equipment (37) and stone (32) had reduced market concentration. Interestingly the electronics (36) industry increased market concentration despite the fact that the industry is one of the most dynamic industries in Mexico.

THE RELATIONSHIP BETWEEN DOMESTIC COMPETITION AND COMPETITIVE ADVANTAGE IN TECHNOLOGY AND TRADE

We now turn to an examination of the relationship between changes in the level of domestic competition and technological and trade competitiveness. In terms of competition the patterns of concentration discussed above indicated that changes in the level of competition were more likely to be influenced by country-specific factors or characteristics than industry-specific ones. Of course there were exceptions. In contrast, changes in technological and trade comparative advantage, as indicated earlier, exhibited a mixture of both country- and industry-specific characteristics particularly with respect to the high-tech industries.

Table 15.2 shows the Pearson correlation coefficients for each industry by country. Although the use of this method is somewhat simplistic, dictated largely by data constraints, it is nevertheless highly indicative of the relationship between the variables concerned. Since these results do not point to the direction of causality however, their interpretation requires a fair degree of caution. With the exception of industries shown in bold italics in Table 15.2, most industries experienced an increase in the level of domestic competition.

The results reveal that there are a number of statistically significant correlations between a change in domestic competition and technological and trade competitiveness. Over 50 per cent of the results were statistically significant except for those between domestic competition and technological competitiveness in the cases of Hong Kong (33 per cent) and Argentina (33 per cent), Brazil (7 per cent) and Mexico (36 per cent), and between domestic competition and trade competitiveness in the United States (47 per cent). In general there are more statistically significant results in relation to trade than technology, suggesting that the level of competition has a more significant impact on trade competitiveness (or trade on competition), than on technological competitiveness. The United States and South Korea are the significant exceptions. It seems that there are no apparent industry-specific characteristics that are evident across the sample economies.

Among the advanced countries, higher levels of competition are associated more with positive changes in technological competitiveness than with those in trade. Those statistics shown in the third from last column in Table 15.2 are for Germany (57 per cent and 17 per cent respectively) and the United States (75 per cent and 14 per cent). In these countries however, higher domestic competition is correlated more with the negative changes in trade competitiveness than with positive changes. In Japan, interestingly, a higher level of domestic competition is correlated more with negative changes in both technological and trade competitiveness than with positive changes. While these characteristics are spread fairly evenly across all industries in these countries, two industries do have a positive correlation between higher levels of domestic competition and positive changes in both technological and trade competitiveness (i.e., paper (26) in Germany and apparel (23) in the United States).

In contrast to the positive correlation, ten industries have a correlation between higher levels of domestic competition and negative changes in both technological and trade competitiveness in the advanced countries. These include electronics (36) and instruments (38) in Germany, textiles (22), apparel (23), wood (24), primary metals (33), fabricated metals (34), transport equipment (37) and instruments (38) in Japan and electronics (36) in the United States. Interestingly the negative changes in technological and trade competitiveness in relatively high-tech industries in these countries (electronics in Germany and the United States and instruments (38) in Germany and Japan) are associated with higher levels of domestic competition. Exceptions in this regard are the correlation between higher levels of competition and the positive changes in technological competitiveness in electronics in Japan and instruments in the United States.

In Hong Kong and Singapore, a higher level of domestic competition is correlated with changes in trade competitiveness (53 per cent and 69 per cent, respectively) rather than with technological competitiveness (33 per cent and 55 per cent). In contrast, in South Korea, higher competition is more associated with technological competitiveness than with trade competitiveness (71 per cent and 64 per cent, respectively). Hong Kong shows a more positive correlation between increased competition and changes in technological and/or trade competitiveness than a negative one. However, only the food industry has a positive correlation between competition and both technological and trade competitiveness. With respect to the other

Table 15.2   Correlation between domestic competition and technological and trade competitiveness

		20	22	23	24	26	28	29	30
Germany	SRCA	0.21	−0.44**	−0.72***	−0.82***	**0.72***	−0.80***	**0.48**	−0.80***
1980–97*1	SRTA	0.10	**0.86**	0.13	0.37	**0.57***	**0.85***	−0.40**	**0.84***
Japan	SRCA	−0.70***	−0.71***	−0.93***	−0.81***	−0.88***	**0.52**	**0.81***	−0.78***
1980–97	SRTA	−0.18	−0.52**	−0.61***	−0.46**	0.14	−0.80***	−0.72***	−0.14
USA	SRCA	0.20	−0.58***	**0.37*	−0.49**	−0.19	−0.94***	−0.10	0.20
1980–97	SRTA	−0.17	**0.64***	**0.65***	−0.23	−0.05	**0.40**	−0.06	−0.32
Hong Kong	SRCA	**0.92***	−0.31	−0.86***	−0.91**	0.30	**0.87***	0.54	−0.83
1983–97*2	SRTA	**0.51**	−0.23	**0.56**	−0.76	0.01	0.20	0.54	−0.95*
S. Korea	SRCA	−0.59**	0.57	−0.54*	na	0.07	**0.77***	**0.70***	**0.89***
1983–97*3	SRTA	−0.23	−0.37*	−0.50*	na	0.04	−0.47**	**0.51**	−0.62**
Singapore	SRCA	−0.67***	na	*0.28*	na	−0.84***	−0.75***	−0.76*	−0.69**
1983–97*4	SRTA	**0.36*	na	*na*	na	na	0.26	0.21	−0.56*
Argentina	SRCA	−0.44	na	na	na	na	−0.87**	−0.73***	−0.16
1987–97*5	SRTA	0.74**	na	na	na	na	−0.38	−0.27	−0.31
Brazil	SRCA	0.34	−0.86***	−0.65*	−0.31	**0.77***	0.29	−0.62**	**0.63**
1989–97*6	SRTA	−0.21	0.53	−0.17	*0.22*	−0.28	0.28	0.02	**0.54*
Mexico	SRCA	−0.23	*0.46**	na	na	0.19	**0.57**	na	**0.83***
1983–97*7	SRTA	**0.65***	−0.23	na	na	0.01	0.03	na	0.43*

Notes:
***, **, and * are statistically significant at the 0.01, 0.05 and 0.10 levels, respectively.
20 = food; 22 = textiles; 23 = apparel; 24 = wood; 26 = paper; 28 = chemicals; 29 = petro-products; 30 = plastics; 32 = stone; 33 = primary metals; 34 = fabricated metals; 35 = industrial machinery; 36 = electronics; 37 = transport equipment; 38 = scientific instruments.
+ % = the percentage of statistically significant positive results in relation to all statistically significant results.
− % = the percentage of statistically significant negative results in relation to all statistically significant results.
Total = the percentage of all statistically significant results in relation to all results, excluding na.
The figures in bold italics are those industries that experienced a decrease in the level of domestic competition (Figure 15.6).
*1: 23=1985–97; 24=1987–97; *2: 24,26=1994–97; 28=1986–97; 29,30=1995–97; 34=1991–97; 37=1985–97; 38=1992–97; *3: 23,30,33,34=1988–97; 26=1993–97; 35=1986–97; 36=1984–97; 38=1989–97; *4: 23=1992–97; 26,30,38=1991–97; 28=1984–93; 29=1993–97; 34=1987–97; *5: 20,37=1992–97; 28=1993–97; 32,34=1991–97; 38=1994–97; *6: 22,23=1991–97; *7: 30=1984–97; 34=1988–97; 35=1992–97; 36=1989–97.

industries, an increase in competition in the chemicals (28), primary metals (33) and instruments (38) is positively correlated with trade competitiveness, while in apparel (23) and industrial machinery (35) the stronger correlation is with technological competitiveness.

With respect to South Korea, the correlation between an increased level of competition and changes in technological competitiveness is characterized by a negative relationship (70 per cent), whereas the correlation

32	33	34	35	36	37	38	+ %	− %	Total
−0.40**	−0.45**	−0.54**	na	−0.86***	0.09	−0.59***	16.7	83.3	78.6
0.12	0.10	0.31	na	−0.71***	0.05	−0.68***	57.1	42.9	50.0
−0.46**	−0.88***	−0.93***	**0.70*****	−0.90***	−0.93***	−0.52**	20.0	80.0	100.0
0.72***	−0.38*	−0.66***	−0.27	**0.69*****	−0.77***	−0.88***	18.2	81.8	80.0
−0.66***	0.16	0.11	−0.39**	−0.68***	−0.12	−0.23	14.3	85.7	46.7
−0.22	−0.35*	**0.34***	**0.96*****	−0.77***	0.20	**0.65*****	75.0	25.0	53.3
−0.41*	**0.76*****	−0.32	0.17	−0.82***	−0.10	**0.70***	62.5	37.5	53.3
0.16	0.32	0.14	**0.41***	0.18	−0.09	−0.68*	60.0	40.0	33.3
−0.72***	−0.03	−0.68**	**0.89*****	**0.60****	−0.35	0.36	55.6	44.4	64.3
0.20	0.00	−0.65**	−0.46*	**0.80*****	−0.75***	**0.77*****	30.0	70.0	71.4
0.22	**0.62*****	−0.15	**0.75*****	**0.42***	−0.75***	**0.95*****	40.0	60.0	69.2
−0.11	−0.50**	−0.68**	−0.59**	**0.72*****	**0.58****	0.04	42.9	57.1	54.5
0.40	−0.83***	−0.65*	na	na	**0.70***	*0.45*	20.0	80.0	55.6
−0.79**	−0.64**	−0.31	na	na	−0.22	*−0.75*	33.3	66.7	33.3
0.39	−0.76***	**0.87*****	−0.50*	−0.95***	0.08	na	33.3	66.7	64.3
−0.30	0.40	0.33	0.23	−0.31	0.32	na	100.0	0.0	7.1
0.45**	−0.09	**0.71****	**0.77****	*0.35*	**0.91*****	na	100.0	0.0	63.6
0.38*	−0.30	**0.79*****	−0.21	*0.55*	−0.08	na	100.0	0.0	36.4

between competition and trade competitiveness is positive. There are some industries where the relationship for technology is positive and these are the medium to high-tech sectors, namely petroleum products (29), electronics (36) and instruments (38). It is also in the medium to high-tech range that competition and trade competitiveness are positively correlated (i.e., chemicals (28), plastics (30) and industrial machinery (35)). Interestingly, in the two cases of petroleum products and electronics, the positive correlation is extended to both technological and trade competitiveness.

In Singapore, generally, more industries are associated with a negative correlation between higher levels of competition and technological and trade competitiveness (60 per cent and 57 per cent respectively). An exception is the electronics (36) industry where competition is positively associated with technology and trade, and the primary metals (33), industrial machinery (35) and the instruments (38) industries where there is a positive relation with trade only. Positive associations with technology alone are found in food (20) and transport equipment (37) for Singapore.

In Latin American countries, higher competition is correlated mainly with trade competitiveness, particularly in Brazil. The association tends to be more negative in relation to both technological and trade competitiveness. Only the transport equipment (37) industry has a positive correlation between higher levels of competition and trade competitiveness. In Brazil, higher competition is correlated more with negative changes in trade competitiveness and only the plastics (30) industry has a statistically significant result with respect to technological competitiveness. Mexico displays a peculiar pattern in which all statistically significant results between higher levels of competition and technology and trade are positive except for textiles (22). Where the correlation is positive for both trade and technology, the industry range is mixed and includes plastics (30), stone (32) and fabricated metals (34).

Following the analysis in the previous section, those industries that moved to the upper right quadrant between the two periods, possessing both technological and trade competitiveness in the last period, are identified in order to examine the relationship between domestic competition and the movements of the industries. The industries that moved from the upper left to the upper right quadrant are: plastics (30) in Germany; petroleum products (29), industrial machinery (35) and instruments (38) in the United States; apparel (23) in Hong Kong; petroleum products (29) and electronics (36) in Singapore; food (20) in Argentina; and stone (32) and primary metals (33) in Brazil. Table 15.2 indicates that all these industries appear to have statistically significant positive correlations between higher levels of competition and the changes in technological competitiveness except for stone and primary metals in the case of Brazil. While Singapore's electronics (36) industry has a statistically significant positive correlation between competition and technological and trade competitiveness, all other industries have statistically significant negative correlations between competition and changes in trade competitiveness except for instruments in the United States, food in Argentina and stone in Brazil, where no statistically significant relationships were found. It can be deduced that the movement of industries between the upper left and upper right quadrants has been influenced by increased levels of domestic competition.

The industries that remained in the upper right quadrant between the two periods, maintaining both technological and trade competitiveness, are also identified as chemicals (28), industrial machinery (35), transport equipment (37) in Germany; electronics (36) and instruments (38) in Japan; paper (26) in the United States; electronics (36) in Hong Kong; and electronics (36) in South Korea. In these cases there is no clear pattern in relation to the correlation between higher levels of competition and changes in technological and trade competitiveness. Only South Korea's electronics industry has a statistically significant positive correlation between competition and changes in technological and trade competitiveness. Chemicals in Germany and electronics in Japan have statistically significant positive correlations between competition and technology but statistically significant negative correlations between competition and changes in trade competitiveness. Transport equipment in Germany and the paper industry in the United States show no statistically significant relationships although the former increased its technological competitiveness and the latter maintained almost the same level of technological and trade competitiveness between the two periods. Japan's instrument industry has a statistically significant negative correlation between higher levels of competition and changes in technological and trade competitiveness, while Hong Kong's electronics industry only has a statistically significant negative correlation between competition and trade competitiveness.

In addition to these two industries, paper (26) in Germany and plastics (30) in the United States, moved from the lower right (possessing technological competitiveness without trade competitiveness) to the upper right quadrant. A higher level of competition in Germany's paper industry is correlated with changes in technological and trade competitiveness whereas the plastics industry in the United States shows no statistically significant result. Thus the role of domestic competition in relation to what may be described as a pure technological push involving industries moving up the right side of the quadrant is unclear and anyway involved few industries.

It is also interesting to examine the relationship between domestic competition and the changes in technological and trade competitiveness in the industries that moved away from the upper right quadrant. The industries that moved from the upper right to the upper left quadrant, losing technological competitiveness while retaining trade competitiveness, are transport equipment (37) in Japan, textiles (22) and instruments (38) in Hong Kong and apparel (23), plastics (30) and fabricated metals (34) in South Korea. In addition, textiles (22) and primary metals (33) in Japan moved from the upper right to the lower right quadrant, losing trade competitiveness but maintaining technological competitiveness and textiles (22) in Brazil moved from the upper right to the lower left quadrant, losing competitiveness in both spheres.

CONCLUSIONS

The analysis has revealed, not surprisingly, that the United States, Japan and, to a lesser extent, Germany have relatively highly competitive domestic markets. Further, that increases in recent years in the level of domestic competition have occurred mainly in the low-tech industries in these countries. In contrast, increases in the domestic level of competition in East Asia appear to have occurred in relation to the medium and high-tech industries within the last ten years. In Latin America reduced levels of concentration have been observed in a range of industries in Brazil and Mexico, and far less so for Argentina, where markets for most industries remain fairly concentrated. The transport equipment industry has witnessed the most significant reduction in market concentration among the Latin American economies reviewed. Explanations for the changes in competition in all countries appear to be country- or regional-specific rather than industry-specific, possibly indicating that domestic or international policy changes have had some influencing effect.

In summary, the analysis of the correlation between domestic competition and changes in technological and trade competitiveness has revealed that on a country basis, the majority of the countries examined have more statistically significant correlations between higher levels of competition and changes in trade competitiveness rather than in technological competitiveness. Only the United States and South Korea have more correlations between higher levels of competition and changes in technological competitiveness. In Germany and the United States, increases in competition are associated more extensively with positive changes in technological competitiveness and negative changes in trade competitiveness. In Argentina, Japan and Singapore higher levels of competition are associated with negative changes in both technological and trade competitiveness. In Hong Kong and Mexico, higher competition is correlated more with the changes in both technological and trade competitiveness, although more significantly with a positive relation in the case of trade competitiveness. In South Korea, competition increases are correlated more with a negative change in technological competitiveness and a positive change in trade competitiveness. Finally, in Brazil, higher competition is associated more with a negative change in trade competitiveness. There is only one correlation with a change in technological competitiveness that is statistically significant and therefore it is difficult to draw a firm conclusion in this case.

On an industry basis, the analysis has also indicated that there is no industry-specific trend or characteristic as to the relationship between higher domestic competition and the movements of the industries in relation to their technological and trade competitiveness. Irrespective of industry and country, higher levels of competition appear to have a crucial role in the movement towards the upper right quadrant, particularly through the positive association with technological competitiveness. In East Asia however, higher levels of competition have also been associated with negative correlations with the industries that moved away from the upper quadrant.

On a country basis, interesting characteristics have been observed among the relatively high-tech electronics industry. Among the advanced countries of Germany and the United States, higher levels of competition have been negatively correlated with changes in technological and trade competitiveness in this industry, while Japan has been associated with a positive change in technological competitiveness. In South Korea and Singapore, higher

levels of competition have been correlated with changes in both technological and trade competitiveness in the electronics sector. In Latin
America, Argentina and Mexico, there have been no statistically significant
results, and in the latter the level of competition has actually decreased for
electronics. Finally, in Brazil a higher level of competition has been associated with a negative change in trade competitiveness with respect to the
electronics sector.

REFERENCES

Aghion, P. and M. Schankerman (2000), 'A Model of Market-Enhancing
Infrastructure', Mimeo, University College London.
Ahn, S. (2002), 'Competition, Innovation and Productivity Growth: A Review of
Theory and Evidence', Economics Department Working Papers No. 317, Paris:
OECD.
Baily, M. and H. Gersbach (1995), 'Efficiency in Manufacturing and the Need for
Global Competition', Brookings Paper on Economic Activity, 307–58.
Balassa, B. (1965), 'Trade Liberalisation and "revealed" Comparative Advantage',
Manchester School of Economic and Social Studies, **32**, 99–123.
Cantwell, J. (ed.) (1993), *Transnational Corporations and Innovatory Activities*,
London: Routledge.
Carlin, W. and P. Seabright (2001), 'The Importance of Competition in Developing
Countries for Productivity and Innovation', Background Paper for World
Development Report.
Carlin, W., J. Haskel and P. Seabright (2001), ' "Understanding" the Essential Fact
About Capitalism: Markets, Competition and Creative Destruction', *National
Institute Economic Review*, **175**, January, 67–84.
Dalum, B., K. Laursen and G. Villumsen (1996), 'The Long Term Development of
the OECD Export Specialisation Patterns: De-specialisation and "stickiness" ',
DRUID Working Papers 96–14, Copenhagen Business School.
Dasgupta, P. and J. Stiglitz (1980), 'Industrial Structure and the Nature of
Innovation Activity', *The Economic Journal*, **90**, 266–93.
Fagerberg, J. (1994), ' Technology and International Differences in Growth Rates',
Journal of Economic Literature, **32**, 1147–75.
Hall, B.H., A. Jaffe and M. Tratjenberg (2001), 'The NBER Patent Citation Data
File: Lessons, Insights and Methodological Tools', NBER Working Paper 8498.
Krugman, P. (1994), 'The Myth of Asia's Miracle', *Foreign Affairs*, **73** (6), 62–78.
Laursen, K. and C. Engedal (1995), 'The Role of the Technology Factor in
Economic Growth: A Theoretical and Empirical Inquiry into New Approaches
to Economic Growth', Unpublished MA dissertation, University of Aalborg.
Metcalfe, J. (1993), *The Economic Foundations of Technology Policy: Equilibrium
and Evolutionary Perspectives*, University of Manchester Press.
Narula, R. and K. Wakelin (1995), 'Technological Competitiveness, Trade and
Foreign Direct Investment', Research Memorandum No. 19, Maastricht Economic
Research Institute on Innovation and Technology, University of Limburg.
Nickell, S. (1996), 'Competition and Corporate Performance', *Journal of Political
Economy*, **104** (4), 724–46.

Soete, L. and B. Verspagen (1994), 'Competing for Growth: The Dynamics of Technology Gaps', in L.L. Pasinetti and R.M. Solow (eds), *Economic Growth and the Structure of Long-term Development*, London: Macmillan.

Uchida, Y. and P. Cook (2005), 'The Transformation of Competitive Advantage in East Asia: An Analysis of Technological and Trade Specialization', *World Development*, **33** (5).

United States Department of Justice (1997), *Horizontal Merger Guidelines*, Washington, DC.

Index